Johnny Van Hove
Congoism

Histoire | Volume 121

Johnny Van Hove (PhD) works as a scientific consultant in the field of migration. He writes for various news media in Germany, the U.S., and Belgium.

Johnny Van Hove

Congoism

Congo Discourses in the United States from 1800 to the Present

[transcript]

This book is based on my dissertation "Congoism. An archeology of Congo discourses in the United States from 1800 to the Present" that I could not have written without the financial support of the International Graduate Centre for the Study of Culture in Gießen.

The pictures shown in the Third Chapter are used with the permission of The Chicago Defender.

Bibliographic information published by the Deutsche Nationalbibliothek
The Deutsche Nationalbibliothek lists this publication in the Deutsche Nationalbibliografie; detailed bibliographic data are available in the Internet at http://dnb.d-nb.de

Cover layout: Kordula Röckenhaus, Bielefeld
Printed by docupoint GmbH, Magdeburg
Print-ISBN 978-3-8376-4037-3
PDF-ISBN 978-3-8394-4037-7

Content

Acknowledgements

I want to thank Stijn Van Herpe for being the most generous friend and interlocutor one can hope for. Thank you Professor Broeck for your guidance, your friendship, and your intellectual mind and open door. Thank you Professor Büschel: You made me a better writer. This book is for you, Noah, my beloved son.

Introduction

Shifting Perspectives on the Congo: Re-Reading Central West Africa

> Congo: 2 different countries are named congo [sic] […]; When u [sic] have dreadlocks, and they start to growtogether [sic] making a big fat dread then u [sic] call it congo […]; A term referred to a black mixed white individual who is stubborn, irrational, arrogant, bipolar, and confusing to many people because of his/her attitude […]; Congo can be best described as the unnecessary display of excessive aggression, severe lack of mannerly conduct or undeserved acts of enthusiasm […]; Person of African descent (from heart of africa [sic]) […]; A great nickname for any of your black friends […]; The stern look of disapproval […]; A racial slur targeting African Americans particularly those who have Portuguese and Angolian [sic] descent […].
>
> BEN E. HAMA, KATTIAA, MOJO12 ET.AL/URBANDISCTIONARY.COM

HISTORY IN "TRANS- MODE"

This is a work of history and a work about history. As a work of history, this book traces the historical trajectories of the word "Congo"[1] within the context of (Afri-

1 Hereafter the Congo will no longer be emphasized through quotation marks. Readers should bear in mind the embattled and fluid meaning and status of the Congo, though.

can) American intellectual texts and milieus. To be more specific: The Congo is not merely a "word", but also, as Reinhart Koselleck's thoughtful distinction has it, a "term" or a "concept". "Concepts" signify the socially entangled and historically loaded, malleable meanings of words (Koselleck 1972: XXI). In keeping with Koselleck's distinction, "terms" like the Congo are based on single events which define the Congo synchronically (at the time when they happen), but also diachronically. As the meaning of these events return systematically in the texts under scrutiny over longer periods of time, they begin to reveal broader socio-political and structural dimensions (cf. Koselleck 2006: 24). This Introduction will constantly come back to this process, highlighting the malleability of the Congo as term. For now, it suffices to state that, as a work of history, this work discusses the term Congo in order to make broader claims regarding the history of the United States in general and Black[2] American communities in particular.

As a work about history, it examines how historians have written about the Congo by relying on particular sources, narrative techniques, and theoretical approaches, as well as by mobilizing and advocating a set of traceable ideological assumptions. "Historian" is a notion that is interpreted widely here: Histories of the Congo have never been created by trained historians alone. The primary and secondary sources taken up here, therefore, are written by scholars and intellectuals – of varying degrees of professionalism as historians – who have indelibly marked the image of the Congo throughout the last two centuries. To examine how history is produced and to investigate its function within certain contexts indeed "reveals", as Ernst Breisach asserts in his Historiography: Ancient, Medieval, and Modern, "that human life is subject to the dictates of time" (1983: 2). Discussing works of history through a historiographical lens is another means, in other words, by which one may discuss socio-political history itself. Historiography echoes the paradigms and political battles of the times in which history was written. In this book, a work of and about history, the Congo is not only discussed as a historically contingent discursive entity, but also in terms of how historical works and sources fashioned it as such.

This work is a history in the "trans- mode", as it is called here, or a history that has been written along transnational, transtemporal, transdisciplinary, and transcultural[3] lines. History in a trans- mode has become quite fashionable in terms of

2 Black(s) with a capital B refers to people of the African diaspora. Lower-case black is simply a color. The terms "Black" and "Black American" or "African American" are used interchangeably here.

3 Transcultural history, as taken up here, is in line with Madeleine Herren's approach, i.e. a history that reflects critically on the way history is constructed, which refuses cultural es-

"space" (i.e. in the form of transnational history). Transnational history, or as Akira Iriye has defined it, "the study of movements and forces that have cut across national boundaries" (2014: 213), has been held an enduring attraction for many American scholars, even before the approach became fashionable. Theoretical reflections on transnational American history began appearing as early as 1916, with Randolph Bourne's "Trans-National America", and continued to appear throughout the following decades, for instance with Laurence Veysey's 1979 "The Autonomy of American History Reconsidered" and Ian Tyrrell's 2009 "Reflections on the Transnational Turn in United States History: Theory and Practice".

The trans- mode, however, is decidedly less popular when it comes to the temporal dimension: "Transnational history is all the rage. Transtemporal history has yet to come into vogue" (Guldi/Armitage 2014: 15). After its heyday in the 1960s and 1970s, long-term history has steadily declined and has only hesitantly returned in the last few years, as Guldi and Armitage argue (ibid: 7-15). In this book, history is executed from the perspective of the "longue durée", as Braudel famously described it in his seminal The Mediterranean and the Mediterranean World in the Age of Philip II. Departing slightly from Braudel, however, longue durée is understood here as the slow and partially cyclical change in "discourse" over time (cf. the discussion on "discourse" below), and not in the natural world, as Braudel originally intended it (1995: 19-21).

This book does take up Braudel's three-tiered temporality, however. The discursive longue durée occurs in dialogue with the gently paced story of states, societies, communities (lentement rythmée; ibid: 20), and the more traditional history of events (l'histoire événementielle; ibid: 21). If this work had limited itself to a history of "events" (see discussion below), it would not have been able to develop an explanation for the particular attention paid by U.S. historians to the Congo. I initially focused exclusively on the 1960s and 1970s of the 21st century, only to discover that the Congo discourse cannot be explained without a broad and deep historical investigation. Moreover, by writing a history in longue durée, this work situates itself in an approach to history written in order to influence public debate (Guldi/Armitage 2014: 8). This is a tradition worth preserving. My work is thus both descriptive and prescriptive: It attempts to describe American discourses on the Congo and, through an in-depth discussion of those agents opposing this dis-

sentialism and asks who has formed history in the past and succeeded in shaping what can be called "the master narrative" (Herren 2012.

course, contemplates ways out of participating in a certain "rhetoricaltiy"[4] on the Congo.

Instrumental in grasping the Congo in a historical and historiographical sense, as well as in a "trans- mode", was the lowering of the disciplinary drawbridge between the fields of history and cultural studies. This type of transdisciplinary approach itself has a long and fruitful history. Philology, economics, sociology, anthropology, and linguistics (among other fields) have entered historical investigations successfully in the past and with great gain, as Richard J. Evans points out (2000: 8-9, 195; cf. Iggers 2007: 101-110). In this spirit, a discourse analytic take will here complement rigorous and broad archival research, as well as critical discussions of a large corpus of primary sources. Bringing cultural studies and history together here is not merely a productive step, but also a necessary one. This has in part to do with the importance of works of "culture", in the sense of "art" (e.g. Joseph Conrad's novella Heart of Darkness), but also with the importance of "culture" in the broad sense of the term as a network of negotiations and power relations across U.S. society, as will be discussed at length below. More effectively than anything else, cultural studies brings useful tools to the table that enable one to interpret these negotiations.

Discussing the Congo requires a methodological approach that goes beyond hermeneutics or source-criticism. Discourse analysis allows seemingly unrelated texts and utterances to be brought together and discussed at eye level through the term that ties them together: The Congo. Henry Highland Garnet's 1843 "An Address to the Slaves of the United States of America" mentioned the "untutored African who roams in the wilds of Congo" (Garnet 2003: 117) to evoke a global, Black humanity. Why the Congo, and not the "Ethiopian" that "roams" the deserts, one may ask? In the same vein, of all the African places that witnessed colonial terror and bloodshed she might call upon, Ida B. Wells-Barnett compared the lynching of two colleagues in the American South in late 19th century to "a scene of shocking savagery which would have disgraced the Congo" (Wells-Barnett 1996: 112). Again, why the Congo? The same can be asked about the monkey brought to the U.S. by author Langston Hughes from his journey through Africa (Hughes 1988: 225), dubbed "Congo devil", as described in his 1940 autobiography The Big Sea. Finally, why did Martin Luther King reject the Congo in 1968 when he told his readers: "The American Negro is not in a Congo" (King 1968: 62). Through a discourse analysis, the details and precise methods of which will be explained extensively below, it is possible to approach the phenomenon of the Congo in an inter-

4 Or how language is bound to be pervasively figurative, and, more often than not, compulsory rhetorical (Richards 2007: 125-133).

textual, socio-political manner. Discourse analysis, focusing on the communication and negotiation that happens between people through language (cf. Iggers 106), has far more potential for ascertaining the "Congo's" significance in U.S. society than other approaches.

The trans- approach in this work has had an effect on how results are presented. Due to the attention to theory and theorization that cultural studies bring to this work, this book can be conceptualized as an empirically-led theorization and historicization of the Congo. Many concepts used to debate this theorization and historicization require extensive definition. These will be provided in the body of the text (not in footnotes), one at a time, and in a context that allows their background and necessity to be explained. At times, this means that the arrival of a clear-cut definition is delayed for some pages, and this is especially the case in the Introduction. This is done with the aim of allowing the reader to journey more informed through the maze of numerous concepts mobilized throughout this book. Another consequence of the trans- mode is enacted on the formal level: The style of reference here is that of American literary scholars. This style integrates references into the body of the text, which allows both for better readability and epistemic coherence. The "constructive and combative activity" usually found in the many footnotes in German works of history (through which these works subtly comment on the works of others; cf. Grafton 1997: 9), is thus transferred to the main narrative. The reason for this particular style of reference is that academics are no mere observers of the Congo: "Academics too have their biases and fads, their preferred topics, and their taboos", as Jan Vansina reminds us in his Paths in the Rainforests: Toward a History of Political Tradition in Equatorial Africa (1990: 25). Contemporary academics, too, this work ultimately hypothesizes, are prone to be part of a particular discourse – i.e. the all-pervading existence of "Congoism". The place to discuss this issue is in the body of the text, not in footnotes.

The trans-mode of writing history points to the "normalized" and "authoritative" discourses produced in scientific, activist, journalistic, and other kinds of communities and institutions – predominantly in the United States, but also beyond it (given the intertwining of these communities on an international level). Attending in more detail to the socially regulated Congo judgments turns the work at hand into a Foucauldian endeavor, the apparatus of which is already echoed in the title of this work. At this point, it may already be useful to spell out how Foucault is used, and not used, in this work. First of all, the early and theoretical Foucault will be incorporated, in terms of his 1969 The Archaeology of Knowledge. It is here that Foucault comes closest to defining his particular take on "discourse" (Willaert 2012: 30), which renders the book useful for empirically-oriented histories like the one at hand. "The purpose of The Archaeology of Knowledge is to suggest how rhetoric can be studied and understood in its relationship with power and knowledge" (n.p.), the cover text of Foucault's seminal theory goes, and it embarks precisely on this enterprise. However, this book is, at the same time, not as Foucauldian as it seems at first. The idea that autonomous rules govern the production of knowledge, as well as that the subject has "died", are rejected in this work, for instance. Empirical evidence in the course of this work shows that subjects have conscientiously operated against the discursive grain.

This Introduction will return to this important topic in due time. For now, however, it is time to move to the question of what this Congo, the subject of our inquiry, actually designates.

TOWARDS THE CONGO: CENTRAL WEST AFRICA AS A U.S. AMERICAN REAL-AND-IMAGINED GEOGRAPHY

The Real-and-Imagined Congo

What does the Congo actually refer to in the American historical record? There can only be a very contextualized answer to this question, which depends on whose Congo we ultimately decide to take up. In this work, the answer is the Congo generations of American intellectuals who published from 1800 onward and whose works found sizable public audiences. Intellectuals are particularly interesting because, on the one hand, they are singular as independent thinkers: They often self-consciously "transmit[ed], modif[ied], and create[d] ideas" (Banks 1996: xvi) about the Congo. On the other hand, they are exemplary as plural entities, too: They are model examples, in other words, of the many voices on the Congo in their respective cultures and times.

Let us dig deeper into this notion of intellectuals in the plural. As such, these thinkers constituted, as Gramsci famously put it, an organic part of their social locus (i.e. their "class", which is broadened to "race" and "gender" in what follows). These "organic intellectuals" are distinguished less by their profession, which theoretically could be anything, than by their function in developing and expressing the ideas and aspirations of their class (Gramsci 1999: 134-135). Gramsci saw, in his own day, the rise of a "new intellectual" (ibid: 141), an intellectual who he opposed to "the traditional and vulgarised type of the intellectual [who] is given by the man of letters, the philosopher, the artist" (ibid). Gramsci suggested that "the mode of being of the new intellectual" lies in "active participation in practical life, as constructor, organiser, 'permanent persuader'" (ibid). Against the background of this "unprecedented expansion" of the role of the intellectual (ibid: 146), this thesis attempts to select wisely from, as well as understand and do justice to, the American intellectual scenes from the nineteenth century onward. As a consequence, intellectuals are examined through their various public roles: As, for instance, journalists, amateur and academic historians, artists, and political activists.

Through the paradigmatic lens of American intellectuals, a Congo will be unpacked that constitutes both a "real" and "imagined" entity, as Edward Soja terms it in his seminal Thirdspace: Journeys to Los Angeles and Other Real-and-Imagined Places. The real and the imagined are produced and maintained by one another simultaneously through their interaction, as is shown in this work. Although Soja argues that the real and the imagined are inseparable, he does divide them in the end. This begs the question: What is this "real" Congo? And what is its "imagined" counterpart? Soja's answer might be that the "real" should be considered the "concrete materiality" of the Congo; the "imagined", in turn, would refer to the "thoughtful re-presentations" of those same material spaces and peoples (Soja 1996: 10). The question remains as to what is meant by this concretely.

The quote at the beginning of this Introduction provides a fruitful entry point for exploring this real-and-imagined Congo in more concrete terms – bringing the real and the imagined together "on equal terms, or at least not privileging one over the other a priori" (Soja 1996: 68). The quote is taken from urbandictionary.com (Hama/Kattiaa/mojo12 et. al), an online slang database that itself constantly straddles the fine line between the imagined and the real.[5] "2 different countries are named congo", claims the first definition – referring to today's The Democratic Republic of the Congo and The Republic of the Congo. These countries are made tangible in the form of government representatives, national soccer teams, armies, embassies, flags, hymns, and, last but not least, official names that appear on the letterheads of official documents. All of these material signs turn the Congo into a very "real" place. However, the history of both nations also reveals how constructed, fluid, and imaginary these material markers of nationhood truly are. This is a trait they share with all other states, as Benedict Anderson points out in his influential Imagined

5 Johnny Davis's 2015 article "In Praise of Urban dictionaries" in The Guardian shows how urbandictionary.com undeniably reflects and shapes the real, despite the fact that the database is characterized by very little "intellectual rigour" (ibid: n.p.), it has been used, for instance, by the U.S. American Royal Courts of Justice, by the Department of Motor Vehicles, and by Fox News to help a judge in a music copyright case, to decide whether to grant certain requests for license plates, and to help determine whether or not to air episodes of The Simpsons and Family Guy.

Communities. How did its status as imagined entity impact The Democratic Republic of the Congo, though, the country upon which this thesis focuses in order to discuss the Congo? And what does this imaginary Congo contribute to a discussion of the Congo as "real" entity?

The imagined Congo allows us to come to terms with The Democratic Republic of the Congo's slightly alienating history (at least from the perspective of those who live in relatively stable Euro-American countries). With the stroke of a pen, or by the barrel of a gun, The Democratic Republic of the Congo was re-named and re-constructed at will (which does not mean without opposition) by those who happened to be in power. The name Congo derives from the pre-colonial kingdom of the Kongo, which had a river flowing through it by the same name (Kisangani/Bobb 2010: Iv-Ixi). Over the decades, the region has expanded and contracted, including and then excluding parts of historical and contemporary Angola (which explains in part why Blacks from the Congo are sometimes called Angolans in slave records – see discussion later on). Through the existence of the Kongo kingdom, inhabitants from that region began to be known by outsiders and insiders alike as Congo or Kongo, Bakongo, or (in colonial times) "Bantu", just as their languages were called similar names, such as Kikongo (Turner 2013: xvi, 75).

In imperial times, the Belgian King Leopold II dubbed and marketed this vast region around the Congo estuary as the Congo Free State (1885-1908; Kisangani/Bobb 2010: Ixi-Ixii). This name promised free trade under the auspices of the king, but soon came to stand for a protectionist horror house of human rights abuse, described in Hochschild's bestselling King Leopold's Ghost: A Story of Greed, Terror, and Heroism in Colonial Africa. The same region was then re-labeled the Belgian Congo (1908-1960), which reflected a power shift from the royal house to the Belgian state with regard to the Congo's governance, as well as a shift from a rationale of trade to one of colonial possession and "paternalism": The Congo became Belgian property and the Congolese its "children" (Gondola 2002: 18-19; Kisangani/Bobb 2010: Ixii).

On June 30th, 1960, the country became the Republic of Congo. Four years later, the Luluabourg constitution changed the name once again to the Democratic Republic of Congo (Kisangani/Bobb 2010: xv). Dictator Mobutu subsequently and unilaterally renamed the country Zaire (1971-1998), a change which was offered to internal and external backers as a means by which the country's authentic past and resources might be reclaimed, but which was discredited soon enough as a huge personal confiscation of the country's wealth (Nzongola-Ntalaja 2007: 171-213). After Mobutu's downfall, the country was re-dubbed The Democratic Republic of the Congo (1998-present), a name which evokes and promises democratic participation, but which can hardly camouflage that the regimes of Laurent and Joseph Kabila – given their track record of handpicked parliaments, unfair elections, and systematic repression of the opposition – constitute "democracy without democrats", as the Congolese scholar and activist Georges Nzongola-Ntalaja described to me in a lengthy interview for the online Belgian magazine rekto:verso (Nzongola-Ntalaja 2010; cf.: Nzongola-Ntalaja 2007: 240-248).

While the official naming of The Democratic Republic of the Congo is pervaded with the imaginary, many of the designations of today's The Democratic Republic of the Congo found in fiction are permeated with the "real", too. The metaphor of "heart of darkness" is a prominent example, deriving from Joseph Conrad's novella of the same title. Even without hinting at the Congo Free State explicitly, the novella was instantly linked to the well-documented "atrocities" committed by Leopold's state and played a substantial role in the international human rights movement against Leopold II's system of forced labor (Hawkins 2006: 373). Subsequently, the metaphor of "heart of darkness" embarked upon a remarkable career, entering the international lexicon as shorthand for crimes that went far beyond the Congo Free State. It came to stand, for instance, for the deplorable imperial appropriation of Africa as a whole (Achebe 2006), for claims of racial superiority (Hawkins), and for extreme human rights abuses in South Africa and South America, exemplified by book titles such as Jacques De Pauw's Into the Heart of Darkness: Confessions of Apartheid's Assassins and Shari Turitz's Confronting the Heart of Darkness: An International Symposium on Torture in Guatemala.

Conrad's text also imposed an enduring way of talking about the Congo itself that is still employed today. Journalists such as the African American veteran foreign correspondent of The New York Times Howard French (cf. Third Chapter, too) have criticized the tendency of many journalists to invoke "overworking clichés drawn from Heart of Darkness" (French 2005: 50). At the same time, French has admitted that he himself has struggled to escape from these same commonplaces in his well-researched A Continent for the Taking. On various occasions, French lapses into a language of blankness, randomness, and naturalness to debate Congolese disasters. Frequently, his rhetoric is reminiscent of Conrad's: "But like nature, politics tolerates no vacuums", French writes, "and politically speaking, Zaire was already becoming an empty pit in the heart of the continent – a pit waiting for someone, by yet another unforeseen process, to fit it up and make the earth level again" (ibid: 56).

An overview of The Democratic Republic of the Congo's recent past thus shows to what extent the Congo has always been thoroughly real-and-imagined, produced through a nexus of material, discursive, and power-filled knowledge. It is through this shift of perspective on Central West Africa (as a real-and-imagined entity) that this book pursues its task.

The U.S. American Congo

The real-and-imagined Congo will be investigated here via a broad corpus of texts by U.S. American intellectuals. The United States was chosen for the following reasons. American intellectuals and political elites have "long insisted on the relevance of the Congo to the United States", as Ira Dworkin observes (2003: 6). These American elites have exerted substantial political and economic influence on Central West Africa, and the Congo's history, in turn, is indelibly marked by American involvement (cf. Turner 2013: 35-42). From the 16th to the late 19th century, with a peak from 1790 to 1803, today's The Democratic Republic of the Congo and its contemporary neighbors The Republic of the Congo and Angola constituted "the single most important source of African slaves" for the New World (Littlefield 2005: 154; Klein 1999: 66-69). Imports from the Congo, many histories argue, accounted for about 40 percent of the slaves shipped forcefully to the Americas and for more than 50 percent of those shipped to British North America specifically (J. Miller 1976: 76; Klein 1999: 66; Gomez 1998: 33). Although this "numbers game" itself must be carefully investigated (cf. First Chapter), the scholarly accounts point unmistakably to the fact that a lot of slaves were presumably imported from Central West Africa to the United States.

America's involvement cannot be underestimated in the colonial era either. Henry Morgan Stanley, for instance, was a Welsh-born U.S. American journalist who claimed territory for Leopold's Congo Free State and who established the first infrastructure of exploitation in that state (Nzongola-Ntalaja 2007: 15-17). Moreover, Stanley wrote bestselling travelogues for the Anglo-American market, such as In Darkest Africa and Through the Dark Continent, which decisively shaped the imagery and vocabulary of the Congo in the international arena (Edgerton 2002: 32). The colonial era also saw substantial lobbying by Leopold's proxies in the U.S., which caused a serious scandal and drew skeptical attention to the king's politics as a whole (cf. Second Chapter). Through this lobbying, the United States government was the first to recognize the king's claims to the Congo in 1884 (Nzongola-Ntalaja 2007: 266). The "plunder [...] slave labor and the crimes of rape, torture, body mutilation and murder" that followed (ibid: 23) were forcefully addressed and communicated in the early 19th century by American activists of the international human rights organization Congo Reform Association (cf. Second Chapter). In the U.S, this organization was aptly represented by both African American intellectuals, such as Booker T. Washington and W.E.B. Du Bois, as well as popular white fiction writers such as Mark Twain (Dworkin 2003: 70, 112; Nzongola-Ntalaja 2007: 24).

The story of American intervention in the Congo continued after the Congo Free State was re-branded the "Belgian Congo". In the early 1940s, the Manhattan Project, the U.S. American research and development program that created the first atomic bomb, could not have been successfully executed without the vast quantities of uranium ore from Central West Africa (Hewlett/Anderson 1962: 85-86). On top of this, in order to secure ongoing access to mineral-rich Central West Africa, consecutive U.S. administrations have both actively undermined and consciously eliminated elected Congolese politicians (Patrice Lumumba, for instance), as well as supported American-oriented autocratic Congolese elites with no social base to hold them nationally accountable. The "America-sponsored coup by Mobutu" in 1965, who was eventually known as "America's Tyrant" and "Our Man in Kinshasa" (Turner 2013: 1, 38), ushered in a regime that lasted decades due to the ongoing financial support of the United States, which bordered on a patron-client relationship (ibid: 38; Nzongola-Ntalaja 2010; Kisangani/Bobb 2010: Ixvii-Ixxxvii). Finally, after the fall of the "Iron Curtain", America turned against the dictator and actively supported those overthrowing Mobutu (and their Congolese proxies, such as Laurent Kabila), through "long-standing and unconditional support" of the invading countries Rwanda and Uganda during the worst episodes of the Congo wars from 1998 onward (Trefon 2011:13). In the transition from war to pacification, the U.S. was the dominant force in guiding The Democratic Republic of the Congo to a "quasi-trusteeship" through international organizations such as the United Nations (UN) and the International Committee in Support of Transition (Turner 2013: 40-41).

The constant meddling by the U.S. in Central West Africa, from slave-catching to coltan-grabbing, has rendered the U.S. the most decisive external power in the region up until today (ibid: 44). This assertion of power from across the oceans has left its material and discursive traces in both places. In this book, the traces of the real-and-imagined Congo in the United States will be focused upon.[6] One striking example of how material, discursive, and transnational semanticizations go together is Congo Square in New Orleans, officially known as "Beauregard Square" until 2011 (Evans 2011: 1-30). This locale originally took its famous unofficial name "from the Congo Negroes who used to perform their dance on its sward every Sunday", to cite William Wells Brown (1880: 121; cf. Thompson 2005b: 285-286). Via

6 Although the transnational Congo will receive some attention – the Congo in Liberia and Haiti, for instance.

the well-known cultural practices performed in Beauregard Square, the Congo came to stand in the following decades for dance performances of various kinds. This real-and-imagined relationship kept reproducing itself in the decades and centuries to come. William Wells Brown's 19th century white contemporaries enjoyed minstrel shows labeled the "Congo Coconut Dance" (Emery 1988: 194). They also performed the "Congo Minuet" themselves (ibid). Choreographers in the mid-20th century, such as Katherine Dunham and Talley Beatty, named parts of their performances or their dancing techniques after the Congo, such as "Congo Tango Palace" and "Congo Paillette (ibid: 271). In Claude McKay's 1928 novel Home to Harlem, "Congo Rose" is a cabaret singer in the Harlem "Congo Club", which was said to be "a real throbbing little Africa in New York" (1928: 29). Clubs and musical groups named after the Congo actually existed, according to the African American newspaper The Chicago Defender, such as the "Congo Rhythm Band" and the "Congo Inn" (e.g. 1931c). The relationship between the Congo, dance, and music continued in the 21st century, as demonstrated by the release of albums by groups like Los Hombres Calientes (New Congo Square), jazz saxophonist Donald Harrison (Spirits of Congo Square), and Wynton Marsalis (Congo Square).

My point of access to the American intellectual archive is the relatively recent history of African American text production. The choice to discuss the real-and-imagined Congo via epistemologies other than the one I was socialized and indoctrinated into constitutes an attempt to pursue a "cross-epistemological" approach, as Obeyesekere terms it (2005: 225). To consciously step inside American and Black American discourses signifies a stepping outside of the "epistemological ethnocentrism" of mainstream Belgian discourse, or a stepping out of the belief that "scientifically there is nothing to be learned from 'them' unless it is already 'ours' or comes from us" (Mudimbe 1988: 15). "Them" in this book points to both African American intellectuals and Congolese. Being raised in The Democratic Republic of the Congo's former colonizer entailed being exposed to an ongoing racist discourse of anti-Black rejection in general and anti-Congolese rhetoric in particular. The reason for this was that the history of the Congo has been dominated by and taught through those personally involved in the "colonial adventure", such as journalists, civil servants, and family members of colonials. In the eyes of large parts of the Belgian public, books written by those closest to the colonial project tell the history of the Congo as it really was, and important advances and works by scholars and intellectuals such as N'Daywel, Stenger, Ceuppens, De Witte, and Hochschild are often neglected (Vanthemsche 2006: 98). Guy Vanthemsche's observations can only be seconded by adding that Belgian discourses have often been framed within an apologetic "model colony discourse", as I labeled it in an online article within the context of the fiftieth anniversary of Congolese independence (Van Hove 2010).[7]

An awareness of Belgian discourses on the Congo, however, does not automatically enable one to fully depart from them. The fascinations of and solutions offered by this work are neither accidental nor incidental. The particular forays into the Black American archive made by this thesis are a reminder that writing hardly constitutes a neutral space and that geo-political, socio-historical, and institutional locatedness deeply mark even the most detached historical analysis (cf. Dirks 2001: 230). This work does not end by mere coincidence with an analysis of Congo: The Epic Story of a People by the Belgian author David Van Reybrouck. Telling as my Belgian infatuations may be, their self-conscious and limited presence also prove that a cross-epistemological approach is the right one: It promises a more detached take on the intellectuals in question. This work profits from the fact I am an "outsider", in the sense of living and working outside of Belgium and the U.S., and these circumstances have helped to at least partially overcome the difficulties involved in metareflecting on one's own "archive" (see discussion below on the term "archive").

To step into a tradition that lies outside the trajectory of hegemonic groups will contribute, as Charles Mills tell us in Blackness Visible: Essays on Philosophy and Race, to a more adequate, more accurate, more complete, subtler, and more "veridical picture" (1998: 28) of the discursive dynamics surrounding the real-and-imagined Congo. Moreover, by looking at Black discourses, the likelihood is higher that "a counterpoint to the myths promoted by the powerful" may be established, as Poletta suggests (2006: 3). Poletta's assumption has proved to be only partly true, however. Accurate as it may be in the case of some intellectuals of the 1960s and 1970s, over large stretches of their history, African Americans were deeply entangled in dominant discourses of and histories by white intellectuals. This led to a systematic "complicity and syncretic interdependency of black and white thinkers", as Gilroy asserts (1993: 31). The title of this work therefore specifies the "United States" instead of "African American", as the processes at work in Black Congo discourse are very much white America's. It will be shown, however, that the "entanglement" of Black and white thought tells more about white power, Black vul-

7 This story operates on the assumption of the innate backwards state of the Congo and focuses exclusively on the positive infrastructural and medical "progress" that the Belgians "brought". The popular model-colony story blatantly downplays anti-Black violence and abuse as "paternalism" and blames the Congolese in overtly behaviorist and deterministic terms for the instability and catastrophic political leadership in the post-independence era (Van Hove 2010).

nerability, and the centrality of categories of differentiation in the U.S. than it does about the motives or complicity of Black elites (cf. Gaines 1996: xv).

Allowing the categories of Black and white to bleed into one another in this way is to discuss "Black" and "white" as social processes that overlap and interact constantly with one another, both nationally and internationally. Recognizing the relational, "doubly conscious"[8] aspect of African American discourse matters greatly in trying to make sense of Congo discourses. Whose discourse are we actually witnessing in a context in which white Americans dominate both materially and discursively over their Black counterparts? Whose thirst for primitiveness is expressed through Congo discourses? These questions are relevant, as the white, transnational influence on African American intellectuals is readily apparent throughout the history of Black American intellectuals. In the 1830s, for instance, the abolitionist movement, dominated by white activists, provided a challenging new stage for African American political performance for a wider audience. While granting political agency, the abolitionist movement also curbed, directed, and restricted Black American intellectuals in what they could say (Banks 1996: 22-23). This Janus-faced situation of white gatekeeping repeated itself frequently in Black American intellectual history. The literary careers of major authors of the "Harlem Renaissance", such as Claude McKay, Langston Hughes, and Zora Neale Hurston, show how dependent these authors were on rich white benefactors for long stretches of their careers, particularly those thirsty for depictions of "primitive" Black culture (ibid: 50-53, 83, 86). Black intellectuals have often acknowledged the effect of white American and European discourses and traditions on their own writing on Africa, and the Congo in particular. Alexander Crummell's 1862 The Future of Africa: Addresses, Sermons, etc., etc. draws from the travel accounts of white African explorers such as David Livingstone and Mungo Park; in The Story of the Negro, Booker T. Washington builds on German-American anthropologist Franz Boas to tell the tale of Africa's history from a diasporic perspective; Du Bois's The Negro cites Leopold critic Edmund Dean Morel, abolitionist Wendell Philips, and Congo explorer Henry Morgan Stanley; finally, Langston Hughes's 1940 autobiography and travelogue, The Big Sea, mentions Joseph Conrad as a significant literary influence.

Given this entangled history, why should one then privilege African American texts over white American ones? The reason is that African Americans have communicated openly how they have been structurally affected by and systematically responded to white American and European discourses. They have done so in ways

8 The often-cited "double consciousness" of many African American intellectuals signifies being both American and part of an African diaspora, as W.E.B. Du Bois famously explained in The Souls of Black Folk (1999: 11).

that non-Black intellectuals have hardly ever achieved, or have hardly ever admitted. As such, the African American archive constitutes a more complete, a more self-reflective, and an overall richer access point than that of white intellectuals. These aspects make a systematic investigation of the much-ignored term "the Congo" easier.

The African American intellectuals I investigate are not only deeply entangled with their white counterparts; they are also deeply engaged with one another. It is in this personal and epistemic sense that they constitute a "community", and by no means in the sense of a homogeneous, unitary group of Black intellectuals. If anything, this book shows the internal divisions within Black American communities along class, gender, and racial lines. Despite this obvious heterogeneity, however, Black Americans do also constitute a community understood more traditionally. Their writings and activities form a network; they exist as a tightly connected group of intellectuals who knew each other personally and professionally. This community created a "vernacular" culture that was marked by continuously appreciating, critiquing, and building upon the texts of one's contemporaries (Gates/Jarrett 2007: xi). A case in point is William Henry Sheppard (cf. Second Chapter), whose travelogues and speeches on Central West Africa, materialized most famously in his 1917 book Presbyterian Pioneers in Congo, exerted considerable influence on African American intellectual circles. For instance, Booker T. Washington's 1904 article "Cruelty in the Congo Country" quoted Sheppard extensively (who was a former student of Washington's Hampton Institute; cf. Second Chapter). Novelist Pauline Hopkins, in turn, drew heavily on William Henry and Lucy Sheppard's story in her serialized 1902-1903 novel Of One Blood (Dworkin 2003: 174). Finally, The Chicago Defender reported numerous times on Sheppard's speeches on Central West Africa (cf. Third Chapter).[9]

Building on Gramsci's idea of the "organic intellectual", African American intellectuals cannot be reduced to a particular list of occupations. Certain professions were more likely to allow for intellectual work than others, of course, depending on the de jure and de facto freedom these jobs provided. The available resources, incentives, and opportunities these occupations promised played a role, too. In times

9 In 1918, for instance, Sheppard was said to have been the principal speaker on the thirtieth anniversary of the Grace Presbyterian Church, as discussed in The Chicago Defender, where he was celebrated as "one of the first men to launch Presbyterianism amongst the cannibals" (1918a: 10). In 1923, Sheppard talked to the students of the all-Black Hampton Institute, The Chicago Defender reported, where he "vividly described some of his experiences with African wild animals and strange peoples, including the cannibalistic Zappa Zaps", and where he showed a valuable collection of "African curios" (1923a).

of slavery, for instance, the abolitionist movement and Black churches provided a secure intellectual working environment for activists and ministers (Banks 1996: 13-14). The rise of individual intellectuals like Henry Highland Garnet, Alexander Crummell, and Frederick Douglass can be explained in this way (ibid: 24). After the Civil War, general and specialized newspapers and magazines began to provide the infrastructure for the systematic development of a viable Black intellectual group. Thus, the African American intellectual landscape not only grew bigger, but also more diverse, because of the increasing influx of educators, scholars, Civil Rights activists, journalists, and authors (Hall 2009: 33-47). Despite the ongoing attempt to integrate marginalized works into this thesis, it undeniably reflects some of the dominance of certain professions, social circles, as well as class and gender biases throughout much of African American intellectual history.

Moving back and forth between widely discussed and "marginalized" texts (in the sense of being ignored by the intellectual gatekeepers of the time), this work discusses a real-and-imagined Congo that has long been a part of the African American intellectual tradition, albeit an overlooked one. This neglect is not due to a lack of traces. On the contrary: Traces are plentiful. As soon as slaves from the Congo entered the "New World", they left their marks on the United States, particularly in regions with high numbers of them, such as South Carolina and Louisiana (Gomez 1998: 136). In these states, a variety of Congo naming practices emerged. Slaves and servants, for instance, were often identified through names that pinpointed their assumed ethnic roots, which they then passed on to their children (Hodges 1999: 53-54). In Louisiana, this practice led to names as "Louis Congo" or "François dit Congo", the latter designating a second generation, "three quarters white", four-year-old slave up for sale (qtd. in Hodges 1999: 53).

Some traces can be detected in the Northeast, as well. Among the first to arrive in New Amsterdam in 1626 were Black men and boys with names such as "Simon Congo" or "Manuel Congo", who appear in the historical record because they were granted land (Hodge 1999: 9) or were punished (ibid: 17). On a slightly different, rather more symbolic note, Joseph Cinque, the prolific leader of the Amistad ship revolt in 1839, was dubbed the "Congolese chief" in Black American publications such as the article titled "Schooner Amistad" in The Colored American, despite Cinque's well-known Sierra Leonine origins (1837). The issue of Congolese captains will return in a discussion of postmodern Congo novels in the final chapter of this work.

Traces of Congo naming practices continued even after the abolition of slavery, as early 20th century obituaries in The Chicago Defender show. In this newspaper, deceased African Americans were mentioned named "C.H. Congo", "Charles Congo", and "Mrs. wn. Congo, wife of Edward Congo" (1931a; 1931 b; 1920a: 1). Many articles in The Chicago Defender show that the Congo was also a name that African Americans would give to themselves or to places in their immediate environment. The boxer Clarence Moulden dubbed himself "Congo Kid" at the turn of the 20th century. Imported gorillas were, moreover, called "Mr. Congo" (1914a; 1925c). These naming practices have continued until today: About 90 Americans are still listed under the surname Congo in the American telephone and address directory White Pages.

Congo naming frequently expanded into the public and geographical arena, too, both nationally and internationally. Near Liberia's capital of Monrovia, a city decidedly shaped by (African) American elites with a self-declared civilizing mission (Beyan 2005: 49-106; Cf. Second Chapter), lies a township called "Congo Town", a place that early 20th century American cruise ships visited on numerous occasions, as The Chicago Defender mentioned (1931: 13). Additionally, in the U.S. national arena, forty-five locations, both geographical and cultural, include the Congo in their official name, according to the Geographic Names Information System, the official repository of U.S. geographic names data (GNIS hereafter; cf. United States Board of Geographic Names). West Virginia, Pennsylvania, Ohio, North Carolina, Alabama, and Arizona all contain at least one locale called Congo; there is a Congo creek in Alabama, a Congo Lake Dam in Arizona, and a Congo Island in Louisiana, to name but a few entries. Educational, cultural, and political institutions have also taken on the name Congo. According to the GNIS, there is a Congo school in Missouri, a Congo church in North Carolina, and a Congo Incline Mine in Wyoming. Other institutions that carried the name Congo included the Congo National Emigration Company, headed by the Black Baptist preacher Reverend Benjamin Gaston, which sponsored forty-two people's emigration to Liberia (Finkelman 2006a: 317). In contrast, no locale is named after other important African geographies such as Ethiopia, Ghana, Gambia, Angola or Niger, and only two villages are called Liberia (in North and South Carolina). Which begs the question that drives much of this book, as well as this Introduction: Why the Congo?

TOWARDS CONGOISM: THE CONGO AS AN IMAGINATIVE GEOGRAPHY

To begin to answer the last question requires looking first at the only African geography mentioned more frequently than the Congo in the African American intellectual text archive: "Egypt". The latter has been a central real-and-imagined geography in the United States, according to Scott Trafton's important work Egypt Land: Race and Nineteenth-century American Egyptomania. In contrast to Egypt, however, hardly any scholarly discussion has revolved around the Congo. This neglect is conspicuous, especially because most of the (African) American intellectuals considered in Egypt Land, to name but one work, are intellectuals who do mention the Congo at some point in their texts. Linda Heywood has a point when she states that the "general interest of the history and cultural impact of Central Africa in the Atlantic Diaspora lag far behind" that of other parts of Africa, especially the Western part (2002: 8). Neglecting the real-and-imagined Congo distorts the overall geography of the Black American intellectual arena. This is because the use of the Congo very often entailed a decision: A decision in favor of the Congo was also a decision against another geography. Thus, it is hypothesized here that whenever the Congo was invoked, a meaningful choice was made. The Congo possessed a set of traits with a particular logic, which may be scrutinized, but also demand specification: Why the Congo, and not another geography?

The Congo term was already recognizable in times of slavery, which is this work's point of departure. The presence of Congo slaves and their descendants led to a vast array of dismissive stories. Narratives about rebellious "Congoes" or "Angolas" – which were ethnic labels employed interchangeably[10] by slave owners to identify their "chattel" from the coasts of contemporary's Angola, The Democratic Republic of the Congo, and The Republic of the Congo (Gomez 1998: 135; Hall 2005: 153) – are numerous in the American historical slave record (Gomez 1998: 137-141). This happened most famously in the 1739 "Stono Rebellion" in South Carolina, one of the largest and costliest slave uprisings in the history of the United States, said to have been started by twenty "Angolan"[11] soldiers (Kolchin 2003: 455-456). One consequence of this violent and rapidly suppressed revolt was that the slaveocracy of South Carolina became even more hesitant in purchasing Angolans and "Kongoes" (Gomez 1998: 136). According to the historical record, these had already been ranked low on the scale of preferred slaves (Kolchin 2003: 19, 67). Slave owners in South Carolina depicted Central West Africans as docile and weak, and agreed that they were best used as house servants (ibid: 19; Littlefield 2005: 13). Others framed them as quite the opposite: rebellious, prone to abscond-

10 Slaves from Central West Africa in particular were called "Kongo" in colonies that were originally French or Spanish – in Louisiana, for instance. British colonies, such as South Carolina, called the same slaves "Angola" (Hall 2005: 153; Gomez 1998: 135, 160).

11 Who, however, were most likely from the Kingdom of the Congo, as Thornton argues in his essay "The African Dimension of the Stono Rebellion" (1991).

ing, and preferably used as "field negroes" for heavy gang labor (Hall 2005: 160; Gomez 1998: 137-141).

These evaluations of Congo slaves from the historical slave record, a deeply biased corpus, cannot be taken at face value, of course, although it frequently is (cf. my discussion of Herskovits and my hypothesis of the existence of an "academic Congoism" in the First and Second Chapters). Ultimately, the supposed disposition of those called Congo is hardly decisive for the overall argument of this book. What matters is that Americans constantly constructed discursive mechanisms that reproduced a group of slaves who possessed negative characteristics. Oscillating between too docile and too rebellious, "Congoes" were caught from slave times onward between a series of binaries which rendered them somehow suspect. If they were perceived as too docile, it meant they could not properly participate in the abolitionist struggle; "too rebellious", in turn, made them undesirable to their masters. Here too, Black and white potentially merged in the formation of a mutual discourse. As the assumptions of slave owners circulated widely amongst slaves and freedmen alike, Gomez reminds us, Black Americans frequently internalized "bits and pieces" of what the slave owners said (Gomez 1998: 215). The result was that no one had a thought to spare for the Congo slave, as is shown in the First Chapter.

The polarizing logic in which the Congo (its people, customs, and geography) was caught returns systematically in the texts of African American intellectuals. The rich corpus of derogatory and stigmatizing Congo utterances contains work by intellectuals as the back-to-Africa advocate Henry McNeal Turner, who stated offhandedly in his 1893 African Letters that the "Congo negro" should stay out of Liberia, since they belong to "the lowest of the African races" (1893: 52). Turner was staunchly opposed to the "Congo negro" – designating, at that point in time, in contrast to the honorable Blacks who should emigrate to Liberia, those slaves that were either freed or "degenerated" (i.e. lower class), or both. "Persons coming here ought to have a little money to start with, and a good-deal of self-reliance, a decent amount of race pride, and considerable common sense", Turner asserted, clearly demonstrating a preference for Blacks with money (the Black "bourgeois", as is shown and discussed in subsequent chapters) over those who have little or none (the majority). Turner continues: "Those who are here from the Congo are ignored by the native heathen, much more by the regular Liberians. They sustain the same relation to the higher African tribes that they do to us in the United States" (1893: 52). The "normative conclusion" (Poletta 2006: 9) of this passage, namely that Congolese (whatever was meant by that at that point in time) are worth less than nothing, will return constantly in the course of this book.

Polarization requires both dismissive claims (which have been plenty), and affirmative ones (which have been few). Within the context of affirmative Congo claims, Pauline Hopkins can be mentioned, who, against the Social Darwinian mainstream of her times, asserted in her 1902-1903 novel Of One Blood: Or, the Hidden Self that the interior of Africa (i.e. the Congo) is a space "at variance with the European idea [of a] howling wildernesses or an uninhabitable country" (1988: 556). During the Harlem Renaissance and in the 1960s and 1970s, the number of affirmative Congo claims increased considerably, as is shown in the Second and Third Chapters. Again, it is crucial to understand that these positive Congo claims are part of a larger landscape of utterances. They are one side of a very tarnished coin. Malediction and canonization, to paraphrase David Spurr (1993: 134), are merely opposing principles of the same, systematic rejection of the Congo.

The Congo can be considered the Central West African equivalent of Edward Said's Orient (an idea suggested hesitantly in Derricourt 2011: vi, for instance). To bring up Said here is also to struggle with the many theoretical problems of his work Orientalism. They need not be rehearsed at length here, as many others have discussed them so aptly (cf. Willaert 2012: 30-31 for a summary); mentioning those issues that are especially relevant to the work at hand should suffice. One problematic aspect in Said's work, for instance, is the tension between the idea of a (mis)representation and the concept of an object-creating discourse. If orientalist discourse created the Orient, how can it misrepresent it unless one reintroduces some kind of "real" Orient (which Said decidedly rejected, cf. Said 2003: 33). Another problem is Said's occasional ahistoricism, or the idea of a stable discourse that spans the entire West and that is present in various forms from Aeschylus until the present. Does the latter not homogenize the West and the Orient alike, it should be asked?

Despite these inadequacies, Said's work does provide plenty of suggestions for approaching the Congo anew. Through Said's concept of an "imaginative geography", a concept which will be defined in the subsequent paragraphs, the Congo can be considered a discursive entity that has historically played the role of the "Other" in the overall "economy of objects and identities" in the United States (Said 2003: 55). Like Said's Orient, the Congo of this book orders knowledge about "us" and "them" via a repertoire of tropes and topoi (cf. below and cf. Said 2003: 55). The Congo thus has constituted the "Other" of African American intellectuals (cf. definition of the Other by Fabian below). The challenge is, of course, that African Americans themselves constituted the "Other" for many white Americans. As such, the Congo would become the Other's Other, via which African American intellectuals could derive a "flexible positional superiority" (Said 2003: 7) in their competition with Black and white intellectuals for the recognition of subjectivity, a "civilized" status, or a political voice.

The idea of the Other's Other denotes a cultural operation that excludes the Congo through stigmatization and metaphorization from any substantial debate about itself. This device is used by African American intellectuals to differentiate themselves from a Congo that is too repulsive, too primitive, too objectionable, in short, too abject, to be discussed at eye level (cf. Berressem 2007: 22, 29 for a discussion on "the abject"). Central West Africa thus turns into a thoroughly reflexive topos, deeply "ego-reinforcing", to quote the African American author Toni Morrison in Playing in the Dark (1992: 8), as well as madly imaginative. The underlying figures of speech hardly aim for accuracy; they are mainly for, and revealing of, "us". This is "Othering" in its purest form. The process of "Othering" highlights that the Congo is never simply given, never just found or encountered, but made. And it is made for a purpose, as Johannes Fabian reminds us (1990: 209):

> [O]ur ways of making the Other are ways of making ourselves. The need to go there (to exotic places, be they far away or around the corner) is really our desire to be here (to find or defend our position in the world). The urge to write ethnography is about making the then into a now. In this move from then to now the making of knowledge out of experience occurs. Both movements, from here to there and from then to now, converge in what I called presence. This is the way I would define the process of Othering.

According to this definition, the Congo provides a means by which African Americans defended their "position in the world" and elevated themselves. Through the Congo, Black American intellectuals knew themselves to be free, not enslaved; civilized and progressing, not savage and backwards; beautiful and desirable, not ugly and repulsive; and historical, not without history. It is this process that is "Congoism", which may be defined here as the amalgam of truth-producing "Otherings" through the interplay of historically contingent discourse and material semanticizations of and through the Congo. Thus, the "Congo's" meaning changes over time (of the Congo), and with it the way in which it is employed (through the Congo).

Congoism has neither, academically or otherwise, been identified properly nor described systematically, although some of its elements have been articulated (cf. Third Chapter and the Conclusion). This should, however, come as no surprise. Whether one looks at primary or secondary texts, the Congo has rarely been considered a clearly separable, distinguishable geography worthy of an empirical or theoretical inquiry through the lens of African American intellectuals. Notable exceptions in secondary texts, mainly in the form of book chapters, predominantly focus on the Congo Free State period or on the 1960s. More elaborate discussions of the former period appear in Füllberg-Stolberg's publication, Amerika in Afrika: die Rolle der Afroamerikaner in den Beziehungen zwischen den USA und Afrika, 1880 – 1910 (2003),[12] as well as Zimmermann's Alabama in Africa: Booker T. Washington, the German Empire, and the Globalization of the New South (2010). These monographs provide valuable insight into the engagement of African American missionaries and educators with the Congo, and the Second Chapter will draw on both.

These works, not to mention others, will be used with caution, however, in terms of how they explain the focus of African American intellectuals on the Congo. Neither Füllberg-Stolberg nor Zimmerman explicitly relate the time period they investigate to the long history of African American Congo discourse, thus providing findings that remain quite limited in their explanatory scope. Amerika in Afrika, for one, misinterprets the response of African Americans to the Congo Free State. The critical Black American norm at the time was not to critique imperialism, as it is suggested by Füllberg-Stolberg (2003: 13-15; cf. Dworkin 2017). The First and Second Chapters, in fact, contradict this claim of African American political anti-imperialism. One of the few long-term investigations, Kevin Dunn's Imagining the Congo: the International Relations of Identity (2003), has equally little to say about African Americans, apart from their alleged feelings of homecoming when they discussed the Congo in the 60s of the previous century. "Images of Zaïre and other African countries became idealized. Muhammad Ali, for example, cried out 'I'm home' upon landing in Kinshasa and told Zaïrians that they, not he, were truly free" (Dunn 2003: 125).

A number of historical works do recognize the importance of the Congo in African American contexts, but they uncritically incorporate the metaphors of the past. Nan Elizabeth Woodruff's American Congo: The African American Freedom Struggle in the Delta (2012) identifies the "American Congo" as a central metaphor for the African American oppression in the Mississippi River Valley at the turn of the century (cf. Second Chapter). But she neither deconstructs nor follows up on this metaphorical practice, thus legitimizing this Congoist figure of speech and reproducing its dismissiveness.

Representative of post-Congo Free State works on the Congo, on the other hand, is James Tyner's research (2006), as well as James Meriwether's (2002), Gerald Horn's (2009), Alvin Tillery's (2011), and Penny von Eschen's (2006) transnational work on the broader influence of African anti-colonial movements

12 America in Africa: The Role of African Americans in Foreign Relations Between the U.S. and Africa, 1880-1910 (translation mine).

within the Black Freedom Struggle – in particular their The Geography of Malcolm X: Black Radicalism and the Remaking of American Space (Tyner), Proudly We Can Be Africans: Black Americans and Africa, 1935-1961 (Meriwether), Mau Mau in Harlem. The U.S. and the Liberation of Kenya (Horne), Between Homeland and Motherland: Africa, U.S. Foreign Policy, and Black Leadership in America (Tillery), and Satchmo Blows Up the World: Jazz Ambassadors Play the Cold War (von Eschen). Meriwether, amongst others, proposes that the assassination of Lumumba caused a long-term schism within the African American community between the reformist Civil Rights advocates and the Black Power militants. He suggests that the internationalism of many Civil Rights and Black Power advocates was both inward- and outward-oriented – an idea that will be addressed and developed in what follows. Further investigations of the 60s mostly acknowledge the significance of the Congo without going into detail. Exemplary among these are Thomas Borstelmann's and Peniel E. Joseph's historical works, especially The Cold War and the Color Line (Borstelmann 2001) and Waiting 'Til the Midnight Hour: A Narrative of Black Power in America (Joseph 2006).

Three case studies are devoted to the Congo through an African American text corpus. This is Ira Dworkin's unpublished dissertation, "American Hearts: African American Writing on the Congo, 1890-1915" (2003), as well as his book chapter "On the Borders of Race, Mission, and State: African Americans and the American Presbyterian Congo Mission" in Borderlands and Frontiers in Africa (2012) and his monograph Congo Love Song: African American Culture and the Crisis of the Colonial State (2017). These studies document and contextualize the engagement of African American intellectuals (educators, activists, novelists, missionaries) with the Congo in the late 19th until the mid-20th century. Despite the differences between our approaches, Dworkin deserves all the credit for recognizing the link between African America and the Congo. "Expressions of love for the Congo", as Dworkin writes (2017: 2), do indeed "take a range of forms within African American culture." But so does the (highly ignored) amount of dismissive utterances. In contrast to Dworkin, this work executes a longue durée reading of both dismissive and affirmative Congo utterances which, in the end, will give us an in-depth analysis of the discursive phenomenon Congo that explicitly spells out the specific epistemic function of Central West Africa in (African) American intellectual circles.

A further distinction between the work at hand and the few others that discuss Central West Africa through an African American lens is the way the Congo is positioned and discussed vis-à-vis "Africa". Although "American Hearts", for instance, attempts to separate the former from the latter, the Congo does occasionally and problematically stand for the whole continent (e.g. Dworkin 2003: 180). This interchangeable use of Africa and the Congo is visible in many studies, both in primary and secondary sources. Historical actors allegedly did not differentiate between, or attached varying meanings to, clearly distinguishable African areas. This is what James Meriwether, for instance, writes in the introduction of Proudly We Can Be Africans (2002: 4-5):

> Twentieth-century African Americans generally did not dissegregate areas of Africa in their transatlantic thinking. The 'imagined' Africa was just that: Africa as a whole. This meant that African Americans responded to events ranging across the entire continent[...] [T]his approach resulted in minimal consideration of the vast ethnic and cultural differences at work on the continent.

Meriwether's statement is particularly striking, and contradictory at that, since he shows throughout his own book to what extent African Americans did indeed differentiate between African geographies. Meriwether's own chapter titles attest to this, including many names of 20th-century political hotspots on the African continent, such as Ethiopia, Ghana, and the Congo.

The interchangeable use of the Congo and Africa might be understood by discussing the Congo as a part of Africanisms in American Culture. This is also the title of a collection of essays in which Farris Thompson's essay, "Kongo Influences on African American Artistic Culture", discusses Central West Africa in a typical Congoist manner. The Second Chapter of this book will refer to this phenomenon as "Congo-as-Culture", which focuses on folklorist leftovers from the Congo in the U.S. through the examination of pottery, languages, music, and baskets, among other artifacts. This is also the focus of Part II of the 2014 collection by Cooksey, Poynor, and Vanhee entitled Kongo Across the Waters (2014), "Kongo in the Americas", which deals in a similarly "culturalist" manner (cf. the discussion below of this term) with Congolese traits in the U.S.A. Overall, in secondary texts, the Congo is often integrated into the signifier "Africa", an operation repeated in the primary texts as well, thus highlighting how Congoism remains an issue even today, not least in scholarly works. The result of this is that the Congo is considered to be just another African ethnicity, or geographical notion – indistinguishable from the others, and as if one "African" geography may substitute neatly for any other. If anything, this book attempts to break with this suggestion and thus critically engages with much of the empirical, historical work done on the Congo.

The Congo has received limited attention in many theory-oriented works. Two cases in point are David Miller's Blank Darkness and David Spurr's Rhetoric of Empire. Building upon Edward Said (who, in fact, takes up Miller's central concepts in Culture and Imperialism, Said 1994: 43-44), Miller suggests that, historically, "Africa" has constituted the blank spot between Europe and it reverse image, the Orient. Because these two interlocking profiles leave no slot open in "our intellectual apparatus" for a third element with a positive shape of its own (Miller 1985: 14), Africa "appears to mean whatever one wants, in the language one wants" (ibid: 11). Miller dubs these imaginations "Africanist", a discourse reproduced via "hints rather than statements, hearsay rather than direct evidence, allegory rather than realism" (ibid: 6). Dual, polarized evaluations of "monstrousness" or "nobility" pervade Africanist discourses (ibid: 5), as well as evolutionary truisms (ibid: 169) and image projection: "as in the clouds[...]you can see anything you wish. The blank slate of Africa, with no past or future, can be made to fulfill the desires of your own present. From there it is only one step to the fulfillment of your nightmares at well" (ibid: 248).

In a manner similar to David Spurr, whose seminal Rhetoric of Empire also uses Heart of Darkness as a "continual point of reference" to debate U.S. American ways of writing about non-Western peoples (Spurr 1993: 3), Miller constructs his theory around Joseph Conrad's novella, which he considers "the strongest of all Africanist texts" that "makes the initial perception of a discourse as 'Africanist' possible" (Miller 1985: 170). Both Miller and Spurr, however, predominantly discuss the rhetoric employed in Heart of Darkness as an allegory for Africa in general (e.g. ibid), not the Congo Free State specifically. As such, both Miller and Spurr use Congo rhetoric as a synonym for Africa and the other way around. Scholars who focus on Joseph Conrad, such as Peter Firchow and others,[13] make precisely the same move.

The work at hand disentangles the real-and-imagined Congo from the real-and-imagined Africa. It avoids using these two signifiers interchangeably and synonymously, although they can and will feed into one another. When this happens, it will be mentioned explicitly. However, Congoism cannot be identified and understood properly if one adheres to the "unanimist mythologies", as Appiah has it (1992: 217), of an epistemic or historical homogeneity of Africa. There is, as Appiah reminds us, no such thing as a unified "African cultural or political or intellectual life" (ibid: 127). As soon as a unified Africa is claimed, writes Appiah, it is the "product, often unintended and unanticipated, of theories" (ibid: 290). When the

13 According to Firchow's though-provoking Envisioning Africa, Conrad intended to write a parable in Heart of Darkness about Africa in general, not the Congo Free State in particular (2000: 22-25). Russell West, in turn, links Heart of Darkness to abjection, but he does so in terms of the whole continent: "the journey into Africa itself is a journey into abjection" (2007: 238).

whole of Africa is monolithically depicted as an "absolute otherness", as one "vast dark cave", "primordial chaos", or "nothingness", as Mbembe suggests (2004: 2-4), the specificity of the Congo (and the discourses, interests, and power relations that go along with it) goes unnoticed. This work attempts to break through this phalanx of "Africa" in order to get to the Congo.

Separating "Africa" and the Congo is especially important since Congoism thrives on internal differentiations within the former. Often it is the Congo, not the whole of "Africa", that is a metaphor for Otherness (ibid: 2) or a "paradigm" of difference (Mudimbe 1994: xii). It is plain wrong to assert that African American intellectuals did not distinguish between African regions and did not transcend the idea, as in current Vice President Joe Biden's famous gaffe at the 2014 United States-Africa Business Forum, that Africa is a "nation" (Chasmar 2015). Congoism turns the Congo into the real-and-imagined underbelly of Africa. It plays Central West Africa out against Ethiopia, Egypt, West Africa, and other regions. It divides Africa into "good" and "bad" parts, of which the former frequently is post-apartheid South Africa and the latter is The Democratic Republic of the Congo, for instance, especially in contemporary discourse.

How does one get through to the Congo without reference to Conradian undergrowth? The focus of the next section is how the Congo might be approached in a manner that is empirically sound.

DISSECTING CONGOISM: METHODOLOGY, METHODS, SOURCES

Congoism is a complex discourse, the subtleties, perseverance, and adaptability of which can be understood by keeping its three C's in mind: culture, capitalism, and (social) class.[14] The pervasive presence and force of Congoism can thus be tackled

---

14 Together with the three C's, the analytic categories of race, gender, and ethnicity will play a role in establishing an understanding of the signifier Congo. It is important to bear in mind that the notions belonging to these categories – "white" and "Black", as well as "male" and "female" and "African" and "American" – will be considered historically contingent cultural constructions rather than biological determinants. Discussing skin color, sex, and nationality as historically contingent emphasizes the dynamic, fleeting, and changeable quality of these notions. This book suggests that power – and the political, social, economic privileges going with it – plays an important role in the transformation of these notions. The term "white", for instance, is more a marker of a certain set

best, first of all, if one focuses on "American culture" as a whole. This does not mean that one can claim to have actually taken into account the whole field of American culture. The best one can do is to attempt to discuss American culture in the manner proposed by Stuart Hall: as the representational field of shared meanings and values that U.S. Americans exchange and negotiate with each other (2003a: 2). Within this cultural field, common meanings, as Hall explains, are produced by binding two systems of representation together: the conceptual and the language systems. Whereas the former enables one to make sense of the world through concepts that classify and categorize, the latter makes use of language signs (words and written texts, as in this book) to communicate these conceptual ideas. To find the regulatory "codes" between concepts and language is part and parcel of this project (Hall 2003c: 29). Otherness is one of these codes, which, like other codes, is "the result of social conventions", as Hall asserts, and therefore "a crucial part of our culture – our shared 'maps of meaning' – which we learn and unconsciously internalize as we become members of our culture" (Hall 2003b: 29). This work maintains that the code of Otherness is produced and reasserted through the Congo, amongst others.

How can one decode the meaning and negotiations that are produced via the Congo? Stuart Hall, building on de Saussure and his structuralist and postmodernist heirs, suggests doing as much by looking at the Congo as a "sign", or as a part of the English language that is used to communicate ideas (ibid: 31). The Congo as sign can be split into a signifier and signified. The signifier is the form (the word itself); the signified, in turn, is the idea, the concept behind this form. As we will see, the signified concepts in this book vary widely – from slavery to notions of Social Darwinian race (e.g. "pureblooded" blackness) to horrendous atrocities (e.g. American lynching, Congo Free State).

Hall reminds us that the relation between signifier and signified is the result of negotiations and agreed meanings "specific to each society and to specific historical moments" (ibid: 32). In this book, this has translated into, on the one hand, clearly distinguishable "text trajectories" (Blommaert 2005: 255), or how the Congo signi-

of power relations than a skin color, although these are intertwined: Economic and social privileges are unequally distributed to those people with the "right" skin color (white). As a power-filled and historically contingent concept, many people can fall into the category of whiteness or blackness under the appropriate circumstances. Building on Charles Mills, it is suggested that these malleable "blacknesses" and "whitenesses" exist by virtue of the establishment of their internal distinctions (Mills: 1997: 80) – some whites are decidedly whiter than others and the same goes for Blacks. In this field of internal distinctions, the Congo will play a central role.

fier moves constantly through American contexts and genres. On the other hand, the historical contingency of the Congo discourse has resulted in a process of "continuous interpretation and re-interpretation" (Said 2003: 332). Thus, phases of signification can be detected, fashions can be traced, and new alliances with major schools of thought can be identified. The sign of the Congo varies and changes depending on the epistemic mainstream to which intellectuals attach themselves at their time of writing.

For instance, in 19th-century American culture, intellectuals drew from various schools of thought – sometimes, but not necessarily, simultaneously – including the sacred and the secular, the academic and the popular, classicist and orientalist thought, and Aryanist and Afrocentrist discourses (Hall 2009: 1-16). The real-and-imagined Congo has thus been produced using different intellectual toolboxes, as will be shown. Despite all of these changes on the surface, the Congo nevertheless remained bound to its underlying code of Otherness. New rhetoric, novel developments in the field of history, and fresh knowledge of Central West Africa have never changed the basic assumptions underlying Congoism. Changes merely highlighted or challenged some traits, suppressed others, and adjusted the rationale behind the "Othering" according to the needs and paradigms of the time.

Capitalist interests have also kept a tight grip on the discursive production of the real-and-imagined Congo. Economic focus on the Congo has taken many forms – from anything as big as colonialism to something as small as decent sales figures for one's own travelogue. Capitalism has risen since the Renaissance as the "single decisive principle" in Euro-American social environments, as Samir Amin has termed it (2009: 152), and yet it has remained largely off the radar in academic and popular Congo investigations. Popular accounts such as Stearns's Dancing in the Glory of Monsters (2011), for instance, avoid mentioning capitalism. In Stearns's work, the international markets (e.g. ibid: xxiii), the black markets (e.g ibid: 39, 117, 157), and the local food markets (e.g. ibid: 35) are treated as derivatives of the principle of supply and demand.

This book asks why particular phrasings are used and not others, especially since some kind of focus on capitalism has been shown in this book to be a an important aspect for coming to terms with Central West Africa. Commercial discourse and capitalist logic provide both the rationale and the discursive justification for, amongst others, colonial conquest (discussed in the First and Second Chapters in particular). "Normalized" capitalist rationale enables conquest executed in the name of "opening" the economies of resource-rich countries. The constantly returning set of thematic fascinations within Congoism has included, amongst others, the necessity of free trade, cheap labor, private and public enterprise, as well as the abundance of resources and a complete lack of economic vision from the Congolese. This is capitalist logic and could be labeled as such. Writing about "the market" in lieu of capitalism runs the risk of regarding local and external markets as equivalent. This strengthens a substantial discursive trait within Congoism: The Congo-as-a-resource (i.e. the Congo as a provider of human and natural resources for the good of, allegedly, all those involved), a topos that is discussed at length in the Second Chapter.

Capitalist commerce is explicitly addressed and spelled out in the following chapters, as it draws attention to issues of power and oppression – through which Othering is enabled – in the name of profit that go beyond the mere buying and selling for the sake of "making a living". As an analytic term, capitalism enables us to critically highlight the far-reaching national and international effects of structuring a society around private ownership, free wage-earning, the expanding accumulation of commodities for profit, and the division of labor (Weinberg 2003: 1). Capitalism is particularly important to highlight because the crystallization of capitalist society went hand in hand with the conquest of the world. Amin asserts, "[T]hese are two dimensions of the same development" (Amin 2009: 151). My book proves this to be correct, both in colonial and postcolonial times. Moreover, capitalism highlights internal social consequences, such as the emergence of social classes, migratory movements, and institutional, legal, and political arrangements implemented to insure a dependable supply of resources and labor (Weinberg 2003: 1). In addition, the term capitalism, as an oppositional term (Kocka 2013: 6), has political dimensions which need to be addressed in the following chapters in order to come to terms with Congoism.

Capitalism comes with a value system, and Eurocentrism is one manifestation of this system. This book wholeheartedly seconds Amin's conviction that capitalism has been a major factor in the development of Eurocentric discourses. These have willingly produced a useless "counterpart", or an equally "artificial conception of the Other" (ibid: 165), in order to legitimize exploitation. Eurocentrism, in the words of Shohat and Stam, "sanitizes Western history while patronizing and even demonizing the non-West" (1994: 3). Furthermore, Stam and Shohat continue, Eurocentric discourse "thinks of itself as its noblest achievements – science, progress, humanism – but of the non-West in terms of its deficiencies, real or imagined" (ibid: 3). This book illustrates how Eurocentrism works in concrete terms, how it gathers or loses steam according to the capitalist needs of the time. To be sure, the Eurocentric rationale has been altered in its most explicit forms over the last decades. Social Darwinism, for instance, is now largely discredited as racist (ibid: 23).

But diluted forms of that same logic do persist, it is demonstrated, albeit wrapped now in a relativist, postmodern vocabulary.

This work also suggests that the reasons for the ongoing persistence of Eurocentrism, albeit in altered forms, are to be sought in the development of capitalism. This is a connection seldom made within the theoretical field of "postcolonial theory", as designated by the theory-producing interpretations, readings, and critiquing of the cultural and material practices of colonialism (cf. Loomba 2005: 1-82). Although postcolonial theories have provided fruitful perspectives from which to tackle the Congo in this work (Edward Said and, to a lesser extent, Gayatri Spivak are used here), they decidedly could not carry the book all the way. Dirlik has a point when he states that many "postcolonial critics have [repudiated] a foundational role to capitalism in history" (1994: 331; cf. Chibber's more recent Postcolonial Theory and the Specter of Capital). Indeed, much can be said in favor of Dirlik's assertion that "the denial of capitalism's foundational status also reveals a culturalism in the postcolonialist argument" (1994: 331). This assertion is quoted and supported here in full recognition, of course, that this book is written with a strong focus on American culture and through the lens of a decidedly Euro-American cultural studies. Investigating "culture", however, is not the same as "culturalism", which, contrary to what is attempted here, largely excludes capitalism from its rationale and replaces it through culture as "the main driving force of inevitably quite different historical trajectories" (Amin 2009: 7). Without capitalism "as the foundation for European power and the motive force of its globalization, Eurocentrism would have been just another ethnocentrism", Dirlik provocatively claims (1994: 331). With this in mind, this book incorporates capitalism as a substantial engine driving many of the findings, and it will be constantly tested and questioned through the primary sources at hand.

Besides culture and capitalism, social class has also emerged as a decisive element in uncovering and understanding Congoism. It is maintained here that through the Congo signifier, Black American intellectuals have outed and constructed themselves as a "class". The term "bourgeois" is used in this book more often than "middle class" when discussing Black intellectuals. The former concept is applied in the sense, defined by Raymond Williams, of "a ruling class" (1983: 48). As such, intellectuals attempted to be spokespeople, as well as organizers and instructors of and for "their" people – on a local scale, but also on a national and international plane. As self-proclaimed mouthpieces of their communities, intellectuals critiqued racist America and did much to strengthen their communities. The heroism of this, as well as the difficulties that were encountered, cannot be underestimated or stressed enough. Amidst this advocating for "their" people, however, processes of self-interest were simultaneously at work. They involved thrusting certain values upon "other" Blacks, through which the latter were kept in their place or forced in a direction that would not serve them best. These processes often drew from white bourgeois thinking and threatened to even out the gains obtain by the activism in which these intellectuals engaged.

Class is understood here in the sense articulated by E.P. Thompson, that is, as an active, historical process that "happens[...]in human relationships" (1995b: 131). Thompson's suggestion is that class is not a given structure, but happens as "a result of common experiences (inherited or shared)" through which "the identity of their interests as between themselves" are negotiated, "and as against other men whose interests are different from (and usually opposed to) theirs" (ibid). Although this definition does not fully encompass the Black American intellectual experience, it does provide a point of departure from which this book may position itself with regard to the category. Black intellectuals did not necessarily share similar experiences, either socially, economically, or otherwise. Although some of them were wealthy and successful, with well-paid positions at academic institutions (e.g. Booker T. Washington), many more could barely make ends meet. "Middle classness", as David Graeber suggests, has never been "an economic category at all", but rather a social and political one (2014: 76). Thus, economic realities, like education, varied immensely among these intellectuals. As a group, however, intellectuals did articulate their own identity vis-à-vis that of others, such as lower-class Americans, Congolese Blacks, and all those who went against their understanding of "normality". Although this struggle (prior to the 1860s) was hardly an open one, many intellectual texts bear its traces.

To investigate how the Congo signifier came into being, U.S. "discourses" on the Congo are examined and interrogated. Due to the amazing proliferation of "discourse babble" in contemporary academia (Henriques et al. 1984: 105), the term 'discourse' has become both omnipresent and maddeningly vague. Sara Mills goes as far as to suggest that the concept "has perhaps the widest range of possible significations of any term in literary and cultural theory, and yet it is often the term within theoretical texts which is least defined" (Mills 1997: 1). As a discourse analytic apparatus is applied throughout this book – including the use of terms such as archive, archaeology, and discourse itself, of course – it is necessary to try to define in as precise and detailed a manner as possible what is understood by these concepts.

The first concept that should be investigated is "discourse" itself. It will not be automatically associated with Foucault alone in this work, although his seminal The Archaeology of Knowledge, as mentioned above, will play a role (more implicitly than explicitly, however). In Sawyer's archaeology of the concept of "discourse", the author concludes that "if one is to attribute the broad usage of the term 'discourse,' it should either be attributed to British cultural studies collectively, to Lacan, or to the French Marxist discourse analysts working in the 1960s and 1970s" (2002: 450). As Foucault's body of work itself does not present a consistent definition of discourse (Willaert 2012: 28), and probably very willfully avoided working out a consistent toolbox of methods, the works of Foucauldian-inspired discourse analysts such as Siegfried Jäger and Jan Blommaert will be mined in what follows in order to arrive at a workable definition and method of "discourse" analysis. The role of Foucault in this work is thus as epistemic provider of important keywords (and the ideas connected to them) – most prominently archive, archaeology, discourse, and power – but he does not serve as an inspiration for the concrete methods necessary to grasp these terms empirically.

Discourse is considered in this work as "language-in-action" (Blommaert 2005: 2). Investigating discourse requires that one attends critically both to language and to action, and recognize discourse as containing myriad forms of meaningful "'flagging' performed by means of objects, attributes, or activities" (ibid: 3). The signifier Congo is a model example of language in action, triggering various historically contingent semanticizations. As shown above, these range from widespread material naming practices to a heterogeneous corpus of metaphors. Given the broadness of these Congo semanticizations, Congo discourse will be narrowed down in this work as an ongoing attention to "language" in the traditional textual sense. Thus, discourse is understood here as the reappearing and socially conventionalized utterances on Central West Africa which provide a normalized language for "talking" about the Congo, its geography, history, and inhabitants (Jäger 2004: 127, 130). The talking in the work at hand is textual, in the sense that Congo utterances are investigated which appear in fictional and non-fictional texts (as well as those falling in between) published for a broader audience. Unpublished work, such as manuscripts and personal letters, is excluded. To ensure comparability between the various time periods and to reduce a large number of sources to manageable proportions, this work refrains from engaging in a systematic investigation of (audio)visuals (e.g. music, images, and film), although they will be alluded to in the Second Chapter to sum up some of the results.

Critics might argue that a discourse analytic approach potentially runs the danger of reducing extremely violent events (such as the ones under scrutiny in this work) and their victims to mere "discourse", thereby reducing these crimes to nothing more than language, invention, and imagination. This is patently not the case because discourse (as language-in-action) is deeply social and contextual in nature.

In other words, if one investigates discourse, one investigates more than just language. "There is no such thing as a 'non-social' use of discourse", Blommaert asserts (2005: 4). From this perspective, discourse analysis enables one to examine meaningful social differences, conflicts, and struggles. This book follows Blommaert in his assertion that "discourse is what transforms our environment into a socially and culturally meaningful one" (ibid). This kind of meaning-construction "does not develop in vacuo", as Blommaert states, "it does so under rather strict conditions that are both linguistic (never call a mountain a 'bird' or a 'car') and sociocultural (there are criteria for calling something 'beautiful' or 'problematic')" (ibid). The social aspect of discourse often requires the discussion of the circumstance that give rise to and perpetuate it, hence the necessity of discussing the Congo via the way it is applied by its language users in various contexts (see below).

This approach to discourse analysis emphasizes the connection between discourse and society writ large. Here, central sociopolitical structures and events in the lives of African Americans – ranging from transatlantic slavery and the missionary movement to Jim Crow apartheid – are taken into account in order to understand the Congo discourse. The analysis of discourse is thus always and necessarily the examination of situated, contextualized language. And vice versa – context itself also becomes a crucial methodological and theoretical issue in the development of a critical study of language. Evans states that "language and grammar" have evolved "through contact with the real world in an attempt to name real things" (Evans 2000: 112). As a consequence, much of this book is dedicated to the scrutiny of context.

And the context, overwhelmingly, has been far from obvious. Wherever possible, the political, social, and cultural surroundings of African American intellectuals is gleaned through their own texts or those of white American or European intellectuals politically sympathetic to their plight (most famously Myrdal in the Second Chapter). Whenever a consistent contextualization through the lens of Black American texts has proved limited or impossible (as is the case in the First Chapter), contemporary academic voices have been added to the discussion. Again, these voices have not simply been taken up wholesale. Their discourse has also been critically scrutinized vis-à-vis my hypothesis of the existence of "academic Congoism".

Building on the contextualization of the Congo discourse, it is essential to understand that the Congo discourse is not a matter of free choice alone: History influences how one talks about Central West Africa. To show the regularities, constraints, possibilities, and rules within this discourse, a large corpus of texts has been assembled, which, in sum, constitutes the "archive" of American intellectual discourse on the Congo. This "archive" should be understood both materially and epistemically. In its material shape, the American archive comprises the entire corpus of texts by American intellectuals on the Congo in any given period, which, theoretically at least, can be bundled and stored (cf. Baßler 2005: 178, 196). In this work, a segment, or a corpus, of the overall Congo archive has been selected, and the criteria according to which this has been done will be described in the course of this Introduction.

In its epistemic meaning, the archive is a highly self-referential system of "intertextual" processes, or processes via which texts constitute the contextual reality of other texts (ibid: 13). Intertextuality thus refers to the fact that, whenever African Americans wrote about the Congo, they drew upon the words of others, constantly citing and re-citing expressions of both colleagues and opponents, as well as continuously recycling meanings that were already available (Blommaert 2005: 46). As Foucault had it in The Archaeology of Knowledge, "All manifest discourse is secretly based on an 'already said'" (2010: 25). As a whole, the archive is the regulator of what can and cannot be said about the Congo in any given time period. It is thus the key to describing the discontinuities and continuities between and within ideas, discourses, and rhetoric.

A Foucauldian "archaeology" will be performed on the Black American Congo archive. Foucault defined this term rather descriptively, writing that "archaeology tries not to define the thoughts, representations, images, themes, preoccupations that are concealed or revealed in discourses" (2010: 138). Instead, Foucault asserted that archaeologists should focus on "those discourses themselves, those discourses as practices obeying certain rules" (ibid). In contrast to Foucault, this work studies both the rules of discourse and the attendant representations. They often cannot, in fact, be disentangled from one another. Topoi such as the Congo-as-Savage, -Slave, -Culture, and -Resource reveal how discourse is regulated through certain figures of speech. They are also indicative of what lies behind the "rhetoric" – a term that signifies the study of tropes, topoi, and figures of style. The study of how these tropes, figures of speech, and topoi are given their internal and external logic (which places them within a larger epistemic framework; cf. Spurr 1993: 8) should shed some light on the "rules for discursive practices" (Foucault 2010: 139) that create a "common sense" about the Congo through "narratives", "stories", "representations", and other practices constituting topoi and tropes. "Narratives" are understood here as texts in which an intratextual agent conveys stories to an addressee (Bal 2009: 5). "Stories", in turn, provide the content of the overall narrative (ibid). Stories and narratives, written down in material "texts", are forms of "representations", which in turn signifies any use of language to represent the world to others (Hall 2003b: 15). All of these processes of narrativization, textualization, and representation combined are mobilized whenever the "discursive" comes into play (Hall 2003a: 6).

A key element in analyzing how common sense about the Congo is produced is what Francesca Poletta has termed the "canonized stories". Canonized stories are stories that masquerade as fact by suggesting coherence, familiarity, and credibility by repeating figures of style, plot lines, normative frameworks, and intertextual references. In other words, Congo stories make sense when one takes into account other similar stories. "We believe a story because it is familiar" (2006: 10), Poletta suggests. This does not mean that these stories are identical. On the contrary: One of their central traits is that they leave room for unpredictability, new interpretations, ambiguity, and alteration (ibid). Thus, far from reproducing a never-ending repetition of identical stories, the Congo discourses in the United States have produced malleable stories that adjust themselves to the parlance and needs of their time.

My archaeology discusses the Congo representations "in their specificity", as Foucault suggests (2010: 139). This is accomplished by attempting to understand the "specificity of its occurrence and to determine its conditions of existence, fix at least its limits, establish its correlations with other statements that may be connected with it, and show what other forms of statement it excludes" (ibid: 28). But how does one execute such a challenging program of archaeological aims? Methodically, this entails capturing the real-and-imagined Congo, first of all, in a longue durée manner, as discussed above. Investigating the evolution of discourse over longer periods of time has involved, to paraphrase Obeyesekere, an ongoing dialectic of reconstruction and deconstruction of the text corpus in this work (2005: 205).

On the level of reconstruction, an attempt has been made to select a representative corpus of texts from the African American archive, comprised of both so-called "truthful" texts and more overtly "imaginative" ones. Factual and fictional accounts occasionally slip into one another, but both groups of texts are, in the end, treated differently. Although both are approached through discourse analysis (thus aligning them with each other methodically and epistemically), this work is not radically postmodernist in that it considers texts as "essentially the same", as Richard J. Evans has phrased it (2000: 114). Fiction is written with its own set of intentions, readerships, and goals in mind. Moreover, "there is a very real difference between what somebody writes and the account someone else gives of it." Hence the split between primary and secondary literature in this work (cf. the list of References), no matter how fluid the borders between the two may actually be. It is through this lens that multiple Congoisms can be identified: The defaming discourse of the primary sources, as well as that of its academic handling (cf. the First Chapter), and the Congoism of fiction and non-fiction. All of them, as will be shown, play into one another.

In the ongoing reconstruction of an African American Congo archive that has been ignored or neglected for so long, this work provides a new reading of a wide variety of texts. Many of them were available in scanned form in large electronic and microfilm databases. Thus, the focus has been less on unearthing "new" texts than on re-interpreting known ones. The archives that were consulted include the online and microfilm archives at the Schomburg Center for Research in Black Culture (New York) and the John F. Kennedy Institute (Berlin). Both of these provided insight into the extent to which Black American intellectuals engaged with the Congo in their monographs, theater performances, and the news media, particularly of the 1960s and 1970s. To access material from the decades and centuries before, electronic databases from the Internet Archive, JSTOR, The New York Times, Accessible Archives, and The Chicago Defender archive were mined.

The method and ambition of this work required an electronic archival approach; time and geography would not have allowed for a systematic analysis of archives other than electronic ones. In the cases where "new" materials, such as John Henrik Clarke's unpublished biography of Patrice Lumumba, were "discovered" in the Schomburg ("The Life and Death of Patrice Lumumba"), more of the same rhetoric marking Clarke's other publicly discussed works was sought out, thus underscoring the similarities between "known" and "new" materials. The publicly discussed texts under scrutiny range from pamphlets to poems and from activist speeches and sermons to novels and travelogues. Transparency is one of the advantages of this electronic archival approach: Anyone who wishes to may consult the databases.

Deconstructing a heterogeneous text corpus has often meant focusing on certain texts and not others in order to create a manageable approach to the overall archive. This has led here to a prioritization of historical accounts about Africa, or, in the parlance of large stretches of the past, accounts of one's own "race". These accounts include works that define themselves explicitly as "history" (e.g. by George Washington Williams, W.E.B. Du Bois, and Lisa Amos Pendleton in the Second Chapter), as well as texts that refrain from claiming a historical status, but do narrate history, such as pamphlets, novels, poems, and plays. Discourse as a language-in-action thus leads to an ongoing broadening of the idea of what constitutes history.

One reason to prioritize historical accounts is their wide circulation among African American intellectuals due to their centrality and "primacy" as a mode of understanding the world and one's place in it (Anderson/Stewart 2007: 43). Another reason is the genre's frequent and openly communicated self-reflectiveness. Whenever African Americans constructed histories of Africa, particularly at times when neither Africans nor African Americans were considered to possess any, they were also writing commentaries on their own times and history, often with a direct political impulse to act against the conditions they were facing – namely, "race prejudice", to quote W.E.B. Du Bois in The World and Africa (1962: x). More so than their white counterparts, who could and would more easily assume a universal and objective historical perspective, African Americans have reflected upon themselves and others as knowledge producers, especially, but not exclusively from the mid-20th century onward.

Examples of this interest-led political self-reflectiveness are legion. "Let me be your guide," the African American veteran Washington Post correspondent Keith Richburg says to his readers in his polemic reflection on his three-year stint in Africa, "and try to follow along as I lay out for you here why I feel the way I do – about Africa, about America, and mainly about myself and where it is I now know I belong" (1996: xvii). Richburg makes it very clear from the start that his interest is in countering the rhetoric of "our supposedly enlightened, so-called black leaders" who hold Africa "as some kind of black Valhalla [...] where black men and women walk in true dignity. Sorry, but I've been there. [T]hank God that I am an American" (ibid: xvii-xviii). The Congo/Zaire figures prominently in Richburg's book as the country where his alienation from Africa's "debilitating effects of corruption" (ibid: 175) and from his fellow African Americans' "near religious pilgrimage" (ibid: 161) to the continent reached an all-time low.

Self-reflectiveness does not mean that these Black intellectuals considered their stories as fundamentally limited, subjective, or flawed. On the contrary, African American historians had no doubts that they were reconstructing a "truthful" Congo representation, no matter how different and personal their stories may have been. Their language, however, betrays the discourse and archive in which they were operating. Geographically, for instance, Congo's landscape ranged from an all-out "swamp" to a "jungle" or a "valley" (as used in, respectively, George Schuyler 1992: 62; Franklin 1952:21; Du Bois 2001:42); Congolese, in turn, designated anything from "Pygmies", "red dwarfs", and "Bantu" to "Negrillos" (Du Bois 2001: 42, 64-65; Washington 1909: 18; Du Bois 1972: 165). Against the backdrop of so many designations, it is the task of the archaeologist to discuss how these constituted and conveyed highly purposeful, and deeply historical and normative meanings. At stake in an archaeology of Congo discourse is uncovering the "unconscious activity that took place [within the author], despite himself, in what he said or in the almost imperceptible fracture of his actual words" (Foucault 2010: 27).

The ebb and flow of African American intellectual discourse on Central West Africa is here followed by investigations of the "discursive events" that drive the Congo narratives. Events become discursive by virtue of receiving broad attention over a short, medial, or long period of time, as Jäger writes (2004: 132-162). The (f)actuality of these events is not what is at stake here, at least not primarily. Foucault writes in The Archaeology of Knowledge: "The description of the events of discourse poses a quite different question: how is it that one particular statement appeared rather than another?" (2010: 27). Thus, the concept of discursive events is used to underline the fact that the Congo, exemplified by today's The Democratic Republic of the Congo, has become in many ways a "heart of darkness" through the cumulative highlighting and repetition of certain events and not others, that is, by discursive selection and self-perpetuating rhetorical strategies and attitudes, and not by the "given" awfulness of things that quite naturally require our attention.

This selective discursive focus has not only created a surplus of dismissive, negative events and statements (cf. Van Hove 2009). It is also a matter of choice and repetition that the Congo Free State, and not the many Congolese abused in the transatlantic slave trade over a span of four centuries (Miller 1976: 101; Klein 1999: 66), has become a primary discursive event. The choices and reiterations involved in transmitting the "atrocities" of the Congo Free State from one generation to the next can be traced step by step in the African American archive, starting with the famous 1890 "[An] Open Letter to His Serene Majesty Leopold II, King of the Belgians and Sovereign of the Independent State of Congo" by George Washington Williams, who, after visiting the Congo Free State, accused Leopold II of being guilty of "deceit, fraud, robberies, arson, murder, slave-raiding and general policy of cruelty […] on the natives" (Williams 2006: 130). Decades of allusions to the Congo Free State followed, either in a direct fashion, such as in Malcolm X's 1964 "[An] Exchange on Casualties" (X 1970b), or offhandedly, as in George Schuyler's satirical 1938 Black Empire, in which the "natives" of the Belgian Congo turn genocidal against the white colonials, a circumstance that had to "be expected in view of the long series of Belgian atrocities" (1991: 129).

What matters for this work is that all of these direct and indirect references contributed to the Congo's strong association with certain "atrocities" (the Congo Free State, that is) and not to others (the slave trade). This one-sided mountain of negative discursive events has produced the Congo's remarkable discursive trajectory – matched perhaps only by its affirmative discursive counterparts "Ethiopia"/"Ethiopianism" (Gruesser 2000: 3-12) and "Egypt"/"Egyptomania" (Trafton). This trajectory made it possible for the Congo signifier to also function independently from discursive events: It remained on the African American discursive radar, often as a metaphor, even when there was nothing new to report about Central West Africa.

The chapters in this book have been organized around the various topoi that underlie the rhetoric used to narrate the discursive Congo events. Topoi designate the fixed combination of various story aspects in Congo texts (e.g. the Congo-as-Slave, Congo-as-Savage, Congo-as-Darkness). These topoi build upon various tropes, taking up literary and rhetorical devices such as metaphor, metonymy, synecdoche, and irony, which all consist of the use of a non-literal use of language (e.g. "Darkness" in the topos of the Congo-as-Darkness). These tropes and topoi will be looked at in order to explain their emergence in epistemological terms. The discussion will revolve around which socio-political circumstances, as well as which trends in knowledge production, have triggered particular representations of the Congo.

Congoism is discussed in all main chapters via three points of analysis: the perceived landscape of the Congo (point one), its people (point two), and its history (point three). Concretely, this analysis is executed based on the building blocks of Congoism: the language of repetition, as hinted at above, but also, and equally importantly, the rhetoric of silence. Repetition can be understood and analyzed in a relatively straightforward manner. It may be recognized through regularly recurring figures of speech, narrative schemes, discursive strategies, and persuasion through rhetoricality. Silence, however, is a more complex matter. It deals with what Allan Sekula has called the "shadow archive" of U.S. American culture (1989: 347), describing the hushed social and moral hierarchy within the U.S. American visual archive (which I will extend to African American texts). Muteness, however, can be investigated because it has a rationale (i.e. silence exists for a reason) and a language of its own: Silence thus leaves systematic traces in the archive, allowing a decision to be made as to whether a "silentium" should be read as an "argumentum". In other words: whether silence is merely coincidental or discursively organized (cf. Ernst 2002: 25; Bührmann/Schneider 2008: 98).

Silences on the Congo will be uncovered via a series of simultaneously executed readings. I read Central West Africa both "widely" and "closely" (Hallet 2010: 294), moving gradually from a broad intertextual reading of the respective context ("wide reading") to a more detailed, text-immanent one ("close reading"). A "contrapuntal" reading, as Said has termed it (1994: 51), is also executed. This entails, to paraphrase Jan Vansina's own methodical considerations in Paths in the Rainforests, "confronting" (1990: 24) Black and white primary texts, as well as marginal and canonized texts, with one another.[15] This confrontation is illuminating in terms of the manner in which it allows for the tracing of gaps in the texts: It allows us to ask whether their claims of knowledge or ignorance were credible vis-à-vis what their sources or what others knew, and what they selectively omitted or underlined. A contrapuntal reading is also enlightening in terms of class. As mentioned before, class positions are hardly ever communicated openly by Black bourgeois American intellectuals (until intellectuals of other classes or with other class aspirations became more prominent; cf. the Third Chapter). How can this allegiance to class be decoded, then, if it is not openly reflected?

For one, class can be recognized because bourgeois intellectuals shared common values which they did communicate frequently. "Bourgeois thought", to paraphrase Amin, makes people responsible for their own conditions, highlighting internal factors along the way and disregarding the external ones that have (co)produced these conditions (2009: 182). Much of this can be detected in Congo discourse. To decode class positions, the "undersides" of African American intellectual discourse are focused upon, to quote E.P. Thompson (1995a: 137). These comprise "petites histoires", such as anecdotes and instances in the text where these intellectuals may be caught off guard. If this had not been done, the current analysis, as E.P. Thompson asserts, would have been in danger of "becoming prisoner of the assumptions and self-image" of those intellectuals under scrutiny, and therefore would have silently accepted and reproduced their class position (ibid).

Silence raises many questions. How is it justified? How does it arise? Are some intellectual circles more silent (or ignorant) than others? To what does silence, as a broader phenomenon, point: the Congo's peripheral meaning or quite the opposite? And how can silence and ignorance be traced and discussed convincingly? As is shown, silence often derived from the Congo's supposed unknowability, no matter how much is actually known about it. To Alexander Crummell in 1862, for instance, the African interior is as unknown in his own time as it had been "two thousand years ago, in the time of Herodotus and Ptolemy" (1869: 288). According to Du Bois in 1910, the Belgian Congo was "a land of silence and ignorance" (1992: 390). Forty years later, he still reckoned that "no coherent account of the millions of human beings who have lived here for thousands of years" can be made (1962: 164). Booker T. Washington discussed the "Kongo Free State" at the start of the 20th century as a region that cannot be known, since it has "never been touched by the influence of either European or Mohammedan civilizations" (1909: 48). John

15 Vansina's full quote goes: "[Texts] can be quite partisan, and as a result quite misleading. This often becomes clear when independent texts are confronted with each other" (1990: 24).

Hope Franklin repeated this argument half a century later in his seminal From Slavery to Freedom: It would be "impossible to trace with any degree of accuracy the political development" of Central West Africa "before Europeanization", as there is "remarkably little available information" (1952: 21). My confrontational readings will discuss what could have given rise to these beliefs and the contradictions inherent within them. Du Bois, for instance, maintained his position up until the early 60s. The Third Chapter investigates what made him change his mind.

Silence turns into ignorance whenever it is unevenly distributed, to paraphrase Robert Proctor – a scholar who advocates the study of ignorance, which he calls "agnotology" (cf. Proctor 2008). Ignorance is by no means understood as a willful act alone. "Ignorance has many interesting surrogates", Proctor reminds us, "and overlaps in myriad ways with – as it is generated by – secrecy, stupidity, apathy, censorship, disinformation, faith, and forgetfulness" (ibid: 2). Proctor subsequently distinguishes three kinds of ignorance: Ignorance as a "native state", ignorance as a "lost realm", and ignorance as a deliberately engineered and "strategic ploy" (ibid: 3). The former implies a kind of deficit, caused by naïveté, improper education or the simple unavailability of knowledge (ibid: 4), while ignorance as a lost realm is based on the idea that inquiries are always selective – "we look here rather than there [...] to focus on this is therefore invariably a choice to ignore that" (ibid: 7). The third kind of ignorance, ignorance as a strategic ploy (or active construct), in turn, focuses on all those instances of ignorance that are made, maintained, and manipulated through active human planning. While tackling why some aspects of the Congo are registered while others are thoroughly neglected (Smithson 2008: 210), an attempt is made in this book to explain ignorance, especially in its first two meanings.

Omission and ignorance are by no means signs of Central West Africa's marginality with regard to geopolitics (as Stearns 2011: xxii-xxiii maintains). On the contrary, deletion and 'unknowledge' are discussed in what follows as discursive strategies employed in order to justify or cover up the constant meddling in the region. If anything, the "alternation between extreme noise or violence and relative silence" (Turner 2013: 3) are indications of the Congo's centrality as a material and epistemic geography in the global history of capitalism. As a prominent supplier of minerals (e.g. coltan, diamonds, copper, and rubber), the Congo has enabled technological advances that accelerated global capitalism over the course of the last two centuries. This has proven as true in contemporary postcolonial times as it did in the colonial period. Until the late 19th century, slaves provided "the capital which financed the Industrial Revolution in England and of mature industrial capitalism", as the 1944 study Slavery and Capitalism by Eric Williams, which remains relevant, maintained (Williams 1944: vii; cf. Inikori 2000).

Each of the three main chapters of this book approaches Congo discourse from a different perspective. Broadly speaking, the "poetics" (Hall 1993a: 6) of Congo representation are examined in the First Chapter, which explains how language produces the Congo signifier step by step, one text at a time. The Second Chapter, in turn, explicitly investigates the epistemic and intertextual aspects involved in Congo signification. By drawing from various epistemic fields, the Congo meanings multiplied and diversified, as is shown, but remained constant in signifying Otherness. In the last major chapter, the near-hegemonic power of historically specific dismissive Congo rhetoric is shown through the failure of many intellectuals to go beyond Congoism, despite striving to do so. The Conclusion confirms this point with a discussion of contemporary white authors. From the point of view of periodization, the three chapters constitute a discussion of precolonial, colonial, and postcolonial discourse. This periodization reflects the major rupture points in the Congo discourse: Colonialism and postcolonialism dramatically affected what was and was not said.

More concretely, the chapters cover the following ground: The First Chapter ("From Slave to Savage") discusses the creation of the Congo topos between 1800-1885 by illustrating how representations of Central West Africa moved from the motif of the Congo-as-Slave (in antebellum America) to the near-monolithic topos of the Congo-as-Savage at the brink of colonialism. With a step-by-step analysis of the repetition and silencing of these topoi, this chapter shows how the Congo reflects African American discursive attitudes towards enslaved and oppressed Others, both of the internal and external variety. Discussing two works of history against the backdrop of their broader discursive context, R.B. Lewis's Light and Truth (1844) and George Washington Williams's History of the Negro (1885), this chapter demonstrates how Congo utterances shift in quantity and quality. These utterances transform from the silenced topos of enslaved abjection to a constantly communicated topos of imperial savageness. The fluidity of the Congo signifier is a leitmotiv, a golden thread throughout the chapter. Its meaning was produced in a complex, supra-individual relationship between contemporary historians and their broader socio-political cultures and social locatedness in terms of class, race, and gender. Through a "close reading" and "wide reading" of some of the African American texts produced in that period, this chapter investigates how African Americans created a Black, bourgeois subject whose textual template of rejection was constituted by the Congo.

The Second Chapter ("Between Art and Atrocity") dedicates itself to the colonial era until 1945 – the time period that saw the internal apartheid of "Jim Crow" and the external colonization and racial segregation of the Congo Free State and the Belgian Congo. Due to the increasing production, variation, importance, circulation, and availability of African American texts (works of history, as well as poetic, activist, and journalistic texts), several competing, simultaneously active Congo topoi emerged, ranging from the Congo-as-Darkness to the Congo-as-the-Vital and the Congo-as-Resource. In contrast to the previous chapter, less focus is put on the "making" of these topoi. Rather, the manner in which these motifs constructed their content and authority from a range of specific epistemologies ("parochial" and "eyewitness" epistemologies, for instance) is discussed. This chapter shows, first, how the canon of American Congo texts is styled by colonialism, and thus preserves a discursive status quo by navigating through familiar cultural oppositions (male/female, Black/white, middle class/lower class, man of action/man of books). Second, the chapter discusses how canonized Congo narratives incited opposition, which began emerging hesitantly (and rather ineffectively) in the 1920s.

"Revolution, Reform, Reproduction", the Third Chapter, deals with the time between 1945 and 2013. This period is marked by the rise and decline of the Black Freedom Movement in the U.S., with which the chapter begins. Examining the stance of select Black American intellectuals at length, the strategies developed by them to de-Other the Congo are discussed. Malcolm X and Pulitzer-prize-winning playwright Lynn Nottage figure prominently in this chapter, along with Black journalists and African-Americanized Congolese. The inherent limitations of modernist and postcolonial strategies become apparent in this chapter.

This work concludes with "Doing Damage, or Re-Writing Central West Africa", a discussion of contemporary Amazon.com bestsellers by Euro-American authors, specifically that by David Van Reybrouck. The broader and continued relevance of the work at hand is shown here, particularly against the background of Van Reybrouck's rather poor reflection of U.S. American sources and discourses. The discussion of Van Reybrouck shows to what extent Congoism is a phenomenon that cuts through national borders due to the increasingly global book markets, of which Amazon.com is both cause and effect. The Conclusion addresses the hope of a postmodern way out of the Congo discourse, which constitutes the latest episode in the long history of Congoism.

First Chapter

From Slave to Savage:

The Realization of a Topos (1800-1885)[1]

> All the religions of the world give the first place to morality. If there are any exceptions, they are at the extremes, Congoism on the one hand and Protestant Christianity on the other
> JOHN MILLER/THEOLOGY 1887

RADICAL DISCOURSE IN RADICAL TIMES: AN INTRODUCTION

Many discursive aspects of the "real-and-imagined" Congo were developed in times when the Central West African Congo was not yet colonially possessed or imperially exploited by Euro-American powers. This chapter traces the discourse surrounding the pre-colonial Congo in U.S. American intellectual texts from the late 18th to the late 19th century (1885, to be precise). This period bore witness to interactions between the Congo and the United States that altered the course of both regions. The massive slave importation from the Congo into the cotton-booming Low South of the United States constitutes one central dynamic that runs through this chapter. Permeating the period under scrutiny were extreme polarization and opposing trends in both the U.S. American and the global economic and social arenas, often revolving around the issues of freedom and civil rights.

This chapter demonstrates how these polarizations often arose from dialectical processes: Discursive action triggered counter-reactions by the key players in these struggles – men and women, Black and white, Americans and "Africans", elite and

1 This title builds on the essay by Dubravka Ugrešić, "The Realisation of a Metaphor."

working-class, and all those in-between that are now understood as agents within the analytic categories of race, class, gender, and ethnicity. This chapter describes the many discursive interactions between these actors by highlighting the often paradoxical and ironic social processes with which they had to deal. For instance, in a time of intensifying anti-Black racism and slavery, both abolitionist sentiments and African American activism, independence, and agency grew. The conservative "cult of true womanhood" presents another case in point: While it thrived, both the Women's Rights movement and "manliness" discourses intensified. Finally, at precisely the same time that ongoing calls for African and American unity were being issued, Black American institutions were organized around the exclusive categories of wealth, color, and middle-class virtues.

Polarizing dialectical processes produced radical discourses, and Congoism was one of them. Congoism's development in the 19th century will be systematically traced in this chapter. This will be done by reading texts by African American intellectuals both "widely" and "closely" (Hallet 2010: 294), moving gradually from a broad intertextual reading of the 19th-century context ("wide reading") to a more detailed text-immanent one ("close reading"). The "wide" contextual reading will describe 19th-century processes decisive for Congoism. Additionally, political trends, discursive themes, and perceived social fault lines in white and Black American intellectual circles, as well as in Central West African contexts, will be discussed.

This chapter attempts to interpret the context of the 19th century "through" primary texts. Thus, contexts are not considered external to the texts they produced, but rather regarded as "produced by and in the texts themselves", as Rebecca Karl phrased it in her seminal Staging the World (2007: 13). The texts through which the multiple contexts of the 19th century are read contain journalistic and popular scientific texts, such as the white abolitionist paper The Liberator and Black weeklies and monthlies like The Christian Recorder, The Colored American, The North Star, Douglass' Monthly, and Frederick Douglass' Paper.

Despite the aim of reading contexts predominantly through 19th-century primary sources, contemporary secondary literature plays a central role as well. Tracing the Central West African context through primary sources was a particularly slippery and elusive business, as the traces and voices of those enslaved, dominated, and destroyed in the 19th century remain either unrecorded or mediated via sources that tell the story of enslavement from the perspective of the enslavers (cf. Hartman 2007: 17). The reading here, ideally, seeks to circumvent the pitfalls of a top-down history by reading my carefully selected literature against the grain. This boils down to asking an uncomfortable, but necessary, question: To what extent can the scholarly works by, for instance, Melville Herskovits be considered part and parcel of a Congoist discourse, albeit an academic version of it?

After examining the various American and Central West African contexts, this chapter turns to Congo discourse in exemplary African American texts. Antebellum and postbellum Congo rhetoric are discussed separately by reading two African American works of history "widely". In the antebellum section of this chapter, the overall narrative, political agenda, and intellectual-epistemic background of R. B. Lewis's 1844 history Light and Truth will be debated. In the postbellum section, George Washington Williams's 1885 work History of the Negro Race in America from 1619 to 1880 is discussed. These works exemplify a number of typical aspects of the African American intellectual "knowing" and "unknowing" of the Congo in 19th-century America. What is known about the Congo is decisively influenced by how it is known, particularly in terms of intellectual traditions, schools of thought, and epistemic trends. Concretely, Lewis could actively "ignore" the Congo by writing a universal history based on the Bible and on antique sources with an agenda that was decidedly Afrocentric. Williams, in turn, could "re-know" the Congo by producing an Americanist history that built upon scientific paradigms and scientific texts of late 19th century. This chapter will show how this worked.

To make investigative claims of "ignorance" and of a "re-knowing" of the Congo requires uncovering the alternatives – what could have been said or written by Lewis's and Williams's contemporaries. A "contrapuntal" reading, as Said terms it (cf. the Introduction of this book), helped to do so by confronting the utterances of Lewis and Williams with the Congo discourses of a) Black newspapers (mentioned before) and b) standardized knowledge produced by white-dominated American dictionaries and encyclopedias (e.g. Lieber's Encyclopaedia Americana, Webster's American Dictionary of the English Language, and Porter's Practical Dictionary). White Euro-American studies, monographs, and travelogues on "Africa" that were known or had been used by Lewis and Williams constitute another source for contrapuntal confrontation (e.g. Reade's Savage Africa; Livingstone's A Popular Account; Stanley's Through the Dark Continent).

After the works of Lewis and Williams have been read "widely", they will be discussed "closely" by highlighting how their "ignorance" towards (cf. Introduction for a discussion on "ignorance") or "re-knowing" of the Congo could be produced and justified. This analysis is aided in particular by an examination of recurring figures of style. In these sections, the Congo signifier is discussed as a double geographical figuration, vacillating between the Central West African Congo and the U.S. American Congo. To illustrate what this meant in 19th-century Congo discourses, one might look to William Still's 1872 work of history, The Underground

Railroad. There, Stills cites from a heart-wrenching "letter dated Lewis Centre, Ohio": "Ohio has become a kind of a negro hunting ground, a new Congo's coast" (1872: 761). How should this quote be read?

The Central West African aspect of the phrase "Congo's coast" is used tropologically here as an analogy for Ohio within the context of the Fugitive Slave Law of 1850, a law that flooded the North with slave catchers from the South. To understand this particular use of the Congo, it is of central importance to come to terms with the Central West African reference behind it. "A new Congo's coast" hardly makes sense without uncovering what the Central West African coast stood for in African American discourses – namely, a slave district. This will be an important task in this chapter and a highly challenging one. Another result of this double figuration is the productive distinction throughout this work between the Congo as a geography and the Congo as a people, which begins to explain why African Americans were described as Congo: The geographical traits attached to the African region along the Congo estuary made them so.

The discussion of Lewis and Williams will be concluded by a more detailed examination, focusing on social power relations in the 19th-century U.S., of why their systematic "ignorance" and "re-knowing" of the Congo occurred. First of all, the silentium of the pre-60s discourses will be discussed via the terms "unknowledge" and "unknowing". These are discursive tools of surpassing or ignoring knowledge about peoples that are considered not worth knowing, since they are perceived as "slaves" whose insulting presence and existence caused free intellectual African Americans to assume "the only reasonable position [...] by a descendant of slaves" (Hartman 2007: 71): Silence, negation, and abjection.

Secondly, to debate the postbellum "re-knowing" of the Congo, the issue of knowledge proliferation and knowledge re-ordering during the rising tide of imperial epistemology in the late 19th century will be taken up. Through the central watchwords of that section – "classification", "progress", and "civilization" (Loomba 2005: 53-62; Burke 2012: 53-77) – Congo people came to stand for the internal and external "savages" that had to be uplifted from their low position in the supposed hierarchy of humanity through colonization, education, commerce, and Christianity.

What connects these ante- and postbellum processes of "unknowing" and "re-knowing" is the discursive creation of a racial, gendered, and classist "subpersonhood" in order to gain a "flexible positional superiority" (Said 2003: 7) towards what one is not – savage, enslaved, ugly, without history.

DIVISION IN BLACK AND WHITE: RACE, CLASS, AND GENDER STRUGGLES

19th-century intellectual America was a house with many chambers and most of them were deeply antagonized and "divided", to paraphrase Abraham coln.[2]Among the white American majority, the coexistence of pro-slavery politics and abolitionist activism led to ongoing sectional fights within the U.S. intellectual antebellum arena. The contradictions between national and state laws are only one example of the many tensions between pro-slavery and abolitionist political forces. For instance, while the Continental Congress3 prohibited the importation of slaves as early as 1774-1776,4 states of the Low South reopened and re-energized the transnational slave trade as soon as "the overpowering practicality" (Zinn 2003: 171) of booming sugar and cotton production demanded cheap labor.[5] This led to the importation of an estimated 250.000 slaves in the 19th century (ibid: 172), 100.000 of whom were imported between 1783 and 1808 (Wright 2001: 196).

Another example of the legal tension between abolitionist and pro-slavery politics was the admission of the Mexican war territories as non-slave states at the same time as the national U.S. government passed the controversial Fugitive Slave Act in 1850. Through this Act, free Blacks in the North had to prove their free status before commissions with little incentive to believe them, as these commissions were paid to return slaves to the South. This led to random arrests and wild accusations

2 Abraham Lincoln's famous speech, delivered upon accepting the Illinois Republican Party's nomination as that state's senator in 1858, is paraphrased here: "A house divided against itself cannot stand. I believe this government cannot endure, permanently, half slave and half free" (qtd. in Foner 2010: 99).

3 Which governed the colonies through the war against the British army (Zinn 2003: 81).

4 As Littlefield shows, the major reason for advocating abolitionism was to put economic pressure on British merchants, rather than to object to the inhumanity of the trade. Nevertheless, none of the states committed to the abolition of the external importation of slaves reopened the trade after the war, apart from those in the Low South (Littlefield 2005: 119). In the end, the policy was confirmed by the United States Federal Law in 1807 (Act Prohibiting Importation of Slaves).

5 Supported by technical innovation, such as Eli Whitney's improved cotton gin in 1793 (which separated the seeds more easily from the strands), cotton became the principle export good of the U.S., accounting for more than half of the nation's agricultural exports (White 2005: 169-170; Zinn 2003: 172).

based on "meager and conflicting evidence", as the African American abolitionist newspaper The National Era decried on January 2, 1851 (1851: n.p.).

Despite the ongoing push against slavery in antebellum America, slavery ultimately became big business again. In the wake of the flourishing cotton and sugar trade, as well as the stern enforcement of anti-fugitive laws, forced internal and external emigration boomed. New slaves were imported from Africa's coasts (mostly the Congo's, as is discussed in subsequent sections), while America-born slaves were directed from the Chesapeake area to the economically revived cotton and sugar regions in Alabama, Mississippi, Texas, and Louisiana (Wright 2001: 196).

To legitimize and stabilize the local slave- and plantocracy, legal defense mechanisms developed to keep both enslaved and free Blacks in check. State and city legislatures integrated "slave codes" into their legal systems at the turn of the century, of which Louisiana's are quite typical. Louisiana, a major importer of slaves from the Congo, declared that those enslaved owed absolute obedience to their masters, whose property they were. The codes outlined what behavior was socially acceptable and denied the freedom to be schooled, to assemble in groups, to travel, or to carry arms (ibid: 180-181). This legalized oppression was rationalized through discourses that condemned Black Americans as morally defect or Biblically cursed (ibid: 173), whereby pro-slavery advocates turned bondage "into something that at its worst was a necessary evil, and at its best a positive good" (ibid: 173). These rationales became attractive to African Americans, too, as soon as they were liberated from slavery; they were eagerly taken up in the context of postbellum African American discourses on Congo slavery, as is discussed in subsequent sections.

Abolitionists tirelessly protested the legal and discursive justifications of slavery, and the life and work of William Lloyd Garrison is exemplary in this regard. As the publisher of the influential abolitionist newspaper The Liberator and as the co-founder of the American Anti-Slavery Society in 1833, Garrison promoted a policy of "moral suasion" – a non-violent, non-political approach to activism that opposed slavery by moral argument (Everill 2013: 5). An excerpt from The Liberator on June 9, 1843 gets to the heart of this stance. "Moral suasion and law won't mix, any way you fix it," the newspapers states, "the moment you begin to talk about the latter, the former loses all its force, and is perfectly useless" (1843: n.p.).

Increasingly, Garrison grew critical of intellectuals who advocated non-abolitionist or violent solutions to slavery. A major target of his critique became the American Colonization Society (ACS). This organization succeeded in depicting itself as the solution to the "problem" of free Black Americans in the midst of slavery. Moreover, the ACS promoted the spreading of "an empire of American culture, civilization, Christianity, and commerce" in Africa (Everill 2013: 25), foreshadowing, as well as actively participating in, the early stages of the colonial era (cf. the final part of this chapter, as well as the next chapter). Boosted by the state funding of Virginia and Maryland (ibid: 57), the ACS eventually gained enough support to establish new colonies in West Africa, which eventually became the much-discussed country of Liberia in 1822 (ibid: 28). Although Garrison initially advocated ACS's emigration plans for free African Americans, he dismissed the ACS in the end. The Liberator wrote of the ACS on November 19, 1831 that it "is the most compendious and the best adapted scheme to uphold the slave system that human ingenuity can invent [...] [I]t serve[s] to increase the value of the slaves, and to make brisk the foreign and domestic slave trade [...] It expressly declares that it is more humane to keep the slaves in chains, than to give them freedom in this country!" (1831: n.p.). While many African American intellectuals joined Garrison in his objections against the ACS, many more of them celebrated the existence of an independent Black state, as is shown below.

Whereas anti-slavery and pro-slavery activism were the major issues that led to a deeply polarizing field of discourses in antebellum white America, of which many intellectuals were very aware,[6] racial polarization was an increasingly large concern as it was stoked by the fires of industrialization, immigration, and the aggressive capitalism of the postbellum "Gilded Age" (Winterer 2002: 99).

The tension deriving from the protection of the rights of African Americans during post-war "Reconstruction" (Wright 2001: 202), via an army of both troops and officials from the Freedman's Bureau, was resolved (at least for white Americans) under the economic and social pressures of the Gilded Age. Under economic pressure, white support for the Thirteenth, Fourteenth, and Fifteenth Amendments, as well as the Civil Rights Act, was withdrawn (Zinn 2003: 198-204). After this withdrawal, white supremacy was re-installed. "Black codes" replaced the former "slave codes" and peonage systems of "sharecropping" which kept African Americans beleaguered and indebted to former slave masters (ibid: 199; Frankel 2005: 256). This re-subordination of Blacks to whites (Burton 2001: 55) re-united the white majority on the anti-Black, racial plane. "By the century's final decade," Donald R. Wright infers, "almost no influential [white] supporters of black equality existed [...] by 1890 the only 'radicals' in race relations were the racist southern whites intent on driving Blacks down into, and keeping them in, their lowly place" (2001: 205).

---

6 Black and white contemporary newspapers frequently expressed their concern about this polarization. A case in point is the condemnation of the "fanatical" Fugitive Slave Law in Black newspapers. The African American weekly Frederick Douglass' Paper wrote, for instance: "If the North and West [...] were calmly united in opposition to the Fugitive Slave Law, there would be no fanaticism among us the subject [sic]" (1851b: n.p.).

The unity of the white majority in terms of self-proclaimed racial superiority by no means turned whites into a social monolith, however. Tensions within the majority were rising, too. Against the background of increasing economic competition and insecurity, white American culture increasingly redefined and differentiated gender roles in terms of true "womanhood" and ideal "manliness". As a moral counterweight to this economic strife, a "Cult of True Womanhood", as Barbara Welter famously termed it, developed in the 19th century, establishing the "female virtues" of piety, purity, submissiveness, and domesticity (1966: 152). True women, therefore, were to be passive and timid responders, silent and dependent "ladies" (Hafter 1979: 14). Domesticity in particular was much prized, firstly because it was considered the "proper sphere" (Welter 1966: 153) for white, middle-class women,[7] and secondly because it could be combined easily with the socially prized notion of motherhood. The cult of submissive, domestic womanhood had far-reaching consequences for the perception of female sexuality. Although American Victorians did not altogether deny the female sexual nature, good Christian women were not supposed to have a sex drive, nor were they supposed to experience pleasure during sexual activity (Newman 2005: 209; Donnelly 1986: 47). This led in American Victorian society to a rhetoric of restraint with respect to sexual practice in general (Donnelly 1986: 41).

In the footsteps of the social Darwinists and male imperial travelers, true womanhood also became an integral part of the discourse on "civilization". This strengthened the assumption that civilized womanhood had to be domestic and asexual, and that the most advanced races were those that divided most perfectly between the male and female spheres (Bederman 1995: 27). Prototypical for this type of discourse was the leading social Darwinist Herbert Spencer, who explicitly debated the link between civilization and gender roles in his popular 1874 Principles of Sociology (1897: 768):

> When we remember that up from the lowest savagery, civilization has, among other results, caused an increasing exemption of women from bread-winning labor, and that in the highest societies they have become most restricted to domestic duties and the rearing of children; we may be struck by the anomaly that in our days restriction to indoor occupations has come to be regarded as a grievance, and a claim is made to free competition with men in all outdoor occupations. This anomaly is traceable in part to the abnormal excess of women; and obvi-

7 Christine Stansell has done a study of white and Black working-class women in antebellum America, City of Women: Sex and Class in New York City, 1789-1860, showing that the construction of separate spheres extended well beyond the white middle-class home.

ously a state of things which excludes many women from those natural careers in which they are dependent on men for subsistence.

To Spencer, the degree of sexual differentiation (marked by the "exemption of women from bread-winning labor") is indicative of the progress that societies have made. Societies have moved from "lowest savagery" to "civilization", Spencer claimed, here making an overt reference to the popular 19th century notion of "evolution", which discussed civilization as a process that went through the stages of savagery and barbarism (Bederman 1995: 25). "Civilized" women, for Spencer, were delicate, spiritual, quietly content, and dedicated to the home. Spencer thus legitimized the ideals of true womanhood, and domesticity above all. Women stuck in the "lowest savagery", in turn, constituted their implied counterparts. In his quote, Spencer also makes clear that he is struck by "the anomaly" of the "grievance" of women concerning their "restriction to indoor occupations" – discursively defaming those opposed to patriarchy.

Spencer had good reason to vilify his female opposition: Plenty of white women challenged the cult of true womanhood. Opposition would come in many shapes and forms. A conservative reaction to the oppression of women was to improve the rapidly deteriorating health of the corseted, inactive middle-class women through health reform and the propagation of physical exercise as a means of increasing their maternal capacities (Newman 2005: 118). More progressive responses came from health advisers and popular writers, who attempted to re-shape the discourse of true womanhood in terms of a tough, (sexually) active, self-reliant woman equal both emotionally and biologically to men – a concept which Francis B. Cogan referred to as "The Ideal of Real Womanhood" (Harris 1988: 331). The most radical challenge came from the ongoing agitation of the Women's Rights Movement, which demanded equality and reform with respect to marriage laws, access to the "public sphere" (e.g. education and work), and suffrage.

The activism of the Women's Rights Movement is illustrated well through Elizabeth Cady Stanton's 1852 speech, delivered at the "Woman's Temperance Convention" in Rochester. In the speech, which was re-published in the Frederick Douglass' Paper, the leading American women's rights activist mobilized the most prominent paradigms and vocabulary of her days to question the validity of "true womanhood". "By the light of science," Stanton proclaimed, "we also see how the salvation of man – the full development of the race, as moral and intellectual beings, the perfect subjugation of the animal, that now wastes and deforms God's perfect image, is all bound up in the freedom of women" (1852b: n.p.). Stanton mobilizes some of the major intellectual paradigms of 19th century intellectual life here, such as "race", "science", "development", as is discussed in more detail later on, after which she continued her speech by claiming that women's "God-given prerogative is to be free, noble and true" (ibid). But instead of freedom, women were held in "a subordinate position, subject to the will and dictation of another," Stanton asserted, "thinking no great thoughts, and feeling no true liberty, always confined to the narrow treadmill round of domestic life, wholly occupied with trifling matters and ministering to the animal necessities, and lusts of the flesh alone, that part belongs not to woman" (ibid). Stanton thus forcefully addresses the oppression of "women" in the middle of the 19th century, ranging from social subordination ("treadmill round of domestic life") to sexual oppression ("lusts of the flesh [...] belong[s] not to woman").

Despite evoking the unifying label of "women", it is clear that Stanton is talking about white (middle-class) women throughout her passage; women in the working classes and those enslaved would surely suffer more under the "treadmill" of exploitative labor than under the drudgery of "trifling matter[s]" (ibid). Read against the grain, Stanton's passage suggests a disconnect between white and Black women too, and Stanton clearly does not address the latter. Moreover, as women's rights activists drew analogies between their own situation and that of slaves, as is the case in the exemplary 1850 announcement of the "women's rights convention" in the African American newspaper The National Era (titled "Women's Rights Convention"; 1850: n.p.), Black and white women struggled to establish a common cause. The National Era, declares that "in the relation of marriage", (white) women had been "actually enslaved, in all that concerns her personal and pecuniary rights" (ibid). Via the metaphor of the "slave" and "enslavement", white American middle-class women constructed a counter-narrative to true womanhood. Unfortunately, this constituted the "double move," as Sabine Broeck suggests, "of propagandistically evoking and disavowing a likeness of woman with slave" (Broeck forthcoming). This double move was executed, according to Broeck, "not in order to create a transgressive solidarity between the figures of 'woman' and 'slave' against the powers that be, but in order to create an enabling distance". White women's activists of the 19th century thus depended heavily on an "evocation of actual enslavement's annihilation of the human" (Broeck: forthcoming) in order to inscribe themselves into full, civilized, able humanness. A similar process can be observed in antebellum African American intellectual circles towards the Congo, as will be elaborated in the next sections.

As a response to the challenges of the women's movement, as well as to those of immigrant and working-class white male workers, bourgeois "manhood" became a topic of ongoing debate in the last third of the 19th century (Bederman 1995: 14).

Produced in a nexus of race, class, and gender, the watchwords of this period became "manliness" and "masculine", terms which marked the difference between any essential characteristics that men mutually shared ("masculine") and the attributes that the Victorian middle class admired in a man ("manly"; ibid: 18). The set of desired characteristics had been formed throughout the 19th century and were communicated and negotiated systematically via popular media such as the monthly gift book Godey's Lady's Book. In its April 1841 edition, the fictional story "A Tale of Domestic Life" described the desired character of a man worthy of being courted by telling its readers what should not be lacking. "Brilliant, intelligent, and amiable, he had not that strength of mind, that fixedness [sic] of purpose, and firmness in the path of rectitude, which are so essential in the formation of character," the author wrote, underlining those essential characteristics that cannot be replaced by other qualities, "however pleasing" they may be (Campbell 1841: n.p.). More than "intelligence" and "amicability", in short, firmness of character, strength of mind, self-reflectivity, and rectitude in life were communicated as the traits of desirable manliness. As with "true womanhood", these "manly" components were part and parcel of the late 19th century discourse of civilization. "Civilized men" had to be self-controlled and independent breadwinners and protectors of women and children, while "savage" men were their alleged opposites, forcing their women into exhausting drudgery such as cultivating the fields and tending the fires.

Like the white majority, which frequently split along racial, class, and gender lines, African Americans throughout the 19th century grappled with each other on many fronts. When the leading African American intellectual and activist Frederick Douglass ended his cooperation with the abolitionist William Lloyd Garrison due to the latter's paternalistic outlook on Black Americans (White 2005: 214), Douglass's newly founded newspaper The North Star would echo some of the disunity amongst African Americans by calling for its opposite in an article titled "To our Oppressed Countrymen": "Remember that we are one, that our cause is one, and that we must help each other, if we would succeed," Douglass reminded his readers (1847: n.p.). According to the author, Blacks were united by misery: "We have drank [sic] to the dregs the bitter cup of slavery; we have worn the heavy yoke; we have sighed beneath our bonds, and writhed beneath the bloody lash" (ibid). To Douglass, these "cruel mementoes [sic]" were indicative "of our oneness". Addressing slaves in particular, Douglass asserted that he and his fellow freedmen "are one with you under the ban of prejudice and proscription – one with you under the slander of inferiority – one with you in social and political disfranchisement" (ibid). The final lines stressed Douglass's desired unity: "What you suffer, we suffer; what you endure, we endure. We are indissolubly united, and must fall or flourish together (ibid).

Douglass's explicit evocation of "oneness" – in terms of being bound together by slavery, by social and political disfranchisement, and by "proscription" – echoed Ralph Ellison's idea of a unifying "identity of passions" founded on a "common suffering more than by our pigmentation" (1966: 255). Since Douglass addressed this "identity of passions" in the first edition of his newspaper, one may infer that this identity needed active confirmation, or was far from being understood as a given. The latter option would not be surprising in a period that saw tensions between light-skinned and dark-skinned African Americans, between emigrationists and integrationists, between free and enslaved Blacks, and between American-born and African-born Blacks. Even more than in the white majority strata, the issue of enslavement was a major fault line in the African American community.

In 19th-century America, the increasing importation of newly enslaved Africans coexisted with a thriving free Black population. The numbers of free Blacks rose from 59.000 to 488.000 between 1790 and the eve of the Civil War (White 2005: 201). This increase was the result of Black children born of free mothers and of Black immigration from the West Indies and Haiti (ibid: 201).[8] From the 1770s onward, free African Americans became considerably more self-organized. This was as much the result of the Black community's resilience as it was of the self-defeating racism of white Americans and their effort to keep Black Americans out of their churches, schools, neighborhoods, and offices. Because African Americans were not allowed to send their children to public schools until after the Civil War, when (mostly inferior) public schools were established via the Freedman's Bureau (Banks 1996: 10-11; Frankel 2005: 274), African Americans founded their own educational institutions. The same process may be observed with regard to the professional market. Since few jobs awaited free, educated African Americans in the 19th century, they created their own newspapers, schools, churches, and other segregated institutions.

Black churches increasingly took the lead in the educational and political organization of free Black life between 1800 and 1860 (Wood 2005: 90) by offering Sunday schools for children and informative presentations on contemporary political events (White 2005: 207). African American benevolent societies, in turn, provided everyday life services and assistance to their members, supporting them financially during during illness or after the death of family members (ibid: 208). Literary and cultural associations expanded the market for Black publications; at the same time, the Black press developed, albeit sporadically, from 1827 onward, offering the small percentage of literate African Americans a Black perspective on national and

8 Haiti gained its much-discussed independence from France in 1804 after a successful insurrection by the free Blacks that had begun in 1790 (Littlefield 2005: 163).

local events (ibid: 215; Hutton 1993: viii). A final phenomenon related to this increasingly organized African American intellectual life was the convention movement. This led to regularly organized political meetings on a state and national level between the 1830s and 1850s (Hutton: xiii; Banks 1996: 17; White 2005: 217). The New York state convention on August 29, 1840 is one such example; it tackled the question of "the extension of the elective franchise to us, as to other men", according to The Colored American in an article titled "The New York State Convention" (1840b: n.p.).

A common trait of many of these free Black institutions and initiatives was their (un)conscious organization around "wealth and complexion" (White 2005: 208-209). There were obvious color-coded, as well as class- and gender-based divisions in most organizations, creating a hierarchy in which light-skinned and fairly well-to-do male Blacks occupied privileged positions. Throughout the 19th century, the "mulatto" population made its power felt. This occasionally took the form of segregating light-skinned African Americans from their darker-skinned counterparts. For instance, light-skinned Blacks formed exclusive social ties and organizations that imposed and maintained a color line within the African American community. This was especially the case in South Carolina and Louisiana – not coincidentally, two states with a high number of Congo slaves who were said to be dark-skinned.

In Charleston, South Carolina, the Brown Fellowship Society was founded on November 1, 1790. This organization admitted "brown men of good character" willing to pay fifty dollars' admission (Lake 2003: 24), resulting in a membership comprised of light-skinned males with considerable economic success. Other Charleston societies, like the Society of Free Dark Men (later called The Humane Brotherhood; ibid: 27), were less marked by color- and class-coded memberships. These societies disdained to some extent the explicit elitism of the Brown Fellowship Society. Ultimately, the Freed Dark Men were as insular in their social relations as other societies (ibid: 19-50). They married within their own class and color lines, owned their own burial plots, established their own schools, and worshiped at their own churches (or worshiped together with white Americans). Some free Blacks from South Carolina also owned slaves, just as other Black elites in Southern states did (ibid: 31-32).

These racial hierarchies continued after slavery ended, thereby consolidating the social and political privilege of the African American upper class (ibid: 39). To Vernon Burton, this division of the African American community along racial, gender, and particularly class lines had devastating effects on the political activism of African Americans in Louisiana and South Carolina – two states with a large population of Congo slaves. "Class differences between the conservative, lighter-skinned, property-owning free blacks [...] and the darker-skinned, formerly enslaved landless laboring class" hastened the breakdown of postbellum Reconstruction, reducing the effective exercise and unity of Black political power (Burton 2001: 54).

The construction of a Black male public "sphere" had substantial consequences for the African American political struggles against slavery and for civil rights. These struggles increasingly took place in a vocabulary that turned the African American struggle into a fight for "manhood" rights. Although Frederick Douglass supported the right to vote for women as well as men (hooks 1990: 90), he simultaneously and systematically equated "Black" with "men". As such, Douglass debated the quest for civic power through the lens of gender. By proving that African Americans were "men", too (Bederman 1995 21) – an assertion that was subject to constant attack by white supremacists (ibid: 25) – Douglass and other male activists equated "Black" with "men", just as women's rights activists had connected "women" with "white[ness]" (hooks 1990: 8).

It goes almost without saying that Black women commented on the use of "Black" as a synonym for "male" by African American spokespeople. In her famous "Address to the First Annual Meeting of the American Equal Rights Association" following the acquisition of Black male suffrage in the District of Columbia in 1867, Sojourner Truth commented on the "great stir about colored men getting their rights, but not a word about the colored women" (Truth 2011: 242). The danger that Truth saw was that if "if colored men get their rights, and not colored women theirs, you see the colored men will be masters over the women, and it will be just as bad as it was before" (ibid: 243). Obviously, the trope of the "master"/"slave" is at work in Truth's postbellum speech, just as was the case in the discourses of white women's right activists, who asserted their own personhood by disavowing the Black slave. A similar process of self-affirmation on the back of slaves can be extrapolated from Truth's paradigmatic quote. Given Truth's own status as a freed slave, her quote acquires particular significance when taking into account the perceived opposition in African American intellectual circles of the difference between "free" and "enslaved" Blacks.

This perceived opposition was debated frequently in intellectual circles. An excellent example of the rhetoric employed by free Blacks with regard to enslaved Americans was the "Colored National Convention" in Rochester, New York, as reported in the Frederick Douglass' Paper of November 25, 1853 in an article titled "Slavery: Colored National Convention" (1853b: n.p.). During this convention, Frederick Douglass pointed "with pride and hope" at the results of the "education and refinement" of Black Americans, leading to Black "mechanics, farmers, merchants, teachers, ministers, doctors, lawyers, editors, and authors against whose progress the concentrated energies of American prejudice have proved quite unavailing" (ibid). These Black professionals, according to Douglass, were "the intelligent and upright free men of color" who would undermine the justifications of slavery by virtue of their "knowledge, temperance, industry and righteousness, in just that proportion" (ibid). Throughout Douglass's speech, these "intelligent and upright free men of color" are opposed to those enslaved, a circumstance that becomes apparent in the lines that follow. "Intelligence is spreading abroad, and light and chains are incompatible," Douglass is reported to have said, continuing, "If it be impossible to keep three and a half million of [sic] people in darkness, it will be impossible to keep them in the condition of beasts of burden" (ibid). With this passage, Douglass constructed an opposition between, on the one hand, "light"/ "intelligence" and, on the other, "darkness"/"beast of burden". By means of this opposition, a distinction and hierarchy is produced between the group of free Blacks and those enslaved: Whereas the former represented themselves as the torch of enlightened hope, the latter were depicted as their dark and ignorant opposite.

At times, the link between slavery and African primitiveness is made explicit. For instance, it becomes clear from Bishop Allen's 1827 letter (titled "Letter from Bishop Allen") to the editors of Freedom's Journal on emigration schemes to Liberia that Allen considered American slaves to be "poor ignorant Africans", who ought to be "civilized and christianized [sic]" as much as the Liberian Africans. The existence and history of enslavement led to harsh statements by Allen about all African Americans. "We are an unlettered people, brought up in ignorance; not one in a hundred can read or write; not one in a thousand has a liberal education," Allen castigated his constituency (1827b: n.p.). "Is there any fitness for such to be sent into a far country, among heathens, to convert or civilize them; then they themselves are neither civilized nor christianized [sic]?" (ibid). Allen obviously thought not. He goes on, "See the great bulk of the poor ignorant Africans in this country; exposed to every temptation before them; all for the want of their morals being refined by education, and proper attendance paid unto them by their owners, or those who had the charge of them" (ibid). This ignorance played in favor of the slaveocracy, Allen asserted pointedly: "It is said by the southern slave-holders, that the more ignorant they can bring up the Africans, the better slaves they make" (ibid). Bishop Allen's quote echoes some of the perceived fault lines running through African American circles in the early 19th century, revolving around the issues of education, Christianity, temperance, civilization, and freedom. Since Black Americans were predominantly ignorant "Africans" themselves who had not reached an acceptable standard in any of these areas, Allen maintained that they should refrain from going to Liberia to try and convert the "heathens" (ibid).

While free Blacks separated themselves from enslaved African Americans, the enslaved blacks were hardly perceived as a homogeneous people, either. Slave owners would differentiate between slaves born and socialized on American soil and newcomers from Africa. The distinction between African-born and American-born Blacks was evoked consistently, for instance in how they were labeled: "Country-born Negroes" would be set apart from "salt water Negroes" (Gomez 1998: 168). Thus, advertisements such as one in The Pennsylvania Packet from the late 18th century, titled: "Two Hundred Dollars Reward", were published which promised to reward anyone who could return "their" runaway "salt water Negro man" (Cockey 1778: n.p.).

It is evident that the interaction between African-born and American-born slaves and free Blacks required considerable cultural negotiation – ranging from learning daily plantation routines and adjusting to social conventions to learning one another's languages (Gomez 1998: 14-15). In an article titled "Native Africans Enlisting" from April 1863 in Douglass' Monthly, it becomes clear to what extent these enslaved newcomers were perceived as different. The article recounts the story of two freed slaves called "Wimbo Congo" and "August Congo" who tried to enlist in the 2nd Regiment Louisiana Volunteers Native Guards ("Native Africans Enlisting" n.p.). Both men are described as "natives of Africa" from the "Congo river" who "give wonderful accounts of Africa, and tell how they were stolen from there and brought to America" (1863: n.p.). The article then tells its readers that both Congo-born slaves were brought to Louisiana "some three years ago on board of the celebrated yacht Wanderer, and sold as slaves to a slaveholder on the opposite side of the river, and were compelled to work until the city was captured by the United States troops" (ibid). Both "patriotic sons of Africa" tried to enlist in the U.S. army "in broken language" to defend their homes, a request that was first declined "because they could not speak the English language plain enough to be soldiers" (ibid). Still, both Congolese were enlisted in the end and "proved as good soldiers as we can find in the whole three colored regiments" (ibid). Despite its happy end, this story is quite telling in terms of the language negotiations and cultural accommodation that had to take place between Congo-born slaves and their environment.

Distinctions between slaves were also determined and enforced by the tasks they performed. In contrast to those working in the master's house, field "hands" were clearly held in lower esteem. A typical demonstration of how this division between "field negroes" and "house negroes" was produced (as Malcolm X would phrase it ironically and critically, amongst others in his speech "Message to the Grass roots" in the early 1960s) can be found in a slave advertisement from The New York Evening Post. This particular advertisement was reproduced in The North Star of January 12, 1849 in order to critique the Post's double standards towards slavery – condemning it in print, but profiting from it via advertisements from slaveholders. This reproduced advertisement indicates clearly how slaves were divided in the slave master's rhetoric. It begins: "THIS DAY, the 14th, at 11 o'clock, at the Mart, on East Bay, will be sold the following family of NEGROES" (1849: n.p.). Subsequently, the advertisement separated the "field hands" (who are explicitly labeled as such) from the rest of the slaves, who are known by their occupation: "viz: Anthony, 40, field hand, and Ploughman. Juliet, about 40, superior Cook, Washer and clear starcher. Caroline, 6, Field Hand, very likely. Mary Ann, 3 years old" (ibid).

The division of field and house slaves often went hand in hand with the deprecation of the former vis-à-vis the latter. In an article in the Frederick Douglass' Paper, from July 6, 1855 ("Profits from Bees"), the low value of field slaves is emphasized in an anecdote by "Mr. Jesse Wilson, an esteemed citizen of Lamar County," who "realize[d] a sufficient amount of money from the industrial pursuits of his honey bees to purchase one good field Negro each and every year" (1855b: n.p.). Furthermore, it becomes clear from the many implicit and explicit utterances in African American newspapers referring to "field hands" that they were considered morally inferior to those working in the house. In the article "Negro Shot" in the Frederick Douglass' Paper from September 3, 1852, the story of how a slave was shot by his overseer is told. In the anecdote, the slave is offhandedly called a "field hand" and conspicuously linked to attributes, such as "insolence", "idleness", and aggression, thus reproducing the divisions instituted by slaveholders in the slave body (1852c: n.p.).

Judging by what we know from African American sources so far, Congo slaves must have ranked fairly low in the slave hierarchy of antebellum Black intellectual circles. Quite often, they were both African-born and field slaves, two aspects which aspiring bourgeois Black intellectuals would have disdained. Several cultural practices testify to the Congo's low position in the American social landscape. Racist and dehumanizing minstrel shows, America's "preeminent form of entertainment" between 1840 and 1900 (Bean/Hatch/McNamara 1996: xii), frequently used the name Congo in their imitations of plantation life. One of the earliest minstrel bands was called the "Congo Minstrels", as The Crest Musical Bulletin wrote in its article "Negro Minstrelsy from its Origin to the Present Day", looking back at the practice in 1908 (2002: 82); minstrel instruments were named after the Congo, too (e.g. "Congo Banjo", Nathan 1996: 36). The link between Congo and "field" slavery was strengthened through reverse language appropriation. Words such as tota, potentially brought to the South by slaves of the Congo region, was turned into "to tote", a "universal Southern term" for "picking up" in times that involved so much lifting and carrying by Congolese slaves (Wood 2005: 88). In Liberia, in turn, slaves recaptured by British anti-slavery patrols came to be called "Congos" rather pejoratively, whether they originated from the Congo or not (Fairhead 2003: 22).

These traces provide good reason to believe that Congo slaves were hardly the most popular Blacks around, facing rejection from whites and Blacks alike. The full picture remains immensely blurred, however, as Congolese will not "speak" for "themselves" for a very long time (cf. the Third Chapter on the chances for and challenges of self-representation). Despite the unbalanced historical record, there has been much speculation with regard to how (many) "Africans" in general (and Congolese specifically, although there is less interest in this) were enslaved during the course of U.S. American history. Research efforts have attempted to grapple with Congo slavery by quantitatively and qualitatively evaluating documents from slave holders (e.g. Gomez 1998) or by executing anthropological research (e.g. Herskovits); others have theorized slavery (e.g. Patterson 1982) or have speculatively imagined the trajectories of Congo slaves (e.g. Van Reybrouck 2014). Read together, the overall discourse of this research and of this popular history is devastating for the Congo slaves, who are cast, for the most part, in gruesome roles in the larger narrative of slavery, ranging from self-enslavers to "socially dead" Blacks, as Patterson would suggest.

As argued in the Introduction of this book, the use of sources produced by those deeply involved in the organization of slavery can neither be reduced solely to the "mistakes" of the historians in question nor to their discipline. Although works of individual scholars are looked at more closely here, they are merely exemplary of a larger, historically contingent discourse. Examining the Congo along Foucauldian lines means, after all, digging into the "episteme, the discursive formation, the regime of truth", as Stuart Hall explains (2003: 55), which produces, regulates, and limits the range of possibilities of what can be said about the Congo (Jäger 2004: 127-130; Maset 2002: 80-81). To Foucault, this meant the radical removal of the subject as the foundation of history as well as the "death" of the knowing and self-conscious subject (including the scholar). Although this book makes a case for a careful return to the subject (cf. Chapter Three), Foucault's premise remains its fruitful starting point. The scholars from various disciplines mentioned here (sociology, history, anthropology, cultural studies) thus function as examples for the rhetorically recurring and socially conventionalized statements on the Congo within academia. Contemporary scholars write within and against an archive and discourse that they did not create themselves – similar to the generation of African American intellectuals throughout the last two hundred years.

Melville Herskovits's seminal 1941 The Myth of the Negro Past constitutes an influential case of what is hypothesized here as "academic Congoism", or the ongoing fabrication of dismissive academic knowledge on the Congo based on deeply flawed source material and on motivations that converge with those found in the primary material (i.e. the Congo archive). A number of attitudes appear in Herskovits's work that are echoed in the work of others. One might begin with his claim of the massive importation of slaves from the Congo basin, for instance. This has been picked up by many researchers (including the work at hand, albeit skeptically), despite the unsolved problem of the fact that regional indications of slaves on traders' ships give "no clue at all as to provenience", as Herskovits himself noted (1941: 47). Even if the provenience is given, one still knows very little, it should be noted, as the Congo at that point had already become a highly malleable signifier – it meant, among other things, a Central West African region, as well as any captured "black from Africa", a runaway slave, and an "Angolan", as will be shown in subsequent sections. To focus quantitatively on what is said in slave records hardly produces a genuine image of the origin of these slaves. Moreover, as African identity was more a matter of "their presence in America" (Kolchin 2003: 41), these are some real difficulties in determining the scope of Congo slavery.

The severe limitations concerning the quantitative aspect of Congo slavery have not limited the claims made in contemporary research. Studies continually produce numbers, such as the assertion that 40 percent of the roughly ten million slaves shipped to the New World began their Middle Passage in the ports of modern-day Angola and The Democratic Republic of the Congo (Miller 1976:76; Klein 1999: 169). With these numbers in mind, the Congo-Angola region in general – and its slave ports Luanda and Loango in particular (Hall 2005: 153) – constituted "the single most important" slave-producing area in Africa from the sixteenth to the late 19th century (Klein 1999: 66; Gomez 1998: 142). Thus, this quantitative story goes, Central West Africa accounted for more than half of slave imports into British North America (Gomez 1998: 33), and these slaves were mostly transported directly to the United States and not via the Caribbean islands (ibid: 169). Due to their large numbers and predominantly young age (Kolchin 2003: 73), prices for West Central Africans labeled and named "Kongo"/"Congo"/"Angola" were comparatively low (Hall 2005. 16).

The numbers game so typical of the overall Congo discourse continues in a large amount of other research projects, as well. For the period between 1800 and

1885, for instance, we may read that of the roughly 100.000 slaves imported from Africa between 1783 and 1807, more than a third to half of them are said to have come from the Congo-Angola region (Littlefield 1991: 154; Gomez 1998: 137). An estimated 380.000 Congolese were shipped across the ocean from the start to the middle of the 19th century (Birmingham 1981: 124-125). This new wave of "Congoes" strengthened the already existing population of slaves originating from Congo-Angola in the U.S. slave economy of the Low South that predominated in the 17th and 18th centuries (Hall 2005: 160; Littlefield 1991: 154). The great majority of Congolese shipped to the United States ended up in the Low South doing intense gang labor (Hall 2005: 160; Gomez 1998: 144). Other research stresses that slave owners saw them as fit house servants because of their alleged weakness (Kolchin 19). General traits attributed to Congolese by their owners thus ranged from docility and comeliness to an inclination to run away (Gomez 1998: 136-141).

Herskovits, for one, was well aware of the epistemic problems involved in his own work and that of others. It made him return again and again to the problem of "not-knowing for sure" in his work (a trait which will return in contemporary, popular accounts of the Congo, too; cf. the Conclusion of this work). In terms of producing truthful anthropological knowledge, Herskovits's hopes were not high. "Deficiencies are greatest for Congo ethnography", he asserted. "The poor quality of the reporting [...] places great difficulties in our way when we search for detail" (Herskovits 1941: 78). Flawed, incomplete information, however, is mostly followed by more truth claims. Rhetorical disclaimers such as "it is said that" indicate Herskovits's doubts, but do not undo the comments made (thus, these comments live on in the archive). Via this strategy, Herskovits conveys to his readers that the Congo was a major slave port, since "it is said that slaves in some numbers were traded from tribe to tribe across the entire bulk of Central Africa, so that members of East African communities found themselves at Congo ports awaiting shipment to the New World" (ibid). Said by whom specifically, one might ask? Led by what interest? Transmitted through what kind of text or oral trajectory?

Skepticism is not out of place when examining how Herskovits arrived at his conclusions. If one looks at the researcher's methods, it shows that Herskovits bases some of these dismissive assertions on writers from the fifteenth century, when the "Portuguese made their appearance" (ibid: 85). Although these writers could be easily dismissed as "untrained observers" – as Herskovits's condemns Mary Kingsley, who was faulted for being "influenced by the period in which she lived" (ibid: 56) – none of this is done in the context of the Portuguese travelers. As is often the case in Congoism, the "rumoring of the archive", to paraphrase Ernst's book, is either taken at face value, or rules of knowledge production are constructed that apply to the Congo only. I will return to Herskovits in the Second Chapter.

Once these Congo slaves entered the U.S., Herskovits's story goes, they could not contribute substantially to American culture. Or, supposing they did contribute, their contributions can be boiled down to folk and other traditional versions of culture. "The vast masses of Congo slaves that we know were imported have made their influence felt disproportionately little," Herskovits claims (ibid: 50). To make this assertion stick, Herskovits suggests that there are few traces of the Congo in the American archive (a claim that will be falsified here). This claim testifies to the irrelevance of the Congolese, despite their great numbers. Except for a "few tribal names, a few tribal deities, some linguistic survivals, and more often the word 'Congo' itself" (ibid), African slaves in general and Congo slaves in particular contributed little to establishing an African cultural trait in the United States, Herskovits asserts.

Instead of contributing to their communities, Herskovits writes, Congo slaves were liabilities to them. He draws here from Caribbean anecdotes in order to underscore the low stamina of Congo slaves, for instance – a trait which reappears in present-day scholarly work on slaves from the Congo. Gomez's work, for instance, reproduces the following anecdote from Herskovits: "In Haiti," Gomez suggests based on Herskovits, "Congo slaves are said to have been more complacent than those from other parts of Africa, and were held in contempt by those Negroes who refused to accept the slave status with equanimity" (1998: 136).

According to Herskovits, "Tradition has it that when the Blacks rose in revolt, these Congo slaves were killed in large numbers, since it was felt they could not be trusted" (1941: 52). Held in contempt by other slaves, Congolese were thus depicted as at the bottom of the planter's hierarchy. This may or may not be true, as the claim is based mainly on "it is said" utterances or some vaguely formulated reference to "tradition". Congo slaves seem to represent the quintessence of what Patterson termed "socially dead" Blacks (1982: 21): Slaves thus stand not merely for forced workers, but for people who depend exclusively on a single person for protection – in contrast to "free" people, who have claims, power, and privileges distributed across a broader community (ibid: 28). With no social ties to speak of outside the relationship to his master (ibid: 38), the slave had no social capital whatsoever. Although slaves were forcibly thrown into a working environment or social community, they remained marginal figures in them, Patterson suggests.[9] This was

9 Through the passing of generations, this alienation and isolation would only gradually decrease, thereby turning slavery into an ongoing production of long-term marginality (Patterson 1982: 46).

particularly true for Congolese slaves, it can be inferred, who were turned into "external exile[s]" through pervasive naming practices (ibid: 39).[10]

Although the empirical base and methods employed by Patterson and others diverge substantially from that of the work at hand, common ground is found in the general function of the slave: It is a category which allowed others to elevate themselves on the back of Blacks from Central West Africa. Some kind of agreement "between master and nonslave" can indeed be suspected, as Patterson asserts, through which "honorable membership" could be claimed for oneself "vis-à-vis the dishonored slave" (ibid: 34). How this worked in concrete terms is the subject of the next sections.

ABSENCE: IGNORANCE AND SLAVE EPISTEMOLOGY IN ANTEBELLUM AMERICA

Drawing on Lewis's Light and Truth, a 400-page tome dedicated to relating the universal history of the "Colored and Indian race", the conspicuous non-presence of the Congo in antebellum African American intellectual discourse may be discussed. To identify the function of the Congo in these discourses, Lewis's book will be read both "widely" and "closely", beginning here with the former. This section then turns to Lewis's narrative, as well as the political agendas and intellectual backgrounds that determine his work. At first sight, Lewis's silence on the Congo (apart from a single instance that will be discussed in more detail later) could be easily attributed to Light and Truth's many structural and factual flaws. This afforded the book a controversial status in African American intellectual circles. Martin Delany's rebuttal of Lewis's work of history in his 1852 The Condition, Elevation, Emigration, and Destiny of the Colored People of the United States echoes the discomfort many intellectuals felt with regard to Lewis. In a chapter devoted to the "Literary and Professional Colored Men and Women", Delany faults Light and Truth in a bibliographical footnote for being "a compilation of selected portions of Rollin's, Goldsmith's, Ferguson's, Hume's, and other ancient histories; added to

10 As Patterson noted, slave-owners tended to rename their human imports according to their alleged origin – Congo, in this case. Since the Congo estuary was very much perceived as a slave-trading geography itself, naming someone Congo would not be a matter of stripping a person of his former identity, one might argue in opposition to Patterson (1982: 85), but constituted an act of re-enforcing an extreme form of fatalistic slave identity these doomed slaves already "possessed".

which, is a tissue of historical absurdities and literary blunders, shamefully palpable, for which the author or authors should mantle their faces" (2004: 143).

Delany's accusation of the usurpation of "Rollin's, Goldsmith's, Furguson's, and Hume's" historical works essentially faults Lewis for being too "white" in his source selection. At the same time, however, Delany takes issue with Light and Truth for being too "Black", although this also constitutes its sole "redeeming quality" according to the man. Thus, the book "is a capital offset to the pitiable literary blunders of Professor George R. Gliddon [...] who makes all ancient black men, white; and asserts the Egyptians and Ethiopians to have been of the Caucasian or white race!" Lewis, in turn, performed quite the opposite operation: He "makes all ancient great white men, black – as Diogenes, Socrates, Themistocles, Pompey, Caesar, Cato, Cicero, Horace, Virgil" (ibid: 143). Delany thus casts Gliddon and Lewis as occupying two sides of the same coin: "Gliddon's idle nonsense has found a capital match in the production of Mr. Lewis' 'Light and Truth,' and both should be sold together" (ibid).

Delany backed up his seething condemnations, which will be taken up in more detail in what follows, by mentioning "learned colored gentlemen", such as "Reverends D.A. Payne, M.M. Clark", who agreed with Delany's "disapproval of [Lewis's] book" (ibid). The deafening silence on Light and Truth by fellow African American historians from the 19th century, as well as African American abolitionist newspapers, suggests that there probably was a broader consensus on the questionable quality of the book amongst Black intellectuals (Ernest 2004: 143). At the same time, some support was given by white abolitionists, who celebrated the publication as a success for the African American intellectual community as a whole, consistent with the broadly paternalistic tone adopted towards Black Americans at the time. In the widely-read abolitionist newspaper The Liberator, Lewis's book was described in an advertisement title "Light and Truth" as a monograph by a "colored man" whose object "seems to be to state who, among the distinguished men of past ages, have been of Ethiopian descent" (1836: n.p.). The rather cool and uninspired conclusion of this review (which was a re-publication)[11] indicated some reservations about the book. The assertion that "the reader will find some facts in it that will probably surprise him" certainly would not have motivated many potential readers to purchase the book (ibid).

Despite his criticism of the book's "historical absurdities and literary blunders", Delany nevertheless found Light and Truth important enough to position himself explicitly and passionately against it. This gave Lewis's book a legitimation that seems quite undeserved for a work perceived as so absurd. One reason for Delany's

11 The review was published first in another abolitionist paper called The Emancipator.

comments may have been, no doubt, the status of the book as a "first", that is, the first published effort by an African American intellectual to produce an extensive work of history (Ernest 2004: 101). Another reason could have been the undeniable success of the book. In his rebuttal, Delany came close to congratulating Lewis for successfully applying the "'Yankee trick'" of publishing a book with the aim of "mak[ing] money" (2004: 143). The publication history of Light and Truth suggests that the book was indeed a commercial success. After the first and second editions were published in 1836 and 1843, the latter twice the size of the former, another revised and expanded edition came out in 1844 (Ernest 2004: 101-102). Lewis seemed to have had ambitions to expand and develop his work systematically by adding maps and more volumes (ibid: 102-103). All the while, Lewis tirelessly promoted his books with tours through New England, thereby turning his book, according to Mia Bay, into one of the most "widely circulated black publications on ethnology" in the 19th century (Bay 2000: 45-46).

When Light and Truth is regarded as a commercial hit, Delany's rebuttal seems more than understandable, particularly since Delany was convinced that Lewis's work was devoid of substance both in terms of content and politics. Some of Delany's critical arguments do, however, appear warranted. Most convincingly, perhaps, was Delany's assertion that Light and Truth looked like a "compilation". Light and Truth indeed cannot be called a closely knit history. Organized in fourteen chapters of varying length, this "volume of collections from sacred and profane history", as the introduction of the publishing committee stated (III), guides its readers both chronologically and thematically through the history of humankind, with the occasional leap to contemporary times. The work started with humankind's biblical origins (Chapter one), then guided its readers through the ancient worlds of Africa, Europe, America, the "Orient", and Israel. It does this by discussing, listing, or providing quotes concerning cities, kings, wars, prophets, "Colored Generals and Soldiers", the arts and sciences, and instances of destruction (chapters two-six, eight, and twelve). Between these fragments and towards the end of his work, Lewis either provides a chronology of the "Great Historical Ages" (chapter ten and thirteen) or takes a contemplative step back to discuss contemporary times, such as "the present state of Judah and Israel" (chapter seven), "Modern Eminent Colored Men" (chapter nine), and "St. Domingo and Hayti [sic]" (chapter fourteen).

Ultimately, Lewis's temporal and thematic back-and-forth produces the strong impression that the historian possesses little coherence in his methodology. Then again, there is too much of a recognizable structure, story, and telos behind Lewis's work for it to be regarded as a mere "compilation" or "a Bakhtinian carnival of documents", as Ernest has suggested (2004: 106). This holds up if one reads the text "widely", looking at the historiographical and intellectual traditions in or against which Lewis was writing. As a historian aiming for a broad audience, Lewis both responded to and worked within the general intellectual trends in U.S. American historiography, leading to a history that was both universal and national, that drew from classicist and biblical authority, and that applied both romanticist and scientific intellectual tools. By evoking all of the aforementioned traditions at once, Lewis created a powerful effect of familiarity, which turned Light and Truth into a bestseller.

It is worth taking a moment to disentangle the various intellectual tools at Lewis's disposal. Universal history, or the history of humankind from its advent to the present (Hall 2009: 19), was a very obvious feature and structuring principle of Lewis's work. Parallel to this, the authority of the Bible and the idea of "Providence", or God as an operating force in history whose actions are mediated via the sacred texts of the Bible, also played an obvious role and served to structure the volume (ibid: 19-20). But Light and Truth is more than a universal history related through a biblical lens. "Next to the historical books of the Old Testament," Lewis writes, "the most ancient history worthy of perusal is that of Herodotus, the father of profane history" (1844: 310). This gives rise to a highly intentional "nexus of Biblical and classical authority" (Hall 2009: 62).

This mixture of classical and biblical texts reflected the broader intellectual atmosphere of much of the 19th century (with its last third excluded as a time in which modern historical scholarship took over; Winterer 2002: 9). Long stretches of the intellectual history of the 19th century were marked by Athens, as well as by Jerusalem, in what Winterer called a "culture of classicism" (ibid: 15-16). This was not an elite phenomenon. The "real and imagined affinity" with the antiques, as Joseph Levine has it (1991: 7), spread rapidly through the expanding public sphere generated by print media (Winterer 2002: 16).

This medial popularization made the classical past appear almost timeless, yet simultaneously modern and "real" – especially since a classical education became standard for any kind of career in public service. Knowledge of Greek and Roman classics was especially important and prevalent in the antebellum South, it seems. Nat Turner's slave rebellion in 1831 led many white southerners to embark on a more studied defense of slavery based on the antiques, for instance. In the 1830s and 1840s, when Lewis was (re-)writing and (re-)publishing Light and Truth, white southern nationalists and northern pro-slavery advocates began to turn to Aristotle and Herodotus to explain slavery and Black inferiority (ibid: 75). Lewis's reliance on classical sources was thus hardly a coincidence, but a way of refuting white supremacist arguments using their own weapons, i.e. Josephus, Herodotus, and Pliny, amongst others (Hall 2009: 62).

Lewis unquestionably also catered to an increasingly nation-oriented readership; history, more and more, was becoming as an essential part of "nation building" (Burke 2012: 192). American Romanticism, another dominant U.S. intellectual movement between the 1830s and 1860s (Hall 2009: 77), played an important part in this process (ibid: 6). Throughout Light and Truth, romantic traits, such as human agency, were stressed by portraying, for instance, "representative men and women", who illustrated that Blacks could be successful, too (ibid: 77). The results of this combination of Romanticism and Americanism can be witnessed in the third chapter, "Antiquity of America", in which Lewis lists the ancient authors, most famously Plato (1844: 125), who "are supposed to have referred to America in their writings" (ibid: 124). The function of such a list is quite obvious – namely, to inscribe America into a universal history through the romantic technique of cataloging its high achievers.

Even more essential to Lewis's effort was the addressing of Black achievement and achievers. These are exemplified by the representational Black success stories listed in chapter nine, which include Alexandre Dumas, amongst others (ibid: 304). These lists of Black successes fulfill a tripartite political agenda, traditionally identified as "vindicationist", "contributionist", and "Afrocentrist" (Hall 2009: 14-21). These three agendas are often all at work at the same time in Light and Truth. They thus lead to the defense of Black humanity against white, racist disparagement (vindicationist); to an inscription of Black achievement into world and local history (contributionist); and to the location of the first forms of civilization in Africa (Afrocentrist).

The "vindicationist" agenda of Light and Truth is overtly announced by the political introduction by the publishing committee, which lauds the book for its opposition to the ongoing trampling of the "weak and defenceless [sic]", in particular those constituting the human "articles of merchandize" (ibid: 3). In the same introduction, the "contributionist" aspect of the book also comes to the fore: Those in chains "in this country" are compared to the accomplished colored men elsewhere who enjoy "every inherent attainment, free from human interference" (ibid). Lewis's contributionist aim, that is, to propagate the achievements of contemporary free Black men abroad, created an ongoing tension between the temporal and thematic structuring in his work, resulting in the ricochet from ancient to modern times and back again. This is exhibited most noticeably by the insertion of contemporary chapters on "Modern Eminent Colored Men" and "Antiquity of America" in a book that was otherwise structured chronologically.

The most obvious aspect of the political agenda of Light and Truth is its Afrocentrism, which leads Lewis to focus heavily on the African roots of human civilization. Lewis does so by tracing humankind back to Black Ethiopia, a region close to the Garden of Eden, which the Bible located "eastward from Canaan, and north from the river Gihon, the land of Ethiopia (Gen. 2:13)". As a consequence, Lewis considers "the first people" to be "Ethiopians, or blacks" (ibid: 10), who he then ties to their most famous descendants: The Egyptians. Subsequently, Lewis "blackens" the ascent of Greece and Rome, as they were, according to Lewis, both colonized by the Egyptians. "It was during the eighteenth dynasty of Egyptian kings, that the first colonization of Greece took place", Lewis writes (ibid: 114). With the authority of the Bible, the antiques, and Rollin's Ancient History of the Egyptians, Carthaginians, Assyrians, Babylonians (which Lewis cites continuously, e.g. ibid: 40, 43, 50, 53, 59, 61, and so forth), Lewis openly contradicts and corrects popular accounts of the "indisputable evidence" of the Asiatic origin of the earliest denizens of the Nile, as claimed, for instance, by Gliddon's popular 1843 account Ancient Egypt: A Series of Chapters on Early Egyptian History, Archaeology, and Other Subjects (ibid: 3).

Since the ancient civilizations inherited their culture from Black Ethiopia and Egypt, a great number of ancient achievers from Carthage, Babylon, Syria, Greece, and Rome are "Africanized". This by no means meant that Lewis casts them uniformly as Black, as Delany suggests in his rebuttal. It is quite probable that Lewis considered Ethiopians and Egyptians, the latter depicted as the descendants of the former, decidedly blacker than the Greeks, whom Lewis viewed as merely colonized by the Ethiopians. It is probable that Lewis adopted a similar position regarding the blackness of Carthage, Babylon, Syria, Greece, and Rome as James W.C. Pennington's Text Book with regard to the Carthaginians. "They were Africans," Pennington asserted, "but African does not mean the same as Ethiopia" (1841: 56). The difference between Ethiopia and Africa was, as Lewis suggests, that "Ethiopia is a name derived from the [black] complexion of the inhabitants, while Africa is a name given to a tract of country inhabited by nations of various complexions" (ibid: 27). Thus, Ethiopia meant blackness; Africa, in turn, was discussed as multicolored.

The subtle difference between "Black" Ethiopia and "multicolored" Africa becomes apparent in how Lewis differentiates between Socrates and Plato. While Socrates is referred to as a "Grecian philosopher – the best of the wise men" (ibid: 303), Plato is labeled both as a "Grecian philosopher" and "an Ethiopian" (ibid: 125, 303), thereby rendering Plato as Black through his "Ethiopianness". Other examples show that Lewis links most of the male achievers of history to Africa, without necessarily claiming that their skin color was black. While Homer is an "Ethiopian" (ibid: 311), and thus probably considered a Black man by Lewis, Moses was merely a "general of Egypt" (ibid: 192), which leaves the question of his skin color open. Thus, although Lewis links all of the historical figures mentioned above to Egypt, Ethiopia, and Africa, he did not necessarily cast them as Black, as Delany suggests.

While drawing on the authority of ancient and biblical sources, Lewis also extensively utilizes popular scientific works and academic paradigms. He does not (or cannot) always acknowledge them openly, however. The attention Lewish lavishes on chronologies, most noticeably in the 70-page thirteenth chapter titled "Periods & C", seems, at first, an odd add-on to the rest of his work, but can be explained in light of the increasing mania for classification in the 18th and 19th century (Burke 2012: 52-66). This mania resulted not only in an extensive division of time, nature, and peoples, but also in a boom of specialized knowledge that was captured in new text genres, such as dictionaries, which Lewis relied heavily upon.[12] The 19th century paradigm of human classification, or the division of human beings into races according to biological, linguistic, and national traits (Gossett 1997: 128), truly pervades Lewis's work. When Light and Truth was written, the "index" of biologically determined racial specifics – most noticeably "blood", skin color, hair, nose, and forehead – had obviously gained currency (ibid: 70-80), as becomes obvious in Lewis's classification of "the blood of Africa" (for which Lewis, according to himself, drew from "Webster's Dictionary"; Lewis 1844: 340):

> Mangroon, is all black, a full blood, (a whole negro).
> Sambo,[13] is three quarters blood, (three quarters negro).
> Mulatto, is one half blood, (one half negro).
> Quadroon, is one quarter blood, (one quarter negro).
> Mestizo, is a half quarter blood, (a half quarter negro).

Lewis emphasizes the importance of this kind of skin color classification by returning to this exact same issue in the final pages of his work. There Lewis produces a racial scale, it appears, for the entire human race – from "Black" to "Mestizo" and "Mangroon" (ibid: 400):

12 These ranged from specialized dictionaries, such as "Dr. Brown's Dictionary of the Bible" (Lewis 1844: 15), to more general ones, such as "Johnson's Dictionary" and "Webster's Dictionary" (ibid: 339).

13 In newspaper articles from the Frederick Douglass' Paper, such as the 1853 article "The Editor", this designation of skin color also reappears, illustrated by phrases such as "our sambo complexioned editor" (1853a: n.p.).

> Between Black and White is a Mulatto.
> Between Mulatto and White is a Quaderoon.
> Between Quaderoon and White is a Mestizo. (After this the color becomes imperceptible to us).
> Between Mulatto and Black is a Sambo.
> Between a Sambo and Black is a Mangroon.
> Between a Mangroon and Black the white hue is lost.
> The complexion of the Indian tribes: Reddish, Copper, Brown, Black, and a white mixed hue.
> We are all one, and oppressed in this land of boasted Liberty and Freedom. "But wo [sic] unto them by whom it cometh."

While distinguishing between black and white by inserting a whole spectrum of variation between them, Lewis simultaneously declares a unity of sorts in the final lines of the second passage: "We are all one". One reading of this line is that the "we" in question designated both Black and white Americans. As such, Lewis could have been positioning himself in the heated debate on the descent of humankind, circling around the "monogenist" and the "polygenist"[14] theses, that is, the debate about the single and shared origin of humankind (mono) versus a multiple and separate origin (poly; Gossett 1997: 57-80).[15] More likely, however, the "we" refers to an imagined Black unity, signifying a self-declared "identity of passion" based on the shared experience of being "oppressed in this land of boasted Liberty and Freedom". This renewed reference to racial unity highlights the paradoxical epistemic background against which Black Americans were writing their histories. Racial in-

14 The work of de Buffon, who substantially influenced Lewis, was foundational for this idea (Roger 1997: 180).

15 When Lewis wrote his book, the debate was still raging, although monogenist thinkers had lost much of their scientific support by this time (Gosset 1997: 58-66). Lewis engaged in a delicate balancing act between both hypotheses. Positioning himself explicitly along polygenic lines would make it hard to mobilize biblical sources with any historical authority, since the Bible supported the monogenic hypothesis (ibid: 44). While catering to biblical authority, however, Lewis at the same time connected himself to the increasingly scientific and oftentimes polygenic belief in the quintessential natural differences between the races (Hall 2009: 62), of which the racial scales mentioned above are but one example. As a compromise, Lewis included nods to both theories by leaning rhetorically toward the monogenic theory, while implicitly applying the principles of the polygenist theory throughout his work.

dexations and qualifications within the white-dominated Euro-American scientific and intellectual circles from the 18th century onward demanded division; Black politics, however, demanded the opposite. The quote thus illustrates that the scientific paradigm of racial differentiation was probably gaining the upper hand in Lewis's work, despite the ideological nod to unity.

There were more signs of Black division in Lewis's color schemes. The idea that "negroes" who are "all black" are more "whole" than their light-skinned pendants[16] (Lewis 1844: 196-197) strongly echoed the vocabulary of many contemporary natural historians. The popular Leclerc, Comte de Buffon, and his Irish spin-off Oliver Goldsmith (who was explicitly and correctly cited by Delany as Lewis's intellectual influence) should be highlighted in this context. That Lewis would be influenced by these authors does not come as a surprise, since both produced works that had become canonical within the scientific circles of the 18th and 19th century (cf. Burke 2012: 101; Gossett 1997 35). If Lewis did not have access to their primary works directly, he certainly would have had the possibility of becoming acquainted with their ideas via popular, best-selling collections of their texts, such as the 1810 A History of the Earth and Animated Nature. In that text, which collected and cited the main ideas of de Buffon and Goldsmith (without separating or marking clearly who said what, thereby evoking the effect of a unified scientific voice), the ongoing fascination with skin color (black, white, red, and everything in between), along with other physical characteristics (height, hair type, lip shape, nose, face, and eyes), can hardly be overlooked. In the chapter on the "Apparent Varieties in the Human Species", a typical passage described the physique of the people of the African continent in great detail. The Egyptian women, for instance, are said to "be very brown; their eyes are lively; their stature is rather low[...]" (De Buffon/Goldsmith et al. 1810: 74). In their appearance, these women diverged from the men in height (the latter are said to be of "good height"), but not in skin color: "Both are of an olive colour; and the father we remove from Cairo, the more we find the people tawny, till [sic] we reach the confines of Nubia, where they are as black as the Nubians themselves" (ibid).

The latter example allows one to infer the extent to which skin color had become a mainstream intellectual concern by the start of the 19th century, having been building since the heyday of the Enlightenment (Eze 2000: 2-5; Winterer 2002: 111). Lewis does indeed align himself with "Goldsmith's, Furguson's [sic], Hume's" work, as Delany mentioned, but he does so in a critical fashion. Although he applies de Buffon's and Goldsmith's rhetoric, concepts, strategies, and methods,

16 A word that Lewis deconstructs and ultimately rejects on the next page, although he subscribes to the underlying idea of blood variation and blood purity.

he simultaneously subverts and inverts their defaming stances towards the African race in general, and that towards the Egyptians in particular.

This is neatly exhibited in how Lewis discusses the "essence" of the Egyptians. This is what is said in A History of the Earth and Animated Nature: "The most inherent defects of the Egyptians are, idleness and cowardice. They do nothing almost the whole day but drink coffee, smoke, and sleep, or chatter in the streets" (De Buffon/Goldsmith et al.: 74). Although Lewis accepted Goldsmith's and de Buffon's stance on the essential character of peoples, he refused to discuss the Egyptians in the way Goldsmith and de Buffon did – in terms of "inherent defects", such as "idleness and cowardice" (ibid). On the contrary, Lewis attributes characteristics such as lawfulness, wisdom, peace, and an "empire of the mind" (1844: 286) to the Egyptians: "Egypt loved peace, because it loved justice [...] She became known by her sending colonies into all parts of the world, and with them laws and civilization. She triumphed by the wisdom of her councils, and the superiority of her knowledge; and this empire of the mind appeared more noble and glorious to them than that which is achieved by arms and conquest" (ibid: 49-50).

The aim of 19th-century processes of categorization, historicization, and racialization was the depiction of the "progress" and "decay" of peoples, which boiled down to depicting the advances (or relapses) of whole societies from primitive to more complex and civilized stages (or vice versa; Hall 2009: 19). This fascination with "progress" and "decay" also had been gathering momentum since the Enlightenment, the thinkers of which provided a very particular vocabulary for discussing historical change and human differentiation through terms such as "race", "nature", "savagery", "civilization", and "progress" (Eze 2000: 2-5). As such, progress had been measured for quite a long time through the alleged static and backward state of others. In his story of Black achievement and empowerment, Lewis discussed Haiti as a model of progress, for instance, as opposed to the story of the "native inhabitant of America". Whereas the latter developed backwards due to "their connexions [sic] with the most degenerate part of the white people" (1844: 263), the former embodied the telos of Light and Truth, ending the volume on a high note. The then-recent events in Haiti were "singularly important" to Lewis, since they were "connected with the establishment and progress of civil and religious liberty and free institutions" (ibid: 386). The rise from slave state to Black self-government was very much the symbol of ultimate Black triumph, particularly for a Black American historian who witnessed the perseverance of U.S. American slavery (Hall 2009: 105). By placing Haiti in the final section of his work, Lewis rounds off the historical story of Light and Truth with the ultimate marker of Black success: an independent, self-governed, slave-free state called Haiti.

Against this complex background of cultural trends, political agendas, and scientific paradigms, Lewis mentioned the Congo only once. He did this in a short, ten-page chapter that discussed the "Ancient Arabians". In this chapter, Lewis tells the story of Abduhl Rahhahman, who was both "a native of the celebrated city of Timbuctoo [sic], in Central Africa" (1844: 344) and heir to the throne of a place called "Footo Jallo", twelve hundred miles from Timbuktu and home of Teembo, which was "now known as one of the largest cities of that continent" (ibid: 344). In this two-and-a-half-page account, Lewis stresses the geography and greatness of Timbuktu, very much in line with his usual vindicationist agenda. "The city of Timbuctoo is situated in the middle of Africa; and has been the object of the European's curiosity for many years" (ibid: 346). Lewis knows this based on the stories of "the slave-traders from the North, East, and West" who have spoken of the city in "marvellous [sic]" accounts (ibid). "Several travelers have attempted to reach it, but none have been able to get so far; and some have sacrificed their lives to the difficulties of the journey. The Prince Abduhl describes the city as surrounded by large and high walls. The government maintains a standing army; and the people are well advised in arts and sciences" (ibid).

Apart from its empowering stance, a striking trait of this quote is that Lewis links the "middle of Africa" to the grand city of Timbuktu, not to the Congo (as will happen later on with Stanley and Conrad, who cemented the idea of the Congo as "the interior" and the "heart" of Africa). But if the Congo was not situated in the middle of the continent, where was it? Lewis answers this question in the final stages of his story, in which he recounts how Prince Abduhl saved a "sick and lame" (ibid: 345) American surgeon in the interior of Sierra Leone. Being the first white man the prince ever saw, Dr. Cox was entertained "with the greatest hospitality" (ibid) for six months by the royal family in Teembo. While Dr. Cox returned to his homeland, the Prince was ambushed by the Hebohs, a slave-trading tribe who sold the prince to the Mandingoes, who sold him to a "slave ship at the mouth of the Gambia" (ibid). The prince ended up in Natchez, Mississippi, where he was recognized sixteen years later by the same Dr. Cox who the prince had saved in the interior of Sierra Leone. Assisted by others, Cox managed to liberate the Prince (ibid: 346). After his manumission, the prince left for Monrovia, Liberia, where he died from a "seasoning fever" a month later. Lewis ended the story and the overall chapter by honoring the "memory of Abduhl". In the final paragraph, the author cites a four-line poem in which the Congo is mentioned (ibid):

The palm's rich nectar, and lie down at eve
In the green pastures of remembered days,

And walk – to wander and to weep no more –
On Congo's mountain-coast, or Gambia's golden shore.

A "mountain-coast" – that is the only reference to the Congo in Light and Truth. In what follows, this reference is read both "widely" and "closely" in order to determine to what extent this utterance constituted the "full" range of discursive possibilities regarding what could be said about the Congo when Lewis wrote his book. To do so, this passage is read against Black and white accounts that serve as counterpoints, ranging from contemporary historians to dictionaries and African American newspapers.

The Political and Intellectual Agenda of Ignorance

"And walk – to wander and to weep no more – / On Congo's mountain-coast, or Gambia's golden shore." Although the origins of the poem are uncertain (Griffiths and Singler 94), it is safe to state that it was widely circulated over a long period within American intellectual circles – especially circles that discussed the colonization of West Africa favorably. As late as 1862, the notable African American intellectual and emigrationist Alexander Crummell cited the poem in his seminal The Future of Africa: Addresses, Sermons, etc., etc. (1969: 285). Three decades prior to Crummell's publication (in 1834), The Colonizationist and Journal of Freedom mentioned the poem in an article on "Abduhl Rahamann" (1834: 31). These texts were published in very different periods, of course. But what connected all of them was that they used this poem to evoke a sense of a carefree African "homeland" in order to legitimize the return of free African Americans to West Africa in general, and Liberia in particular. As such, the Congo appeared to be mobilized as just another, random region in Africa to signify the continent of origin.

At the same time, it is unlikely that the specific geographies relied upon in this poem – the Congo and Gambia – were used completely at random. There are qualitative differentiations between the Congo and Gambia in the poem, after all. While both regions are designated as regions near the sea, the terms used to communicate this were not quite synonyms. In contrast to Gambia's "shore", the Congo was labeled as a "coast". This differentiation may seem too subtle to be noticed, but if one looks at the entry "shore" in Webster's 1834 American Dictionary of the English Language, some substantial differences appear. Webster's defined "shore" rather generally as "land adjacent to the coast or sea" (Webster 1834f: 752), while "coast" was discussed as a particular "country near the sea-shore" (Webster 1834a; 156). The central term in the latter's explanation, "country", designated "any region, as distinguished from other regions; a kingdom, state or less district" (Webster 1834c:

200). Thus, Webster's assigned to "shore", via its central noun ("country"), a specificity and organizational depth (e.g. kingdom, state) that "land" did not possess, since it merely designated any "fixed part of the surface [...] any portion of the solid, superficial part of the globe", whether it was a "kingdom" or a "real estate" or any "superficial part of the earth or ground" (Webster 1834e: 484).

In keeping with the differentiation between "shore" and "coast", the adjectives used to describe the Congo and Gambia differ greatly, too. While Congo's coast is referred to as a "mountain", Gambia's shore is described as "golden". While the former designation is a geographical add-on, the latter reference is a judgmental and moral one, explained by Webster's American Dictionary as "excellent; most valuable", "happy; pure", and "preeminently favorable" (Webster 1834d: 381). Gambia's favorable shore was therefore pitched nominally and morally against the Congo's, of which it was implied (via the term "shore") that there was more to know than its relatively sparse description suggested. There are many questions that should be raised in this context: If there was more to know about the Congo, what was it? Where can it be learned? And why is this knowledge not imparted in Lewis's history? In discourse analytic terms, these questions aim to address the other socially and discursively conventionalized possibilities and knowledge that were at Lewis's disposal, but were not used (cf. Hall 2003c).

A first step in mapping the discursive possibilities and choices made by Lewis involves looking at the texts of other African American historians from the antebellum period. What one learns, however, is that they produced texts quite similar to Lewis's. In short, if African American historians mentioned Africa, they wrote almost exclusively about Ethiopia, Liberia, Babylon, Carthage, and Africa as a whole. Many of the works by fellow historians – Easton, Penningon, Garnet, Delany, and Brown, to name but a few of the major ones that will be cited in what follows – suggested a willingness to talk about "Africa", but in reality produced a discourse on Egypt that underlined its civilization, achievements, and political and scientific greatness.

A number of historians incorporated strong critical traits about Egypt, too, however, mostly to complement their main points. David Walker's famous 1830 "Appeal, in Four Articles" discussed slavery in the "ancient and heathen nation[s]" of Egypt at length (1830: 3). Walker's main point in his "Address" was to show that "the condition of the Israelites was better under the Egyptians than ours is under the whites" (ibid: 12). However, the "Appeal" simultaneously developed an overt story of Egyptian decay, which he considered a region of "Africans or coloured people" (ibid: 10). Walker explained the Egyptian "destructions" (ibid: 6) by mentioning heathenism and slavery, a thought that Ann Plato took up when she stated that

"Egypt, that once shot over the world brilliant rays of genius, is sunk in darkness" (1988: 30). Others developed similar images and ideas.[17]

Against the background of these discourses of Egyptian degeneration, much can be said for Trafton's hypothesis, in his seminal Egypt Land, that Egypt constituted a "figure of the double" (2004: 240), signifying both the "dark land, the land of Hebrew bondage and the home of slavery" and the "black land, a great African civilization" (ibid: 225). How Egypt was signified, according to Trafton, depended on the political agendas that were being advocated (ibid: 226). Strong vindicationist and contributionist agendas, such as those in Light and Truth, would typically lead to a strong emphasis of Egypt's greatness, for instance. Walker's "Appeal" suggested, however, that the rejection and embrace of Egypt could coexist; empowering political agendas and critical stances towards slavery in Africa were, therefore, not mutually exclusive.

In comparison to the "Egyptomania" of the antebellum 19th century, silence towards the Congo plagued all works of history. Early works, such as John Marrant's 1789 sermon "You Stand on the Level of the Greatest Kings on Earth", were as silent about it as Nathaniel Paul's 1827 "Address, Delivered on the Celebration of the Abolition of Slavery, in the State of New York". Book-length historical overviews – ranging from Hosea Easton's 1837 Treatise on the Intellectual Character, and Civil and Political Condition of the Colored People of the U. States to Pennington's 1841 A Text Book of the Origin and History of the Colored People and Martin Delany's 1852 The Condition, Elevation, Emigration, and Destiny of the Colored People of the United States – literally did not mention the Congo once. To my knowledge, no 19th-century female writer with an interest in history ever mentioned the Congo (until Amanda Smith in her 1893 Autobiography). The reason why these female intellectuals ignored the Congo went beyond their restricted access to the male-dominated public intellectual sphere (Hall 2012: 45), since it can be noted that women did mention and write about other African regions, as the example of Ann Plato illustrates (cf. above). As such, ignoring the Congo seems to have been a matter of selection for Black intellectual women as much as for their male counterparts, although their motivations for doing so were not necessarily the same.

17 William Hamilton's 1815 oration "O'Africa" is also a story of Egyptian decay. Hamilton tells us that Egyptians have sunk from "honest, industrious, peaceable and well-disposed people" (1998: 93) to a level beyond good and bad: "Look at the present state of the present inhabitants of Egypt. Sunk, and they shall continue to sink, until they are on a level with the worm they crush beneath their feet; no effort can save them" (ibid).

If fellow historians did not write about the Congo, who did? Did standardized 19th century works of knowledge do so? Lewis was no stranger to encyclopedias and dictionaries. Along with Johnson's Dictionary, which does not refer to the Congo,[18] Lewis mentioned and actively used Noah Webster's Elements of Useful Knowledge (e.g. 1844: 399). Webster discussed the Congo in its description of the African continent, which mainly emphasized Egypt, Northern Africa, and the Cape of Good Hope, just as Lewis had done. However, in a subsection called "Western Coast of Africa" (which was incorporated into the article about "Morocco"), the dictionary did turn its attention in a lengthier passage to the Congo. The text began, "Along the western coast of Africa are numerous kingdoms or states, and countries of which it is needless to give a particular description" (Webster 1806: 256). Despite the fact that the dictionary did not show an urge to describe the states in Western Africa, Webster ultimately did provide a depiction. It mentioned "the principal countries and tribes" which are "inhabited by blacks" called the Jaloffs, Foulahs, Guinea, Benin, Loango, Congo, and Angola, "who resemble each other in their persons and features [...] They are mostly pagans and great believers in witchcraft, inchantment [sic] and magic" (ibid).

After a short description of the climate and the wildlife of West Africa, the entry in Webster's Dictionary concluded by alluding to the local economy. This consisted of the exportation of "gold dust, elephant's teeth, ostrich fethers [sic], and some other commodities, but chiefly slaves" (ibid). The latter economic sector is elaborated upon in more detail by claiming that "the traffick [sic] in slaves commenced in 1517 under a patent from the emperor Charles V. and has been extended to other nations, who supply their colonies in America with blacks to cultivate the lands" (ibid). In this passage, the Congo is once again identified as a "country", just as it was in Lewis's work. Beyond that, however, the Congo was explicitly named and framed as a slave economy that was said to be providing a slave "supply" to the "colonies in America [...] to cultivate the lands". It is at this point that the Congo-as-Resource in a capitalist world economy comes to the fore.

Although dictionaries like Noah Webster's American Dictionary of the English Language or Lieber's Encyclopaedia Americana were not mentioned by Lewis, they were very likely accessible to and used by him. The former dictionary explains the Congo as "a species of tea from China" (Webster 1834b: 178), which is understood by the Encyclopedia Americana in its 1835 edition as a "black tea" (Lieber

18 While at the same time integrating plenty of references to Egypt in its section "Chronological Table of Remarkable Events, Discoveries, and Inventions" (Hamilton 1810: 263-276), which constitutes a mixture of biblical and ancient events quite similar to Lewis's time lines.

1835: 161). Although this might seem trivial at first sight, the Congo as a black tea does confirm the connection between "blackness" and the Congo.

Lieber's Encyclopaedia Americana, in turn, included a lengthy entry on the "Congo", which provided detailed information on this "kingdom in Lower Guinea, under the sovereignty of the Portugese [sic]" (Lieber 1830: 425). In terms of natural geography, the article mentions the river "Zaire", as well as mountains and coastal regions, all of which are in line with what Lewis's poem transmitted. In contrast to the poem, however, the article also mentioned an interior Congo where the wildlife flourished and the Congo's slave economy boomed. According to the article, the peoples of the Congo "seem less intelligent than the other Negro tribes" (ibid: 426). Their "great indolence" was considered a significant "obstacle to their civilization" (ibid). Another obstacle was their ongoing engagement with the slave trade, for which they "sell their wives for a glass of brandy to a European" and with which they punish criminals (ibid).

In a similar vein to Webster's Dictionary, the article repeatedly emphasized the importance of the slave trade for the Congo. "Though this country abounds in all the productions of the tropics, there appears to be no commerce carried on, except that in slaves, of whom vast numbers are annually carried to Brazil" (ibid). Again, the link between slavery and the Congo is made, just as in Webster's Dictionary. After the description of its main provinces, the article describes how the kingdom of the Congo was founded in 1487 and subsequently Christianized by the Portuguese, which was a rather unsuccessful enterprise, since "idolatry [...] is more comfortable to their savage state" (ibid). The article concluded by again stressing the importance of the Congo in terms of slavery: "[T]his kingdom has been important to the Portugese [sic], on account of the slaves which it afforded. Among slave-dealers, the Congo men are generally not considered so strong and powerful as slaves from some other parts of Africa" (ibid).

As these dictionaries show, select information about the Congo, its geography, political organization, economy, and peoples was readily available to Lewis. Given the information that was there for the taking, ranging from a banal tea called Congo to a specific country labeled as such, why were African American historians led to ignore these options? To discuss the issue of silence among African American historians, Black newspapers will be used as a counterpoint to discuss what was known about the Congo in African American circles and why it was ignored in works of history. Central to this analysis of newspaper articles is the issue of "people, places, and processes" (Miller 2012: 28).

Ignorance and Slave Epistemology

Like works of history, Black newspapers communicated little about the Congo. The handful of articles that did address it, however, provide valuable clues as to why the Congo had become an ignored entity in antebellum African American intellectual discourses. The geography of the Congo primarily stood for a river, a coast, and a "country". As a coastal country – a depiction already evoked by the poem that Lewis cited – the Congo was typically located on the "Western coast of Africa [...] occupying a line of coast of less than three hundred miles in length", as the Frederick Douglass' Paper suggests in an article titled "The Slave Trade" on September 4, 1851 (1851a: n.p.). The port of Loando constituted the sole concrete place mentioned in these articles. This reduction of the geographical Congo to its "watery" regions – its coast and major river – was reinforced by how the "banks" of the river Congo were depicted, namely as a ship-oriented economy of "piers" and "wharfs", in the Douglass' Paper of March 1861 (1861c: n.p.).[19] In this lengthy letter from a reader of the Douglass' Paper, the Congo river was discussed as a tightly-organized commercial arena in which a ship, as it is told, "sails unmolested some thirty miles up the river, and with all the bustle of a new arrival, hauls into a pier opposite the 'factory' and warehouse belonging to the Havana Company" (ibid).

Within the commercial infrastructure of the Congo made possible by the water, only one economic activity attracted systematic African American interest: The slave trade. The "discursive events" that led a description of Congo's geography almost exclusively related to events in which slave ships, slave ports, or slave factories were involved. The Congo's geography, typically, would be mentioned within the context of ships that took slaves from the Congo coast or were captured while attempting doing so. An article titled "Capture of a Slaver" from January 5, 1848 in The North Star, for instance, recounts the story of a slave ship that was "taken at Congo river, at which place it appears she had been delivered to Brazilian purchasers" (1849a: n.p.). Other and mostly shorter articles in Douglass' Monthly in the early 60s, for instance the article from December 1861 titled "Conviction of a Slave Trader", tell the story of how slave-traders shipped "900 Africans at Congo River" (1861b: n.p.).

What sets the Congo apart from other slave-catching geographies is that it was considered one of the last bastions of the transatlantic slave trade. "The slave trade on the coast of Africa is nearly extinguished," the Frederick Douglass' Paper wrote

19 This quote comes from an excerpt from the article "Secret History of the African Slave Trade", reproduced from the Evening Post in Douglass' Monthly in March, 1861 (1861a: n.p.).

in the article "The Slave Trade" on September 4, 1851, with the exception of "Lagos, Poto Novo [...] and eight or ten factories in the Congo country" (1851a: n.p.). Given the ongoing abolitionism of African American newspapers, the slave ports of the Congo were a continual annoyance, particularly since these ports were frequently used to bypass the anti-slave trade blockades by the British Navy. In an article from The North Star on January 16, 1851, a letter from the Boston Journal is reprinted titled "The African Slave Trade" in which "an officer on board of one of our ships on the African station" expressed skepticism about the "suppression of the slave trade by the present system of blockade", particularly in light of the dubious role of the U.S. Navy (1851: n.p.):

> I very much regret to say, that for a long time the greatest facilities for carrying on the slave trade have been afforded by the prostitution of our flag. I believe full one half of the negroes shipped from the Congo southward, have been made in vessels under its cover. The position which the United States occupies upon the right of visitation and search, is such that a "bona fide" American vessel, cannot be molested by a British cruiser, even with a full cargo of negroes on board. England by treaty or convention, has secured the right, under certain restrictions, of visiting and searching all suspected vessels, except those wearing the American flag; – such, are sacred, and thus guarded, may embark hundreds of slaves under the guns of the British Commodore himself, avoid all interruption from foreign countries, and by hoisting the Brazilian flag may escape capture by our own. Now, I believe I know my duty as an officer too well to find fault with the acts of my Government, but after two years' service and experience as an African cruiser, and not wholly without observation, I am free to say that could the United States, authorities consistently make an exception to the general rule, so as to allow vessels notoriously engaged in the slave trade to be detained by British cruisers and delivered up to own, the disgraceful traffic would be greatly curtailed, and especially would the vile prostitutiion [sic] of our flag be prevented.

In this significant quote, the real-and-imagined Congo stood as a physical place from which slaves were shipped and as a marker of "the prostitution of the American flag". The Congo was thus more than just some place in Africa: It stood for the active non-commitment of the United States to end the external and illegal slave trade by refusing to be controlled by British vessels, even when the American ships were clearly transporting "negroes shipped from the Congo southward". In this quote, the real-and-imagined Congo geography stood for the political and moral disaster of slavery.

Various metaphorical operations transferred the "slavery" characteristics of the Congo to other geographical entities, particularly those in the United States. The Colored American explained to its readers in an article titled "Power of the Free

States" on May 18, 1839 that the internal slave trade in the United States was enabled by "northern slaves states" happy to sell their Blacks to the South. By doing so, those states became "the Congo and Guinea of America", according to the paper (1839a: n.p.), therefore transferring the real-and-imagined slave qualities of the Congo to the northern states.

A more minor aspect of the topos of the Congo-as-Slave was the trope of the Congo as "a home country", a feature that will return in subsequent decades. The Colored American, for instance, discussed the recaptured slaves of the famous and hotly debated schooner Amistad in an article titled "From the Herald of Freedom" on September 28, 1839.[20] In it, the human cargo was said to be heading to "their dear lost Congulese [sic] country and home" (1839b: n.p.). This idea of the Congo as a "mother-land", a term used by the Frederick Douglass' Paper on January 12, 1855 in an article titled "Our Correspondents" (1855a: n.p.), was already at play in the poem cited in Lewis's Light and Truth and would return in other poetic utterances, too. For instance, the 1849 poem titled "The Captive Dreams", published in The North Star on May 4, depicted a family of Tennessee slaves, with the father dreaming of freedom on African soil, where he could again chase "the Congo bird / Amid the cocoa bowers / Again his parents voices heard, / And danced away the hours: / Back through the lapse of years he passed" (1849d: n.p.).

People called Congo in antebellum African American intellectual discourse were rarely free Blacks.[21] That the Congo as a slave district also stands for the Congo-as-Slave is not "natural", but the result of a discursive strategy that aimed at merging those referred to as Congo with their slave environment. Living in a slave district could have easily opened up the possibility of framing people named Congo as both "victims" and "perpetrators", too, as would be the case in postbellum discourse (cf. next section) or the era of the Congo Free State (see next chapter). References to Congo people in Douglass' Monthly vary from "cargoes of Congos" in the article "Slave Breeding" (1859c: n.p.) to "Congo Africans for sale" in the article "Miscellaneous News Items" (1859b: n.p.). These slaves are discussed in ways that still reduced them to merchandise, in other words.

A slave could be identified as Congo by skin color: The blacker the slaves, the more easily they could be labeled as Congo. How this link between Congo and blackness discursively played out can be witnessed in an article from The Liberator titled "American Civilization Illustrated: A Great Slave Auction", reprinted April, 1859 in the Douglass' Monthly. The article critically described and discussed the

20 This was a reproduced from the Herald of Freedom.

21 One free Black called Congo was a supporter of the National Reform Convention: "Emmanuel Congo", as The Colored American records it on July 25, 1840 (1840a: n.p.).

slave sale of the "Butler stock", including "but very few" who were "a shade removed from the original Congo blackness" (1859a: n.p.). The article makes clear that Congo blackness was a label reserved to those who "have been little defiled by the admixture of degenerate Anglo-Saxon blood" (ibid). Full-blooded blackness was considered favorable "in the eyes of the buyer" since "pure blooded negroes are much more docile and manageable than mulattoes, though less quick of comprehension, which makes them preferred by drivers, who can stimulate stupidity by the lash much easier than they can control intelligence by it" (ibid).

In the same vein, other journalistic articles overtly linked physical blackness to intellectual darkness. In an article titled "Dealings with Slavery and the Contrabands: Facts, Scenes and Incidents" from December 1861, Douglass' Monthly separated slaves with "genuine Congo physiques" from those "as white as their masters, and as intelligent" (1861c: n.p.). An extreme case of this connection between Congo blackness and low intellectual capabilities is the story of Tom, the mentally challenged and untutored slave who was something of a musical Wunderkind, since he could play several instruments as well as any schooled musician. In an article reprinted from Dwight's Journal of Music from St. Louis, Tom is described in the African American The Christian Recorder on June 22, 1861 as "a grinning, idiotic, Congo boy [...] more like an ape than a man" (1861a: n.p.). Through this animalistic terminology, Tom's "blackness" and stupidity are stressed. The fact that Tom, as a Black "Congo boy", played the piano with the gusto of "a master" caused the narrator of the story to be "astounded, I cannot account for it, no one can, no one understands it" (ibid). The disbelief in Tom's skills did not only reflect amazement towards a gifted disabled person, but mainly towards a Black, animal-like Congo.

Real-and-imagined people called Congo were as transnational as the slave trade. Slaves called Congo were thus located discursively in both America and Africa, most prominently the area around the Congo estuary and Liberia. There were considerable differences between geographies and people called Congo in the United States (internal) and elsewhere (external). As we have seen, the internal entity of the Congo constituted a metaphor for racial abomination and abolitionist perversion (that is, by signifying "pure-blooded" blackness and ongoing enslavement, the Congo constituted the perversion of American liberties guaranteed by the Constitution). This internal Congo could only be turned into an abominable entity by reference to an external Congo in Central West Africa that was discursively reduced to a slave factory and a slave coast populated by incorrigible and morally defective pagans. Liberian "Congoes" strengthened this imagery. In Liberia, Congoes constituted both a "class" and a "tribe". The North Star of April 13, 1849 gives us an idea of how this "class" of Congoes is related to the "tribe" by discussing the Liberian apprentice system in an article titled "Extracts" (1849c: n.p.):

> But there is another class, who live in the families of the colonists, and are bound to them for a term of years. Some are recaptured Africans taken off the Pons. They are of the Congo tribe. There are others from the tribes within the Republic. These are bound under what is called the apprentice system. I enquired how long the term of their service was, and learned that the Congos had to serve seven years. I asked if they were bound to educate them. They told me they were not, unless they choose to; but when there was a native school convenient they generally sent them.

The social order in Liberia clearly segregated the class of "Congos" from other Liberians by organizing a "native school" and by providing religious education "especially among the Congo negroes that are flocking in", as The Christian Recorder reported in an article from May 30, 1863 titled "A Bird's Eye View of Missions in Africa" (1863: n.p.). The reason for this segregation was that those people called Congo were undesired folk, both in Liberia and beyond. Their "real-and-imagined" enslavement would make them incompatible with the central beliefs, norms, and paradigms of those in power.

Congoes also presented an integration challenge to Liberian elites because of their "paganism". In a period that saw the "Great Awakening", or the opening and intensification of the "religious marketplace" for African Americans and their Black churches (McDonald 2001: 12), paganism was a cardinal sin. Thus, when a late 18th-century sermon summoned Black American believers to keep on progressing in faith, it also warned against what was left behind and should not be returned to: The Congo. "You are a people who have walked in darkness," the re-published sermon titled "A Sermon Delivered in Saint Thomas' Church, Fifth Street, Philadelphia, July 17th, 1794" went in The Christian Recorder on October 19, 1861 (1861b: n.pag.). The reason why the preacher called his African American congregation descendants from heathens was their supposed roots in "Benin, Congo, or Angola" (1861b: n.p.), and to remind them of what they once were: Unchristian and untaught. What was in the past for African Americans was a bitter reality for those contemporary "tribes" called Congo. To these tribes were sent "Bibles, missionaries, well qualified teachers, and as many Christian families as can be spared" for the purpose of "advancing the missionary enterprise", as the historian Pennington is reported to have said about the "Mandingo and Congo" in a public speech, reported in the Frederick Douglass' Paper of February 5, 1852 (titled: "Meeting of the Colored People of New York"; 1852a: n.p.).

From the latter suggestion that one send bibles to them, one should conclude that there was hope for the Congoes, as a class and a tribe, both in Africa and America. They were clearly not considered completely beyond education or salvation. It becomes clear from many newspaper passages, however, that this hope placed in the progress of the so-called Congo people was often more of a theoretical assumption that satisfied one's own interests than a practical belief in the Congolese's ability to improve their status. For instance, in an article on "The Law of Human Progress", September 14, 1849, The North Star explicitly incorporated "the Fegee Islander [sic], the Bushman, the Hottentot, the Congo negro" into its discourse of progress, since "no term of imagined 'finality' can arrest it" (1849e: n.p.). It is quite clear, however, that the Congo is addressed in this passage in order to validate the theoretical universality of "human progress" rather than to concretely exemplify the ability of the Congo people to advance. This strategy is also applied in the 1843 "An Address to the Slaves of the United States of America" by Henry Highland Garnet, who only mentions the "untutored African who roams in the wilds of Congo" (2003: 117) to emphasize his universal demand for liberty. Garnet's silence about the Congo in his lengthy historical work The past and the Present Condition, and the Destiny, of the Colored Race (1848), published but a few years later, shows how little interest he actually had in addressing the Congo as a topic in its own right.

Despite their (theoretical) ability to progress, people called Congo were conceived of as fairly inert, particularly those from Africa. An article on marriage customs around the world appearing in Freedom's Journal on October 5, 1827 titled "Marriage Customs, &C. of Various Nations" states (1827a: n.p.):

> The converts to Christianity among the Congoese, in their nuptial ceremony adopt the manners of the Portuguese; but no persuasions can prevail upon the most religious Congoese Catholics to renounce the custom of keeping as many women as their circumstances will enable them to maintain.

Obviously, this quote was not very optimistic about the ability of "Congoese" to denounce polygamy, since "no persuasions can prevail". Minor changes in their behavior aside, the external "Congoese" could not, according to the article, be redeemed. The inertia of external "Congoese" contrasts with those called Congo in African American realms. Instances of inner-American people called Congo conceived of as unable to adapt were therefore rare. If this suggestion was made at all, it was evoked via humorist allegory. In an article describing the internal workings of the newspaper in an overtly ironic manner (February 18, 1853), the Frederick

Douglass' Paper asked why its "colored editor" did not "learn to read". Its answer denounced less the editor than the entity to whom he was compared to (1853a: n.p.):

> It is a singular defect in our colored editor, a sort of bizarre make-up, which reminds one of the dear old Congo King, stalking abroad under his own palm trees, dressed in a red military coat and golden spurs, with a dusky hiatus between, an object for the profound admiration of himself and his very colored subjects.

The humorous absurdity of the editor's refusal to learn is highlighted by comparing him to the preposterous "dear old Congo King", whose unchangeable penchant for ignorant and tasteless pomp matches the editor's alleged pompous ignorance. An interesting side-effect of this allegory is that the Congo was implicitly inscribed in historical processes by reference to the institution of the king, which was never actually done beyond this passage. As such, when the history of the Congo was mobilized at all in Black newspaper articles, it was done so in order to ridicule and negate it. The complete silence about the history of the Congo did not mean, in other words, that newspapers considered the Congo to have none; it merely meant that they considered it too ridiculous to be dealt with in a serious and systematic manner. To what extent did this change in the postbellum period? This will be investigated in the following section.

PRESENCE: IMPERIAL EPISTEMOLOGY AND THE CONGO'S RE-EMERGENCE IN POSTBELLUM AMERICA

On the surface, postbellum Congoism was significantly different from its antebellum manifestation. To discuss this, George Washington Williams's History of the Negro Race in America From 1619 to 1880 will serve as a continuous point of reference. This work was chosen, amongst other reasons, because of its immediate success and enduring and wide circulation. John Hope Franklin's assertion that "at the outset few blacks knew of the existence of the work by Williams" (1998: 120) is thus questioned. Franklin's claim rests upon the obvious demise of the African American press in the 1880s, supposedly preventing works of history by Black Americans from being discussed or announced properly (ibid).

The disappearance of Black newspapers in Boston, Philadelphia, and Chicago was no doubt a serious blow to the circulation of Black knowledge. The work at hand, however, has insisted on white and Black intellectual "entangledness" (cf. Introduction). Seen from this perspective, it seems very likely that Black intellectuals would have known of Williams's book despite this. When Black media ceased publishing, Black intellectuals still had to remain informed, and would thus have consulted white media channels. Chances were very high that they would read about Williams's book, since more than three hundred magazines and newspapers – ranging from the American The New York Times and the Magazine of American History to the British Spectator and Westminster Review – considered Willams's history worthy of critical acclaim, as Franklin himself noted (ibid: 117-119). This remarkable amount of attention can be partially attributed to the fact that the reputable publishing house G.P. Putnam's Sons published all editions,[22] both in New York and London (ibid: 119).

The willingness of the white press to discuss the book was matched by the serious interest exhibited by what African American local press was still left, and this took forms as diverse as reviews in media outlets such as the Huntsville Gazette to editorial comments in the Washington Bee (ibid: 120). The Christian Recorder also published a lengthy review of the first edition of the book on January 18, 1883. On top of that, after the book's initial publication in November 1882, it ran a three-week ad campaign from January 4, 1883 to January 18, 1883. The ad titled "A History of the Negro Race in America from 1619 to 1880 Negroes As Slaves, as Soldiers and As Citizens" announced the book as "a Great Work for the Negro Race!", thus overtly inviting African Americans to read the book as an act of racial solidarity, since it was billed not only as a history of the "negro" race, but also for it (1883a: n.p.). At the same time, the advertisement attempted to emphasize the importance and authority of the book by quoting supporters from the white N.Y. World. That publication describes the book as a "prodigious work [...] one of the most cheering books of recent times". Furthermore, the N.Y. World lauded the book's "philosophic breadth of vision" and finished by saying that "the author has presented with an almost poetic force one of the greatest problems that await human solution" (ibid). This quote from the N.Y. World again exemplifies the interdependence of white and Black intellectual thought: It shows how Black intellectuals tapped white authority in order to assert their own worth and quality. On top of publishing ads for the book, The Christian Recorder offered a deal for the two-in-one version at "the low price of $4.00" on September 10, 1885, as it concerned a book "which should be read in the home of every colored family" (1885h: n.p.). Other news media offered free copies of the two-in-one-volume edition in 1885 to new

22 Putnam's Sons also published the second volume of Williams's work, A History of the Negro Troops in the War of the Rebellion, 1861-1865, as well as the 1885 two-in-one-volume titled A History of the Negro Race in America 1800-1880. It is the latter volume that has been consulted in this book.

subscribers (Franklin 1998: 126), as in the case of the Bostonian Advocate or the New York Freeman (ibid).

What is behind these odd (and plainly false) claims by John Hope Franklin?[23] Much of Franklin's skepticism about Williams's success is caused by the alleged "complete obscurity" of The History of the Negro Race among Black and white intellectuals in subsequent generations (ibid: xix). Williams's alleged disappearance – another assertion that does not hold ground; cf. subsequent sections and chapters – clearly did not begin until some years after his book's initial publication. In the review in The Christian Recorder, "Williams History [sic] of the Negro", the book was consistently lauded, and in the end recommended without reserve: "It were to be wished that Mr. Williams would give the public a cheap edition of his invaluable work, assured as we are that it ought to be in every library, and on the table of thousands" (1883b: n.p.). If the book was criticized at all, particularly by condescending authors in the white press, it was due to Williams's tendency to repeat himself or to write in a "declamatory" fashion (Franklin 1998: 119). Another critique was that the history was lacking, in that it did not tie the great amount of facts together to produce a compelling narrative (ibid). This was also echoed by The Christian Recorder: "Mr. Williams is less of an analyst. He gives little evidence of knowing how to interpret a fact" (1883b: n.p.).

In general, however, Williams's history was very well-received. His perceived obscurity by Franklin was therefore probably caused by Williams's controversial personal and professional life. Accusations of embezzling subscribers' money from his short-lived Washington journal The Commoner hurt his reputation considerably in subsequent decades, for instance. The same went for the ongoing suspicion surrounding him because he was perceived as an opportunist who hopped from one profession to the next, leading to short-lived careers as a Baptist pastor, state representative, lawyer, and human rights activist. Enough accomplishments remain in the end to save Williams from obscurity: His engagement with the Congo is still remembered, especially his activism (cf. next chapter), as is his merit as a historian: W.E.B. Du Bois's 1888 laudatory comments on Williams as "the greatest historian of the race" surely helped his cause (qtd. in Franklin 1998: 133).

There are many reasons why white and Black readers found Williams's book appealing. In what follows, the intellectual influences and political agenda that

23 Who is, after all, considered by the Oxford Encyclopedia of African American History to be a deeply transformative figure in the American historical profession (Finkelman 2006b: 265), as well as the "most influential African American historian of the twentieth century" (ibid: 263).

guided Williams will be addressed, allowing, as with Lewis in the previous section, the man and his work to be seen in its broader context.

(African) American Progress as Program

One reason for Williams's success was that his work focused on the history of the United States, and especially its great dramas (the American Revolution and the Civil War, amongst others). Whereas Lewis's Light and Truth took a look at the present and future through an ancient, universal, and Afrocentrist perspective, Williams remained close to home, both temporarily and geographically, just as many of his late 19th-century contemporaries did. Williams, for instance, devoted the entire second part of his two-in-one-volume to "slavery in the colonies" and focused solely on the "Negro in the Revolution" in part three, in which he examined Black soldiers and intellectuals – their military employment and achievements, their "intellect" as astronomers, mathematicians, and physicians, and their overall legal status. Williams maintained this focus on the United States in subsequent parts by covering topics such as "anti-slavery agitation", the role of Blacks in the Civil War, and the rise and decline of Black institutions and African American achievers up until 1880.

The only part of the epic, 1000-page tome that departs from this America-oriented narrative is the roughly 100-page "Preliminary Considerations" (part one). The title already suggests the status of this chapter in Williams's larger narrative, i.e. as a primer for the story that really mattered: The U.S. and its Black population. In this section, Williams discusses numerous international topics. He debates the merits of Egypt and Ethiopia in the chapter "Primitive Negro Civilization" (chapter 3) and integrates a discussion of the "Negro Kingdoms of Africa" into chapter four (Benin, Dahomey, Yoruba). The Ashantee empire receives particular attention (chapter five), as do Sierra Leone and Liberia (chapter nine and ten). In between these chronologically organized African case studies, Williams devotes himself to discussing Africa as a whole – its "Negro Type" (chapter six), its "Idiosyncrasies" (chapter seven), and its "Languages, Literature, and Religion" (chapter eight). It is in chapters six to eight that the Congo is mentioned and discussed.

Through an American lens, Williams systematically inscribes Black Americans in U.S. history. The author announces this "vindicationist" and "contributionist" aim in the introduction (see previous section for a discussion of these terms), in which he states that "the history of the Colored people in America was required" (Williams 1885: v) due to a number of reasons, including the lack of "historically trustworthy material" (ibid); because "colored people" had been, historically speaking, "the most vexatious problem in North America" (ibid: vi); because "Colored people had always displayed a matchless patriotism and an incomparable heroism in the cause of Americans" (ibid); and because Williams's history "would give the world more correct ideas of the Colored people, and incite the latter to greater effort in the struggle of citizenship and manhood" (ibid).

These openly communicated political agendas have much in common with those of Lewis's Light and Truth. To set the historical record straight, or to provide "more correct ideas of the Colored people", is an obvious goal of the work. Williams pursues this aim by integrating Black Americans into American history and by staging and listing them as American patriots, heroes, and scholarly people, which was a quintessential romanticist tool already at work in Lewis's work. Williams's history contains strong vindicationist traits, as well, in the form of what one could call a "pushing b(l)ack" strategy – in other words, by pushing back against the racism that distorted the "ideas of the Colored people" and by pushing Black to elevate the race in terms of "citizenship and manhood".

This double vindicationist strategy was very much understood and taken up in the many reviews of the book. Exemplary here is The Christian Recorder. The newspaper reported in "Williams History [sic] of the Negro" from January 18, 1883 that, until Williams, "[The American negro] could not look with any pride upon the past, as that past had been told him by those whose first business as an excuse for themselves was to blacken and defame it" (1883: n.p.). The result was devastating, according to the paper: "American black men holding Africa and all that relates to it, even the color of their faces and the texture of their own hair, in downright contempt; seeing with the whites beauty only in a white face, and 'good' hair, only in hair that is straight" (ibid). Thus, Williams's work is lauded for studying Black Americans "as part of the nation" (ibid).

This passage indicates that Williams's history was considered as a corrective for the "contempt" and the "prejudice" about and of Black Americans, their African roots, and "the color of their faces and the texture of their own hair". These views were clearly internalized by African Americans, the quote suggested, by virtue of "seeing with the whites beauty only in a white face". On top of that, The Christian Recorder read Williams's story as an internally unifying narrative of "our common manhood and our common civilization". With the reference to "our", African Americans are meant, especially since The Christian Recorder hardly considered the Blacks in Africa as equals. Paganism marked the difference between African Americans and Africans, according to The Christian Recorder, which openly asked in this review whether "the African" would have been as "far advanced as any pagan or Mohammedan power on earth, as far as Morocco, or Turkey, or the inferior powers of East Asia" if "Christianity been given him" (ibid). The review's highlighting of African inferiority should hardly come as a surprise, as Williams's work constituted an ongoing devaluation of Africa in history, particularly as compared to Light and Truth. Whereas Lewis was concerned with locating the Urform of humankind in Black Ethiopia, Williams refrained from discussing Africa in these terms. Although he describes Ethiopia as "the cradle of civilization" (Williams 1885: 40) and suggested that "Greece went to school to Egypt" (ibid), he did so offhandedly. Unlike Lewis, Williams never aspired to celebrate Egypt and Ethiopia as a major benchmark of Black achievement.

Although it might sound paradoxical at first, the reason for this reluctance to develop an Afrocentrist discourse is Williams's reliance on 19th-century "civilizationist theory" (Hall 2009: 155), casting history even more strongly than Lewis as periods of "advance" and "decline". More explicitly than in Lewis's account, progress could be achieved (or lost) via Christianity as well as through secular agents – "nations", "empires", "kingdoms", and "republics" with "different nationalities, and hence different languages" (Williams 1885: 2). The most notable examples of the latter were to be found in Liberia and Sierra Leone, which Williams discusses at disproportional length. Nations were truly considered by Williams as the "lighthouses" on the "Dark Continent" (ibid: 109). As such, Liberia and Sierra Leone were obvious exceptions to the common decline of the post-antique "negro races" – the embodiment of which was to be found in Egypt and Ethiopia, where progress was stalled by heathenism. "It is asked", Williams states in the chapter titled "Primitive Negro Civilization", "what caused the decline of all this glory of the primitive Negro? Why this people lost their position in the world's history?" Willams's answer: "Idolatry! Sin!" (ibid: 41). In addition to the lack of Christian socialization, the former antique nations were also steadily declining, according to Williams, due to their emigrational drive, a trait they shared with other African "cosmopolitan people" (ibid: 35). This trait will return within the context of the Congo, as well.

Williams used late 19th-century "civilizationist theory" to demonstrate his compatibility with the dominant strands of the American intellectual culture of that period, which argued strongly along national, racial, and linguistic lines (Gossett 128). But he also used the concept of "civilization" to challenge the notion that white Americans, and whites in general, constituted its apex (cf. Hall 2009: 155). Williams addressed this topic via a little intellectual detour. By discussing the "unity of mankind" on the very first page of his book, he dismissed the "absurd charge that the Negro does not belong to the human family" (1885: 1), which rendered Blacks unable to civilize. Williams believed that God gave "color, language, and civilization" to all humankind (ibid). "It is fair to presume", he reminded his readers, "that God gave all the races of mankind civilization to start with" (ibid). Despite this omnipresent ability to civilize, some peoples were, for Williams, clearly more apt to develop and advance than others. Although Williams never spelled it out, it becomes clear from his narrative that the "dark and woolly-haired people who inhabit Western Africa" (ibid: 31) are less prone than other Blacks to achieving what was understood as civilization.

To start understanding this, Williams's particular framing of "blacks" and "Negroes" must be explained, especially since Williams clearly distinguished between the two. This differentiation had been marked since ancient times by the hair: "Negroes" have "curly or woolly hair" (ibid: 32); "blacks", in turn, have "straight hair" (ibid). Based on ancient sources, furthermore, Williams comes to the conclusion that there "were nations who were black, and yet were not Negroes". He thus combines a national outlook with a thoroughly racialized one, as was the case with Lewis.

To Williams, Western Africans are exemplary representatives of the "Negro" type, not only because of their physical appearance, but mainly because of their essential inability to progress beyond the vice of slavery (ibid: 45). Williams underscores this difference by describing the "Negro" as "the lowest strata of the African race" (ibid: 117): "The genuine African has gradually degenerated into the typical Negro", Williams asserts. He goes on: "His blood infected with the poison of his low habitation, his body shrivelled [sic] by disease, his intellect veiled in pagan superstitions, the noblest yearnings of his soul strangled at birth by the savage passions of a nature abandoned to sensuality, – the poor Negro of Africa deserves more our pity than our contempt" (ibid). This typical "Negro" is thus depicted as a physical, social, and psychological disaster. Williams's point was to connect the "least civilized" blacks of Africa to the "worst" among African Americans. William begins by asserting, "It is true that the weaker tribes, or many of the Negroid type, were the chief source of supply for the slave-market in this country for many years" (ibid). However, he does not leave it at that: Slaves in the U.S. had bettered themselves through suffering and education, his story goes. Through the "severe ordeal through which to pass to citizenship and civilization", the African American, Williams asserts, moved from "idolatry" to "an extreme rationalism" (ibid).

Williams's passage did not deny the ability of West African "Negroes" to progress because the "slumbering and dying attribute in the Negro nature" could supposedly be awoken through tough, but necessary "ordeals", such as slavery, allowing them to pass from "pagan superstitions" and "savage passions" to "citizenship and civilization" (ibid). African Americans were therefore congratulated by Williams for having turned misery into salvation through (first) "extreme religious exercise", followed by an "extreme rationalism" (ibid). Apart from overtly separating primitive and backward Africans from highly advancing Black Americans, this passage is particularly revealing in terms of the epistemic background against which Williams was writing. It is striking that "extreme rationalism" figured as the final stage of African American progress. This reflected what Peter Burke labeled the "knowledge revolution" of the late 19th century (2010: 256-258), which saw the ongoing substitution of theological and classical thinking for "rational" and scientific reasoning and methodology.

The coexistence of biblical and classical authority that dominated many antebellum works of history (Winterer 2002: 9) was increasingly replaced by "science" (ibid: 104-108). Science understood time as "progressive". As such, it comes as no surprise that the major engine of history in History of Negro Race is both "science" (e.g. Williams 1885: 36) and progress. Although Williams did discuss classical and biblical texts, he did so mainly to counter the defenders of slavery and racial oppression who still sought authority in both of them. As a general rule, however, Williams did not draw from the Bible or the antique texts as a historical guide to reality. "While I am a believer in the Holy Bible," Williams stated in the introduction, "it is not the best authority on ethnology" (ibid: 5), a stance that reflected the "liberal Protestantism" typical of the late 19th century, as Winterer called it (2002: 121). This kind of Protestantism designates a nonsectarian and non-dogmatic strand within American Christianity that defined and applied religion as set of ethical ideals rather than a trustworthy historical compass (Winterer 2002: 121). The end result can be seen in Williams, who favored "scientific", "objective", and "truthful" sources over others (cf. Hall 2009: 124; Winterer 2002: 104-105).

In the same vein as the mainstream historical scientists of his days, Williams aimed to "write a thoroughly trustworthy history" (1885: 7) that would "record the truth, the whole truth, and nothing but the truth" (ibid). We can trace through his footnotes how he did this and which branches of the scientific revolution he mobilized. What obviously constituted dominant epistemic threads in Williams's work were the "twin sciences of anthropology and physical geography" (cf. Eze 2000: 2). Similar to Light and Truth's fascination with the different shades and meanings of skin color, Williams flirted with ideas of racialized physical indexes ("curly or woolly hair" vs. "straight hair", for instance). This reproduced select Enlightenment rhetoric surrounding Africa, which, as Winterer argues (2002: 111), was experiencing a revival in the late 19th century. As in Kant's "Physical Geography", for instance, Williams makes the distinction between "blacks" and "Negroes". To quote this Enlightenment icon. "One can say that the only true Negroes are in Africa and in Guinea. Not just the evenly smoked-black color but also the black woolly hair, the broad face, the flat nose, and the thick lips constitute the characteristics of these people, in addition to clumsy large bones" (Kant 2000: 60). In this passage, Kant uses most of the buzz words that return in Williams's text – "true negro", "black", "woolly hair".

In all fairness, Williams never mentioned Kant, but he did overtly refer to other champions of the Enlightenment – Blumenbach and Cuvier in particular (e.g. Williams 1885: 23-24), who, due to the highly intertextual trading of ideas amongst Enlightenment thinkers, evoked Kant's racial ideas and discourse on "civilization" as opposed to terms such as "nature", "degeneration", and "savagery" (Eze 2000: 6-7). Williams plainly alludes to this rhetoric when discussing "the genuine African" as a "degenerated" being whose soul is "strangled at birth by the savage passions of a nature abandoned to sensuality" and who could only be brought to "citizenship and civilization" through slavery, which re-awakened the civilization abilities "in the Negro nature" (ibid: 117).

In contrast to the Enlightenment thinkers above, however, Williams left open the possibility that Blacks might become civilized. For this idea, Williams sought scientific support and authority in the work of James Cowles Prichard, one of the leading anthropologists until the mid-19th century (Petermann 2004: 400), mentioned frequently in Williams's footnotes. Prichard considered civilization a human trait, although he did see a correlation between light skin color and the ability to develop. Since the original "stock of men were Negroes" (qtd. in Petermann 2004: 401), Pritchard believed that those with a light skin color were further removed from their original states of primitiveness than those who were black (Petermann 2004: 401; Gossett 1997: 55). In other words, for Pritchard, the likelihood that a people might become civilized increases with the lightness of skin. Williams agreed, as is discussed in what follows.

Pritchard's (and Williams's) intellectual horizon thus mapped the ability to progress according to skin color. This orientation was influenced, but not caused, by the natural environment in which people lived. 19th-century intellectuals genuinely debated the effects of geography, climate, and nature on physical appearance and the ability to historically and morally progress. In the same vein as Prichard (but contrary to Kant and Blumenbach), Williams refrained from making the environment the ultimate determinant of skin color and hair type. He considered many of the theories which advocated this theory as "speculation [...] one theory is about as valuable as another" (1885: 37).

Yet, at the same time, Williams did not shy away from linking "low habitation" to the debased qualities of the "typical Negro" in Africa (ibid: 117). "Low" should be read both literally and metaphorically, since the correlation between flat or low locations and moral debasement – often framed racially through claiming someone's "blackness" – was quite strong by the late 19th century. This idea had been gaining traction since the Enlightenment. In Kant's words: "[T]hose that live in the flat parts are blacker than those who live in the high altitudes. That is why the blacker people live in Senegal than in Congo" (2000: 62). The point of Kant's remark was to link flat or low geography to the low and weak character of the "typical Negro", who is quintessentially black.

Williams combined Kant's rhetoric and arguments with the social Darwinian convictions of his times. He did this by discussing the "negroid type" as a member of the "weaker tribes" (1885: 106) which could be more easily enslaved than other Blacks. "Weaker" tribes suggested that there was a hierarchy among the tribes, comprised of "weaker" and "stronger" ones. This evoked the scientific paradigm of "the law of the survival of the fittest", to quote Williams, which "carried the rubbish to the bottom" (ibid). It is no coincidence that Williams wrote "survival of the fittest" to make his point, as this was an increasingly popular catch phrase of the social Darwinist Herbert Spencer, who articulated the social-biological dimension of the "struggle for existence" and the "survival of the fittest" in his 1864 Principles of Biology (1867: 48-60). As a theory of natural selection in the social and civil arena, Spencer's theory had a "tremendous" influence on the American academy viewed broadly, and on many individual intellectuals in particular (Gossett 1997: 153).

Obviously, Williams was one of them, along with African American intellectuals of generations that would follow, as is shown in the next chapter. The "unworthy Colored people" in Liberia, amongst others, were proclaimed by Williams to be "rubbish," opposed to "the better, wealthier class of free Colored people" – a reference indicative of the class divisions in Liberian communities (1885: 106). This happened in spite of Williams's rhetorical efforts to give the impression of racial unity. It will not be the last contradiction in Williams's history arising from his drawing so heavily on white Euro-American intellectual thought, as will become apparent in the discussion of Williams's depiction of the Congo.

Signifying by Any Means Necessary

Working in the same progressive,[24] profane, romantic,[25] and male-centered[26] manner as Williams, many works of history by African American intellectuals that mention the Congo clearly exhibit a new level of qualitative interest in Central West Africa. Williams himself returned a number of times to the Congo in the

24 Postbellum African American historians who mentioned or discussed the Congo wrote works that were permeated with the idea of temporal and social progress. A second similarity to Williams was that they, too, embodied the shift from the primacy of biblical and classical sources to the primacy of profane texts. Many titles of major African American works of history reflected both tendencies. Obvious examples are E.W. Blyden's co-authored 1871 The people of Africa. A series of Papers on Their Character, Condition, and Future Prospects (Blyden/Taylor/Dwight 1871) and William Wells Brown's 1874 The Rising Son; or, the Antecedents and Advancement of the Colored Race, whose key words ("future" and "advancement") imply that these are histories of progress. Moreover, many works in Williams's vein had a strong contributionist and revisionist take on the nation's history, as may be seen in William Still's 1872 The Underground Railroad (which inscribed the clandestine network of white and Black Americans who helped fugitive slaves escape to Canada) and William Wells Brown's 1867 The Negro in the American Rebellion, His Heroism and His Fidelity (which addressed and celebrated Black contributions in the American revolutionary era).

25 The quintessential romantic tool of listing representative men and women was applied in many works. William Wells Brown, who truly dominated the market of Black historical works in the postbellum period, was a notable example of this tendency. His 1863 The Black Man: His Antecedents, His Genius, and His Achievements contained a series of lists of Black achievers, many of whom were eighteenth- and nineteenth-century American contemporaries, such as the activist Henry Highland Garnet, the revolutionary Nat Turner, the poet Phillis Wheatley, and historians Martin Delany, William Nell, and James Pennington.

26 The female Black authors consulted for this work refrained from discussing or mentioning the Congo altogether. Frank A. Rollin comes closest in her 1883 biography Life and Public Services of Martin R. Delany, in which she discussed Delany's maternal grandfather as "an African prince from the Niger valley regions of Central Africa" who, in his youth, was captured "during hostilities between the Mandingoes, Fellahtas, and Houssa [sic]" (1883: 16). While Rollin ignored the Congo, she did mention Egypt and Ethiopia a number of times. One encounters the same omission in Sojourner Truth's 1878 biography Narrative of Sojourner Truth; while Egypt and Ethiopia are gestured towards, the Congo is silenced.

chapter titled "Preliminary Considerations". The privilege of being discussed independently from other African topics is granted only to Sierra Leone and Liberia in Williams's story, together with some of the "Negro Kingdoms of Africa" (Benin, Dahomey, Yoruba) and the "Ashantee Empire". The Congo appears in Williams's more general dealings with the African "Negro Type" (chapter six), "African Idiosyncrasies" (chapter seven), and African "Languages, Literature, and Religion" (chapter eight). In the "Appendix" of the book, Williams returns to the Congo by quoting from Pigafetta's sixteenth century travel account, as is later discussed later.

To tell the story of the Congo, Williams again turns to the scientific and empirical paradigms of his days. His sources range from the natural histories of Prichard and Blumenbach to the travel accounts of Livingstone and Henry Morgan Stanley (Dr. Livingstone's Expedition to the Zambesi and Through the Dark Continent especially), and from contemporary and popular scientific literature on Africa, such as Wilson's 1856 Western Africa and Wood's 1870 Uncivilized Races of Men, to Du Chaillu's 1861 travel report Explorations & Adventures in Equatorial Africa. However, one book that truly sticks out in Willams's list (and which constitutes an odd bedfellow amidst the rest of the literature used) is Winwood Reade's 1864 Savage Africa. This book was a written report on the author's travels in Equatorial, South-Western, and North-Western Africa, mainly compiled from "letters written to a friend at monthly intervals" (Reade 1864: n.p.), as the Preface suggests in defense of the somewhat "familiar and sometimes egotistical tone" (ibid) of his book.

By taking up Savage Africa, Williams was relying on a book that was quite popular in his own days. Since then, however, it has largely disappeared from the historical archive. Since the book meanders between the genres of travel narrative and imaginative fiction, many twenty-first-century historians virtually ignore Reade as a subject of inquiry (Driver 2001: 92). In his own days, however, Reade's books found a wide readership amongst white and Black intellectuals. Reade's 1872 Martyrdom of Man was hailed as a masterwork by contemporaries as various as H.G. Wells, Cecil Rhodes, W.E.B. Du Bois, and Charles Darwin (ibid). Although Savage Africa was not as lauded and accepted as Martyrdom of Man, it was nevertheless part of a critical debate that provoked serious reviews in respectable magazines, as illustrated by the Anthropological Review from May 1864. Although this review criticized the author's liberal drawing on accounts other than his own, particularly from "anecdotes of former travelers" (1864: 123), the final evaluation of Savage Africa is far from negative. The book, in the end, is praised for "the somewhat rare merit of honestly describing what the author saw, and not what he would have liked to have seen" (ibid: 126).

Williams clearly considered Reade's Savage Africa as an authoritative text on Africa. The African American historian quotes him in his History in lengthy passages that are introduced without qualification or explanation. By introducing these passages with lines like "Mr. Reade says of such government [...]" (1885: 55) or "Mr. Reade says of the musicians he met up the Senegal [...]" (ibid: 78), Williams aligns himself quietly with Reade's assertions, raising them to the level of fact. Williams values Reade as an eyewitness of the African continent. "We have quoted thus extensively from Mr. Reade" (ibid: 61), Williams writes, "because he has given a fair account of the peoples he met" (ibid). Although Reade announced in his Preface that he had no "pretensions to the title of Explorer", but sought to travel "with no special object [...] to flaner in the virgin forest; to flirt with pretty savages, and to smoke his cigar among cannibals" (1864: n.p.), he could nevertheless successfully claim authority on Africa due to his rhetorical commitment to the "sacred facts of science" (ibid: 399). Through this positivist position, which Reade shared with Williams and the academic mainstream of his days, it seems his success was ensured. As a flaneur with a scientific posture, Reade inscribed himself successfully in the 19th-century "culture of exploration" (Driver 2001: 10) because he could credibly claim to provide accurate and credible observations (ibid: 51) of what he saw in Africa. Reade's empirical factuality was provided by his name, background, and class, among other characteristics, which formed the emerging standard for believable knowledge production. Despite his failure to graduate from Oxford, he was a member of a well-to-do and well-known family (his uncle was the famous novelist Charles Reade; Hargreaves 1957: 306). This would make his observations quite believable indeed.

Savage Africa found favor with Williams because of Reade's story of the United States and Britain. Both are depicted as the epitome of 19th-century civilization. Reade labeled the United States a "model land of liberty" (1864: 36) and Britain a secular paradise: "The earth should be a reflection of heaven, and heaven is an empire" (ibid). Reade held numerous stances, concerning progress and race particularly, which aligned with Williams's. Reade's assertion that the "African slave-trade has done its work in assisting the progress of civilization" finds strong parallels in Williams's account. Similar to Williams's Spencerian division of the Liberian population into "rubbish" and a "wealthier class of free Colored people", Reade divided Sierra Leone into "Africans of the highest grade" and the "rubbish" to be found in the recaptured African slaves sent over to the English colony (ibid: 27).

Though he describes him as a "good writer" (Williams 1885: 61), Williams does not buy into Reade's whole account. At particular points in the story, in fact, Williams criticizes Reade. While discussing Sierra Leone, Williams faults Reade for being "somewhat prejudiced against the Negro" (ibid: 89).[27] Indeed, Reade considered the Blacks there to be nothing more than "trained animals", Williams asserts, and were depicted by Reade as merely capable of showing a "display of imitative faculties, with an utter barrenness of creative power" (ibid: 32). Imitating "the white man as the ape imitates the negro", inhabitants of Sierra Leone were thus reduced by Reade to "a caricature" (ibid: 30). Williams clearly objected to this depiction, since he considered Sierra Leone to be "a renewed spot on the edge of the Dark Continent" in which "civilization is at its noonday tide, and the hopes of the most sanguine friends of the liberated Negro have been more than realized" (ibid: 103). Williams thus contradicts Reade's assessment of Sierra Leone, also taking issue with Reade's condemnation of all former slaves in the Americas as the offspring of "the dangerous classes of Africa, the destitute and the criminal" (Reade 1864: 237). There, too, Williams opposes Savage Africa by stating that "many of the noblest types of mankind in Africa, through the uncertainties of war, found their way to the horrors of the middle passage" (Williams 1885: 43). Thus, while valuing Reade's work on many fronts, there were also clear limits in what Williams was willing to accept, particularly when it ran counter to his political outlook.

As ambivalent as Williams might have been towards some passages and attitudes in Savage Africa, the African American historian clearly considered Reade a reliable source for descriptions of the Congo, as did Williams's contemporaries. For instance, Reverend J.G. Wood's 1870 Uncivilized Races of Men of All Countries of the World,[28] which was also taken up by Williams, referred to Reade while discussing the Congo in his entry "The Bubés and Congoese". "The following account is mostly taken from Mr. Reade's condensation" (Wood 1870: 614), it is stated as a matter of fact. Williams adopted a similar factual attitude towards Reade. This is quite remarkable, as Reade did not, in the end, visit the Congo and could not claim the authority of an eye-witness – the premise on which his authority was normally constructed. After a "certain tribe at the mouth of the river" had robbed a schooner and "had declared that they would in future kill any Englishman they could get hold of", Reade gave up on his "Congo enterprise, and took a passage to the islands of the Cape de Verd [sic]" (Reade 1864: 282-283).

The information presented by Read in the twenty-seventh chapter, on the ancient Congo Empire, therefore drew from sources other than his own observations,

---

27 A suggestion also made by the Anthropological Review, which faulted the author for talking "nonsense" in that same context (1864: 124).

28 Which had the self-declared aim of collecting the information from "many travelers [...] scattered rather at random through their books, of the habits and modes life exhibited by the various people among whom they have travelled [sic]" (Wood 1870: I).

treading on very thin ice from a 19th-century scientific point of view. Reade suggests, for instance, that he derives his knowledge from the "writings of Jesuit and Capuchin missionaries" (ibid: 285) and Portuguese explorers such as Antonio Pigafetta, whose 1591 Report on the Kingdom of Kongo was re-published in English in 1881. As such, Reade claims authority on a subject that he only knew from texts produced hundreds of years prior to his account and that contradicted his own standard of knowledge production. Williams either did not fully realize this or did not care. Either way, the implicit result was twofold: First, the Congo was turned into a static, unchangeable entity that could be re-constructed via age-old sources; second, it opened up the possibility of a re-construction of the Congo via texts that did not meet contemporary standards of quality. Both strategies of (re-)knowing the Congo will return frequently in the course of this book.

Although drawing from "old" sources, the information Williams used was apparently "new" enough to both reproduce and substantially alter some of the central aspects of the antebellum discourse on the real-and-imagined Congo. In terms of reproduction, the Congo geography was labeled in ways that echoed the antebellum narratives. Via the many quotes George Washington Williams incorporated in his History from Savage Africa, the Congo was discussed both as a "country" (56) and a "land" (1885: 45), situated on the "other side of the equinoctial line" (ibid: 447). That the Congo is referred to as a "country", as opposed to a "nation", is significant. Since Pigafetta discussed the Congo as a kingdom with its own governmental customs, the term "nation" would have been a more accurate designation; the contemporary Webster's Complete Dictionary of the English Language, for instance, explained the term "nation" as "a body of people under the same government, and generally of the same origin and language" (Goodrich/Porter 1886c: 875). This would have described the old "Kongo kingdom" fairly accurately.

Instead of calling it a "nation", the Congo was a "country", which, according to that same Dictionary, primarily meant the "region of one's birth, permanent residence, or citizenship" (Goodrich/Porter 1886a: 303). Through its secondary connotations, a derogatory aspect might be suspected, since "country" could also mean "destitute of refinement; rude; ignorant" (ibid). With this label, the country of the Congo could convincingly signify, on the one hand, a home country of some sort and a place of ignorance – designations already in place in antebellum discourses on the Congo, as has been discussed in the context of Light and Truth.

Besides being a "country", the Congo also signified "land" in Reade's account, which, according to the Dictionary of the English Language, designated the "earth, or the solid matter which constituted the fixed part of the surface of the globe, in distinction from the waters" (Goodrich/Porter 1886b: 749). In contrast to earlier

Congo discourses, the watery land of the Congo had suddenly become solidified: It obtained more depth and its profile became more defined. Other designations also changed: The "slave coast" suddenly became a "swamp", although these representations would alternate. Williams refers to the Congo as a "low, swampy land at the mouth of the Congo" (1885: 45). William Wells Brown's The Rising Son even gave the Congo an interior,[29] building on travel accounts such as the one by "Captain Tuckey, of the English Navy" (1882: 73) who, according to Brown, "penetrated" the "heart of the continent" (ibid).

In postbellum America, Congo could refer either to individual Black Americans or groups of Africans. Williams mentioned an African American individual named "Congo Zado" in his History who was part of a "company of colored infantry" during the Civil War (1885: 361). That a Congo could be named, given human qualities, and lauded was hardly imaginable in antebellum America. In postbellum America, however, African individuals called Congo were still next to non-existent. Whenever people in Africa are designated as Congo, this entailed a whole group of "inhabitants" or "tribes" of the Congo "country" (ibid: 84). There is one exception to this rule – the Congolese "judge" in chapter seven, who is said to sit on a "mat under a large tree, and patiently hears the arguments pro and con. His decisions are final. There is no higher court, and hence no appeal" (ibid: 56). Despite being an individual, the lack of personal characterization in this short passage is striking. The judge is thus more a metonymy than a clearly distinguishable human being. He stands in this passage, in short, for the "African idiosyncrasies" announced in the chapter's title surrounding primitiveness and autocratic rule. Being an important entity, the judge sits nevertheless on "a mat under a tree" (which can be considered idiosyncratic); while being a balanced evaluator ("hears the arguments pro and con"), his decision cannot be challenged (and is thus autocratic). As an individual non-individual, the judge is "drowned" in the "anonymous collectivity" (Memmi 1991: 87) of traits that point to the character of a whole "African" people instead of a single Congolese.

"Congo Negroes" function as a malleable, abstract idea in Williams's History (1885: 447). Congo demarcated, for instance, the lowest position on the scale of the African "races", both in Central West Africa and Liberia. This was done by linking human traits, morality included, to geographical ones. In a telling passage on "the Negro Type", Williams cites Reade's African typology and racial categorizations

29 William Wells Brown's 1874 Rising Son located the Congo "along the western shore southward", containing both a coast and an "interior" that had both a "shallow" and "deep" quality, of which the former is constituted by "tablelands" (Brown 1874: 70) near the coast and the deep quality is represented by the "far interior" (ibid).

extensively. In this passage, the "typical Negro" is located in "the low, swampy land at the mouth of the Congo" (Williams 1885: 46). Not coincidentally, geography and humans are described in a similar fashion; it was no coincidence that the "typical negro" of the "low" Congo constituted the "lowest" strata of the African race, which Williams (through Reade's book) divided into "three grand types – the Ethiopian, the intermediate, and the Negro" (ibid). The "typical negro" was the lowest group among the latter, described as an "exceptional race even among the Negroes, whose disgusting type it is not necessary to re-describe" (ibid). According to Williams's passage, the "Negroes" are found "chiefly along the coast between the Casemanche and Sierra Leone, between Lagos and the Cameroons, in the Congo swamps, and in certain swampy plains and mountain-hollows of the interior" (ibid).

The "typical Negro" of the "Congo swamps" highlights the tendency of the intellectual mainstream of the 19th century to connect geography to human traits. "Low" countries were thus populated by "low" people. Williams spelled this out in a more overt and detailed fashion by elaborating on this "Negro", who is found in the "low, marshy, and malarious [sic] districts" (ibid: 47). In this lowly district, no honorable human can live (either physically or socially), the passage assumes. On the "descending scale" of "Negroes", Williams asserts that "the African who moves from the mountain regions down into the miasmatic districts may be observed to lose his stature, his complexion, his hair, and his intellectual vigor: He finally becomes the Negro." "Pathologically considered," Williams asserted, "he is weak, sickly, and short-lived. His legs are slender and almost calf-less: The head is developed in the direction of the passion, while the whole form is destitute of symmetry" (ibid). The spatialization of human vices and virtues was thus clearly common sense to Williams: "That climate has much to do with physical and mental character, we will not have to prove to any great extent" (ibid: 46).

The favoring of "white" and "light" over "black" and "dark" was a process very much at work in the African American community of the 19th century, as was shown in the contextualization of this chapter above. Not surprisingly, this opposition was constantly in play throughout Williams's History, too. The more distant from the "Caucasian somatype" one was, as Charles Mills reminds us (1999: 61), the less acceptable one became. A notable example was the comparison of the "ancient Egyptians" to the "Negro", which boiled down to the comparison between a "debased caricature" to a near-perfect complexion "of a warm and copper-colored tint" (Williams 1885: 48). As a "typical Negro", or the lowest form of "Negro", the Congo Black could be rejected as a "disgusting type" by virtue of "its" dark skin color. William Wells Brown spelled out the connection between the Congo and blackness even more explicitly than Williams. While describing the skin color of the different "nations" of the world in Rising Son, Brown described the people in "Briton and Germany" to be "fair" and those in Arabia and Egypt to be "tawny or copper-colored" (1882: 79). As an example of blackness, Brown mentioned the Congo: "They are 'black at Congo, in Africa'," Brown told his readers (building on Prichard, as his footnote suggested; ibid), stirring up a whole load of anti-Black connotations.

Those called Congo were not only perceived as black and woolly-haired (and thus "disgusting" and "ugly"), but at the same time also enslaved. This was another discursive trait that was carried over from the antebellum era. Williams, for instance, understood "the typical Negroes" as Blacks from African societies "with whom the slavers are supplied" (1885: 47). A special mention was reserved for the "brutal and debased [...] slaves of the Portuguese" who were "brought for the most part from the Congo" (ibid: 46). The significance of the Congo as a slave arena, however, was clearly waning, since neither Williams nor others called much attention to it anymore. Williams could easily have done as much, since Savage Africa repeatedly framed the Congo as a former and a contemporary slave region, culminating in Reade's claim that "the [contemporary] trade is now confined almost entirely to Congo" (1864: 244). The days of the topos of the Congo-as-Slave were numbered, it seemed, as its meaning had shifted to "savage" in postbellum African American intellectual circles. "The typical Negro is the true savage of Africa" (Williams 1885: 48), it is asserted, using a term that Williams and other historians related to discursive traits of debasement, brutality, patriarchy, or all three combined.

Who was this "savage"? The "savage" was a "typical negro" who "dwell[s] in petty tribes", according to Williams (ibid: 48). "Dwell" echoed the verb "roam" used by Garnet's 1843 "An Address to the Slaves of the United States of America" (2003: 117) and suggested an undirected, aimless quality in the Congo people. This idea was reinforced by his use of the term "tribe". "Tribe" is understood by Webster's 1886 Complete Dictionary of the English Language as a people merely united by means of having the "same progenitor" (Goodrich/Porter 1886d: 1411). Thus, the savage "typical Negro" was basically unbound by geographical borders, thereby embodying the quintessential "cosmopolitan" trait of African people in general (Williams 1885: 35). Webster's Dictionary added another explanation to "tribe" – "a nation of savages or uncivilized people" (ibid) – which appointed to the debased status of the "typical negro". In the same vein as the Dictionary, Williams framed "the typical Negro" as "unrestrained by moral laws" and as spending "his" days "in sloth, his nights in debauchery" (ibid: 48). Debasement of the Congo savage was exemplified by the consumption of "palm-wine", as well as "hashish till [sic] he stupefies his senses or falls into convulsions" (ibid).

It is clear from the ongoing use of the word "his" that this uncontrolled "typical Negro" is a male figure, who, above everything, was a perverted father and a controlling patriarchal husband. "He abuses children," Williams stated in a lengthy passage from Savage Africa, "and makes a trade of his own offspring" (ibid). As such, the male Congolese savage was the polar opposite of the respectable and protective American father, as described in the contextualization. "The typical Negro" was represented as a promiscuous partner with "savage passions" and a systematic taste for polygamy, which was "almost universal in Africa", according to Williams (ibid). Woman, in turn, is "the greater sufferer" from this system, "drained of her beauty [...] like the fragile rose [passing] into the ashes of premature old age" (ibid: 58). Another reason for her premature aging is the miserable laziness of her husband, who "stab[s] the poor brute of a woman whose hands keep him from starvation". In the end, the husband dies "tardy" anyway, since his wife can "no longer care to find him food" (ibid: 48).

Much of the debasement of the Congo and its inhabitants is negotiated through perceived gender transgressions. The scandal in terms of sexual differentiation in Victorian America lies both in women as breadwinners (albeit unstable ones) and addicted, do-nothing males. "Without her industry man would starve," Williams told his readers (ibid: 58), which would likely be read as an undesired reversal of roles. Tellingly, this gender division was discussed in vocabulary that called to mind slavery. "Everywhere man's cruel hand is against her. Everywhere she is the slave of his unholy passions," Williams stated, and he finished this assertion by claiming that women were "the merest abject slave everywhere" (ibid). Within the Victorian cult of true womanhood, this subversion of spheres, in which women dominate the professional sphere while men committed the cardinal sin of "intemperance", would have been considered both a sign of deviant masculinity and an undesirable femininity under which the women would particularly suffer.

Two Congolese women transcended their oppressed state in Williams's History. Since these two were framed as the only female rulers in Africa, according to Williams, they constituted aberrations right from the start. The first woman, "by the name of Shinga", ascended the throne of the Congo empire in 1640. "She rebelled against the ceremonies sought to be introduced by Portuguese Catholic priests, who incited her nephew to treason," Williams wrote (ibid: 54). "Defeated in several pitched battles, she fled into the Jaga country, where she was crowned with much success. In 1646 she won her throne again, and concluded an honorable peace with the Portuguese" (ibid: 54-55). In this quote, Shinga is obviously far removed from being depicted as the "victim" of men, since she successfully won and re-won the throne of the Congo empire via "pitched battles". At the same time, the impetus behind her ascent is explicitly anti-Christian, as she "rebelled against the ceremonies [...] introduced by Portuguese Catholic priests" – highlighting once again that in 19th-century intellectual discourse, the Congo was quintessentially and stubbornly pagan. The second queen, named Tembandumba, is also said to have "fought many battles", leading to many "great victories" (ibid: 55). This victorious and militant agency of Tembandumba, however, was counter-balanced by a set of traits problematic for Victorian Americans, ranging from descriptions of insatiable sexuality and brutality (cf. Loomba 2005: 131) to engaging in "bloodthirsty" and cannibalistic practices. In the end, she was "poisoned", adding another element of brutality to her Amazonian[30] story of a harsh reign (Williams 1885: 55).

The stories of the two queens are also noteworthy in what they reveal about the information that Williams had at his disposal and what he chose to use. Williams offhandedly refers to the Congo as an "empire" in his passage on Shinga – a piece of information that he derived from Reade's ten-page chapter on the same topic. In that chapter, Reade elaborates on the royal household of the "great empire" of the Congo (1864: 285). He tells anecdotes about its legal and tax system, provides details regarding the "remarkable customs" of Congo culture (ibid), recounts the above-mentioned queens in a five-page section, and hints at Portugal's extensive religious and economic engagement with the Congo.

Reade relied extensively on Filippo Pigafetta as a source (whose 1591 History of the Kongo Kingdom was re-published three years prior to Williams's work). Williams also mentions this early Portuguese explorer in his appendix, which includes additional comments on "The Negro Type". Williams states here that "Pigafetta declares" that the "Congo Negroes [...] have not thick lips or ugly features" (1885: 447). The quote concluded by stating that "except in colour they [the Congo Negroes] are very like the Portugese [sic]" (ibid). Although this passage does not refer directly to Pigafetta's translated account, the quote did reproduce Pigafetta's stance accurately. This is what the Portuguese stated: "The men and women are black, some approaching olive colour [sic], with black curly hair, and others with red. The men are of middle height, and, excepting the black skin, are like the Portuguese" (Pigafetta 1881: 13). Pigafetta continued his description by noting that "the pupils of the eyes are of various shades, some black, others of the colour of the sea. Their lips are not large like the negroes, and their countenances vary, like those of

30 The story of Tembandumba could be certainly read as "Amazonian", or as a postbellum adaptation of the ancient Greek myth describing the Amazonas, the nation of militant femininity (cf. Loomba 2005: 131).

people in our countries, for some are stout, others thin, and they are quite unlike the negroes of Nubia and Guinea, who are hideous" (ibid). This quote from the History of the Kongo Kingdom clearly contradicted the majority of derogatory claims in Williams's work about the Congo and its inhabitants. In contrast to the "disgusting type" in the History of the Negro Race (Williams 1885: 46), Congolese were represented as more similar to the Portuguese than to "the negroes of Nubia and Guinea, who are hideous".

Despite this open contradiction, however, Williams did integrate the statement in the end, albeit hidden in the appendix. Reasons for only including this observation in the margins ought to be sought in the intersection of Williams's vindicationist political agenda (which explains the mentioning of Pigafetta) with his scientific positivism (which explains the marginalization of the Portuguese). Thus, on the one hand, Pigafetta's was a useful text for Williams's vindicationist agenda, especially within the specific discursive context of this passage, i.e. the appendix, is examined. Keeping in mind Williams's aim to re-align the "Negroes" in the Congo ("independently of the woolly hair and the complexion") with "the rest of mankind" (Williams 1885: 434), Pigafetta becomes a textual asset that could be quoted. On the other hand, this could not be done very prominently, since the Portuguese traveler was pre-modern.

The translator's preface to the History of the Kongo Kingdom, written by Margarite Hutchinson, exemplifies how problematic Pigafetta's pre-modern status was to late 19th-century intellectuals. While lauding the work of the Portuguese – "we cannot fail to observe," she wrote, "how much of truth was contained in them" (Hutchinson 1881: ix) – she cannot help but raise her eyebrows in response to many factual issues. She seriously questions the truth value of Pigafetta's maps, for instance, due to the "imperfect scientific knowledge of these earlier travellers [sic]" (ibid). Hutchinson then explains that these pre-modern ways of knowing "prevented their determining with accuracy the position of their various discoveries, and led them into errors with regard to the hydrography of the continent, which are apparent on their maps" (ibid). It seems very likely that Williams, a believer in "science", dismissed Pigafetta because his investigations were not exactly scientifically rigorous, while nevertheless integrating him into the appendix in order to fulfill the ambivalent vindicationist agenda of hist History.

The marginalization of Pigafetta, however, can hardly be reduced to 19th-century scientific chauvinism and Black vindicationism alone. Another major factor led to the specific accumulation of knowledge about the Congo in (African) American intellectual circles: The rising tide of imperial-style knowledge production. This both shaped and drew upon the "sciences", as well as African American political agendas, in order to bulldoze pre-modern ways of knowing. It is this epistemological project that will form the subject of the next section.

Re-Appearance and Imperial Epistemology

Although African American involvement in the imperial and colonial projects of the U.S. will be looked at in more detail in the next chapter, it is already necessary to begin elaborating upon this topic in order to explain the break between antebellum and postbellum Congo discourse (from slave to savage) and to demarcate early imperial rhetoric (until 1885) from the narratives that were developed in the period when imperialism was in full swing (from 1885 onward).

By the end of the 19th century, empire was no longer "a shadowy presence" but a "central area of concern", as Edward Said states in his groundbreaking Culture and Imperialism (1994: xviii). Indeed, the United States did have a less concerted, state-authorized imperial agenda than many European countries until the embattled annexation of the Philippines at the turn of the century (Harvey 2001: 20). Nevertheless, the traveling vanguard of imperialism alluded to earlier – above all, explorers and missionaries – were well-known and well-regarded in (African) American intellectual circles. In his depiction of the Congo, George Washington Williams, for instance, drew systematically upon authors who openly advocated imperialism and, at times, colonization.

Reade's Savage Africa promoted the re-modeling of African commercial systems along European and British lines. This influenced Williams, too, culminating in his stating that as soon "as the interior of Africa becomes better colonized, a direct trade will be established" (1885: 76). Williams also confided in his work that he had "utmost confidence" (ibid: 110) in both Henry Morgan Stanley and David Livingstone, of whom he wrote that "the noble life-work of Dr. David Livingstone, and the thrilling narrative of Mr. Henry M. Stanley" sparked his interest "on behalf of Africa" (ibid: 76). Although Williams turns the stories of these travelers into personal accounts of bravery, self-sacrifice, and moral victory, the truth of the matter was, of course, that Stanley and Livingstone were the vanguard of state-sponsored imperialism.

Many of the major expeditions, embodied by Livingstone's exploration of the Zambesi, were supported by the Royal Geographical Society, which was "part social club, part learned society, part imperial information exchange and part platform for the promotion of sensational feats of exploration", as Felix Driver pointedly describes it (2001: 25). Livingstone himself was quite open about his intentions and supporters, as well. "The Government have supported the proposal of the Royal

Geographical Society," Livingstone wrote in the preface of his narrative on the Zambesi expedition, "and have united with that body to aid me in another attempt to open Africa to civilizing influences, and a valued private friend has given a thousand pounds for the same object" (1875: vi-vii). The "unprecedented" flood of images and ideas surrounding the Congo generated by Livingstone and others was orchestrated and legitimized, in short, by both state-sponsored organizations and private initiatives (cf. Loomba 2005: 54). This increasingly frenzied and institutionalized push for best-selling knowledge in the service of empire explains the "sudden" re-knowing of the Congo after it had been rendered abject and actively "unknown" merely a few years before. Williams echoed Livingstone's rationale throughout his own work in the analysis of Africa's problems and solutions. Thus, the problem of "African geography", as well as the paganism of the "savage tribes" (Williams 1885: 111), could be approached by broadening knowledge on the African continent and spreading Christianity there.[31]

The "watchwords of Livingstone's mission [were] information, resources, cultivation, and commerce", as Driver observed (2001: 86), which had won official sanction at the highest level: Livingstone explicitly mentioned in his introduction that he had received "instructions from Her Majesty's Government" (1875: 2). Livingstone's commercial goals in East and West Africa are repeated constantly in his book, despite his secondary desire of "securing the happiness and prosperity of tribes now sunk in barbarism or debased by slavery" (ibid). He hoped to lead those tribes to "the introduction of the blessings of the Gospel" (ibid). Producing knowledge in the commercial service of empire, however, was the most conspicuous elements in Livingstone's work, but also in other reports on Central West Africa, ranging from the early-19th-century accounts by Tuckey and Parks to Stanley's late 19th-century one. As all of them were actively used by African American historians and journalists, a deeply commercial and capitalist streak was introduced into their discourse (which remained there, as is discussed in the next chapter).

The rise of imperial-style knowledge production in postbellum America can be traced in detail in African American journalistic publications. Exemplary is the Philadelphia weekly The Christian Recorder, which was one of the few Black papers that successfully weathered the Civil War (Franklin 1998: 120). The reason for

31 Livingstone described his aims in the Introduction as follows: "To extend the knowledge already attained of the geography and mineral and agricultural resources of Eastern and Central Africa – to improve our acquaintance with the inhabitants, and to endeavour [sic] to engage them to apply themselves to industrial pursuits and to the cultivation of their lands, with a view to the production of raw material to be exported to England in return for British manufactures" (1875: n.p.).

its robustness was that it was published by the African Methodist Episcopal Church, through which it became the first paper that actively built upon the financial and human resources of an institution instead of relying entirely upon subscribers, philanthropists, or the "variable fortunes and interests of an individual owner" (Lapsansky-Werner 2006: 268), as was the case for the many papers that went under during and after the Civil War. Although published by a religious organization, The Christian Recorder did not see itself as the mouthpiece of Christian doctrine – particularly not after the Civil War when so many other Black periodicals had ceased to exist. Writing for the Black, literate community at large was its goal. Thus, The Christian Recorder developed and maintained a strong focus on Black politics, science, literature, and morality (ibid). For this reason, the newspaper provides a fruitful source on imperial knowledge circulation in terms of particular rhetorical patterns in late 19th-century African American society.

One of the most striking elements in the Congo news reporting of The Christian Recorder was the sheer amount of detailed Congo information produced by the paper (especially in comparison to historians such as Williams and Brown). The driving force behind this knowledge production on the Congo were discursive events directly related to the twin issues of exploration and exploitation. In terms of exploration, the Congo was known through articles titled "African exploration" (January 22, 1874) describing a series of expeditions, such as the "German expedition organized by Dr. Bastian and the Berlin Geographical Society" (1874: n.p.). Others included Stanley's "circumnavigation of Lake Tanganyika" and Cameron's "Livingstone Relief Expedition" (1877: n.p.; 1875a: n.p.; 1875b: n.p.; 1876b: n.p.). Despite the fact that the interior was becoming increasingly well-known to the Euro-American public, the fixation on Congo's "watery" regions underlies the articles and remains intact, albeit with a clear drive inward. The Congo was no longer reduced to a coast or a swamp, but became a "network of lakes and rivers of the water system" that provided the side-rivers with water (1875b: n.p.).

Like Williams's History, the articles on the expeditions were written as self-congratulatory narratives of historical and scientific progress. The article "Central Africa", which recounted the history of the quest for the origins of the river Congo, serves as a typical example. The efforts of Livingstone, Sir Samuel Baker, and Colonel Long were recounted, culminating in the line "Stanley is on his way there; and it will be a great glory to American explorers in Africa, if they finally establish the exact truth so many have tried to learn, for more than twenty centuries" (1875b: n.p.). The "great glory" of establishing "the exact truth so many have tried to learn for more than twenty centuries" harks back to the belief in the pervasive truth-producing power of science. This language returns in the article from March 22,

1877, titled “Further from Stanley”, discussing “Stanley’s circumnavigation of Lake Tanganyika” (1877: n.p.). In the article, Stanley’s expedition was evaluated in terms of the new knowledge it would bring home through “accurate observations and measurement” (ibid).

The Christian Recorder tended to inscribe itself into the general excitement surrounding the scientific progress of knowledge regarding the origins of the Congo. But there were limits to how much imperial-style knowledge could be adopted and accepted. For instance, the newspaper never went so far as to actually rename the river Congo in its articles. When the explorer Cameron suggested in early 1876 that “the Congo River be changed to Livingstone, in honor of the great missionary who in reality discovered its sources” (1876a: n.p.), the newspaper reported this request but never acted upon it. By sticking to the “old” name, the newspaper demonstrated that the “new” knowledge produced, and the attendant suggestions made by the traveling “men of science” (Driver 2001: 10), had some limitations. What information and suggestions were accepted from these exploring “men of science” in the 19th-century “culture of exploration” (ibid) depended on the moral and scientific integrity of the individual explorers. The “great missionary” Livingstone (1876a: n.p.) is clearly more acceptable to the newspaper than Stanley, whose “circumnavigation of Lake Tanganyika” is said to be (one should read: merely) “a repetition of Cameron’s undertaking” (1877: n.p.).[32]

The Christian Recorder also took issue with Stanley’s militant methods, which “will forever tarnish the really great accomplishment of this traveller” (1878a: n.p.). The Christian Recorder lauded “that section of the Royal Geographical Society” and the English public in general, “which shows a determination to ventilate his doings” (ibid). “In England,” according to The Christian Recorder, “shooting ‘niggers’ is not tolerated like it is in America” (ibid). As indicated in these quotes, The Christian Recorder’s reservations with regard to Stanley were telling of a much broader resistance to Stanley in the United States and Great Britain. Whereas Livingstone was a “saint” of the anti-slavery movement in Britain (Driver 2001: 139), Stanley was mainly portrayed as everything Livingstone was not (ibid: 143). Despite Stanley’s achievement of settling the long-running dispute over the sources of the Nile by synthesizing the fragments of knowledge gathered by his predecessors

32 This differentiation can also be found in the History by George Washington Williams, who, despite praising Stanley for possessing a “noble, brave soul” (1885: 71), charged him with producing “a repetition of the experiences of Drs. Livingstone and Kirk” (ibid: 157). Livingstone, in turn, was considered by Williams as England’s “courageous son, who, as a missionary and geographer spent his best days and laid down his life in the midst of Africa” (ibid: 113).

(ibid: 117), he was an extremely contested figure. On the one hand, he was presented as a "man of action" and as a representative of "science of action", who embodied the cultural style of a new sort of imperialism – bold, brash, and uncompromising, most noticeably embodied by his support of Leopold II's imperial politics (ibid: 125). On the other hand, Stanley was considered by many philanthropists to be exemplary of "exploration by warfare" (ibid: 123). Stanley's critics thus presented him as a warlord rather than a gentleman scientist in the service of truth (ibid: 127-129).[33]

Despite critiquing Stanley's tactics, The Christian Recorder did accept, and often applauded, his imperial aims and claims. From the 1880s onward, an enormous increase in interest in Stanley's imperial project as a whole may be noted. On June 16, 1881, The Christian Recorder published an article titled "The Twentieth Century" permeated with general thoughts on the issue of progress. To exemplify the issue of progress, Stanley is mentioned. Concretely, it is stated that "the United States Commercial Agent at Gaboon reports to the Department of State that the knowledge of the Congo or Livingston River, derived from Stanley's discovers is already bearing practical fruit" (1881a: n.p.).

The "practical fruits" were both secular and religious in nature, as may be derived from other articles. Quite telling with regard to the interrelatedness of secular and religious progress is an article titled "It Looks as if Ethiopia Would Stretch Forth her Hands" from May 8, 1884, reporting on "a steam launch to Africa for use on the Upper Congo" (1884b: n.p.). This technical improvement was related against the background of a newly-founded missionary station at "Stanley Pool", of which "Mr. Stanley writes to the mission authorities in London that the station [...] is well located and the buildings are the neatest and most complete he has seen on the Congo" (ibid). The passage concluded with the hopeful message, building on Psalm 68:3 that "it looks as if Ethiopia would stretch forth her hands". The article continued by stating that "the world will be greatly indebted to Stanley for the apparently successful effort he is now making to open up the rich valley of the Congo to the advancing tide of civilization" (ibid). The "advancing tide of civilization" mostly signified infrastructural projects, such as the construction of "the Livingstone lock Canal" (1881a: n.p.) and the railroad "Henry M. Stanley is said to be engaged in" around the rapids in the Congo "preparatory to the establishment of a line of steamboats to navigate the upper levels of that river, which extend at least a thousand miles" (1881b: n.p.). In other words, despite the occasional religious undertones in

33 Condemning some of the effects and leaders of imperialism, many philanthropic Societies did not condemn imperialism as such (Driver 2001: 132).

the articles on the Congo, what drove The Christian Recorder's interest was the technical "improvement" of Central West Africa.

The Christian Recorder's interest in progress was described in terms of commerce, competition, conquest, and, ultimately, colonization. An examination of articles on or alluding to the Congo hints at the increasing acceptance of an imperial rationale. Articles increasingly focused on "Stanley's mission" in terms of "open[ing] certain districts in Africa to commerce", which was not to be expected as a successful enterprise "until the companies in whose employ he is, are ready for publicity", as The Christian Recorder wrote on November 23, 1882 (1882e: n.p.). In that same commercial vein, the newspaper announced in an article titled "A Society has been Established at London" on June 7, 1883, the establishment of a railroad society in London called "the Congo and Central African Company" with a capital of "250,000 livres sterling" that was said to traffic along the western side of Africa, especially in the Congo, using the road constructed by Stanley (1883c: n.p.).

Articles focusing on discursive events indicative of the military competition for the Congo began appearing in The Christian Recorder, too: "It is reported from the Congo River that Henry M. Stanley has arrived at Brazzaville with 1000 men. M. de Brazza has a force of 200 men and has made little progress" (1883e: n.p.). Stories like these were indicative of the increasingly numerous territorial claims made by Europeans, also embodied in the quote from the explorers Pierre Savorgnan de Brazza and Henry Morgan Stanley, who operated in the service of Paris and Brussels, respectively.

Within the context of this military competition, The Christian Recorder suggested a distinction between "good" and "bad" imperialists. Portugal's inclination "to have her say in the affairs of the Lower Congo" (1883f: n.p.) amazed the newspaper, as it clearly considered this ailing empire less than eligible to make such claims: "One would think that after making such a medley of things in Western Africa, she would be willing to stand aside and let nations of more vitality attempt the regeneration of that region" (ibid). The competition between less and more "vital" nations was discussed by The Christian Recorder in a vocabulary that cast imperialism as akin to the social Darwinist "survival of the fittest". "The next best thing is to waylay some of the weaker powers," The Christian Recorder reported on Germany's imperial militancy on June 7, 1883, "and this she has been doing with a vengeance. Tunis has already been conquered, while war is being made upon Annam, the tribes of the Congo, and Madagascar" (1883d: n.p.).

In the relatively short time period of five years, starting at the turn of the 1880s, the idea of a struggle between suitable and unsuitable competitors became firmly established in The Christian Recorder. Often these ideas took the form of overt colonial fantasies, as may be glimpsed in an 1885 article titled "The Destiny of the English-speaking Race" reproduced from Harper's Magazine. The author of the article, John Fiske, was pleased to see that "colonial blue-books" were circulating everywhere. "The natural outcome of all this overflowing vitality," the author claimed, "is not difficult to foresee" (1885a: n.p.). In an analogy between North America in the 17th century and contemporary Africa, the author expressed his wish that Africa – which he considered "rich in beautiful scenery, and in resources of timber and minerals, with a salubrious climate and fertile soil, with great navigable rivers and inland lakes" (ibid) – will not "much longer be left in control of tawny lions and long-eared elephants, and negro fetich-worshippers [sic]" but will be turned over to the "pre-eminently industrious, peaceful, orderly and free-thinking community" (ibid). The model example of such as an "industrious, peaceful, orderly and free-thinking community" was the United States, which, as Fisk maintained, had previously liberated its own territory from "scalp-hunters" and turned it into a booming economic, political, and social order. In the same vein, Fisk hoped that Africa would be "occupied by a mighty nation of English descent, and covered with populous cities and flourishing farms, with railroads and telegraphs and free schools and other devices of civilization", including those regions along the "the course of the Congo and the Nile" (ibid). It is clear from the publication policy of The Christian Recorder (i.e. re-publication without critical commentary) that the staff of The Christian Recorder seconded Fiske's stance.

In the five-year boom in imperial-style Congo articles from 1880 onward, a new way of talking about Central West Africa emerged. Whereas Williams, who wrote prior to and in the midst of this boom, still framed the Congo as an undesirable geography (a "swamp", that is), shifting economic desires with regard to Central West Africa in the 1880s required a new language. Since a "swamp" was difficult to exploit and undesirable to occupy, this metaphor had to become a more attractive one that could also legitimize imperial politics (embodied by the traveling "men of science"). This shifting of gears is obvious in The Christian Recorder, which mobilized a new metaphor reflective of changing geopolitics: The Congo became a "valley".

The trope of the Congo "valley" was both a continuation and a radical break with some of the discursive traits that preceded it. Porter's 1884 A Practical Dictionary of the English Language explained "valley", first of all, as a "tract of low ground, or of land between hills: Valley; dingle: dell; dale; a little trough or canal". This explanation echoes the Congo's depiction in the articles of The Christian Recorder, where it is described in terms of the "Livingstone lock Canal" and "Stanley Pool". The "valley" was also a continuation of the discourse on the Congo as a watery and lowly place, which would make this new metaphor of the "valley" more credible and familiar. This familiarity is important, as Poletta reminds us: "We believe a story because it is familiar" (2006: 10). The same goes for tropes and topoi (see Introduction). The second definition of the term "valley" in Porter's A Practical Dictionary of the English Language highlighted it as a "space inclosed [sic] between ranges of hills or mountains". The high-low opposition underlying this explanation – low lands surrounded by high mountains – can be observed in The Christian Recorder's suggestion that the Congo was "an open country with metalliterous [sic] mountains" (1874a: n.p.).

This inscription of the Congo as "valley" opened up possibilities for radically re-imagining it. As soon as "trade and revenue" entered the discourse on the Congo – which was reportedly legitimized at the highest political level by President Chester A. Arthur (see next chapter) – the adjective "rich" entered the discourse and was systematically applied. One finds evidence of this in a review of the book The Congo Valley: Its Redemption by D. Augustus Straker, the Black "Dean of the Law School of Allen University", as the article titled "Bethel A.M.E. Church"sgoes (1884a: n.p.).[34] In this review of January 21, 1884, the book is said to provide

> a picture of the beautiful, rich Congo Valley, the recent movements of the great powers with reference to its redemption, the ill methods by which mean and nations have dealt with Africa in the past, ye [sic] the wonderful worth discovered in the "Dark Continent" even under these methods, the wealth and wonders that may yet be found in the "Dark Continent" and its dark people when God's due time shall come and the wilderness shall be made to blossom.

Through the lens of Straker's book, the Congo was radically re-imagined as a "beautiful" and "rich" valley. As with Reade and Williams, the "ill methods" of the past – by which slavery was meant – were justified by the good that allegedly emerged from them, namely the discovery of the Congo's "wealth and wonders". In this passage, the commercial and exotic re-signification of the Congo was far removed indeed from the past representation of Central West Africa as an unfruitful and debilitating "swamp". Yet at the same time, the Congo "wilderness" had to be "made to blossom". With this attitude, the necessity of colonizing the "'Dark Continent' and its dark people" was established.

---

34 Straker seems to have actively discussed the insights from his books in public speeches, for instance at Selma University in 1885. The Christian Recorder takes note of a talk by him entitled "The civilizing and Christianizing influences upon Africa by the establishment of commercial agencies in the Congo Valley under the auspices of the International Association" (1885g: n.p.).

This need to colonize was based on the "darkness" of Congo's people, which entailed a list of variable faults quite similar to those articulated by Williams. In an 1875 poem titled "Livingstone, the Friend of Africa", The Christian Recorder cataloged some of the well-known ills of the people who "dwell along the Niger and the Nile, / The Congo and Zambezi, Senegal". "Fetish superstitions" and "slavery" rank high. As always, these can be combated, according to the poem, with the twin healers of Christianity and "commerce" (1875c: n.p.). The "darkness" of the Congo was discussed here as indistinguishable from that of the rest of the continent. Far from contradicting the idea of Congo as home to the lowest grade of the "Negro" race, this shows the malleability of the Congo as signifier: It was both part of the continent and a separate geography, depending on the function it had to perform in African American discourse. In the poem "Livingstone, the Friend of Africa", the Congo serves merely as a random African region. The point of the poem was namely to declare the whole of Africa "open" for partition and illumination.

Despite being sometimes treated as only one marker among many on the continent of Africa, the Congo simultaneously indicated something specific. Its particular "darkness" derived from its signifying a certain kind of African "blackness" to The Christian Recorder. Its darkness was applied to Africans and Americans alike, creating a kind of reverberation effect. This was hardly the case for other African regions. The American take on Congo blackness can be gleaned from an article titled "Something About Woman's Work" from June 16, 1866 in The Christian Recorder on "woman's work", in which a "meek-eyed maid" is featured "who will attract the attention of Congo Coolebs" by virtue of being "dark-skinned" and "dusky" herself (1866: n.p.). Another example from the American arena may be found in the article "Princeton: A Difference" from July 23, 1874, in which journalists from The Christian Recorder visit the University of Princeton, where light-skinned Black men are treated as "black as the blackest Congo" (1874b: n.p.).

Thus even in The Christian Recorder, as in Williams's History, Congo blackness occupied a lowly rank on the perceived scale of civilization. In an article from May 18, 1882, titled "The Colored People – Different Races", The Christian Recorder identified "three distinct sorts of American negroes" (1882a: n.p.). Apart from the "the brown negroes" and the "the black negroes with good features", a third group of "black negroes" is presented with "bad" physical and intellectual traits (ibid):

> The black negroes, with flat noses, thick lips, low forehead, and ill-shaped skull. If any of these show high intelligence, the cases must be very rare. And unfortunately the overwhelming majority of American negroes are of this class. They come from the coast of Guinea and

Congo, where they were captured by the superior races of the interior and sold to the slave-ships, or were easily caught by slave hunting parties. They are a low grade of savages.

Apart from establishing the well-known link between the Congo's coast and slavery, this passage relies upon the external and internal hierarchies expressed in the social Darwinist opposition between "superior races" and their "inferior" counterparts. Inferiority had both an "internal" and an "external" aspect. Internal inferiority enters this passage in the separation established between the descendants of the Congo slaves ("the overwhelming majority of American negroes") and an unnamed "rest". That "rest" may be read as the Congo's opposite. And read as such, one ends up with a counterpart to the majority of American "Congoes" that possesses light skin and thin lips – very much how African American elites of the 19th century perceived themselves.

Internal inferiors were probably not addressed by the phrase "a low grade of savages", however, although it might be read this way. More likely to be denounced here was the Central West African Congo "negro". The Christian Recorder did differentiate between American people called Congo and Africans labeled as such. In an article titled "The Outlook's View of American Slavery" on the subject of slavery re-published from Outlook on September 14, 1875, The Christian Recorder explicitly announced the superiority of American Blacks to those in the Congo: "The Virginia negro is far superior to the negro of Congo" (1875d: n.p.). This superiority could "only" be achieved, the article suggested, "through such a process as slavery" (ibid); thus, as George Washington Williams also argued, the article considered slavery a "blessing to the African", despite "all its cruelties" (ibid). "Had the negro, cast upon the coast of Africa, been left to himself, he would have remained in his native heathenism, and would never have reached the degree of civilization he now possesses [...] he would very likely never have learned to work, and would today be a thriftless savage", The Christian Recorder added (ibid).

The superiority of Black Americans is mainly constructed via the tropes of "tribes", "natives", and "Congo savages" (e.g. 1878a: n.p.), all of which are reserved for Central West Africans. One notable exception was William Wells Brown's description of the "Congo negroes" on Congo Square in New Orleans in his 1880 autobiography My Southern Home, "who used to perform their dance on its sward every Sunday" and who were Africans "stolen from their native land [...] New Orleans was the Center" (1882: 121). Although they are said to be divided into "six different tribes [...] named after the section of the country from which they came", it becomes clear from Brown's story that these "curious people" were only considered "tribal" by virtue of their ethnic roots. As such, the Congo also stood for "the remnants of [the] African jungle" (ibid) brought to Louisiana by these Congo slaves, not as an actual tribe-driven differentiation in African American communities. Labelling these dancers as Congo indicates the existence of an "imagined" Congo that was a variation on an antebellum theme: The Congo as the original African home.

Although it is seldom stated explicitly, African American intellectuals felt very qualified to enlighten the Congo darkness. Blyden's 1882 letter to The Christian Recorder, for instance, reads (1882c: n.p.):

> The American descendants of Africa have not yet realized the fact that their face shines on the continent of Africa. The natives descry the illumination in the distance and are anxious to welcome them not only as missionaries but as colonists on the coast and in the extensive districts of Soudan as well as on the Niger and the Congo, and will second instead of opposing their efforts to destroy the brazen calf of superstition and ignorance with its attendant drawbacks.

Blyden's point was to highlight the desired possibility of emigrating to Africa – any part of it – as "missionaries" and "colonists". Blyden, a prominent advocate and organizer of Black American emigration to Liberia, tied the typical imperial attitudes of the late 19th century explicitly to the "American descendants of Africa" whose "shin[ing] face" was opposed to the "darkness" permeating Africa. The population of the Congo was one of many "native" groups in Africa who "descry the illumination in the distance". The rationale behind sending African Americans as "missionaries" and "colonists" is, according to the author, that "natives" are "anxious" to "destroy the brazen calf of superstition and ignorance with its attendant drawbacks". African American emigrants, the idea went, could turn "elephant hunters from the vicinity of Congo" (1880: n.p.) into Christians through systematic schooling. Ideally, this led to a situation in which "men were preparing for the ministry" (1872: n.p.), or for being "profectures apostolic [...] of Congo", as The Christian Recorder suggested (1876a: n.p.). The next chapter discusses the extent to which African Americans were in fact involved in the missionary project.

Congoist Strategies in the Age of Discursive Extremes: A Conclusion

The concept of Congoism is not a postmodern neologism, but has its roots in 19th-century America. The inscription at the beginning of this chapter, from John Miller's monograph Theology, underlines this: "All the religions of the world give the first place to morality," Miller asserted, continuing, "if there are any exceptions, they are at the extremes, Congoism on the one hand and Protestant Christianity on the other" (1887: 26). In this quote, "Congoism" marks a religious extreme, and draws on the belief that "Congoese" are people who "serve the Devil" (ibid). For Miller, Congolese thus constituted the opposite of an organized religious movement such as Protestantism: "To call it worship is absurd. They [the Congolese] serve him [the devil] because he is so wicked" (ibid). The vilifying of Congolese in a discourse of polarization and defamation returns again and again in 19th-century American culture. This chapter has shown when, how, and why this was the case within African American intellectual circles. To grapple with these discursive extremes, this chapter has focused on the changing forms and functions of the Congo signifier, the results of which will now be discussed.

In terms of "form", Congoist discourse exhibited extreme malleability, epitomized by the topoi of the Congo-as-Slave and the Congo-as-Savage, as well as the tropes of the "coast" in the antebellum period and those of the "swamp" and "valley" in postbellum America. All of these figures of style constitute both continuations of and radical breaks with antebellum discourse. The move from the "coast" to the "swamp" turned water into a register unto itself, granting the "swamp" a familiar feeling, as well as credibility and "realism". The substitution of the swamp with the valley, however, constituted a shift that was decidedly more extreme. This rhetorical move was not just the result of an ongoing deepening and broadening of geographical knowledge triggered by Euro-Americans setting foot on Congolese "land" instead of merely navigating its "watery" regions. In-depth knowledge of and interest in the Congo was available before Stanley and Livingstone "opened" the Congo, as is illustrated via the 16th-century example of Pigafetta and 19th-century encyclopedias and dictionaries. Since detailed knowledge about the Congo was already available, the geographical metamorphosis of the Congo is reflective more of how than what African Americans knew about it (and wanted to know about it). In the antebellum period, African Americans were thus silent about the Congo, because the authorities on which they relied – the Bible and antique sources – had nothing to say about it. Through the secularization, proliferation, and modernization of authoritative sources in the late 19th century, the possibility of "re-knowing" the Congo arose.

In terms of "function", discourses on the Congo were highly reflective of the extremely polarizing powers that shaped African American intellectual communities in the 19th century, both from within and without. The list of polarizing powers is long: Slavery and dehumanization had to be dealt with in antebellum America, as did legalized apartheid and other structures that produced hierarchies after the Civil

War; white Euro-American intellectual power, ranging from de Buffon to Reade, provided a set of bigoted ideas and vocabularies to which intellectuals had to respond; and intellectual Black communities, which were divided along gender, class, and racial lines, had to be addressed and held together by common interests. In this field comprised of extreme tensions, an extreme discourse on the Congo developed that was both reflective and constitutive of these strains.

Although the form the Congo took clearly varied throughout the 19th century, its function remained stable: Signifying that which "we" are not and do not want to be. Therefore, Congoism functioned as a discourse of rejection, both of internal and external Others, and along the axes of gender and race as well as class and ethnicity. What underlies these strategies is the creation of a subpersonhood called Congo that is either too ugly or too dangerous to be integrated into the world view of the African American elite of light-black, male African American intellectuals. In the antebellum period, the Congo quintessentially stood for the thing that was loathed (and feared) the most by free African Americans: "slavery"; in postbellum America, Congo signified the opposite of how Black intellectuals came to see themselves: "savage".

What are the logical operations that undergird the Congo-as-Slave and the Congo-as-Savage? What strategies give these figures coherence and credibility, despite their shaky empirical foundations or tendentious rationales? How have African American intellectuals succeeded in creating "natural" images of a superior "us" and an inferior "them"? In what follows, an attempt has been made to sum up the answers this chapter has offered to such questions. This will be done by focusing on the strategies of Congoism, which operate on multiple levels, including the planes of language, logic, and knowledge production.

One central Congoist strategy in antebellum America (which will return in subsequent chapters, too) was the Congo's separation from, and unification with, the signifier "Africa". This logical operation can be observed in the untitled poem in Lewis's Light and Truth, for instance. The point of the text was to evoke the longing of Black Americans for "Africa" – a longing that was undermined by the division of Africa into different regions, and namely into "Congo's mountain-coast" and "Gambia's golden shore" (Lewis 1844: 346). Although this sentence aimed merely to demarcate two randomly chosen areas of potential return, the specificity of the language register used ("mountain-coast" versus "golden shore") reveals a substantial difference and establishes a hierarchy between these two areas. The strategy of evoking an "African" homogeneity while at the same time dividing it into favorable (Gambia) and less favorable (Congo) parts reappears in many works by antebellum and postbellum African American intellectuals, who claimed to write about "Africa" in general, but focused solely on parts of it that were particularly interesting and/or deplorable to them and their political agendas.

Another strategy is catering to the epistemic mainstream. Congoism, as was shown, is an extremely conformist discourse. It thus attached itself to the intellectual standard and forced the Congo to fit into the frameworks offered by it. This turned the Congo into a recognizable and understandable signifier that reflected the dominant politics and paradigms of those days. In the discourses of antebellum America, for instance, the Congo had to be rejected, since it constituted nothing to which one could epistemically relate or which one might consider politically desirable. In a culture steeped in classicism, romanticism, and Egyptomania, the Congo could hardly be mentioned or discussed. Moreover, the idea of the Congo as a slave coast was an ongoing offence to the abolitionism of African American intellectuals, as well as to their refinement: As a marker of "pure" blackness, the Congo would rank low in African American color schemes. Seen altogether, these dynamics resulted in a discourse that transformed the Congo into the negative underbelly of the knowledge production on, as Gilroy has it, the "Black Atlantic" (whose positive counterpart was alternately played by Liberia, Haiti, Egypt, or whatever region best matched the ruling paradigms of progress and vindicationism).

As the underbelly of the "Black Atlantic", the Congo could (or had to) be met with the strategy of ignorance and silence in the antebellum period. As a systematically discarded geography, the Congo constituted a model example of "unknowledge", an entity actively ignored and forgotten despite all the knowledge available about it. As Alcoff suggests, ignorance is a truly powerful tool for shaping and cementing social interactions and relations (2007: 44). In 19th-century America, these social negotiations took place between white majorities and Black minorities, as well as within both groups themselves. In the arena of white-Black interactions, an "epistemology of ignorance", as Charles Mills terms it, protected the privileges and supremacy of the white majority by consensually unknowing the racist world these whites themselves had created and profited from (1998: 18). According to Mills, this white ignorance resulted in "white mythologies, invented Orients, invented Africas, invented Americas, with a correspondingly fabricated population, countries that never were, inhabited by people who never were" (ibid: 19). To counter some of the aspects of these white mythologies, "vindicationist" contributions by African Americans, such as Lewis's Light and Truth, were necessary political antidotes (cf. ibid). However, while correcting white "unknowing" of Black achievement via their writings, African Americans simultaneously acted as producers of their own epistemology of ignorance by tapping into this deep reservoir of white epistemologies for their own negotiations.

While as little as "one drop" of blood constituted blackness for the white majority, African Americans intellectuals themselves maintained Black-white constructions by systematically dividing blackness, as Lewis did in Light and Truth, into many shades, ranging from "Mulatto" to "Quaderoon" and from "Mestizo" to "Mangroon". The African American ignorance towards the Congo, therefore, opened the door for the active production of what Charles Mills called "subpersonhood": The condition of people who, due to racial phenotype, genealogy, or culture, were considered not fully human (1998: 56).

Congoism also thrived on the strategy of hierarchization. Black and white intellectuals employed "science" to generate an unprecedented volume of data on a global scale on the "Other". The chauvinistic paradigms of "objectivity of observation" (Loomba 2005: 57), as well as "classifying" human kind and nature at large into "types", provided a clarity regarding Central West Africa hardly achievable in previous times. Classification reduced a vast number of objects and peoples into simplified and frequently stereotypical types and generalizations (Said, Orientalism 119). The original binaries between Christians and the rest of humankind were increasingly complemented by the proliferation of categorizations based on skin color, origin, temperament, and character (Said 2003: 120). One of the tools to impose hierarchy via classification was stereotyping. The notion of the "typical Negro", the category to which peoples called Congo belonged, serves as the prime example of the process of reducing images and ideas to a simple, manageable, and mostly vilifying and racist form (Loomba 2005: 55).

As a "typical Negro", the Congo could be reduced to a certain objectionable phrenology and to a loathsome moral character redeemable only, if this was considered possible at all, through long and hard missionary work. The stereotypical representation of the Congo as a black African savage with thick lips, a low forehead, and woolly hair converged or contrasted sharply with his surroundings. Either Congolese fit their environment (when it was depicted as a disgusting "swamp") or they existed in opposition to it (whenever the Congo was described as a "rich valley"). In the former case, the Congo could be ignored (as was the case in the antebellum period); in the latter "he" had to be helped to overcome "his" heathenism, slavery, and patriarchy in order to finally reap the fruits of the natural riches of his region.

Various discursive strategies lent credibility to this narrative of Euro-American "helping". By depersonalizing people called Congo and rendering them as an undifferentiated mass, they were homogenized into a collective "they". Single individuals were metonomics, functioning merely as an example of the collective. Knowing the character of one Congo in "his" essential pagan and primitive character sufficed to know them all. Arguments about the benefits of systematic law, Christianity, traditional gender roles, and modern capitalist commerce could be easily made in this way. As inferiors, the Congolese thus deserved to be ruled, which constituted a well-known pattern in "imperial culture", as Edward Said shows (1994: xii).

The Congolese human monolith was termed a "savage", a label that had a long and varied cultural history, as Andrew Sinclair's seminal work The Savage: A History of Misunderstanding shows, but that remained consistent in one aspect: The savage was inferior. From the mid-19th century onward, this inferiority was legitimized by Darwinian thought and early anthropology that turned the savage into the lowest example of human evolution (Sinclair 1977: 93; Brantlinger 1985: 186). People who were lost in intellectual and moral "darkness" required enlightenment from external superiors. The more explorers, missionaries, and scientists went to the Congo in the name of imperial "knowing", as this chapter showed, the darker its people grew and the more need there was for the "light" of science and Christianity (cf. Brantlinger 1985: 166). By re-casting the Congo's geography as an attractive "rich valley" rather than a suffocating "swamp", capitalist exploitation was legitimized. The metaphor of the "valley" turned the Congo into a "good" space that could easily be contrasted with its "bad" population, once again legitimizing the conquest of Central West Africa that would soon take place. Because the Congo turned out to be a rich valley and not a wild, unfruitful "swamp", as the parlance prior to the 1880s had it, the human inability to make use of natural riches turned the people of the Congo into a particularly "low grade of savage" on the Dark Continent. As incapable capitalists, the Congolese were both typical and atypical of the "darkness" of Africa.

The trope of "darkness" draws attention to the strategic continuities and breaches within the Congo discourse between the antebellum and postbellum period. Congoist discourse shows itself to be an accumulation and repetition of past ideas, as well as a rephrasing of these same thoughts executed through new epistemic authorities. The perceived antebellum darkness of the people called Congo was triggered by abolitionist propaganda that thrived on revealing the atrocities of the European slave trade when handling the agency-less, pagan Congolese. In contrast, postbellum African American discourse considered the Congo's darkness a matter of the pagan's savage own doing, no longer victimizing "him", as "he" was considered his own source of misery. Euro-Americans thus no longer played the role of oppressive enslavers, but that of the leaders of "a crusade that would vanquish the forces of darkness" (ibid: 198). Through this strategy of blaming the victim, American slavery was no longer an inhuman brutality, but rather a civilizing tool from which African Americans in the end profited. As beneficiaries of slavery, albeit ones refusing to forget its horrors, African American intellectuals would now inscribe themselves in the imperial epistemology of "salvaging" the pagan Congolese from their home-made misery – which included everything from the slave trade to tribal savagery, the lack of a work ethic, shameless sexual customs, "unnatural" gender relations, and a general primitiveness.

The metaphors of "light" and "darkness" perpetuated the supposed difference between an "enlightened" self and a "dark" Other (cf. Loomba 2005: 55). Whoever this Other might have been, whether external or internal, its characterization was always determined by reference to what "we" were not: "Who are we? We are non-savages" (Mills 1998: 43). The achievement of imperialism was to bring the world closer together and at the same time separate it (Said 1994: xxiv), which, in the African American antebellum period, resulted in a clear separation of oneself from the pagan African, as well as the African American labeled Congo with the characteristic physical features. Despite their separation, these Others existed as intertwined entities because they would reciprocally produce and influence one another's signification. "Black tea" could stand for Congo only because pitch black Americans, who themselves were named after their alleged home country, would be referred to as such.

By buying into the epistemology of epistemic "whiteness" and "Americanness", African American intellectuals in the late 19th century actively tried to tie themselves through race, class, capitalism, and citizenship to those people in the United States who mattered because of social privilege: white Americans. In an attempt to disrupt the equation of Americanness with "whiteness" (Mills 1998: 58), African Americans produced and pushed for an entity that constituted their alleged opposite: an entity called Congo.

Second Chapter

Between Art and Atrocity: Epistemic Multiplications and Standardization (1885-1945)

> First, we were informed that Africa, as a country, for the most part, was a dry barren, sterile desert of shifting sands. Now, Stanley comes out and informs us that Africa is the richest of all the continents.
> Then again, we were told by old geographers that it was largely unwatered. But we are now told by later authorities that the same country abounds with lakes and rivers, and that these are among the largest in the world. As for its people, we were told that they were simply a lot of dwarfs, abnormally constituted, with heads, arms and feet peculiarly different from those of other peoples. But now we are told, with, as it were, bated breath of astonishment, that there are men stalwart and beautifully formed, brave and warlike, in Africa. Which of these statements shall we receive as true?
> HARVEY JOHNSON/"THE QUESTION OF RACE" 1891

TEXTUAL PLURALIZATION AND THE DAWN OF NEW EPISTEMOLOGIES: AN INTRODUCTION

Harvey Johnson, the African American Baptist minister from Baltimore, wrote these words in a pamphlet responding to derogatory comments on the "black race" by William Cabell Bruce – a U.S. Senator and the infamous author of the racist monograph The Negro Problem (1891). Here, taking up discussions of the Bible,

Africa, and the slave trade, Johnson forcefully refuted Bruce's claim of "the superiority of the white to the colored race" (Johnson 1891: 6). One of his arguments in defense of the "colored race" is alluded to in the passage above, which discussed the uncertainty and changeability of white knowledge about Africa. Explorers such as Henry Morgan Stanley proved, according to Johnson, that the history and geography of Africa as it "has come down to us from the 'kith and kin' of the white man" (ibid: 9) was far from stable, objective, or accurate. Instead, Johnson saw "a vast array of misrepresentations, and historical, geographical and ethnological contradictions" (ibid). Was Africa a desert, he asked? Or was it a watery region? Were its people abnormal and loathsome, or quite the opposite? "Which of these statements shall we receive as true?" (ibid).

Read superficially, Johnson seems to have addressed Africa as a whole in this passage. His readers, however, would have understood that he was implicitly differentiating between regions. Through terms such as "Stanley" and the "rich" and watery country (that "abounds with lakes and rivers" which are "amongst the largest in the world"; ibid), the Congo region silently surfaces here as a separate geography. Johnson confirms this a few lines later when he discusses "the language of the African". Whereas it was previously held that Africans "had no language that was above the gabble of the goose" (ibid), there had clearly been some developments on that account: "Now, Dr. Grattan Guinness says he has found in the Congo and Soudan countries, languages having as many as forty tenses to the verb." These forty tenses meant to Johnson "forty modes of expressing one's thought" (ibid).

Johnson's pamphlet echoes the old adage "the more things change, the more they remain the same". The epigraph, in other words, reflects both the great stability and malleability of (African) American Congo discourses. Johnson's pamphlet indicates that the pre-colonial imagery of the Congo (as a "watery" region; cf. previous chapter) had been both transferred to and altered in the colonial context. What had changed, in contrast to precolonial times, was the more positive depiction of the Congolese, as well as Johnson's recognition that the Congo constituted a historically contingent signifier in dire need of epistemic critique. Precolonial Black historians, in comparison, hardly engaged in oppositional epistemic meta-thought; they shifted from one hegemonic Congo meaning to the next and did not express much doubt about those they employed. The Congo-as-Slave was silently replaced by the Congo-as-Savage in the late 1870s, a shift that hardly any African American intellectual cared to address. The epigraph here by Johnson suggests that this monolithic trait of the Congo discourse – moving from one coherent topos to the next – was beginning to be viewed critically at the dawn of the colonial era.

Was Johnson's representation of the Congo the exception to the Congoist rule? Or did he constitute the avant-garde of those adhering to a new set of discursive rules, potentially anti-Congoist, in African American intellectual Congo rhetoric? Was he, in other words, inaugurating the dawn of a rhetoric that was more meta-reflective, affirmative, and oriented toward the epistemic? This chapter attempts to answer these questions by identifying the leading Congo topoi in the texts of publicly active (African) American intellectuals in the heyday of colonialism (historians and journalists specifically), that is the period between 1885 and 1945. The function of the discursive Congo motifs will be analyzed by addressing the events that triggered them, discussing the epistemologies from which they stem, and by tracing the rise, evolution, and disappearance of these topoi and epistemologies. To avoid redundancies with regard to the previous chapter, this chapter discusses some of the methodical differences between itself and the rest of the work, rather than rehashing what has already been laid out in detail in the Introduction and the First Chapter.

This chapter begins with a contextualization, considered broadly, of Congo discourse in the U.S. from 1885 to 1945. Against the background of a ruthless intellectual and material onslaught against Black people on a global scale, the proliferation of Congo meanings is discussed. The chapter also takes as its subject how this onslaught was triggered and rationalized by Social Darwinian theory, exemplified by its opposite intellectual poles, Arthur de Gobineau and Franz Boas, and how its genocidal effects were rhetorically opposed and lamented in strikingly similar ways. Euro-American authors and activists who called international attention to the bloody rubber trade in the Congo Free State (such as E.D. Morel and Joseph Conrad) utilized rhetoric similar to that of Black American intellectuals, decrying the lynching epidemic in the American South, as the work of Ida B. Wells-Barnett and James Weldon Johnson demonstrates.

The existence of mutually shared, oppositional tropes, such as "redness", "horror", or "civilized barbarism", gestures towards the existence of a language shared by Black and white intellectuals. Did they share Social Darwinian arguments, too? In an age of perpetually discussed economic crises, accompanied by waves of internal and external migration and deepening social stratification, supremacist thought claiming a superior Anglo-Saxon or African American "stock" could indeed have proven particularly useful for securing one's own social status on the ladder of "civilization". This chapter asks whether, parallel to securing internal privileges, Social Darwinian thought could have also been considered a useful intellectual tool for the imperialist "open door" policies of the United States. It investigates, as well, how

Social Darwinism may have served to justify civilizing missions performed by both Black and white missionaries.

The contextualization performed in this chapter underscores, once again, the dialectics of African American history: When anti-Black oppression grew, opposition against it mounted correspondingly. Heightened activity in the political, journalistic, missionary, and artistic arenas – coined in those days as the emergence of the "New Negro" – led to an amount of textual production far exceeding previous periods. This proliferation of African American intellectual texts has proved as much an opportunity as a hurdle to overcome in this chapter. On the one hand, this explosion of texts has allowed for a detailed content analysis to be conducted based largely on primary sources. As white and Black Americans increasingly addressed their relationship to one another more directly and discussed their shared interest in the Congo, the interconnections between discourse and social structures can be established more easily in the language and terms employed by the intellectuals of the period (this is in contrast to the heavier reliance on secondary texts in the contextualization of the previous chapter). On the other hand, the sheer volume of primary texts necessitated reducing an oversized corpus to manageable proportions. To solve this problem, African American historians are once again taken as a starting point for analysis, ranging from William Alexander's 1888 History of the Colored Race in America and Booker T. Washington's 1907 The Story of the Negro: The Rise of the Race from Slavery to Leila Amos Pendleton's 1912 A Narrative of the Negro, James Weldon Johnson's 1927 Native African Races and Culture, and Carter Woodson's 1936 The African Background Outlined.

These works of history are once again approached through both "wide reading" and "close reading". This chapter thus moves constantly back and forth between the broad Black American "archive" – containing journalistic, poetic, and historical texts – and individual works of history (cf. the Introduction and the First Chapter for a discussion of these terms). The discursive events were filtered in order to demarcate what could and could not be said about the Congo. In this wide reading, four discursive events returned systematically: (one) African American missionaries in the Congo, (two) atrocities in the Congo Free State, (three) Belgian colonialism, and (four) the ethnic art and culture of the Congo. Given the increased text production within intellectual African American circles, this chapter asks whether some of these events are evoked more easily in certain texts than in others. It investigates, moreover, whether the high volume of African American texts produced led to competing Congoes, and, if so, what these signified.

These questions are answered by comparing statements made by historians on the Congo both to those of other historians and to "counterpoints" within other text genres (cf. the Introduction for a discussion of "counterpoints"). In this way, the particularity, selectivity, and ideological interests of these works are identified. Newspapers such as The Christian Recorder, The Chicago Defender, and The Colored American Magazine are here considered counterpoints to the works of history, along with the works of authors such as Langston Hughes, Jessie Redmon, Claude McKay, and George Schuyler. Black missionaries, including Clinton Boone, William Sheppard, and Charles Smith, round off this contrapuntal reading, which ultimately highlights the intertextual trajectories and circulation of ideas between missionaries, historians, artists, and journalists. At the same time, the silences in the texts raises the question of why these exist. For instance, amidst a flood of information in white media on the Congo "atrocities" in the Congo Free State, both Black historians and journalists remained mute on the issue, despite the activism of groundbreaking Black historians like George Washington Williams and African American intellectual gatekeepers like Booker T. Washington. This chapter attempts to find out why this was the case.

Through a "close reading", the particular textual representations of Central West Africa are discussed. As in the previous chapter, the characterization of and language used to describe the people, geography, and history of the Congo are the main analytic points of interest. The language and figures of speech used in these depictions are condensed into four topoi that regulate the overall Congo discourse in the time period under scrutiny: namely "the Congo-as-Darkness", "the Congo-as-Example", "the Congo-as-the-Vital", and "the Congo-as-Resource". These topoi demand the discussion of the truth-generating epistemologies from which they emerged and drew their authority. They also raise larger questions: To what extent did the sum total of these discursive events, topoi, argumentative strategies, and epistemologies constitute a colonial-style "Congoism"? Did discourse between 1880 and 1945 once again create a Black (sub)geography and (sub)persona called Congo, as it had in the previous century? Or were new, more critical times, spearheaded by Harvey Johnson and others, to come?

SUPREMACY IN THEORY AND PRACTICE: SOCIAL DARWINISM IN THE AGE OF COMPETITION AND GENOCIDE

The Age of Competition

The period between 1885 and 1945 was marked by a succession of structural economic crises, leading up to the stock market crash of 1929, which brought the

American and European economy to a decade-long standstill and set off what later would be labeled the "Great Depression" (Zinn 2003: 286). Although this crisis was more disastrous than its predecessors – closing down about 5.000 banks, cutting industrial production in half, and putting one third of the labor force out of work (ibid: 287) – it was only a sign of how "fundamentally unsound" the global economy had become, to quote John Galbraith (2009: 177).[1] A popular, non-governmental response to the "unsoundness" of increasingly unstable global capitalist markets and the misery caused by them was mass migration (Hobsbawm 1991: 36). People from what is today Russia, Italy, the Balkans, and Greece poured into the United States at an even faster rate than the Irish and Germans had in the preceding decades. About five and a half million newcomers entered the United States in the 1880s, and another four million in the 1890s (Zinn 2003: 266). By 1920, which saw the rise of anti-immigration campaigning that put a "national origins quota" in place (which favored English, Irish, German, and Scandinavian "races" over those from Southern and Eastern Europe, Gossett 1997: 406),[2] more than 14 million had migrated to the United States (ibid: 382).

White and Black American intellectuals alike were alarmed by these waves of migration. The 1905 monograph Italian in America warned in its preface that "no concern of this country is more momentous and urgent than the national dealing with the problems of immigration" (Lord/Trenor/Barrows 1905: n.p.). The problem, according to the authors, boiled down to "congestion, distribution and education" (ibid), through which "American laborers" were "crowd[ed] out" from "avenues of employment" (ibid: 18). Contemporary authors predicted what Howard Zinn refers to as "desperate economic competition" (Zinn 2003: 265), especially amongst the have-nots. Southern and Eastern Europeans, contemporary authors feared, set in motion a wage race to the bottom that the more vocal American-born workers could not win. Frank Julian Warne's 1904 monograph The Slav Invasion and the Mine Workers described immigration as a "tremendous influence upon labor conditions" (1904: 39) in the anthracite coal fields of Pennsylvania. English-speaking immigrants (such as the Irish) were increasingly unwanted, according to Warne, since they were considered an "easily excited race, quick to resent oppression, whether real or imaginary [...] the Irish have been the leaders, or agitators, of every labor or-

1 This "unsoundness" had already caused an economic crash in 1893, driving one in four Americans into unemployment (Zinn 2003: 277). As early as 1888, industrialization resulted in what was perceived by contemporary economists and businessmen as a prolonged "depression of prices, a depression of interests, and a depression of profits" (qtd. in Hobsbawm 1991: 36).

2 These quotas were legislated through the Immigration Acts of 1921 and 1924.

ganization" (ibid: 54). Warne predicted that immigrants could be used as strike-breakers, thereby undermining the increasingly organized and politicized American workers.[3]

Quite often, intellectuals of those days actively favored native-born Americans over the foreign newcomers. The influential African American intellectual Booker T. Washington, for instance, advocated the use of African American workers, not those "of foreign birth and strange tongue and habits" (2011: 207). Home-grown workers and not foreigners should be used to expand the "prosperity of the South", as he told his audience in the famous "Atlanta Exposition" in 1895 (ibid). Southern business leaders should "cast down their bucket" at home by relying on local and cheap Black labor, according to Washington. These workers would not be prone to "strikes and labour wars", Washington promised (ibid).

Black workers did not adhere to Washington's stay-at-home advice, though. Mass internal migration by African Americans was a central component of American history of that period. This served to further heighten the sense of competition for employment in the United States. Although an overwhelming number of Blacks – 90 percent of the six and a half million in the country – made their homes in the South after the Civil War (Bair 2005: 3), a massive exodus from Southern rural regions into urban areas in the North gained momentum in the 1880s. In his groundbreaking 1899 sociological study The Philadelphia Negro (one of the first academic studies by a Black American), W.E.B. Du Bois estimated that "the majority of the present immigrants arrived since 1887, and nearly 30 per cent since 1892" (1899: 79). These internal movements intensified during and after World War I, a period defined by the "Great Migration" to Chicago, Philadelphia, Detroit, Cleveland, New York, and Pittsburgh. This mass relocation of 500.000 Black Southerners from 1916 to 1919, and another million during the 1920s (Bair 2005: 108), continued during the "Great Depression". As late as 1944, as indicated by Gunnar Myrdal's monumental An American Dilemma: The Negro Problem and Modern Democracy, "Negroes ha[d] not stopped coming to the urban North" (1944: 189). The work did note, however, that this was not to the "same extent as during the period of the World War and the 1920's" (ibid: 197).

Many incentives to "push" out of the South, as well as "pull" factors from the North, led to "accumulated migration potentialities", Myrdal noted (ibid: 193). Whereas Southern white, supremacist contemporaries considered migration to be the "negro's character" (Grossman 2005: 73), Myrdal stressed economic and social

3 In the peak year of 1886, 500,000 workers actively participated in strikes, who used their power in numbers to unionize and to advocate labor reform (Zinn 2003: 265, 273-74; Hofstadter 1993: 105).

factors. These included, amongst others, the relocation of the cotton industry from South to West, drought, and the "infiltration of whites into the types of work formerly monopolized by Negroes" (1944: 193). At the same time, increased employment opportunities offered by industrial expansion and an enlarged service sector pulled Blacks to the North. Once there, these Blacks would be pitted against other immigrants in a ruthless low-wage competition. "In many places," as Myrdal noted regarding the early 19th century, "it was a fashion among the wealthy to hire Negroes as servants in preference to European immigrants [...] many middle class whites also come to prefer Negroes – largely because they did not object to the hardest work and did not expect much in wages" (ibid: 191-192). The economic battle between Black and white immigrants frequently had the opposite outcome, as well, as Du Bois observed regarding the Philadelphia barber market.[4] A second important pull factor for Black migration to the North, as Myrdal suggested, "came from the big industries when white workers went out on strike" (ibid: 192). As usual, however, the "industrial employers found their demand for unskilled labor well filled by European immigrants. The workers themselves often resented Negro competition" (ibid: 192-193).

The influx of thousands of Black and white migrants in such a brief period not only greatly complicated the existing labor market, but also the general living and housing conditions in Philadelphia, Chicago, and other fast-growing urban centers (Tuttle 1970: 106). This led to over-crowded environments in quickly expanding urban centers – of which the "slums" of the 7th Ward in Philadelphia at the turn of the century and the rat-infested cellars of Harlem in the mid-20th century serve as prominent examples (cf. Du Bois 1899: 81; Zinn 2003: 404). These dense living environments would eventually become hotbeds for a variety of Black expression – musical, visual, and political – through which the gravity of African American culture shifted increasingly from the South to Northern cities (Grossman 2005: 108). Subsequent sections will return to this point, especially within the context of the Harlem Renaissance, a movement that deeply marked the cultural signifier Congo.

Against the background of an unsound and crisis-ridden global economy that continuously triggered mass political mobilization, mass migration, and ruthless economic competition, Euro-American "imperialism" and "colonialism"[5] blos-

4 Blacks withdrew increasingly from this profession due to the "competition of German and Italian barbers [who] cut down the customary prices and some of them found business co-operation and encouragement which Negroes could not hope for" (Du Bois 1899: 116).

5 "Imperialism" denotes here the practice and theory of a dominating metropolitan center that rules a distant territory in order to control both the labor and resources of the latter;

somed, itself strongly driven by the idea of economic and nationalistic competition. Between 1880 and 1914, most of the world outside Europe and the U.S. was partitioned into territories under the formal rule or informal political domination of a handful of states (Hobsbawm 1991: 57), of which the Congo Free State was but one of many examples. The U.S., which, from its early beginnings, might be considered an imperial power because of its pattern of ongoing expansion and foreign intervention (Pease 1993: 22), followed the imperial trend of dominating overseas markets against competing industrial economies (Hobsbawm 1991: 67; Zinn 2003: 313). In the wake of the 1898 Spanish-American war over Cuba, the remnants of the old Spanish empire were annexed (the first "victim" of the process of slicing up the world into new chunks) – including Puerto Rico, the Hawaiian Islands, Guam, and the Philippines (Hobsbawm 1991: 57). This expansion and intervention overseas had its internal equivalent in the annexation of Texas from the Mexicans (1845) and the massacre of Native Americans, for instance at Wounded Knee in 1890, which guaranteed access to the internal frontier (Zinn 2003: 126, 298).

Successive administrations in the U.S. strongly advocated an "open door" economic policy, through which America's rising economic strength could dominate large parts of the world via an "informal empire" (Zinn 2003: 301-302). Frequently, this policy led to an "imperial anticolonialism" (Sexton 2011: 5), which was anticolonial and philanthropic in theory, but deeply imperial and commerce-driven in practice – best illustrated by the "Monroe doctrine".[6] U.S. "imperial anticolonialism" and the politics of the "open door" determined the role of America in the foundation of the Congo Free State. On April 22, 1884, President Chester A. Arthur became the first head of state to recognize Leopold's claims on the Congo, after the king had obtained cessions from local Congo leaders through Henry Morgan Stanley and lobbied the U.S. government efficiently through Henry Shelton Sanford

"colonialism", in turn, designates the actual implanting of settlements on distant territory (see Said 1994: 8; Loomba 2005: 11; Seymour 2012: xiii).

6 Issued in 1823, when the countries of Latin America were winning independence from Spanish rule (Sexton 2011: 3), the Monroe doctrine made it clear to European countries that the United States considered the Western Hemisphere its "zone of influence" and no longer open to European colonization and political intervention (Sexton 2011: 3). While the doctrine proclaimed American opposition to European colonialism due to its own experience under British rule, there also lurked a strong American imperial ambition in it (ibid). As such, the Monroe doctrine opened the door for worldwide American "zones of influence" (Hobsbawm 1991: 57) – commercial and political – that were aggressively imposed on Latin America, China, and in the Caribbean, amongst other locations (Zinn 2003: 408-409).

(Füllberg-Stolberg 2003: 200-209). Through Arthur's recognition, Leopold's strategic position in acquiring his private empire in Central West Africa was decisively strengthened (ibid). Arthur decided to back Leopold after evaluating the claims of Leopold's International African Association (IAA) in a report titled "Occupation of the Congo Country in Africa", written by the influential Committee on Foreign Relations. The report collected the Congo evaluations of academics, diplomats, and travelers, many of whom were linked to pro-imperial institutions, such as the American Colonization Society (cf. previous chapter), the Chambers of Commerce of both Manchester and New York, and the IAA itself. A number of treaties with Congo chiefs are incorporated into the document, as well (signed with an "X", tellingly). The head of this Committee, Senator John Tyler Morgan, alluded to "open door" policy throughout the report (Congress of the United States of America 1884: 7):

> After Stanley had made his journey of exploration of nearly 7,000 miles across the continent of Africa, and had revealed to the world the extent and importance of this great river Congo, all the great commercial nations at once began to look earnestly in that direction for a new and most inviting field of commerce, and with the high and noble purpose of opening it freely to the equal enjoyment of all nations alike. The merchants of Europe and America insist upon this equal and universal right of free trade with that country, and their chambers of commerce have earnestly pressed upon their respective governments the duty and necessity of such international agreements as would secure these blessings to the people of Africa and of the entire commercial world.

Given the importance for the U.S. of establishing an open commercial door to the Congo (discussed here as the "universal right of free trade"), the claims of the IAA and its successor, the Congo Free State, were favored over those of the protectionist Portuguese empire (ibid: 4). The IAA and Congo Free State, in other words, were viewed as more conducive to the economic and industrial interest of a U.S. attempting to gain the upper hand over European rivals in a crises-ridden capitalist system (Hobsbawm 1991: 45, 65). Portugal's tolerance of slavery (ibid: 7) rendered it unacceptable, as the capitalist, pro-colonial argument of the United States was systematically balanced by its moral opposition to slavery. As such, the colonization of the Congo would be a win-win situation, or a blessing to "the people of Africa and of the entire commercial world", as the report wrote (ibid: 7).

Anti-slavery rhetoric constituted an integral ideological part of Morgan's report,[7] which justified the subjugation of the Congolese and the reorganization of

7 And the pro-colonial argument in general (see Grant 2005: 26).

their social, economic, and religious structures. In the name of a Euro-American civilization that rallied around anti-slavery (which it had practiced on a global scale for centuries itself; cf. previous chapter), the "50,000,000 people" of the Congo were soon to become "most useful factors in the increase of the productions of the earth and in swelling the volume of commerce" (ibid: 2). Ultimately, the open door politics of the United States – as well as its anti-slavery advocacy – were acknowledged at the Berlin West Africa Conference of 1884-1885.[8] Here, representatives from the United States actively helped to legitimize Leopold's claims and legalized the borders of his Congo Free State (Füllberg-Stolberg 2003: 210-216). True to its imperial anti-colonialist leanings, however, the U.S. never ratified the outcome of the conference (ibid: 225).

Imperialism has always been more than merely a way of securing the raw materials necessary to keep up with the rapidly developing technological and consumer innovations of the age – i.e. railroads, steamships, cars, and department stores (Hobsbawm 27-28). Amidst serious internal social upheaval and competition, it was also engaged in to diminish domestic discontent. Empire, as Hobsbawm reminds us in his seminal The Age of Empire: 1875-1914, has always been "social imperialism", as well (69), as it promises economic improvements funded by semi- or fully colonial dependents (Hobsbawm 1991: 64). In short, empire offered "glory rather than more costly reforms" (ibid: 70). In "Occupation of the Congo Country in Africa", the colonization of the Congo was discussed, for instance, as a solution to the internal "problem" of African Americans (Congress of the United States of America 1884: 7):

> We owe it as a duty to our African population that we should endeavor to secure to them the right to freely return to their fatherland [...] looking to their re-establishment of their own country. The deportation of their ancestors from Africa in slavery was contrary to the now accepted canons of the laws of nations and now they may return under those laws to their natural inheritance.

In this quote, the Congo is openly imagined as the "potential dumping ground for both America's manufacturing surpluses and her unwanted blacks", as the head of the Committee, John Tyler Morgan, once phrased it (qtd. in Füllberg-Stolberg 2003: 209). Cast as a matter of doing right by those formerly enslaved, the interference in the Congo is again presented as a win-win situation. By sending "our African population" back to the Congo, white Americans could make up for slavery and for

8 The conference was initiated by France and Germany with the aim of stimulating and securing free trade in the Congo region (Füllberg-Stolberg 2003: 211).

breaking "the now accepted canons of the laws of nations" (Congress of the United States of America 1884: 7). Black Americans, in turn, could resettle in their "fatherland", to which "they may return under those laws to their natural inheritance" (ibid). The categorization of Black Americans as "Africans" who live by "natural" laws (instead of "Americans" who live by the Constitution) demonstrates how the ideology of empire might appeal to white Americans. Because it tapped into and actively shaped the idea of white superiority and domination over Blacks, both at home and abroad (Hobsbawm 1991: 70), racism's place in 19th- and early 20th-century imperial thinking cannot be overemphasized (ibid: 252). Scientific racism and Social Darwinism in particular played a fundamental role in this process, as is show in the following section.

Supremacy in Theory

In order to explain and defend their privileged position and advocate investment in global imperialism, the white American bourgeoisie actively incorporated bits and pieces from a heterogeneous corpus of scientific and pseudo-scientific texts which justified the belief in their own racial superiority. This corpus, usually labeled "scientific racism" in contemporary research, drew from anthropology, history, and sociology, among other disciplines, to construct human typologies and divide these into "races" with a set of fixed positive or negative traits, or often a combination thereof (During 2005: 161-163). Within this context, "Social Darwinism" (as those in the 19th century referred to it, too) was the leading theory; it was explicitly invoked and systematically drawn from for more than a generation, as Richard Hofstadter shows (1993: 4).

In comparison to its reception in England, Social Darwinism was eagerly and sympathetically received in the United States (ibid: 22-25). In the late 19th century, it was imperative for intellectuals to master the basics of Herbert Spencer's theoretical approach to humankind – even more so than in the previous decades (in which Darwinian thought was clearly gaining traction, as explained in the previous chapter). Spencer applied Darwin's evolutionary theory to the social arena (ibid: 33) and exerted a decisive influence on the founders of American sociology, psychology, ethnology, and ethics, in addition to deeply affecting both Marxist and liberal thought (ibid: 143, 116). Books by Social Darwinian adepts and advocates of Spencer's work enjoyed bestseller status in the United States by the turn of the century (ibid: 33-34), testifying to Social Darwinism as the leading intellectual stream in American thought during this time.

What did Social Darwinism mean to U.S. intellectuals at the turn of the century? A 1907 essay dedicated to Social Darwinism by Dartmouth College sociology professor Collin D. Wells provides at least one idea. By Social Darwinism, a term the author used explicitly, Wells understood the "general doctrine of the gradual appearance of new forms through variation; the struggle of superabundant forms; the elimination of those poorly fitted, to the given environment; and the maintenance of racial efficiency only by incessant struggle and ruthless elimination" (Wells 1907: 695). Through the notion of "gradual appearance of new forms through variation", Wells highlighted Social Darwinism's conception of American society as a slow-moving natural organism (cf. Hofstadter 1993: 7). Despite being a sociologist who grappled with the connection between biological and social factors (such as education and alcohol), Wells did not doubt that biology trumped social environment in his favorable summary of Social Darwinism.

This winner-takes-all philosophy befitted the age of competition. In terms of politics, Social Darwinism was deeply classist. As a theory, it was as if tailor-made to safeguard the bank accounts and the everyday privileges of the white bourgeoisie, as well as to deal with the "practical problem" of geographical and social movement in the U.S., that is, of Black and white mass migration (see Gossett 1997: 174). The perceived challenges that went along with this social fact – criminality, pauperism, and ghettoization (ibid: 155) – were thus explained by hereditary inferiority. Social Darwinism was thus mobilized systematically against the variety of forces that might disrupt the bourgeois status quo. As social life was framed as a "struggle" for the "survival of the physical units that are competing" (Wells 1907: 702), the losers of this struggle, along with their genes, were themselves to blame. Advocates of those not belonging to the bourgeoisie were dismissed as a danger to the "race". Socialism, as well as trade-unionism, were considered by Wells "aberrant, and it is to be hoped temporary, manifestations [since] these tend to afford an equal chance of survival and of parenthood to the incapable and weak" (ibid). Taxation was also questioned by Wells because he perceived it as having a negative "effect upon vital phenomena" (ibid: 703). The categorical repudiation of state interference in the "organic" growth of society had led advocates of Herbert Spencer's work to oppose all state aid to the poor, deeming them unworthy of attention that might slow their elimination (Hofstadter 1993: 41). Although generally dressed up in lofty scientific rhetoric – "gradual appearance", "superabundant forms", "racial efficiency", and so forth (as showed through the example of Wells) – Social Darwinian language continuously broke down into more blatantly genocidal language such as "ruthless elimination", including comments as "each species is the food of others" (Wells 1907: 695) and "those poorly adapted to their life-conditions are eliminated" (ibid: 696).

It is important to note that, although the idea of racial inferiority gained broad legitimacy and considerable strength from Social Darwinism, it did not depend on it. Claims of racial inferiority circulated widely in the pre-Social Darwinian debates surrounding slavery and warfare against Native Americans throughout the 19th century (Hofstadter 1993: 171), as alluded to in the last chapter. This kind of racism found official sanction through concepts such as "manifest destiny", which emphasized the virtues of the American people and their institutions and highlighted America's mission to redeem and remake the world in the the special image of America under God's direction. The idea of manifest destiny was ultimately connected to Social Darwinism in the late 19th century, allowing Anglo-Saxon racial superiority to truly "obsess [...] many American thinkers in the latter half of the 19th century" (ibid: 174-175).

Arthur de Gobineau's Inequality of Human Races must be considered as an influential early pamphlet in the remarkable career of Social Darwinism. As Stephen Jay Gould describes it, Inequality of Human Races turned the French aristocrat into "the most influential academic racist of the 19th century" (Gould 2014: 379). This pamphlet, written before Darwin's seminal works, exerted considerable influence in the U.S., too, and will be taken up in what follows as a way to measure the Social Darwinian influence on white and Black intellectuals. Re-published in the United States in the early 20th century when the immigration question arose, it was in fact originally translated and published half a century earlier (its first translated edition ran from 1853-1856, almost immediately after its original French version appeared; cf. Gossett 1997: 352).

Inequality of Human Races explained to its readers that the fate of civilizations is generally determined by the purity of the races that compose them; their decline and fall are attributable to dilution of "pure" stocks by interbreeding. De Gobineau divided the human species hierarchically into three types, "the black, the yellow, and the white" (1915: 152). Whereas the "negroid variety" is located at the bottom of the human ladder, whites, considered broadly, are positioned at its height. Among the latter group, de Gobineau differentiated between the various white "races", too, which are "as unequal in strength as they are in beauty" (ibid: 191). On his "descending scale" of whites, all of whom are assigned an essential and "special character" (ibid), de Gobineau placed the English, French, and Germans at the top, due to their "strength of fist" (ibid: 152). The "nameless mixture of Italians and other Latin races", were put near its bottom (ibid: 93), despite the redeeming fact that they were considered slightly more beautiful than the Germans (ibid: 152).

By dividing the white race along these lines, de Gobineau provided ready-made arguments for American anti-immigration activists. The ongoing disparagement of Italians as an inferior subgroup of the white race by American-born elites serves as a case in point. In Italian in America, a monograph written in defense of Italian immigration by three civil servants from the Census and Prison Department/The Immigration Committee (Lord, Trenor, and Barrows), the objections against labor congestion and slumification raised against Italian immigrants were critically discussed. These objections, according to Lord, Trenor, and Barrows, had been "amplified and more bluntly and bitterly urged in a current outcry against Italian immigration" (1905: 17).

The authors then examined this anti-Italian discourse in detail, identifying and explaining the rhetoric and rationale behind this "outcry" (ibid). At this point, the impact of Social Darwinian thinking on the prejudice of the time is revealed: "It is urged that the Italian race stock is inferior and degraded; that it will not assimilate naturally or readily with the prevailing 'Anglo-Saxon' race stock of this country" (ibid: 18). On top of that, the authors noted that opponents of Italian migration sought to prevent "intermixture", as this was said to "be detrimental" due to the Italian's "servility, filthy habits of life, and a hopelessly degraded standard of needs and ambitions" from centuries "of oppression and abject poverty" (ibid). This led, according to the authors' opponents, to the inability of the immigrants to espouse "any adequate appreciation of our free institutions and the privileges and duties of citizenship" as they "are illiterate and likely to remain so" and thus will "inevitably lower the American standard of living and labor and citizenship" (ibid). Many of de Gobineau's central ideas were mobilized against Italian immigrant communities here. Italians were painted as hopelessly inferior in terms of their intelligence, citizenship, and predilection to progress, and therefore their "hopelessly degraded standard of needs and ambitions" were well-deserved. Their presence was depicted as a danger to the Anglo-Saxon "race stock". Against this background of Italian inferiority and Anglo-Saxon superiority, the "wide-ranging exclusion" (ibid) of the former by the latter seemed inevitable.

De Gobineau's tendency to pitch one "inferior" group against another provided a white American supremacist bourgeoisie with powerful munition against white migrants and African Americans alike. In a striking passage of The Inequality of Human Races, de Gobineau compared Italians to "young mulattoes who have been educated in London or Paris" (1915: 191) in order to illustrate that nature always trumps nurture. Although the educated "mulattoes" may show a certain "veneer of culture superior to that of some Southern Italian peoples, who are in point of merit infinitely higher", they can never actually surpass them. "Once a mulatto, always a mulatto", de Gobineau maintained (ibid). As a product of "intermixture", "mulattoes" constituted the worst-case scenario within a framework that went to great lengths to promote the preservation of pure race stocks.

This mixing was considered particularly dire by de Gobineau because he viewed the so-called black race in almost entirely negative terms. He states, for instance, that "the animal character, that appears in the shape of the pelvis, is stamped on the negro from birth, and foreshadows his destiny" (ibid: 205). For the author, the Black's intellectual abilities are low and "will always move within a very narrow circle" (ibid). Despite his "dull or even non-existent" intelligence, a Black man is, however, no "mere brute, for behind his low receding brow, in the middle of his skull, we can see signs of a powerful energy, however crude its objects" (ibid).

The quality that makes this Black man less useless is thus "intensity of desire, and so of will, which may be called terrible. Many of his senses, especially taste and smell, are developed to an extent unknown to the other two races. The very strength of his sensations is the most striking proof of his inferiority" (ibid). This inferiority leads him to be "careless of his own life and that of others: he kills willingly, for the sake of killing; and this human machine, in whom it is so easy to arouse emotion, shows, in face of suffering, either a monstrous indifference or a cowardice that seeks a voluntary refuge in death" (ibid). Throughout this passage, de Gobineau transforms Blacks into simple-minded, murderous, morally defective "human machine[s]" that are, in essence, the exact opposite of whites.[9] As a true

9 This, for instance, is how de Gobineau discussed white people in The Inequality of Human Races: "We come now to the white peoples. These are gifted with reflective energy, or rather with an energetic intelligence. They have a feeling for utility, but in a sense far wider and higher, more courageous and ideal, than the yellow races; a perseverance that takes account of obstacles and ultimately finds a means of overcoming them; a greater physical power, an extraordinary instinct for order, not merely as a guarantee of peace and tranquillity [sic], but as an indispensable means of self-preservation. At the same time, they have a remarkable, and even extreme, love of liberty, and are openly hostile to the formalism under which the Chinese are glad to vegetate, as well as to the strict despotism which is the only way of governing the negro. The white races are, further, distinguished by an extraordinary attachment to life. They know better how to use it, and so, as it would seem, set a greater price on it; both in their own persons and those of others, they are more sparing of life. When they are cruel, they are conscious of their cruelty; it is very doubtful whether such a consciousness exists in the negro. At the same time, they have discovered reasons why they should surrender this busy life of theirs, that is so precious to them. The principal motive is honour [sic], which under various names has played an enormous part in the ideas of the race from the beginning. I need hardly add

Social Darwinian, albeit writing in pre-Darwinian times, de Gobineau came to his conclusion via biology. In other words, he diagnosed intellectual and sensual abilities by reading physical attributes: The shape of a pelvis, a receding brow, a skull. With his emphasis on Black physical characteristics, de Gobineau anticipates the popular eugenics movement of the 20th century.

De Gobineau's distinct notion of racial purity and Anglo-Saxon white supremacy clearly struck an enduring chord in the post-Reconstruction era of Jim Crow. His influence, along with Darwin's and Spencer's, cannot be overlooked in the avalanche of anti-Black books, such as Carroll's The Negro: A Beast (1900), Tillinghast's The Negro in Africa and America (1902), and Shufeldt's The Negro: A Menace to American Civilization (1907; cf. Gosset 1997: 280), all of which are highly sympathetic to these scientific racists. In The Negro: A Menace to American Civilization, for instance, one of the major arguments revolves around (white) racial purity. This is discussed against the background of the "sensual instinct" of Blacks, or their ongoing "copulat[ing] solely for the gratification of the passion – for the erotic pleasure it affords them" (Shufeldt 134). One can also find this argument in de Gobineau's assertion, referred to above, of the "strength of [a Black's] sensations" (1915: 205).

In the same vein as de Gobineau and other Social Darwinian anti-Black thinkers, The Negro: A Menace to American Civilization contains frequent and overt calls to violent action. "To sustain a high standard of morals and refined ethics," the argument goes, "we must rid ourselves of the source of the immorality, of the cause of our retrogradation in good conduct with respect to the negro, this evidently remains for us to do. Suppression has never been known to eliminate or eradicate vice, or crime, therefore, we must, for the sake of mankind, resort to other means" (Shufeldt 1907: 123). One of the solutions was proposed a few pages later: "It would doubtless be a capital thing, if it could be done, to emasculate the entire negro race and all of its descendants in this country, and effectually stop the breed right now, and the horrors of their crossing continually with the Anglo-Saxon stock" (ibid: 145).

Although de Gobineau and his proponents insisted on denigrating the black race as a homogeneous whole, he indirectly produced a hierarchy within it. In comparing

that the word honour, together with all the civilizing influences connoted by it, is unknown to both the yellow and the Black man. On the other hand, the immense superiority of the white peoples in the whole field of the intellect is balanced by an inferiority in the intensity of their sensations. In the world of the senses, the white man is far less gifted than the others, and so is less tempted and less absorbed by considerations of the body, although in physical structure he is far the most vigorous" (1915: 207).

the physique of the yellow, black, and white races, de Gobineau held up the character of the "negro from the West Coast of Africa" (1915: 106) as prototypical for the black race. His description recalls the phrenological Congo types discussed in the last chapter: "[H]is colour is [...] entirely black; his hair [is] [...] thick, coarse, woolly, and luxuriant" (ibid). Adding to this alleged aesthetic insult of "the self-love of human kind" are the flatness of this "negro's" feet and hands, long bones, and a lower jaw that "juts out" (ibid). "When we look for a moment at an individual of this type," de Gobineau noted in his typically dehumanizing, anti-Black rhetoric, "we are involuntarily reminded of the structure of the monkey" (ibid: 107). This type of Black had a label: "Congo negro", who is only exceeded in including the "most ugly, degraded, and repulsive specimens of the race" by the "Australian tribes" (ibid).

Statements singling out and rejecting Congolese specifically can be found in many Social Darwinian works. The Negro: A Beast illustrates the innate inability of the black race to civilize by pointing to the "negro's facile relapses, as in the Congo nation, into a state of abject barbarism" (Carroll 1900: 327). In The Negro: A Menace to American Civilization, the same assumption is made for the sake of lambasting Blacks in the United States: "Throughout the entire historic period of man's career upon earth the chapter on the negro is practically a record of the lowest savagery, soon lapsing back into mere tradition of wild and untutored tribes" (Shufeldt 1907: 42). The list of "negro" flaws was a long one, including "undiluted fetichism [sic], with the worship of ancestors for a religion, coupled with torture, cruelty, slavery and cannibalism, and a common belief in sorcery" (ibid). The model example for this lowest savagery is found in the "Congo Basin", which must be "checked by the presence of the European" (ibid). Because "many of these people see their near relatives in the negroes of the United States" (ibid: 42), the message of The Negro: A Menace to American Civilization was clear: As members of the same race, African Americans were guilty of the same crimes Central West Africans had supposedly committed throughout their history. As such, they must be kept in check by white people (just as the Congolese needed to be controlled by Europeans).

The hegemony of militant Social Darwinian thought in the political arena was undermined by the economic havoc it caused among the middle and working classes. Nothing is as unstable as economic success within a crisis-ridden capitalist mode of production, it turned out, and nothing as malleable as the stance of people whose livelihood is threatened by the menace of unchecked competition. As the middle classes shrank in numbers under the laissez-faire economic and social policies of the day, so did the glorification of Social Darwinism (Gould 2014: 202). "The figure of the great capitalist entrepreneur, hitherto heroic, lost much of its glamour", Hofstadter notes (1993: 119). World War I dealt another serious blow to Social Darwinism when biological determinism, the rhetoric of superiority, and the expansionism of Germany required discrediting.

Despite these significant setbacks, by 1915 Social Darwinism had thoroughly pervaded American intellectual thought (ibid: 150) and served as the decisive inspiration for a new fad: Eugenics (ibid: 161). As a scientifically and politically motivated attempt to improve the quality of the original "racial stock" of Anglo-Saxons (ibid: 163), it became a major movement in the first half of the 20th century, particularly in 1920s Great Britain, Germany, and the U.S., whose efforts mutually influenced one another (Kühl 1994: 4). Although eugenics came in many political fractions, shapes, and forms (ibid: 84),[10] professors, legislators, and activists joined forces in their belief in genetically transmissible qualities (ibid: 4-5), which, as the story went, resulted in superior and inferior racial stocks. Like the followers of Social Darwinism, adherents of the eugenic mainstream argued that all of these races should be kept apart.

Academics critical of the biological determinism espoused by Social Darwinians and eugenicists struggled to liberate themselves from the theories, which held them in a tight stranglehold after World War I. Anthropologist Franz Boas's work in opposition to Social Darwinism is particularly revealing with regard to Social Darwinism's staying power. By questioning the hereditary and hierarchical premises of the academic mainstream, Boas stood at the vanguard of the scientific revolt against Social Darwinism (Gossett 1997: 423; Trotter 2005: 145). Specifically, he criticized the method of comparing cultures by standards foreign to them and advocated the examination of cultures on their own terms (Gossett 1997: 423).

More than the majority of white academics before him, Boas attempted to redefine the so-called "Negro problem" in the United States as a problem with the white majority and not the Black minority (Boas 1921: 273-278). Through his systematic attack on Darwinian dogma, many central African American intellectuals – ranging from W.E.B. Du Bois and Carter Woodson to Alain Locke and Zora Neale Hurston – corresponded and collaborated closely with him or sought his intellectual

10 American immigration laws in the 20s (cf. above), which were designed to keep people from non-Northern European countries out of the United States, won special approval in Nazi Germany (Kühl 1994: 37-38). The same can be said about legislation for compulsory sterilization and euthanasia – starting as early as 1899 in Indiana and spreading rapidly from 1909 onward to California, New York, and Michigan – which forcibly affected 64,000 individuals, a majority of whom were Black women (Ward 1996: 95). Reform eugenics took over in the 30s, but the inherent belief in inferior and superior people remained intact (Kühl 1994: 84).

support in helping to counter racist attacks on their communities from a scientific point of view (Williams 1996: 37-54). It is telling that thinkers as different as Booker T. Washington and W.E.B. Du Bois quoted him extensively in their seminal works The Story of the Negro: The Rise of the Race from Slavery and The Negro.

While he did question the "degeneration" of the "pure stock" of Anglo-Saxons through its intermixture with other races, Boas's language and arguments remain marked by Social Darwinism's powerful orientation towards hierarchy (ibid: 4). His highly influential 1911 classic The Mind of Primitive Man[11] illustrates how Boas both critiques and reproduces the hegemony of Social Darwinian hierarchical thinking. On the one hand, Boas deconstructs at great length "the naive assumption of the superiority of the European nations and their descendants" (1921: 2). Differences, to Boas, should be explained in reference to "distinct economic, social, and other environmental conditions" (ibid: 40). Although openly opposing Spencer, de Gobineau, and other Social Darwinian thinkers vis-à-vis "the higher hereditary powers of the white race" (ibid: 100), in the end Boas does not abandon an essentialist and hierarchical framework. Rather, he reinforces the opposition between the inferior and superior: "The fact deserves attention that at present practically all the members of the white race participate to a greater or less degree in the advance of civilization, while in none of the other races has the civilization that has been attained at one time or another been able to reach all the tribes or peoples of the same race" (ibid: 10).

This inherent belief in the inferiority of non-white races reappears in his discussions of African Americans. Although "no proof could be given" of their inferiority (268), Boas nevertheless deems it possible that "perhaps the race would not produce quite so many men of highest genius as other races" (ibid). Boas returns to this point in his summary chapter, titled "Race Problems in the United States". "There is every reason to believe that the negro when given facility and opportunity, will be perfectly able to fulfill the duties of citizenship as well as his white neighbor" (ibid: 273), Boas notes. This relativist idea is followed, however, by a deeply hierarchical one: "It may be that he will not produce as many great men as the white race, and that his average achievement will not quite reach the level of the average achievement of the white race" (ibid), although he finishes by noting that "there will be endless numbers who will be able to outrun their white competitors, and who will do better than the defectives whom we permit to drag dawn and to retard the healthy children of our public schools" (ibid). By this point, if not prior to this, this linking of "race" and "health" indicates a return to Social Darwinian rhetoric.

11 As its multiple revised editions attest, the wok remained highly relevant throughout the period between the World Wars.

Boas had no doubts that the average Black American could "fulfill the duties of citizenship as well as his white neighbor". At the same time, he did not expect them to produce "as many great men as the white race". He held on to this belief until his death (Williams 1996: 13). While lacking confidence in great Black men, Boas also doubted that the "average achievement" of Blacks could match that of the white race, although he did allow for the prospect of the black race doing better than the "defectives" who debilitate other "healthy" American children. Boas's reasoning thus collapses into the militant health and degeneration discourse of his days. This may also be seen in his discussion of the Congolese as the underbelly of the black race, i.e. "the pygmy Negro types", which formed "a separate division" (Boas 1921: 109).

This essential belief in the inferiority of the cultures under scrutiny persisted in the works of Boas's many influential pupils and collaborators, including Robert Lowie,[12] Melville Herskovits,[13] and Margaret Mead[14] – decisive thinkers in the fields of anthropology, as well as African and African American study departments in the U.S.

Supremacy in Action

Social Darwinian theory crucially informed practice, helping to advocate and justify the ongoing disenfranchisement, expropriation, and massacre of Black people on a global scale. This is demonstrated here by deaths in the United States from mob vi-

12 In the same vein as Mead, Robert Lowie's chapter on "Subsistence" in Boas's 1938 General Anthropology differentiates between "complex societies" and "simpler peoples" (1938: 282).

13 Herskovits, like Mead and Lowie, at first dismisses the favoring of one culture over the other in his 1941 The Myth of the Negro Past as "poor ethnology and poorer psychology" (1941: 296). This recognized, Herskovits argued, that many of the terms applied to African societies should be discarded. When examining "the cultures of West Africa, Senegal, and the Congo", however, Herskovits described them as "nonliterate, nonmachine societies" comparable "in many respects to Europe of the Middle Ages" (ibid).

14 Her bestselling Coming of Age in Samoa (1928) is particularly instructive in this regard. This influential work, with a foreword by Franz Boas, defined the method of the anthropologist as traveling to a "different civilisation and mak[ing] a study of human being under different cultural conditions in some other parts of the world" (1928: 7). Her insistence on framing the cultural conditions she found through the relativist term "different", however, did not stop her from discussing her subjects as "primitive peoples, whose society has never attained the complexity of our own" (ibid).

olence in the North and lynchings in the South, as well by the large numbers that died in Central West Africa from mutilation, starvation, or (imported) diseases in the wake of the region's forced entrance into global capitalist markets at the turn of the century (Hochschild 1998: 225-234). In the midst of global competition for resources to fire up Euro-American national economies (Hobsbawm 1991: 63), Social Darwinian ideas became imperial ones.

Tyler Morgan's report "Occupation of the Congo Country in Africa" (cf. section above) serves as one example of how the occupation by King Leopold was justified via the hegemonic narrative of hierarchy between peoples. "If the laws of Christian nations give any effect to the discovery by the subjects of a Christian power, of a country inhabited even by savages, they also require that discovery shall be followed by continuous subsequent occupation" (Congress of the United States of America 1885: 5), the document urges, distinguishing plainly between "Christian nations" and "savages". "If such occupation ceases," Tyler Morgan continues, "it is justly considered as being abandoned" (ibid). The reason for this perceived abandonment is, according to Morgan, that "the only foundation of reason or of justice" derives from those occupying it, not those that were already there. "It is," in Morgan's words, "better that the savages should have the advantages of Christian instruction and laws, than that they should continue in darkness to rule the country in their own way" (ibid). Through this official report by Morgan, Belgium received its blessing from the United States to occupy a vast region for the "benefit" of the Congolese, who were framed as "savages [who] should have the advantages of Christian instruction and laws" (ibid).

Despite its benevolent, diplomatic rhetoric, Social Darwinian thinking permeates the document, particularly the passage recommending Western intervention. It does so by imposing a hierarchy between superior Euro-American nations and the inferior Congolese, who, as soon as the Christians retreated from their country, would purportedly wander in a "darkness" devoid "of reason or of justice". Just how this "900,000 square miles of fertile territory and its 50,000,000 of people" should be turned into the "most useful factors in the increase of the productions of the earth and in swelling the volume of commerce" (ibid: 2) remained unaddressed throughout the report.

Friedrich Nietzsche, however, had foreshadowed how capitalism was to be imposed on Central West Africa. The German philosopher is noteworthy as a Euro-American intellectual who Black Americans knew, used, and discussed. Black American intellectuals loved to both loathe and embrace his writings. The discussion of the link between the German philosopher and Black America continues until today, as the essay collection Critical Affinities: Nietzsche and African American

Thought indicates. There is much truth in editor Gooding-Williams's assertion in his foreword to the volume that, at first sight, Nietzsche and Black America may seem like awkward bedfellows. "Let us assume that some of Nietzsche's writings express racialized colonialist fantasies," he begins. "Does it follow from this assumption that black and other progressives have no use for Nietzsche's writings except to castigate them?" (Gooding-Williams 2006: ix-x). Based on what was found within the scope of my own study in the African American newspaper archive, Black Americans did indeed find some value in the philosopher's thinking.

The Chicago Defender quoted him affirmatively, for instance, to condone the Black and white men in power in the mid-20th century, such as the Black Dean Kelly Miller and President Franklin D. Roosevelt, who were both considered redeemers of "accident unto order" – an adage explicitly linked to Nietzsche (e.g. 1940c: 14; 1940a: 14). Going back a few decades in The Chicago Defender's archive, however, Nietzsche was discussed quite differently. He stood "for a sullen, ivory tower thinker of hierarchy and the "materialistic 'superman'" (1915: 3). Nevertheless, it seems as if Nietzsche was not dismissed entirely. "All men are still divided as they ever have been, into bond and free," The Chicago Defender wrote, alluding to Nietzsche's binary thinking in another article, "whoever has not two-thirds of the day to himself is a slave, no matter what he may be otherwise – statesman, merchant, official or scholar – Nietzsche" (1912: 7).

As a philosopher of hierarchical oppositions (e.g. slave vs. free), Nietzsche was representative of the times in his intellectual treatment of colonized people. In The Will to Power, compiled and published posthumously from his notebooks between 1901 and 1910, the philosopher wrote: "What means one has to employ with rude peoples, and that 'barbarous' means are not arbitrary and capricious, becomes palpable in practice as soon as one is placed, with all one's European pampering, in the necessity of keeping control over barbarians, in the Congo or elsewhere" (1969: 487). Nietzsche's idea of "barbarous means" was echoed by prominent U.S. anthropologists actively involved in the eugenics-oriented Galton Society, such as Clark Wissler. He justified the superiority of the Nordic race by proudly declaring it comprised of the "wild untamed barbarians of Europe" – manifest in historical "conquest and pillage" (qtd. in Barkan 1992: 110).

Intellectuals more critical of the excessive violence in the colonies took up the idea of Euro-American barbarity, as well. Confronted with the ruthlessness of colonial policy, Edmund Dene Morel, for instance, crusaded against the Congo Free State by actively and critically taking up Nietzsche's idea of "'barbarous means" in his seminal Red Rubber (1919: 192). Morel's work is worth a closer look, as it quite illustrative of how Social Darwinian disasters were discussed by white and

Black intellectuals alike: They not only employed similar tropes, but also followed common lines of reasoning.

Red Rubber was truly a groundbreaking account of the Congo Free State and raised mass awareness of the abuses of Leopold's regime. Although the book was an abridged version of Morel's major 1904 work, King's Leopold's Rule in Africa, its catchy title and accessible writing turned it into an instant bestseller (Cline 1981: 30). It became a powerful text in the struggle against the bloody ("red") economic and social realities of the Congo Free State. As the co-founder of the highly influential Congo Reform Association, which was active predominantly in Great Britain and the United States, where it attracted the support of major American intellectuals such as the writer Mark Twain, sociologist Robert E. Park, and educator Booker T. Washington (Dworkin 2003: 70, 112). Morel truly became the "chief propagandist of the crusade, but also its theoretician, strategist, and organizer" (Cline 1981: 30). In African American intellectual circles, Morel's major works and achievements were repeatedly lauded in newspapers such as The Chicago Defender. "A champion of justice to [the] Race", he was called in an eulogy on Nov 29, 1924 titled "Darker Races Lose Friend as Congo Hero Passes out" (1924:1).[15]

In its sixth and revised edition, Red Rubber described the "civilised barbarism" (Morel 1919: 76, 192) of the Congo Free State in the period between 1890 and 1910. "Barbarous", however, meant something different to Morel than the necessity of using "arbitrary and capricious" violence to control the "barbarians" of the Congo (to paraphrase Nietzsche). Like many contemporaries, Morel used it to designate a force that was "cruel", "merciless", and "brutal", as in the definition for "barbarian" and "cruel" from the 1899 American Dictionary of the English Language (Lyons 1899a: 29; Lyons 1899c: 87). This kind of barbarity was civilized and could not be mistaken for what the same dictionary termed "savage", which was reserved for those who were "wild: uncivilized: fierce: cruel: brutal – n. a human being in a wild state: a brutal person: a barbarian" (Lyons 1899k: 377). The example the dictionary used was: "N. American Indians and other savages" (Lyons 1899m: 475). Morel's "civilized barbarism", in contrast, was applied to the cruelty of those in the Congo who were considered civilized, i.e. white Europeans, who could not be mistaken for the "savage" Congolese barbarians.

Morel was a pivotal figure in the constitution of the discourse on the "atrocities" of the Congo Free State. His narrative was decidedly critical towards Belgian imperialism without being anti-imperialist per se (cf. Gehrmann 2003: 110). This stance

15 Cf. the following articles in The Chicago Defender, in which Morel was lauded years after his death in 1924: "Edmund D. Morel Freed Belgian Congo Slaves" (1929b: A1) and "From the Defender Files" (1935c: 16).

was the standard rather than the exception at the turn of the century, as can be seen in Joseph Conrad's novella Heart of Darkness. Given the manner in which they influenced one another (ibid: 120-129), a number of parallels between Heart of Darkness and Red Rubber may be drawn. Conrad's text was published a few years prior to Red Rubber and was considered by Morel as "the most powerful thing ever written on the subject" (qtd. in Gehrmann 2003: 122). Morel held Conrad in high esteem as an authority, corresponded extensively with him, and publicly called the Congo a "heart of darkness" in his History of the Congo Reform Movement (ibid: 121).

As in Conrad's story, the coercive transition to capitalism in the Congo is depicted by Morel as a singular imperial disaster – a disastrous aberration in the imperial everyday. "Everything is abnormal", Morel writes (1919: 187). Like Conrad, he does not discuss violence as a mutually shared aspect of the many empires that coerced Africa into becoming a part of the global capitalist market (Grant 2005: 29). By framing Leopold's Congo Free State as "civilized barbarism" and those advocating it as the "protest of civilisation" (1919: 187), Morel's story aimed for a reform of Belgian imperialism along the lines of (morally sounder) nations such as Britain, rather than the abandonment of the Belgian colonial project as a whole. Heart of Darkness defended imperialism, too – for instance, by drawing a parallel between the Roman conquest of the savage darkness of Great Britain and imperialism in Africa (Conrad 2006: 6). The "violence, aggravated murder on a great scale, men going blind" was judged by Conrad as "very proper for those who tackle a darkness" (ibid: 7). Still, it was nothing to boast about, since it was referred to as "just an accident arising from the weakness of others" (ibid). Confronted with the murderous reality in the Congo, however, this imperial theory crumbles much in the same way as in Red Rubber. In light of what the profit-driven Belgian imperialists made of colonialism, the "sepulcher" (ibid: 9) capital city of which fittingly houses its ruthless, rubber-grabbing colonial administrators, the novella ultimately dismisses the Belgian colonial enterprise. The necessity of imperially civilizing Africa, however, is never seriously abandoned.

In Morel's Red Rubber and Conrad's Heart of Darkness, the "civilized barbarism" of the Congo Free State hinges on the topos of "horror", as in Kurtz's famous last words in the novella: "The horror, the horror" (ibid: 69). In Red Rubber, "horror" appears continuously in its collage of eyewitness accounts of the Congo Free State's economy in order to underline "the horror of it, the unspeakable horror of it" (Morel 1919: 89; cf. Morel 1919: 40, 53, 86, 164, 187). Against the background of a booming rubber market (Nelson 1994: 81-85), Morel recounts the massive appropriation and domination of the vast Congolese land by Leopold's police and military forces, leading to the division of it into economic zones ruled by concession holders (ibid: 89).[16] As these failed to gain the support of the local leaders of the Congo, the collection of rubber had to be ensured by coercive means (ibid: 105). The tax system imposed on the Congolese and the bonus systems that were developed to motivate the agents of the Congo Free State (Morel 1919: 30, 64) constitute the pillars of the abusive system as described by both Morel and Conrad.

The failure to meet the rubber quota imposed by the private companies on the local populations (in order to pay their taxes) was punished corporeally. The range of coercions appear in great detail as reported by Morel's selection of eyewitnesses – missionaries, diplomats, travelers, and those otherwise interested in the Congo, such as the African American historian George Washington Williams (Morel 1919: 40; cf. previous and subsequent sections). The sum total of these horrific stories of violence, abuse, and sexual violence might be described as "pornographic" (cf. Baaz/Stern 2013: 92), in the sense that the reports aim at arousing emotions of pity for the victims by depicting them in demeaning ways which potentially reflect or promote racism. The next chapter will touch upon this representational ambiguity, as well.

There was plenty of material that could be used by Morel to evoke pity. Punishing the Congolese into submission had its genocidal aspects. "We must fight them until their absolute submission has been obtained, or their complete extermination" (1919: 35), Morel quotes from the diary of the Belgian district commissioner Jules Jacques. The statement comes close to Kurtz's infamous line: "Exterminate all the brutes!" (Conrad 2006: 50). The result of this genocidal method is described as an "atrocity" throughout Red Rubber (e.g. Morel 1919: 40, 46, 50, 66, 69), a label to be found in the works of American intellectuals as well.

An exemplary account of how these atrocities are described is found in the parts dedicated to the Swedish missionary Sjöblom, who wrote about his experiences from 1895 to 1897 in the central region of the Congo Free State: "I saw the dead bodies floating on the lake with the right hand cut off, and the officer told me when I came back why they had been killed. It was for the rubber. In fact the officers have always freely told me about the many who were killed, and always in connection with india-rubber [sic]" (Morel 1919: 43). It is a striking element in many of these accounts how authority is produced and maintained by "seeing", experiencing, and talking with those involved in the horrors – an epistemology of "the eyewitness" that will return in the accounts of Black missionaries. "In one village which I passed through," the missionary continued, "I saw two or three men on the

16 The crown domain – King Leopold's private fiefdom (established in 1896) – was the most profitable of all the sectors (Nelson 1994: 94).

wayside quite recently killed – about an hour before. The sentry who had to oversee the gathering of the rubber told me they had killed the men because they had not brought in the rubber" (Morel 1919: 43).

Here, as elsewhere, Morel points at the Black troops as the willful executioners of the dirty work of the Congo Free State. Under the auspices of non-commissioned white officers (Nelson 1994: 106), whose casual attitude towards Black casualties was immortalized in Conrad's novella (cf. below), Black soldiers punished those who had not "brought in the rubber". Sjöblom concludes his horror story by describing the perversity of the rubber trade (Morel 1919: 43):

> When I crossed the stream I saw some dead bodies hanging down from the branches in the water. As I turned away my face at the horrible sight one of the native corporals who was following us down said, "Oh, that is nothing, a few days ago I returned from a fight, and I brought the white man 160 hands and they were thrown into the river."

Revolting[17] mutilations (e.g. cutting off hands) were standard procedure in the Congo Free State under Leopold – a process executed by Blacks themselves, as Morel stresses. Throughout his work, he describes with indignation how "a large body of troops [was] recruited from the most savage tribes in the Upper Congo", who, after being drafted to "'camps of military instruction'", were "equipped with modern rifles of precision" (ibid: 24). Morel underscores that these soldiers were themselves forcefully "obtained by armed raids upon villages, differing in no degree from the raids of the Arabs except that they were accompanied by greater loss of life" (ibid), thus also effectively casting them as slaves. This discursive template is reinforced by Morel's explicit assertion that those captured were "a portion of the libérés – so-called free slaves" (ibid).[18]

Morel's depiction of the Black soldiers as "free slaves" fits in with his representation of the Congo Free State as a slave region, a well-known topos already discussed in the previous chapter. The other topos from the last chapter, the Congo-as-Savage, also appears often in Red Rubber. Morel's repeated condemnation of the Congolese as "savages" with guns is a case in point. "The soldiers are themselves savages," a Baptist missionary of the crown domain is cited as saying, "some even

17 Photographic evidence of these mutilations re-energized the CRA in 1904 (Grant 2005: 66).

18 Those forcefully captured belonged to the "outcasts and inferiors" of Congolese society, as Nelson notes (1994: 106-107), many of whom were people with low status, thus adding another defaming description to the large archive of negative comments about Congo slaves within academic Congoism.

cannibals, trained to use rifles, and in many cases they are sent away without any supervision, and they do as they please" (Morel 1919: 47). An independent English explorer goes beyond even these descriptions, calling them "the lowest type of natives, almost invariably cannibals" (ibid: 58). "The savage" slips often in these accounts into the "cannibal", and this is also the case in Heart of Darkness. The passages concerning the Congolese "fireman" with "filed teeth" (Conrad 2006: 36-37) testify to this slippage, as well as anecdotes from the "enlisted" ship crew of "twenty cannibals" who were considered "fine fellows – cannibals – in their place" (ibid: 40-41). In Conrad's story, the lowest of Blacks (cannibals) serve the brutal Congo Free State, and in doing so, were considered by Conrad and others "in their place" – their alleged inhuman behavior (devouring people) was not out of place in the murderous Congo Free State.

Despite these occasional references to the Congo-as-Savage (and its variation Congo as a cannibal), however, the Congo-as-Slave is most apparent in Morel's Red Rubber. Leopold was repeatedly depicted as the "absentee landlord" (Morel 1919: 36, 133), a well-known topos associated with British planters and slaveholders in the West Indies (Morgan 2007: 34, 39; Ryden 2009: 21, 33). Leopold is said to have systematically organized and condoned slave raids in order to mobilize the necessary labor forces for his "rubber slave trade" (Morel 1919: 98). The problems with this slave economy were manifold, according to Morel. For one, the coercive, concession-driven policies of the Congo Free State had negative effects on the morality of the white man. One may point here to the cynical, laconic "white man in an unbuttoned uniform" in Heart of Darkness, whose hospitality and cheerfulness remained intact after just witnessing "the body of a middle-aged negro with a bullet-hole in the forehead" (Conrad 2006: 20). The Congolese, in turn, were, according to Morel, also wronged by Leopold and the Belgian state. When the latter took over the Congo Free State, Belgium's tactics were similarly oppressive, Morel found; both authorities, the Belgian state and the king, according to Morel, degraded the lives of the Congolese.

Morel depicted the "Congo slave" in Red Rubber as a "broken man" (1919: 217) by continuously referencing Congolese imprisoned in the hostage house, flogged by the Chicotte, raided and forced into slavery by the servants of empire, exploited in chain-gangs, and living "under the shadow of the sentry's rifle" (ibid: 86-87). A passage in which Morel attempts to paint a picture of their wretchedness serves well as an example of how the author describes the Congolese: "See these men in whom the very manhood seems stamped out dragging themselves back from the bush at the day's end after a weary search through partly submerged forest, knee-deep, waist-deep, in fetid swamp" (ibid: 84-85). As when quoting from Congo missionaries like Sjöblom, Morel emphasizes "seeing" and "experiencing" in discussing these Congolese "men" whose "very manhood seems stamped out" (ibid: 84). Morel wrote in order to evoke the surroundings – as if he stood next to the Congolese as they experienced these horrors. This is particularly apparent when Morel continues his story by describing the miserable living conditions of these workers and the effects these had on them: "The rain invades their scanty shelter, and the night-wind chills their naked bodies racked with rheumatism and fevers, their minds a prey to superstitious fears [...] exposed, unarmed and helpless, to the attack of some roving leopard. What thoughts are theirs!" (ibid: 85). Morel did not know, but it did not keep him from making calculated guesses: "Day after day the year round until death in some form – by violence, exhaustion, exposure, or disease, or mere weariness and sorrow – closes the term of an everlasting and to them – mysterious visitation" (ibid). Morel knows little about these men, but he does know, in the end, that they do not understand death.

Through passages such as these, Morel's Red Rubber depicts the Congolese as an innocent, ignorant, helpless, and superstitious population that worked itself to death without even understanding that "mysterious visitation" (ibid: 85; a claim already at work in de Gobineau's writing). Morel balances this picture of innocence with the violence of how "in the distant village wives and children live at the mercy of the capriciousness, cruelty, and lust of the armed ruffian set there by the white man" (ibid: 84). Morel describes these soldiers as "fierce, all-powerful, speaking another tongue, tribal enemies perchance, or maybe the worst malefactors in the community" who were "specially selected for that very reason as the most fitting instruments of oppression: men whose lightest word is law, who have but to lift a finger – they and their bodyguard of retainers – and death or torture rewards protest" (ibid). Morel subsequently listed the crimes of these "exotics introduced by the white man's 'civilisation'" (ibid), ranging from "rape of the newly-married wife" (ibid) to "bestialities foul and nameless" that "satanic[ally] crushed" the Congo – the "body, soul, and spirit in a people – crushing so complete, so thorough, so continuous, that the capacity of resisting aught, however vile, slowly perishes" (ibid: 85). The discursive event of sexual violence – "rape of the newly married wife" – endures, and this story will return in the next chapter, with almost the exact same wording.

By contrasting these bestial, rapist Black helpers of white civilization to the innocent bulk of the population, Morel constructed a framework of Congolese dualities in which the worst and the best could be expected – oscillating between innocence and viciousness, between untouched by white civilization and too thoroughly permeated by it, and between a people oriented toward family and sexual predators.

Although Red Rubber undeniably attempted to incorporate Congolese into a "black humanity" (ibid: 91), the "primitive simplicity" of Congolese (ibid: 94) reduced them to ciphers for misery and victimhood. Indeed, through his friendship with Mary Kingsley and other relativist anthropologists and travelers, Morel probably did consider "African" culture worthy of respect, as Grant suggests (2005: 33). However, the essentialist opposition between "the European" and "the inhabitant of Tropical Africa" in the "actual stage of our evolution" (Morel 1919: 185) highlights that Morel's "black humanity" rang hollow. Morel's pleas for empathy by reminding the reader of the manhood, familial privacy, and social life of the Congolese by no means offset his essentialism.

The rhetorical strategy employed by Morel – "watching" and "feeling" the suffering of the Congolese – harkened back to 19th-century abolitionist discourse. Emblematic of this discourse was the 19th-century anti-slavery medallion, which depicted an enchained Black man in a supplicant posture asking the (white) viewer: "Am I not a Man and a Brother?" (Hall 2003b: 250). Morel's use of this kind of strategy was not wholly surprising, given that many Victorian anti-slavery organizations and their leadership integrated themselves into the Protestant missionary societies in Britain, which, in turn, embraced abolition as a central cause in their civilizing mission (Grant 2005: 26). As missionaries played a central role in mobilizing popular support for the Congo Reform campaign in Britain, protests against the "new slaveries", as Grant called them, reawakened paternalistic discourse expressing neo-abolitionist sympathy for the Congolese (ibid: 41). Bearing this in mind, it was no coincidence that Morel used a quotation from American abolitionist William Lloyd Garrison as the epigraph of his book.[19]

While the forced labor system under Leopold and the early Belgian colonial regime caused a bloodbath among the Congolese, Blacks in the American South were facing "Jim Crow" apartheid. Disenfranchisement laws "swept like a tide over the Southern states during the period from 1875 to 1910", as the influential 1944 study An American Dilemma: The Negro Problem and Modern Democracy by the Swedish economist and sociologist Gunnar Myrdal noted (1944: 580). Through "grandfather clauses", poll taxes, literacy tests, and "white primaries", voting registration and political participation increasingly depended on free ancestry, education, and income. These restrictions were overwhelmingly anti-Black, although poorer whites were forced out of the political machinery as well (ibid: 480-484, 489). Jim Crow

19 "The standard of emancipation in now unfurled. / Let all the enemies of the persecuted blacks tremble / I will be as harsh as truth and as compromising as justice. / I am in earnest; / I will not equivocate, / I will not excuse, / I will not retreat a single inch: / And I will be heard. / Posterity will bear testimony that I was right" (Morel 1919: n.p.).

discrimination was justified through the "separate but equal" doctrine – separating schools, railroad cars, hotels and restaurants, and other public places along perceived racial lines. Black infrastructure throughout the era, if it existed at all, was mostly underfunded or of poor quality (Bair 2005: 25; Myrdal 1944: 579-580). The rapid "restoration of white supremacy in the late 'seventies" (Myrdal 1944: 580) through Jim Crow legislation led to a renewed and steep decline in the political, civic, material, and social status of Blacks in the Southern states in the post-Civil War and post-Reconstruction era. As in the Congo Free State, the Jim Crow laws were based on coercion and violence. In an attempt to restore labor conditions to what they had been in times of slavery (ibid: 228), white supremacist Southern elites passed "lien laws"[20] and "vagrancy laws",[21] both of which were initiated to keep the labor of freedmen cheap and available. Everyday threats of psychic and physical violence towards Blacks served to further justify Jim Crow laws (Gaines 1996: 52). Given the "weak legal tradition" (Myrdal 1944: 229) of the South, police forces and courts were active agents in upholding peonage systems by supplying the necessary labor forces for white employers.

Another result of the "weak legal tradition" was that planters and other whites had few scruples about taking the law into their own hands in order to impose sanctions on the Black opposition. "Threats, whippings, and even more serious forms of violence have been customary caste sanctions utilized to maintain a strict discipline over Negro labor which are seldom employed against white labor", Myrdal notes

20 Lien laws regulated a credit system widely applied to cotton farmers from the 1860s to the 1930s. Sharecroppers and tenant farmers who did not own the land obtained supplies and food on credit from local merchants, who, in turn, held a lien on the respective crop (Bair 2005: 3). While production levels and charges for seeds and equipment were high (ibid), the prices paid by those merchants frequently and unjustly were not, therefore creating a debt cycle sharecroppers and tenant farmers could hardly escape. The lien laws enabled debt peonage, or compulsory labor based on indebtedness (Myrdal 1944: 228-229).

21 Vagrancy laws allowed for the forced labor of apprehended vagrants (those homeless, unemployed, or involved in petty crimes, often due to the debt trap they were in; Bair 2005: 16). Convicted loiterers and vagrants were hired out to planters, mine owners, road contractors, and turpentine farmers, sometimes in chain gangs (Myrdal 1944: 228; Bair 2005: 16-17). The brunt of this "convict-lease system" was borne by African Americans, as they constituted 60 to 90 percent of the prison population in Southern jails (Bair 2005: 16-17). Although these numbers gradually declined at the turn of the century, by 1940, Blacks still represented 44 percent of the male prisoners in the Southern States, though only 23.8 percent of the total population was Black (Myrdal 1944: 554).

(1944: 229; cf. Bair 2005: 28-29). Without fear of legal reprisal, a pattern of violence against Blacks developed (Myrdal 1944: 559). Lynching constituted one type of extralegal violence, increasing in the late 1880s after its initial rise from 1830 to the 1850s as a way of punishing white men (ibid: 560). In addition to escalating this violence to "epidemic" numbers (Grossman 2005: 81)[22] and contributing to the dehumanization of Blacks, it had a devastating effect on the Black opposition and its white supporters, as well as on the legal and political mainstream.

Anti-lynching activists in the United States took up topoi and employed argumentative tools similar to those of Morel and Conrad. Eyewitness accounts of horror, savagery, barbarism, and extreme violence were also used in the influential work of Black journalist and Civil Rights leader Ida B. Wells-Barnett, the 1895 pamphlet "A Red Record", which tackled lynching in the South. She addressed the subject via statistical evidence (not regarding the number of victims, but the rationale behind the violence) of "Negroes [being] whipped, scourged, exiled, shot and hung whenever and wherever it pleased the white man" (Wells-Barnett 1996: 77).

She also discussed case studies based on reports from white newspapers: "Out of their own mouths shall the murderers be condemned," she wrote (ibid: 82). In the main body of her pamphlet, Wells-Barnett provided detailed descriptions of the lynchings. Moving case by case, Wells-Barnett turned to white newspapers, such as the Memphis Commercial, for information on how, for instance, prisoners were taken from the "county jail" with little to no resistance against the "patrolmen" to be hanged on a "telegraph pole just north of the prison" (ibid: 113). In that same case, Wells-Barnett quoted the newspaper's description of how the alleged rapist was "half dragged, half carried to the corner of Front Street and the alley between Sycamore and Mill, and hung" (ibid), all the while being beaten, cursed, spat at, and cut into pieces by the mob. The newspaper wrote in gruesome detail, "One or two knife cuts, more or less, made little difference in the appearance of the dead rapist, however, for before the rope was around his neck his skin was cut almost to ribbons" (ibid: 114). Nauseating eyewitness reports like these were used frequently by Wells-Barnett to make her point.

Wells-Barnett often described the stabbing, burning, and mutilation of Black people as "horrors" and did not hesitate to label it in ways that stung contemporaries: She called lynching a savagery and a "Southern barbarism" (ibid: 76) that was executed by "barbarous people" (ibid: 106). The barbarism of lynching was fre-

22 While the lynching of Black people averaged near two hundred a year in the 1890s, by the 1940s it had dropped to 4 (Myrdal 1944: 561). In the end, lynching cost the lives of about 3,800 Blacks (Gossett 2005: 270).

quently referred to by her as a "revolting savagery" (ibid: 108) or "savage orgies" (ibid: 100) which demonstrated a "contempt of civilization" (ibid: 82) that would not have gone unnoticed in "non-civilized" areas of the world. "If it were known that the cannibals or the savage Indians had burned three human beings alive in the past two years," Wells-Barnett wrote, "the whole of Christendom would be roused, to devise ways and means to put a stop to it" (ibid: 74). Since the lynching did not occur "in the wilds of interior Africa" but in the "American civilization" (ibid: 112), it could "be passed by unnoticed, to be denied or condoned as the requirements of any future emergency might determine" (ibid). While these comments aimed at highlighting the one-sided interest of white Americans in oppressing minorities, Wells-Barnett implicitly created, or at least gestured toward, a dichotomy between American civilization and the "cannibals" and "savages" from interior Africa.

Wells-Barnett and journalists from The Chicago Defender mobilized a vocabulary similar to Morel's to address white cruelty, too. On September 27, 1930, the article "Southern Savages" reported on the lynching of two accused robbers while they were being transferred to another town for a court hearing. These "chaps were murdered [...] to satisfy the blood lust of brutal, cruel, stupid men, far closer to the beast – nearer the ape –than their black brothers" (1930a: 14). This explicit reversal of stereotypes (Blacks calling whites "apes" instead of the other way around, as seen in de Gobineau's writing) is reinforced by the final statements made in the article. "Southern whites are given to ranting about their superiority over the Negro race," the article maintained, but "that boast becomes a hideous joke when they sink to such barbarism as this" (ibid). This appropriation of supremacist slander and vocabulary is even more demonstrable in "On with Democracy", an article published on June 30, 1928, two years prior to Wells-Barnett's pamphlet and just after another lynching in Houston. In this case, the article ended by openly ridiculing "the better class of white people of Houston" (1928b: A2). Because this "better" class distanced itself from the lynchings by "white hoodlums", but did not manage to produce adequate legislation against this kind of violence, The Chicago Defender accused them of being "Hypocrites – Anglo-Saxons, Nordics, southerners, aristocrats, whites, Democrats – Hypocrites" (ibid).

This bold language returned in the context of urban violence as well, in both the North and the South. Although instances of this violence were referred to as "race riots" by many contemporaries, Wells-Barnett maintained in "A Red Record" they were as much an "appalling slaughter of colored people" (1996: 73) as in more rural areas. She stated: "It was always a remarkable feature in these insurrections and riots that only Negroes were killed during the rioting, and that all the white men escaped unharmed" (ibid). The list of riots shows how big of a national problem this actually became in the early to mid-20th century, including riots in New York City in 1900, Springfield (Ohio) in 1904, Atlanta and Greensburg (Indiana) in 1906, Springfield (Illinois) in 1908, Tulsa (Oklahoma) in 1921, Watsonville (California) in 1930, and Detroit in 1943 (cf. Tuttle 1970: 11). Standing out in this period of mass violence and death was the "red summer" of 1919, as James Weldon Johnson famously called it in his autobiography Along this Way, which saw "bloody race riots" between April and October 1919 in "Chicago, in Omaha, in Longview, Texas, in Philips County, Arkansas, in Washington, and other communities" (1969: 341). About 120 people died, the majority of them Black (Tuttle 1970: 14).

Like the lynchings in the South, riots in the North had a decisively corrective, disciplinary trait. In Chicago, for instance, the tensions surrounding the housing and job markets had been made worse by the influx of thousands of returning veterans (about 50.000, Tuttle 1970: 106 suggests) and Black Southern immigrant workers drawn to the job opportunities in the booming war economy of the Illinois metropolis. Mob violence aimed at keeping these Blacks "in their place", as James Weldon Johnson phrased it in his autobiography (1969: 341). In the competitive post-war economy, marked by rising unemployment and the worst labor strife since the 1890s (Tuttle 1970: 19), Black and white Chicagoans battled the streets for five days. The riot was set in motion by the death of eighteen-year-old Eugene Williams, who was knocked into Lake Michigan on Sunday, July 27, 1919. His drowning, and the lack of assistance by a white police officer, ignited "a battle royale", as The Chicago Defender had it in its article "Riot Sweeps Chicago" (1919a: 1), resulting in the death of twenty-three Blacks and fifteen whites. Over 500 Chicagoans were injured, and the homes of thousands, Black and white, were burned to the ground (Grossman 2005: 119). In its discussion of the "underlying cause" of this "disgrace of American civilization" (1919b: 16)), The Chicago Defender explained the riot by pointing to white prejudice, economic and social discrimination, and renewed Black confidence. It was one of the first times that Blacks pushed back violently, the newspaper suggested, thus leading to the death of fifteen whites. The Chicago Defender stated: "America is known the world over as the land of the lyncher and of the mobocrat. For years she has been sowing the wind and now she is reaping the whirlwind" (ibid).

The reason why Blacks pushed back, even through counter-violence, was that World War I had, according to The Chicago Defender, changed things. "The Black worm has turned. A Race that has furnished hundreds of thousands of the best soldiers that the world has ever seen is no longer content to turn the left cheek when smitten upon the right" (1919a: 1). The newspaper thus connected the confidence that many African American soldiers brought home from their tour of duty in

World War I to the increased political and social activism at home. The Chicago Defender went on to assert that particularly "the younger generation of black men are not content to move along the line of least resistance as did their sires" (ibid).

Thus, despite living in the land of the "lyncher and of the mobocrat" (ibid), African Americans had gained new self-confidence from their constructive contributions in the military and as a labor force in the war economy of the United States, according to the paper. This explained why Blacks resisted the violence of the whites. "We have little sympathy with lawlessness, whether those guilty of it be black or white," the editorial continued, "but it cannot be denied that we have much in the way of justification for our changed attitude" (ibid). This changed attitude pervaded the 20th-century African American communities, which bore witness to what would be labeled the "New Negro".

Supremacy Opposed (and Re-affirmed)

African American intellectuals responded systematically to the omnipresent anti-Black stereotypes and derogatory naturalizations in American culture described in previous sections. To derail cultural stereotypes was an enormous task, however – especially because Black Americans possessed limited control over the mass media, despite the successful establishment of major African American newspapers such as The Washington Bee, The Richmond Planet, and The Chicago Defender (Bair 2005: 53). A new leading catchphrase among African American intellectual activists was the "New Negro". Like many Black American activisms before and after, the New Negro employed a double strategy of "Pushing B(l)ack" – or Blacks fighting back against white "social terrorism", as Locke phrased it in his introduction to the collection The New Negro, while at the same time strengthening their own identity through "race pride" (Locke 1992: 6-7).

The figure of the New Negro circulated constantly and was propagated by authors with widely differing ideological programs. For instance, Marcus Garvey rejected Booker T. Washington by calling him "the great Sage of Tuskegee" (2006: 41) and criticized him posthumously for failing to strengthen the "political voice of the Negro" (ibid). The nationalist organizer claimed: "No leader can successfully lead his race of ours without giving an interpretation of the awakened spirit of the New Negro" (ibid). Garvey overlooked however, at least rhetorically, that the accommodating Washington actually had addressed the New Negro in his collection A New Negro for a New Century in 1900. Other works addressing this figure would follow: William Pickens's The New Negro: His Political, Civil and Mental Status and Related Essays (1916), and Alain Locke's seminal collection The New Negro:

Voices of the Harlem Renaissance (1925) were books by highly educated authors who mobilized the topos of the New Negro as much as Garvey and Washington.

Differences in how the New Negro concept was used cannot be overlooked, either. Washington and Pickens employed it as a quintessential "contributionist" tool for discussing (inter)national Black achievers in the field of industry, education, and particularly the military. Locke, on the other hand, took up this topos for his very local, "romantic, apolitical movement of the arts", as Gates and Jarret describe it (2007: 13). Locke thus focused on the cultural production of Black artists in Harlem, which constituted the self-proclaimed "pulse of the Negro world" (Locke 1992: 14).

Despite their differences, central ideas kept returning in the discussion about the "New Negro". On the one hand, the New Negro expressed a "concern with time, antecedents, and heritage", as Gates and Jarrett suggested (2007: 4). On the other hand, it indicated "a concern for a cleared space, the public face of the race" (ibid). Against this framework of glorious pasts and fresh starts, the proclamation of "newness" asserted a conscientious beginning that depended fundamentally on a negation of an earlier type of Black American (ibid) – "new" is constantly pitched against "old". The "Negro of to-day," as Washington's introduction to A New Negro for a New Century states, "is in every phase of life far advanced over the Negro 30 years ago" (1900: 3). Those old Blacks were the "ignorant Negros" from the "Reconstruction days", as Pickens also claimed (1916: 38).

"Old Negroes" included those of the slave period. Fannie Barrier Williams's contribution on the Black women's club movement,[23] "The Club Movement Among Colored Women of America", which appeared in Washington's A New Negro for a New Century, provides an excellent example of how this distance from the slave era was established. In her essay, Williams discussed the movement as the producer and hotbed of a "new" Black woman who "succeeded in lifting herself as completely from the stain and meanness of slavery" (1900: 424). For Williams (and other "New Negro" thinkers), slavery was more than an economic system; it was a submissive subjectivity inherited from the past that strongly marked contemporary mentalities. Locke wrote, for instance: "The day of 'aunties,' 'uncles' and 'mam-

23 The club movement itself was a model example of newness, of course, since it contributed strongly to the ascent of female voices in the debates in African American bourgeois communities. This manifested itself in a wide variety of political and cultural societies, such as the fast-growing and influential National Association of Colored Women (Grossman 2005: 91). On top of this, it enabled the emergence of numerous authors of fiction and non-fiction, such as Ida B. Wells-Barnett and Fannie Barrier Williams, mentioned above (Bair 2005: 57-66).

mies' is equally gone. Uncle Tom and Sambo have passed on" (1925: 5), referring to the dismissive and dehumanizing labels employed by white and Black Americans in times of slavery and the Jim Crow laws.

The case against the slavish "Old Negro" was made repeatedly in this period. For instance, George S. Schuyler's essay "The Rise of the Black Internationale" still alluded to this image of slavery in 1938 when he wrote that the New Negro, with whom he associated both African Americans and their "cousins in India, Malaysia, the Caribbean and China", is "no longer blindly worshipful of his rulers", as opposed to those "who dropped [their] shackles in 1863" (2007: 153). Although he also claimed that the New Negro was "no more courageous than the Old Negro" (ibid), it cannot be overlooked that the New Negro was, at least in Schyler's discourse, an entity superior to the old one. The "ignorance" and "lethargy" of the past was substituted for the slickness of the New Negro, who was "better informed, privy to the past, understanding of the present, unafraid of the future" (ibid).

Turning away from the "Old Negro" – including the "patient, unquestioning, devoted demi-slave" from Reconstruction times (Pickens 1916: 236) – signified a move towards the embrace of a "self-conscious, aspiring, proud" Black persona (ibid). The notion of self-help abounded in this discourse. While Fannie Barrier Williams stressed the autodidactic quality of the women's club movement, Locke highlighted the idea of transcending the racist status quo through "self-expression" (1925: 5), which would finally bring an end to the "old epoch of philanthropic guidance, sentimental appeal and protest" (ibid: 7). The "New Negro" would no longer take the ongoing racial derision lightly. This was exemplified by Fannie Barrier Williams's story in her essay "The Club Movement Among Colored Women of America" of the nation-wide response by Black women to "some obscure editor in a Missouri town" who published a "libelous article in which the colored women of the country were described as having no sense of virtue and altogether without character" (1900: 397). By contrasting this overwhelming response with the probable lack of one "twenty years prior to this time [when] a similar publication would scarcely have been noticed" (ibid), Williams elevated her own times, describing how this "vulgar attack" was met with "mass meetings [...] held in every part of the country to denounce the editor and refute the charges" (ibid). It is this "frankness and open expression of opinion", as Pickens termed it, that was the overt expression of the "New Negro" (1916: 37).

Another dominant idea was that the "New Negro" should be an interracial persona. One might turn here to Fannie Barrier Williams's assertion that the club movement in general, and the National Association of Colored Women in particular, aimed to emancipate Black and white women alike. The aim was to integrate

Black women in the "classification of progressive womanhood in America" and to help white women to "emancipate" themselves from "the fear and uncertainty of contact and association with women of the darker race" (1900: 402). Education was the path to freedom. "In considering the social advancement of these women," Williams noted, "it is important to keep in mind the point from which progress began" (ibid: 382). That starting point was self-education. These women, Williams asserted, "have been mainly self-taught in all those precious things that make for social order, purity and character" (ibid). The "progress" announced (and practiced) here, as well as the emphasis on "order, purity, and character" (ibid), also highlighted the staying power of Victorian mores. Respectable reproductive sexuality, as practiced within the safe confines of marriage and the home, were still very much de rigueur, it seems (cf. Gaines 1996: 12), along with restricted entry to professions beyond teaching children.[24]

Locke, too, emphasized education, albeit with quite a different slant than Williams's. In his introduction to the collection The New Negro, education was considered to liberate "the minds of most of us, black and white" from the stereotypes of oppression, which barred the road to "true social self-understanding" (1992: 4). Education, however, meant formal education to Locke, not self-schooling (which African American female leaders advocated). Locke, instead, asked for a "scientific rather than an emotional interest" to be invested in Black America (ibid: 8) – a view that was seconded by Pickens, among others, who underscored the need for a "scientific spirit, which seeks the facts, all of the facts, and faces the full meaning of those facts, regardless of prejudice or preconception" (1916: 206). The insistence on the primacy of "scientism" (Hall 2009: 192) blocked those who lacked academic credentials from entering public discourse (Jardins 2003: 122). "Self-taught" women were among the first who suffered from the opposition between thinkers and doers, the trained and untrained, and professionals versus amateurs. These oppositions were created by first-generation academics like Locke and Du Bois (ibid), and, as a consequence of these oppositions, they distanced themselves from women as interpreters of social and historical processes (ibid).

This epistemic gatekeeping by, and shifting of authority to, roughly two percent of the Black male population (Gaines 1996: xiv), was highly noticeable in the academic field of history, which was a closed, male world until the 1940s, when Black women obtained their first PhDs in the field (Jardins 2003: 141; Dagbovie 2010:

24 Exemplified by the skepticism and hostility of Black ministers to Ida B. Wells-Barnett's anti-lynching campaign (Gaines 1996: 13).

101).[25] Black women did write histories, however. Many were "historians without portfolio", as Dagbovie noted (2010: 103). They taught and wrote about Black history as schoolteachers, club women, reformers, novelists, authors of children's books, or journalists for local newspapers (ibid: 123-124). The works of the novelist Pauline Hopkins and of educators such as Leila Pendleton (e.g. A Narrative of the Negro) and Drusilla Houston (e.g. Wonderful Ethiopians of the Ancient Cushite Empire) testify to the hands-on approach applied by African American women as "disseminators, populizers, researchers, and catalogers" (Dagbovie 2010: 147). However, gender bias deeply affected the professionalization and institutionalization of science and Black literacy in general, the resources and jobs required for which (those of librarians and school teachers excepted) were overwhelmingly controlled and taken by Black men (Jardins 2003: 122-124).

This was particularly visible in the thriving discipline of history, which was dominated by male historians (Hall 2009:190). These men gained prominence in the broader context of the proliferation of academic departments from the 1870s onward (Burke 2012: 169). Noticeable markers for the success of history departments in the United States were the foundation of Black historical organizations at the turn of the century (e.g. Association for the Study of Negro Life and History in 1915), as well as university presses (e.g. Tuskegee's Yearbook Publishing Company in 1913), journals (e.g. Journal of Negro History in 1916), Black libraries (e.g. at Atlanta University between 1907-1919), and the strengthening and development of history departments in Black colleges and universities (e.g. Howard University by 1905; cf. Hall 2009: 88-198). The historical work of the handful of Black PhDs in white elite institutions, such as Du Bois and Alain Locke at Harvard, was distinctly different from the avocational work of the earlier Black intellectuals, although they were still required to build upon these earlier histories (Hall 2009: 191).

All of these institutional, content-related, and personal changes and achievements, however, were made possible by a broadening of the base of literate and educated Blacks. Between 1870 and 1910, literacy rates went up from 19 percent to 61 percent (Grossman 2005: 81), which led, among many other changes, to the long-term establishment and proliferation of the Black press. The journalistic landscape was diverse – from independent weeklies such as the "fearless" Chicago Defender (Grossman 2005: 109) and monthlies such as the Colored American Magazine to institutional publications like The Crisis from the civil rights organization National Association for the Advancement of Colored People (NAACP hereafter).

25 Social activist Anna Julia Cooper became the first Black American woman to receive a PhD in history, awarded by the Sorbonne University in Paris (Dagbovie 2010: 117).

The underlying philosophy of the ongoing Black organization and institutionalization – from the women's club movement to the male-dominated Black history movement – was the ideology of "uplift". "Among colored women," Fannie Barrier Williams explicitly wrote in "The Club Movement Among Colored Women of America", "the [black women's] club is [...] only one of many means for the social uplift of a race" (1900: 383). "Uplift" continually reappeared in later writings on the "New Negro". For instance, the increasingly left-leaning W.E.B. Du Bois remained loyal to this concept from the early 20th century all the way up to the middle of it – addressing the concept both in "The Negro Mind Reaches Out", Du Bois's contribution to Locke's collection The New Negro (1925: 390-397), as well as in his essay "Prospect of a World Without Race Conflict" two decades later (1944).

"Uplift" reflected heavily the idea of the "progress of civilization", as Pickens phrased it (1916: 13). The role of the "race" was discussed through the lens of "race solidarity" (Locke 1925: 7). Despite this call for unity, uplift ideology also reflected and reproduced the social tensions within the African American community. Class stratification pervaded the "New Negro" discourse. "Among colored women," Fannie Barrier Williams asserted, "the club is the effort of the few competent in behalf of the many incompetent" (1900: 383), subsequently discussing the latter as the "many unprotected and defenseless colored girls to be found in every large city" (420). The same dichotomy of many versus few is evoked by Locke, who distinguished between the "multitude" and the "thinking few" (1925: 4). This "thinking few" consisted of the "more intelligent and representative elements of the two race groups" (ibid: 9). A similarly elitist split is produced for white America by Pickens, who, in discussing the critical public opinion makers regarding Blacks, boiled the problem down to "the ignorance of the better class of white people" towards the "better class of colored people who live in their community" (1916: 225).

In his seminal The Negro of Philadelphia, which does not employ the label of the "New Negro" (it appeared too early) but already alludes to its major characteristics, Du Bois openly called for interracial solidarity between the "better classes" (e.g. 1899: 39, 348, 350, 357), identifying them as the Black "middle class" throughout his work (e.g. ibid: 7, 58, 117, 317, 444). Du Bois wrote, "In their efforts for the uplifting of the Negro the people of Philadelphia must recognize the existence of the better class of Negroes and must gain the active aid and co-operation by generous and polite conduct" (ibid: 397). In the typical interracial, classist vein of "New Negro" discourse, he added: "Social sympathy must exist between what is best in both races and there must no longer be the feeling that the Negro who makes the best of himself is of least account" (ibid). Du Bois ended by stating who belonged to this better Black class, namely "men and women educated and in many cases cultured [...] but their active aid cannot be gained for purely selfish motives [...] and above all they object to being patronized" (ibid).

All in all, the trope of the "better" classes suggested a common ground between white and Black middle classes based on a bourgeois morality and social capital. Education and culture, self-sufficiency, and individual ambitions are returning elements that bridge the territory of white and Black. Pickens added another set of elements to the list – "pride, ambition, self-respect, un-satisfaction with the lower positions of life, and the desire to live in a beautiful house and to keep his wife and children at home and out of 'service'" (1916: 229).

The dominant ideology of material and professional progression through self-help, racial solidarity, temperance, thrift, chastity, and the accumulation of wealth (ultimately leading to a "beautiful house", as Pickens imagined it), allowed for little solidarity with the "happy-go-lucky life of the lowest classes", as Du Bois phrased it in The Philadelphia Negro (1899: 60). Describing the lowest strata of Black life as "cheerful" and "good-natured" (ibid), Du Bois came close to evoking the minstrel stereotypes that saturated American popular culture throughout the period. By occasionally and strategically embracing these stereotypes, Black opinion asserted the superiority of their own class. Crime, prostitution, and dependence on aid organizations (Blair 2005: 14) could be sharply contrasted to the (allegedly) independent middle-class way of life. Black independence, however, as the critical sociologist Franklin Frazier wrote in his "La Bourgeoisie Noire" at the end of the 20s, was mainly rhetorical, especially for large parts of the Black intelligentsia. Whereas the "Negro business [...] can boast of the fact that he is independent of white support," Frazier wrote, "the Negro artist still seeks it" (2007: 140).

Frazier wrote these words in the heyday of the Harlem Renaissance, when New York-based Black artists successfully claimed their turf in mainstream American culture. More books by Blacks were published during the 20s and 30s than ever before (Singh 2004: 25-26). The central figures of the movement were deeply dependent on and indebted to the white middle and upper classes, who acted as patrons and were instrumental to the financial survival and intellectual development of the Renaissance (Kellner 2004: 53). Despite the "New Negro's" push for independence and self-empowerment through control of the imagery of Black people (Feith 2004: 278), the taste and preference of white boosters, publishers, and audiences did ultimately greatly affect the overall production of the Renaissance. Claude McKay's exotic urban Bohemia, as presented in his bestselling novel Home to Harlem, was clearly favored above the down-to-earth bourgeois Black characters in Jessie Fauset's Plum Bun. In the milieu of the Harlem Renaissance, Black authors sought means of self-expression while white sponsors simultaneously nurtured a taste for the exotic and celebrated a Black primitivism and vitality that reduced Blacks to their bodies, otherness, and instincts (ibid: 283). It is against this background of Black sensualization, idealization, and downright cliché that a set of images of the Congo could emerge.

Apart from interracial cooperation and dependence, elite Black rhetoric was deeply marked by conservative gender politics, allocating women to the domestic arena and men to the public sphere. Amidst the continual push by Black women to gain access to the male-dominated public discourse, "uplift" often pitted Black men against Black women, in the process reflecting and reproducing the prevailing misogynist and late Victorian attitudes (Gaines 1996: 13). "To keep his wife and children at home and out of 'service'", as Pickens described it (1916: 229), clearly belonged to the core of required discursive attitudes. Fannie Barrier Williams would cater to this stance by discussing "colored women as mothers, as home-makers" (1900: 379). The male counterpart to this domestic, "pure" womanhood was the role of the Black protector – both of women and of the country (cf. Gaines 1996: 52). The central topos in this context is the confident, reliable, able, and patriotic African American soldier, which was a continuation of the late 19th-century fascination with military prowess and national loyalty as a rare outlet for courageous masculinity (ibid: 27). In this "New Negro" rhetoric, Black soldiers figure prominently. For instance, they are discussed in the context of the Spanish-American War in Washington's A New Negro for a New Century. Pickens saw the "Negro soldier" as the "decisive blow" against the Confederates in the Civil War (1916: 135).

The ideology of "uplift" did not merely pertain to the national arena; it also manifested itself in a view of international politics that had strong imperialist and colonialist motives. As an ideology rooted in class, gender, and ethnic inequality, "uplift" neatly fitted into U.S. imperialism (Gaines 1996: 4). Black nationalists such as Martin Delany linked Black progress and humanity strongly to territorial expansion and nation building, civilization, and patriarchal authority (Gaines 4; cf. last chapter). In an 1877 speech, Alexander Crummell voiced strong support for the efforts of King Leopold II's AIA (Association Internationale Africaine) as "eminently practical, both with respect to the physical and moral needs of the continent" (qtd. in Füllberg-Stolberg 2003: 228).

Other intellectuals were in touch with colonial powers more directly. At the turn of the century, European powers such as Germany and Belgium flirted with cooperation with internationally renowned Black American intellectuals, such as Booker T. Washington. His focus on uplift, physical and practical work, thrift, and sobriety in Tuskegee's industrial education was seen as a panacea for the "negro problem" within colonialism (Zimmerman 2010: 21-22, 176). The racist American South, and

Washington's accommodation of it, became a model for European colonial rule because of its high agricultural productivity enabled by submissive, hardworking, segregated, and poorly paid Blacks. Washington sent an expedition to Germany's Togo in 1901 to investigate the possibilities of a cotton economy in what Germany planned as a "model colony" with ostensibly humane and "progressive" rule (ibid: 172). Washington would go along with this scheme, as he (and the African American mainstream in general) believed that Black American intellectuals could lead "underclass" Blacks at home and abroad.

Washington and the slave-free "New South" became important landmarks for liberal colonialists who were attempting to build a "humane colonial system in light of the patent economic and social failures of the Congo Free State, whose crimes were increasingly revealed at the turn of the century" (ibid: 204). The Congo Free State, in turn, attempted to revamp its own public profile by associating itself with African Americans in general, and all-Black institutions like Tuskegee and Hampton specifically. Leopold and his proxies, for instance, planned to recruit African American workers as early as 1877 (ibid: 179). Later on, Leopold II approached Washington multiple times (both in 1903 and 1905) to develop a Congolese cotton industry and sent an invitation for him to speak in Brussels (which Washington ultimately declined). Leopold also offered Hampton a collection of books (ibid).

Leopold II's ongoing interest in African American elites was partly due to the fact that the Congo was becoming more and more like the American South. When the rubber economy finally collapsed through the genocidal exhaustion of the Congolese labor force and the over-tapping of rubber vines (Nelson 1994: 115), Belgium assumed sovereignty over the Congo in 1908. It responded to the breakdown by imposing a Southern-style plantation economy on the Congo via its Programme Générale in 1909 (Zimmerman 2010: 116). In 1912, Belgium even announced, though never executed, a plan that it would set up a Tuskegee institute in the Congo (ibid: 179). It strengthened its plantation efforts when commodity prices fell in the 1920s due to the worldwide market crisis and because Katanga's "mineral revolution" (Nelson 1994:126) could no longer finance the colonial state. The 1933 plan for a "total civilization" included the vast expansion of infrastructure and palm, rubber, and coffee plantations based on compulsory, low-wage workers, just as in the American South (ibid: 132-165).

Another similarity between the Belgian Congo and the "New South" was its overt racism. Institutionalized racism and the vast number of statutes and regulations that defined the do's and don'ts of the interaction between the different "races" were the most obvious commonalities. In the Congo, as in the South, the ideology of white supremacy led to de jure racial discrimination, including limitations on the free movement of the Congolese in white areas, restrictions on Black ownership of land, punishment in cases of disrespect towards Europeans, separate labor legislation, and a ban on the consumption of hard liquors for the Congolese. De facto forms of the color bar resulted in the segregation of the public sphere – including trains, hotels, and soccer stadiums – and an unofficial ban on interracial sex, which did not apply to white men (ibid: 183). This was very reminiscent of the American South indeed.

American-Congolese interaction also took place through the Black missionary movement. This was another result of the outward-oriented "uplift" philosophy of the Black American elites. In the wake of worldwide Christian expansionism in the late 19th century, through which the number of American missionaries of all denominations doubled from 1885 onward, at least 113 Black American missionaries were sent to Africa between 1877 and 1900 (Williams 1982: 4-5, 85). These missionaries were overwhelmingly middle class and highly educated in predominantly (white-sponsored) all-Black institutions, such as Lincoln University, which was co-established by northern Presbyterians with the aim of training Black American missionaries (ibid: 41). Since tropical Africa was considered the white man's grave, it was predominantly Blacks who were sent to areas, where the death toll through disease was substantial. This was very much in accordance with the genocidal anti-Black atmosphere of those days, which, in turn, made it difficult to convince well-educated African Americans to go to Africa (ibid: 9, 35).

Starting with the missionary work of Amanda Smith in Liberia (ibid: 14), who promoted her profession continually through speaking tours, African American missionary sentiment seems to have developed in the late 19th century. By the end of the century, the African American missionary movement was in full swing, twenty representatives of which went to the Congo (the second largest contingent, after Liberia)[14] and founded the American Baptist Congo Mission in 1881 (ibid: 19, 85). It is the accounts of (and on) Black missionaries that considerably shaped and influenced the broader Congo discourse at the turn of the century.

FRESH TOPOI, NEW EPISTEMOLOGIES, OLD MEANINGS

First Topos: The Congo-as-Darkness

The arrival of Black and white missionaries constituted a distinguishable discursive event in the overall Congo discourse in the late 19th and early 20th centuries. This continuous attention was part of a larger missionary hype to which most historians and journalists responded affirmatively – at least roughly up until the late 1910s. Although there were notable exceptions to this celebratory attention, such as the reverend Rufus L. Perry's 1888 pamphlet The Cushite; or the Children of Ham (The Negro Race), which flatly ignored the subject,[26] there clearly existed a consensus among Black historians on the desirability and importance of the missionary movement.

The response of Black intellectuals to the movement was instantaneous. Although hardly any Black missionaries worked on the African continent at the time when William T. Alexander published his 1888 History of the Colored Race – Amanda Smith in Liberia, Susan Collins in Angola, and Theophilus E. Scholes in the Congo Free State were the exceptions (Williams 1982: 14, 19) – the author nevertheless lauded the missionary drive of "colored schools" (1888: 530). These schools, Alexander suggested, were "the great hope of Africa's evangelization by her children in America" (ibid). Other historians, spearheaded by Booker T. Washington, sought to integrate this educational connection between Black schools and Africa's evangelization as well.[27]

---

26 This book aimed at proving the ability of Black Americans to progress based on biblical and "ancient literature and archaeology" (Egyptian and Ethiopian ancestry of Black Americans in particular). In the same vein as mid-nineteenth century forefathers such as Lewis with his Light and Truth, Perry used biblical and classical narratives to make a number of theoretical claims about the "the oneness and brotherhood of the human family" (1887: 7) and to draw attention to the fact that "ancient Cushites were the world's magnates and the world's schoolmasters. Those of Ethiopia taught art, science, and theology to the Egyptians, and the Egyptians taught the Eastern nations and the Greeks and the Romans" (ibid: 25). Through his Afrocentric and contributionist approach, Perry aimed at "inspiring the Africo-American with an ambition to emulate his forefathers" (ibid: 31).

27 The 1909 Story of the Negro described Washington's own Tuskegee mission to Togo at length. Washington frequently alluded to Black missionaries (such as Alexander Crummell) in his work, basing his own agricultural and social knowledge on accounts produced by white missionaries (such as Leighton Wilson: Washington 1909a: 44-48, 72). This embrace of missionary work can also be seen in Crogman and Kletzing's 1898 Progress of a Race (the expanded 1920 edition of which is consulted in this work), which incorporated the missionary efforts of the various religious African American churches into its story – such as the "praiseworthy work" of the Baptist missionary societies, leading to the applauded establishment of "mission stations" (1929: 321). William H. Ferris's 1913 The African Abroad referred to the work of missionaries in much the same way, identifying with approval an "aggressive missionary spirit" stirred up by what he identified as the "missionary movement" (1913a: 34).

This considerable discursive attention to Christian expansionism was encouraged by the Black journalistic newsmakers of the time, illustrated here by The Christian Recorder. As discussed in the First Chapter, The Christian Recorder was a widely disseminated, nearly nationally distributed Philadelphia newspaper that was sponsored by the African Methodist Episcopal Church. The Christian Recorder had always shown interest in (mainly Methodist) missionary work in Liberia (Lapsansky-Werner 2006: 268), but an all-out endorsement and advocacy of the missionary ideology first developed at the turn of the century. Through reporting on events such as "Missionary Day" on March 5, 1885, The Christian Recorder itself became an advocate for the missionary movement. It noted that the time of "visionary talk so popular a few years ago" (1885a: n.p.) had become insufficient and openly called for the support of a mission on the "'dark continent'" (ibid). The paper argued, "There is no estimating power that can calculate the good we might do there" (ibid). A few weeks later, on March 26, 1885, The Christian Recorder reproduced a speech which announced the establishment of "an African Fund", asking for financial support from the readership. "The fields are already white unto harvest and the laborers are ready to go, but where is the money?" (1885b: n.p.), the paper asked.[28] Throughout these early years of the missionary movement, The Christian Recorder maintained a steady flow of reporting on missionary efforts.

Secular African American journalistic publications, such as the Boston-based The Colored American Magazine or the weekly The Chicago Defender, joined The Christian Recorder in its frequent reporting on Black missionaries. The Colored American Magazine became the "most widely distributed Black-oriented journal" in its short-lived career between 1900 and 1909 (Aberjhani/West 2003b: 65). Alongside it bourgeois orientation and expressed faith in educational "uplift" (see previous sections), the magazine alluded to missionaries in the context of colleges such as Spelman and Talladega, just as subsequent sections here will show many other historians did as well. The latter college, according to William Pickens, the author of the article "Talladega College" from April, 1906, (as well as the 1916 The New Negro: His Political, Civil and Mental Status and Related Essays, discussed above), had been "brought forth in that day of American history when the spirit of patriotism and the spirit of Jesus Christ were running exactly parallel" (1969: 244). This "spiritual impulse", Pickens continued, had carried the college "through one generation and now sweeps it along the second with a power for good that is felt in every section of the United States and among the heathen of the Congo" (ibid).

28 This appeal for funding would return in many contexts, for example in the travelogues that individual missionaries would write to attract financial support for their work overseas.

With remarks such as these, the magazine mobilized the real-and-imagined geography of the Congo to highlight the depth of Black involvement in the missionary movement. In doing so, it also linked the Congo to heathenism and African American, male-dominated institutions to the "power for good".

The interest and support for this movement among historians, as well as other intellectuals, had waned by the 1920s, after a period of growing doubts. Brawley's 1918 Africa and the War demonstrates the skepticism increasingly expressed towards missionaries. On the missionary upside, Brawley dedicates a full chapter to David Livingstone's thirty-year scientific-religious contribution and applauds Livingstone's "scientific exploration" of the "interior of Africa" as well as his "'unwearied effort to evangelize the native races'" (1918: 18). While praising the explorer, however, Brawley raises serious questions about the potential for progress in these areas through missionary efforts: "To what extent after sixty years have we advanced toward [Livingstone's] ideals? With what justice are we the inheritors of his renown?" (ibid). By reminding colonial nations to take up their educational responsibility in order to turn "Africans" into intelligent citizens (ibid: 41), Brawley called for "education given by missionaries, but also something broader than that" (ibid: 40).

The skepticism towards the missionary movement that crept into Brawley's story only acquired strength among many of his successors, who stopped focusing on the movement altogether. Whereas Carter Woodson's 1922 The Negro in Our History still discussed in passing the missionary phenomenon, James Weldon Johnson's 1927 Native African Races and Culture abandoned the topic altogether. The strong decrease in interest in missionary topics suggests that the missionary ideology as a whole was under pressure. Historians grew increasingly impatient with the missionaries' inefficiency in bringing morality to Africa. The army of traders that trailed behind them was cause for major concern, for instance. Du Bois's 1915 The Negro praised "white missionary societies" for "accomplishing much good", particularly in the educational arena (2001: 139). Traders, however, were harshly criticized. In contrast to the missionaries, "white merchants are sending at least twenty million dollars' worth of European liquor into Africa each year, and the debauchery of the almost unrestricted rum traffic goes far to neutralize missionary effort" (ibid: 139).

The discursive event of missionaries received less attention over time, but Black missionaries did not stop going to Africa and, more specifically, to the Congo. This we know because newspapers such as The Chicago Defender did continue to focus on them, although the subject received dwindling attention there, too, and the tone surrounding it was less and less celebratory. Founded in 1905, The Chicago Defender had become one of the most influential Black American publications in the first half of the 20th century with a national circulation that peaked at a quarter of a million publications in the 1920s and 1930s (Aberjhani/West 2003a: 62). If literate African Americans knew any newspaper, in other words, this would be the one. As late as 1943, the paper discussed the considerable success in the schooling of African natives by Methodist "church schools and in probationary classes" in Southern Rhodesia, Angola, and South Africa (1943d: 22). In the preceding decades, considerable attention was given to a Spelman-trained "native African girl" who visited the U.S. in 1938 (1938: 3). The seventy-seven Presbyterian missionaries on the "dark continent" in 1926 also appeared in the news, four of which, The Chicago Defender announced, "are members of our race" (1926: 2). Increasingly brief and anecdotal as they may have been, articles such as these kept the discourse on missionary engagement alive.

Although historians and journalists grew impatient with missionaries, the question remains as to what drew them to the topic in the first place, especially in late 19th and early 20th centuries. To examine this in more detail, this work turns to A Narrative of the Negro, a text book published in 1912 by Leila Amos Pendleton. While contextualizing the book with regard to the literature of the time, the stakes that African Americans had in the missionary movement will be discussed: How did they explain their engagement? And what does this say about Black intellectuals in the broader discursive context?

Pendleton's book is an interesting case study, as it was published in a time when critical voices towards the missionary movement were gaining strength, but had not yet led to the silencing of the discursive event as a whole. A Narrative of the Negro also stood as both a deviation from and an affirmation of how history was written in Black intellectual circles in the early 20th century. Pendleton was one of the few female African American historians of that time firmly dedicated to inscribing Black female achievers in the American historical record. She focused particularly on women involved in the larger struggle against slavery – such as Sojourner Truth and Harriet Tubman (Pendleton 1912: 114-115, 140-141) – as well as those women active in the "women's club movement" or "the National Association of Colored Women" (ibid: 185-186). Pendleton was also interested in contemporary female writers, most notably Frances Ellen Watkins Harper (ibid: 142).

Typical for the time in which she was active, Pendleton was hardly taken seriously as a historian. She was important and well-known enough to be granted an entry in the 1915 Who's Who of the Colored Race. In it, however, only those of her roles considered befitting to women at that time were discussed: She was described as a "teacher in public schools" and the founder and leading member of the Alpha

Charity Club and the Social Purity League in Washington (Mather 1915: 214). As a female historian without a portfolio (and a husband who was her publisher), she produced a very modest mission statement in her own book. In the preface, she announced "a sort of 'family story' to the colored children of America" (Pendleton 1912: n.p.). With such humble rhetoric, she was easily dismissed by fellow historians (Dagbovie 2010: 110-112).[29]

How can we explain Pendleton's particular interest in the missionary movement? Put bluntly: Pendleton and others felt that an inferior Africa was in dire need of salvation by more enlightened Blacks. How did she, and others, pull this off, it must be asked, in times when the unity of the "black race" dominated contemporary rhetoric?

To be sure, Pendleton was committed to overhauling the rhetoric on Africa. Though it assumed a less personal tone than Booker T. Washington's, her vindictive and contibutionist "race story" attempted to save the African "Motherland" from degrading imagery, including that of the "'the Dark Continent'" (1912: 7, 16).[30] There were a number of other strategies, too, through which Pendleton and others[31] engaged affirmatively with Africa and its diaspora. For instance, she proudly highlighted "the Egyptians and other people of northern Africa" (ibid: 15), peoples from whom "the neighboring countries of Europe obtained their first instruction in the arts and sciences and received their first ideas of a written language"

29 Pendleton received some attention as a historian through an article in The Crisis by fellow female author Jessie Fauset, who saw in her a "historian who has arisen in answer to our need" (qtd. in Dagbovie 2010: 112).

30 Washington, too, made this point by contrasting his old, unlearned beliefs to those he acquired through education. "I had always heard Africa referred to as the 'Dark Continent'," he wrote in The Story of the Negro, "I pictured it to myself as a black, sunless region, with muddy rivers and gloomy forests, inhabited by a people, who, like everything else about them, were black" (1909a: 18). Through his "study of the native races of Africa" (ibid), however, Washington claims he revised his opinion.

31 Others used their own strategies. In his Progress of a Race, Crogman aligned "personalities and careers of men" as different as Benjamin Banneker, Frederick Douglass, and Alexandre Dumas (Crogman/Kletzing 1920: 14). Washington's strategy, in turn, was to stress those alleged elements in African peoples that were laudable or recognizable in Black Americans, such as a "distrust for the city, not unlike that distrust of the Africans in the bush for the coast towns" (1909: 62). It goes without saying that Washington's assertion was interest-driven: As he focused in his life and work on the African American rural community, he obviously had a stake in it.

(ibid). What lay beneath this evaluation of Egypt was the ideology of the unity of the race.

The unifying ideology employed by Pendleton and others explicitly rejected absolute racial inferiority or superiority in theory, but failed to do so in practice. Crogman, for instance, asserted in his monograph Progress of a Race, or the Remarkable Advancement of the Afro-American Negro that "there is no absolute or essential superiority" (Crogman/Kletzing 1929: 14) in short sections such as the one entitled "No Inferior Races". However, this claim is followed by its outright denial: "[T]here are races with inferior conditions and these may be black or white" (ibid). Against this discursive background, it hardly comes as a surprise that Pendleton's work also produced dichotomies between Africa and the rest of the world. She did this through the idea of historical degeneration: "What has been in modern times called the Dark Continent [was] in olden days a light which lighted the world", she wrote (Pendleton: 15-16). According to Pendleton's story, however, those glorious ancient days were over. In fact, the tables had turned: "Civilization moved northward into Europe rather than southward into the heart of Africa" (ibid: 16). As this chapter will go on to demonstrate, this "heart of Africa" was a common way of discussing the Congo.

Historians such as Pendleton were not alone in their belief in "African" inferiority. The idea of an uncivilized African darkness produced by degeneration returned systematically in journalistic texts, as well, thus suggesting an attitude that was pervasive in Black American intellectual contexts. The Christian Recorder published speeches and articles that continuously referred to Africa as "the dark continent", which had to be restored "to its primitive glory in art and lead in civilization" (1886c: n.p.). Africans were discussed in ways that pitted them against the light of Christianity: "The attitude of the Christian world toward the darkest, we do not say the darker, race is a significant, loud and certain call to our church to go in and possess the land" (1889a: n.p.). The Christian Recorder thus divided Backs into "darker" and the "darkest" races, demarcating "darker" African Americans from the "darkest" Africans.

In contrast to the "dark continent", African Americans and other Blacks in the Americas (Jamaicans and Brazilians, for instance) had developed rapidly from the 18th century onward, according to Pendleton's textbook. This progress was achieved through various forms of "racial uplift" by "Negro churches, schools, benevolent societies and other organizations" (Pendleton 1912: 180). Via the rhetoric of "light" in her chapter titles – which range from "The Dawning Light" to "The Light Grows Brighter" and "The Light Diffused" – A Narrative of the Negro stressed that African Americans were bearers of civilization (represented by the trope of "light") due to their perceived progress since the time of slavery.

With this global uplift narrative – African Americans who were enlightening "Africans" – Pendleton aligned herself with other historians and journalists. Booker T. Washington openly discussed African Americans as a Black avant garde that could light up African darkness.[32] The Christian Recorder, in turn, echoed Washington's and Pendleton's stance in a range of articles in 1885, that is, on the brink of factual colonization. It contended that "there is a bright destiny awaiting [Africa] in the near future, when her exiled and once lost, but now free and enlightened children, will return home and carry with them the civilization which has been imparted to them through the two hundred years of training" (1885d: n.p.). In the article "The Duty of the Hour" from April 23, 1885, The Christian Recorder elaborated upon the characteristics of those who should go to Africa, turning uplift issues (such as temperance) into a key aspect of the missionary discourse: "We need men who will unfurl the banner of intemperance, drive out the drunk fiend," the paper intoned, "men who can tame the Red Dragon of lust, who will open fire upon pride, vaulting ambition, heartless avarice, scorpion slander, velvet-lipped falsehood" (1885e: n.p.). Seen alongside the bourgeois ideals of temperance, chastity, and general ambition, the perversity of the rum trades, which came along with the missionaries, becomes particularly obvious.

It was in this broader context of racial hierarchies refuted and re-affirmed that the missionary movement found its advocates among historians and journalists alike. The two-volume 1913 history The African Abroad or His Evolution in Western Civilization, by the historian William Ferris, connected notions of racial superiority with missionary movements. Ferris urged African Americans here to "acquire the aggressiveness and tenacity of purpose of the Anglo-Saxon race", whom he

32 For instance, Booker T. Washington told his readers in The Story of the Negro that Africans "are watching closely the progress of these American Negroes" (1909a: 35). The reason for this observation was that Africans "are beginning to realise that if it is possible for the ten million black men in America, surrounded by modern machinery and all the other forces of civilization, to get into line and march with the procession that it is also possible for them, in time, to follow, somewhat more slowly, perhaps, but in the same direction" (ibid: 35). Washington's story was awash in the vocabulary and argumentative strategies of the Social Darwinian dogma of his days. One discursively unified group of people ("black men in America") is compared to another alleged homogeneous group of that same race in Africa. While the former is said to lead the "procession" of "progress" and the "forces of civilization", the latter is discussed as barely able to march along, let alone at the same tempo.

considered the "advance guard of civilization" (1913a: 34). According to Ferris, from this Anglo-Saxon attitude "the great missionary movements have sprung", from which he hoped a crossover between white and Black would develop for the benefit of the latter "stock", leading to an improved specimen called the "Negrosaxon" (ibid: 34-35).

By invoking the light-dark dichotomy between Africans and Black Americans, at times in crude evolutionary terms, the rhetorical superiority of the latter was established. This found its clearest expression in the Black American historiographical discourse, as the next section shows.

Human Darkness: Cannibals, Drunks, Murderers

Central West Africa played no substantial role in Pendleton's missionary account (nor in the works of others), despite harboring the second-largest missionary contingent in the early 20th century. When they were mentioned, Congo missionaries mostly served as a template for ideas and interests reflective of African American sensibilities rather than Central African ones. Given the obvious underrepresentation and particular framing of the Congo missionaries in works of history, one is prompted to ask why this was the case. I will again turn to Pendleton's textbook to elaborate on this issue, discussing her intertextually vis-à-vis other works of history and journalism.

Apart from Pendleton, no historian reached a rhetorical level of specificity in their claims regarding the geography, history, or people called Congo within the context of Black American missionaries. Reductiveness, allusions, metaphors, and general vagueness were the standard. Booker T. Washington's first 1909 volume The Story of the Negro is a case in point. In his story of early missionary efforts in the "Kongo", with which he presumably meant the Kongo kingdom region around the "Kongo river", [33] Washington explained that "the Catholics were the first to

33 Geographical vagueness pervaded Washington's texts and those of fellow intellectuals. The Congo was reduced to its river. Reading Washington's passage alongside others highlights to what extent this had become the standard. Like Washington, who focused on the area of the "Kongo" river, The Christian Recorder also approached the Congo via its watery parts, discussing it as "a rich region watered by the wide Congo and its twenty tributaries" where missions were established "on the banks of the Congo" near places called "Stanley Pool" (1885f: n.p.). The newspaper assigned contradictory traits to the river, simultaneously painting it as a source of legitimate pride and an embarrassment. According to The Christian Recorder, the Congo belonged to the "three great river systems" of Africa, along with "the Nile and the Niger". In this September 10, 1891 article,

send missionaries to Africa" (1909a: 271). Washington added that the Catholic Church was "the First Christian Church into which Negroes were received as members" (ibid). He continued by taking his readers back to the time when it all started for the Catholics in Central West Africa: "As far back as 1496, two years before the discovery of America, Catholic missionaries visited the mouth of the Kongo River. For several centuries after this a Negro Catholic kingdom existed in that part of Africa" (ibid).

Through quotes as these, the Western presence and activity in the Congo right now was legitimized by Washington through the longevity of Western engagement back then. Through this long-term engagement, the continuation of Euro-American meddling with the region was justified. Moreover, the Congo was strongly linked to the slave trade; Washington continued his account by reporting that this Catholic Congo kingdom was "eventually overthrown, as a result of wars with neighbouring peoples [...] Some of the first Negroes to reach America were Catholics. They came over with the early Spanish discoverers" (ibid).

Washington strongly instrumentalized missionary history to highlight the progress of African Americans. His suggestion that internal "wars with neighbouring peoples" brought down the century-old "Negro Catholic kingdom" of the Congo, highlights that a religious standard was destroyed by the natives themselves. This breakdown of Christianity is implicitly contrasted with the Black community in the Americas, which had turned itself into a religious success. "The first Negroes to reach America were Catholics" (ibid), Washington states, stressing the humble and dire beginnings of his enslaved ancestors in order to aggrandize African American achievements through time. Washington mentions the existence of "great Negro organisations" (such as the Black church) in this passage, which supported the "progress of the masses" (ibid: 278). Thus, by contrasting the failure of Christianity in the Congo with African American advancement, the author's message was clear: African Americans progressed from slavery to highly organized religious state, whereas the Congo was in a state of retrogression and in urgent need of re-evangelization.

The sole instance of concreteness to be found in Washington's discussion of the Congo occurs in his mention of the African American missionary William Shep-

"Africa – Its Resources and Possibilities", the Congo river clearly bore the promise of progress through capitalist trade. "Stanley, in tracing the course of the unknown river and proving it to be the Congo," the article stated, made known "the possibility of reaching the heart of the continent by a waterway instead of by a long, tedious and dangerous land march, has conferred a benefit on Africa, on the world, the result of which only future years can measure" (1891: n.p.).

pard in the second volume of The Story of the Negro, who, according to Washington, was "one of the most successful of the missionaries of Africa today" (ibid: 338). Washington's interest in Sheppard was clearly not impartial: He noted, "[W.H. Sheppard] was a student in my day at Hampton Institute, and later at the Stilman Institute at Tuscaloosa, Alabama" (ibid). Washington wrote with pride on the interracial cooperation between Sheppard, who "went out to the Kongo in 1896 with Reverend Samuel N. Lapsley, of Alabama, as a missionary of the Southern Presbyterian Church [...] Mr. Lapsley chose a station to establish his mission at Luebo, far in the interior of Africa, and Mr. Sheppard remained and worked with him there until Mr. Lapsley's death" (ibid). Washington celebrated Sheppard as the embodiment of aspects of "uplift" and the "New Negro", celebrating Black-white cooperation and Sheppard's autonomy and success, even after the untimely death of his white supervision (an aspect celebrated by Crogman as well, albeit with respect to another missionary).[34]

A final outstanding element in Washington's passages is his awe for the discursive authority with which Sheppard discussed his work in Africa "throughout the South". "Mr. Sheppard has returned to America several times [...] and spoken throughout the South in the interest of his work in Africa. Everywhere I hear him referred to with the greatest respect, and even affection" (ibid: 338-339) What Sheppard actually related about the Congo was hardly of any interest to Washington or others. What mattered was that he had been in the Congo and talked about it as an authority.

In contrast, Pendleton's A Narrative of the Negro went beyond Washington's instrumental interest in Congo missionaries. She focused on Sheppard as "a colored man and a citizen of the United States" (1912: 33) who possessed discursive authority and brought pride to his colleagues and community, stating, "in 1911 he returned to America from the Congo region and tells many interesting things" (ibid). But she did more with Sheppard; she also hinted at the content of the Black missionary's story. When she talked about his tribal experiences, we gain potential insight into why many historians felt uneasy integrating concrete information about the Congo into the missionary strand of discourse. Pendleton writes (ibid):

34 Crogman evoked this sense of a self-confident, self-sacrificing missionary service by narrating the story of "Miss Gordon", a Spelman Seminary graduate who "was appointed missionary to the Congo, in 1890, where she remained until 1894, when she was compelled by ill health to leave her work, and returned to Spelman. She hopes again to take up her chosen work after regaining health" (Crogman/Kletzing 1920: 409).

> Among them [Congolese tribes] there was a tribe which he was the first civilized man to visit. The king of this tribe had heard of foreigners and their cruelties to the natives, and as he thought they were all alike, he issued an edict that no foreigner should enter his kingdom. But Dr. Sheppard had won the love of the tribes around Stanley Pool, and accompanied by some of them, he finally made his way into the forbidden land. He found the natives weaving their own cloth, making their own farming and domestic implements, and living very contentedly. He also came into contact with a tribe of cannibals, whose lives were, as a matter of course, on a much lower plane. He preached to them the Gospel, and after many years has the happiness to know that he and his helpers have been the means of bringing many to Christianity and civilization.

A Narrative of the Negro created a strong dichotomy here between Sheppard and the Congolese people, who were labeled both as a "tribe" and as "natives". The latter designation turned them into "original inhabitant[s]", as the 1899 The American Dictionary of the English Language testifies in its entry of the word (Lyons 1899j: 280). Natives were not citizens and could not be treated as such, although discussing the Congolese as citizens with certain rights was a potential discursive path that could have been taken: Pendleton, after all, did also label and discuss the Congo (i.e. the Congo Free State) as a state, in her work. As "natives", however, Congolese could be more easily subjected to the arbitrary rule and random cruelness of "foreigners".

Central to Pendleton's work was casting the Congo as "tribal" – a highly charged notion that turned Congolese "natives" into people in desperate need of evangelization. The American Dictionary of the English Language clarifies that "tribe" had strong ethnic and racial connotations, defining it as "a race or family from the same ancestor: a body of people under one leader: a number of things having certain common qualities" (Lyons 1899l: 455). It becomes apparent from the use of the word throughout the dictionary that this straightforward and balanced definition, however, did not apply for every "race or family from the same ancestor". Contemporary Euro-American races were not included in the descriptor; it pertained only to those from a distant past such as the "Franks" (Lyons 1899e: 181) or non-Euro-Americans in the present who were described as "savage", "primitive", "migratory", or "wandering" (Lyons 1899h: v; Lyons 1899b: 67; Lyons 1899g: 224).

Contemporary tribal people, according to The American Dictionary of the English Language, were in a "state of having husbands or wives in common" and were ruled by a king, "the father of a tribe" (Lyons 1899b: 67; Lyons 1899i: 257). In its more general meaning, tribes signified animals of the same kind, such as pelicans and other water birds, or gorillas (the "largest of the monkey tribe, found on the west coast of tropical Africa"; Lyons 1899f: 201). As savage, stateless people who were autocratically ruled by a king (and were also linked to animals), tribes were not worth much as far as the dictionary was concerned. In its explanation of the word "Extermination", for instance, The American Dictionary used as an example for the "destruction of the prevalence or influence of anything", explicitly exemplified by "the extermination of inhabitants or tribes" (Lyons 1899d: 135). At this point, the ideological convergence between the dictionary and texts from its contemporaries cannot be overlooked – Joseph Conrad's Heart of Darkness, for instance, also alluded to tribal extermination, invoked king-like figures (i.e. Kurtz), and dehumanized, as well as assigned animal characteristics to, the Congolese.

Through the tribal label, Pendleton successfully framed the Congolese as untouched by "civilized man" (exemplified by Sheppard). The so-called civilized man was thus framed as the first to enter "the forbidden land" in order to bring "Christianity and civilization" (Pendleton 1912: 33). The tribal aspect of the Congolese defined Sheppard's civilizing place in the world, as a bearer of light. This was done through the notions of civilized/uncivilized, heathen/Christian, and known/hidden. In a typical Congoist move, Pendleton split the Congolese into the worst and the best possible. On the one hand, she highlighted agreeable, industrious Congolese people who were "weaving their own cloth, making their own farming and domestic implements, and living very contentedly" (ibid). On the other hand, she used "cannibals" who were "on a much lower plane" (ibid) than the thrifty weavers as counterparts to this – hardly inspiring – image of native craftsmen.

Pendleton's weavers would be acceptable to many Black American contemporaries. Booker T. Washington was interested in them as well; while referencing "Mr. Verner's mission station" in "the heart of savage Africa" (1909a: 48), Washington identified people who have "never been touched by the influences of either the European or Mohammedan civilisations" (ibid), but who were remarkably gifted blacksmiths and craftsmen. Washington did not praise the Congolese for qualities inherent to them, of course, but rather in order to explain the notable Africanness of Black American craftsmen in the South, the privileged territory of Washington's activity. "Just as everywhere in the Southern states today, especially in the country districts, at the crossroads, or near the country store," Washington wrote, "one finds the Negro blacksmith, so, in some of the remote regions in Africa, every village has, according to its size, from one to three blacksmiths" (ibid).

Like Washington, Pendleton hardly mentioned the Congolese craftsmen and farmers in question for their own sake. She granted them the ability to perform self-sustaining manual labor to keep themselves afloat. She did this to underscore that

Congolese were not beyond redemption (brought to them by Sheppard). Pendleton did not breach the subject of whether Sheppard's salvation actually succeeded. "He preached to them the Gospel," Pendleton remarked, "and after many years has the happiness to know that he and his helpers have been the means of bringing many to Christianity and civilization" (1912: 33). The happiness of faith belonged to Sheppard, in other words, not to the Congolese, who, for all we know, may have been wandering in darkness ever since.

The "cannibals" who were "on a much lower plane" (ibid: 33) than the thrifty weavers and the farmers further testify to Pendleton's evolutionary framework. At the same time, these Congolese cannibals indicated that rock bottom had been reached in terms of human decency, as well as Christianity and civilization. The frequent "cannibal talks" in Euro-American intellectual thought, as Obeyesekere has noted, were effective in turning barely-known people into utter savages (2005: 1). The obsession with groups of people threatening to eat a Western traveler or missionary constituted a fantasy with little foundation in empirical fact (ibid: 15-17).

Cannibals were nevertheless an important cultural topos in American intellectual culture when Pendleton wrote her history. Almost every white or black intellectual cited in the contextualization sections of this chapter alluded to cannibalism, whether The Negro: A Beast to Red Rubber, "A Red Record", or Heart of Darkness. Additionally, numerous books linked the Congo specifically to cannibalism, such as Herbert Ward's Five Years with the Congo Cannibals (1891), Melville William Hilton-Simpson's Land and Peoples of the Kasai; Being a Narrative of a Two Years' Journey Among the Cannibals of the Equatorial Forest and Other Savage Tribes of the South-Western Congo (1911), and John H. Week's Among Congo Cannibals: Experiences, Impressions, and Adventures (1913). The cannibal was a discursive figure that justified any number of actions, including violent conquest and a sustained conversion effort. This is why Pendleton inserted the mention of cannibals from Sheppard's account – to re-affirm and stress the need for civilization and evangelical redemption in the Congo, on the one hand, and to elevate Sheppard's bravery and willingness to sacrifice himself for the greater good of enlightening the savage heart of the continent, on the other.

Central West Africa was not only "the shame of a christian Nation" (Crogman/Kletzing 1920: 175) due to cannibalism; the alcohol trade, too, turned it into a disgraceful geography. Alcohol abuse was used both as an affirmation and a rejection of evangelization by foreign missionaries. The historian Crogman wrote: "It is estimated that Christendom has introduced 70,000 gallons of rum into Africa to every missionary" (ibid). This was particularly the case in the Congo Free State, where there were, according to the historian, "one hundred drunkards to one convert" (ibid). Crogman concluded his passage with a devastating critique of the alcohol-induced violence of the Congo: "Under the maddening influence of intoxicating drink sent from New England two hundred Congoans [sic] slaughtered each other. One gallon of rum caused a fight in which fifty were slain" (ibid). As a land permeated with alcohol, Crogman described the worst of possible missionary scenarios. Instead of bringing light in this case, they exacerbated the darkness of the place.

The Congo played a central role in the questioning of the missionary movement. From 1888 onward, The Christian Recorder illustrated the disastrous influence of alcohol on Africa through the signifier Congo in an article titled "The Dark Continent Made Darker" from May 24. It featured statements such as the following (1888b: n.p.):

> Better, a thousand times, that Livingstone and Stanley had never gone to Africa; that King Leopold, the founder of the 'Congo Free State,' had never lived; that the millions of poor, ignorant savages, who have thus been brought into contact with European civilization and commerce, had been left in the darkness of the 'Dark Continent' than that they should now be deluged by millions of gallons of vile intoxicants.

It is not to expand the market for alcoholic beverages, The Christian Recorder lamented, "that these brave, and, we hope, Christian explorers 'hazarded their lives' for years, amid arid waters and burning sands, in peril of wild beasts and more savage men" (ibid). Articles such as these framed the Congo as a disappointment to the original idea of bringing civilization to Central West Africa by the founding fathers of the Congo Free State, such as Livingstone, Stanley, and Leopold. The "stealthy serpent of intemperance", caused by the importation of "one million of gallons of intoxicants" (ibid; 1890a: n.p.) led to the image of a Congo thoroughly drowned by alcohol. This topos never left the missionary discourse as a whole, contributing to the gradual disappearance of support for the movement as a whole among historians and other Black intellectuals.

This questioning of the legitimacy of Black missionary efforts in light of massive transgressions called into question the larger discourse surrounding "the dark continent". As soon as missionaries stopped being bearers of light, could "Africa" be re-framed too? Newspapers such as The Chicago Defender certainly began deviating from the standard derogatory stance assumed towards Africa as a whole. Articles that openly questioned the idea of the "dark continent" and the "darkest race" appeared with increasing frequency. Telling titles such as "Natives of Africa not Uncivilized" (Graham 1925: A1) and "How Africa is Rising" (1925a: 13), as well as "Dark Continent Lures" (1928a: 2) and "Says Africa Not A Dark Continent" (1935a: 10), indicate that the image of the "dark continent" was challenged.

If one reads all statements about the Congo in the works of history and journalism together, very little concrete information was transmitted in the context of the missionary movement. Geographically, the Congo was imagined through metaphors of "darkness" and the "heart". A tangible feel for the Congo cannot be extracted from historical accounts, despite the occasional reference to places such as the "Kongo" river, "Luebo", or "Stanleyville". As far as the Congo's environment was concerned, Central West Africa was discussed as a space of disease and death. Historically, the Congo was reduced to a defeated "Christian kingdom" that was turned into a Free State with abusive tendencies. Socially, the Congolese were depicted as cannibals, murderers, drunks, or craftsmen (the latter analogous to African American workers). In accord with the missionary narrative (bringing Christian light to Congolese darkness), Central West Africa constituted both a place of horrible failure and near-hopeless natives: It was a thoroughly vague place, without any concrete or affirmative traits. The Congo's only redeeming quality was its rich environment and the missionary women and men overseas who sought to save it.

This begs the question: Were there alternatives to this discourse? In the following section, this will be discussed by reading the missionary discourse against eyewitness reports by Black American missionaries. What kind of knowledge did these missionaries disseminate and to what extent do their accounts differ from historical narratives that did not build on personal experience (such as Pendleton's and Washington's)?

Eyewitness Epistemology and the Textuality of Experience

Until the late 1880s, Black writers drew from the works of white journalists, travelers, and explorers, such as Stanley and Livingstone, to make "truthful" claims about the Congo and its supposed darkness. The "opening" of Central West Africa, as well as the push factors of oppression in the U.S. under the Jim Crow laws, motivated Black Americans to leave their homes to visit the Congo or work in it, in the process producing additional reports on Central West Africa. Missionaries, in particular, transmitted their thoughts to the wider Black world through various media, including newspapers (illustrated here by The Christian Recorder), travelogues (embodied in the accounts of Smith, Sheppard, and Boone), and public speeches (which, in turn, were reported in media outlets like The Chicago Defender).

Text production on and by missionaries who were sent to Africa already began to appear at the start of the missionary boom. The Christian Recorder instantly incorporated their experiences and voices into its pages, whether these missionaries were from one's own denomination or not. Human interest was a central aspect of these articles. Two personal stories in particular were followed by The Christian Recorder: L.C. Fleming's and Charles Smith's. "Miss Fleming" sailed for a three-year mission to the Congo "under the auspices of the Baptist Missionary Society", The Christian Recorder noted in 1886 (Fleming 1886: n.p.). It published Fleming's letters to the Black historian William Still, informing readers about her health, her words of farewell, and her first impressions of the Congo (Fleming 1886: n.p; Fleming 1887a: n.p.; Fleming 1887b: n.p.).

Fleming's reports and letters contain many personal anecdotes. Of particular note is the petite histoire of Bishop Taylor's broken "Congo steamer" (1887b: n.p.). Fleming tells her constituency how "two men out from America" failed to repair it. In the end, "the boiler-maker" was "discharged", which provoked a strong reaction in Fleming: "We were all very sorry for him. Has no work as yet" (ibid). The letter continues in this personal tone by describing the mission station, the general mood ("we are all very well"), her housing situation ("I am not situated at all as yet"), and the classes she taught aimed at civilizing the local population (ibid). In her letters, Fleming relies on a rhetoric of uplift, advancement, and "savagism" (Obeyesekere 2005: 2) characteristic of the mainstream of her day: "I asked one of the boys of my class to write you a letter, which you will find enclosed [...] The letter is poor English, but when you think of the dear little fellow being a wild savage ten years ago you would look in wonder on him now" (1887b: n.p.).

Money is also a frequent subject in Fleming's letters, which highlights one of the purposes of these eyewitness texts: to rally for funding. The failed efforts to repair Taylor's ship were significant to her since it was considered "a waste of time and money" (ibid). In her letters, the cost of her house in the Congo is openly announced and legitimized. Fleming writes, "A very loving English lady, whose husband died here last Christmas and whose companion I am in the school work, kindly opened her doors until I could build, or have built, a house" (ibid). Then, in the following lines, Fleming shows her spirit of the "New Negro's" self-reliance by stating that "I have written to friends asking that they afford my house. It will cost only two hundred dollars" (ibid). As she imagined she would be more at home in a house "given me by friends out of love and sympathy than have my Board make an appropriation for it" (ibid), the appeal for adequate funding could not be ignored. The money issue came up often in eyewitness accounts by Smith, Fleming, Sheppard, and Boone, too – the latter two writing for this reason a considerable time after their experiences: Boone's account, written in 1927, announced his fund-raising ambitions right at the start of his book (1927: vii).

The level of human interest in the Black missionary Charles Smith was such that when he prepared to leave (a process discussed in detail), The Christian Recorder listed the possessions he took along, such as a "large number of Bibles, hymn books, love feast tickets, church and Sunday School class books, local preachers' and exhorter's licenses, catechisms, handy songsters, primary lessons, children's day lithographs, souvenirs, dedicatory services" (1894: n.p.). More so than in its articles on Fleming,[35] The Christian Recorder bathed the atmosphere surrounding Smith's departure in the rhetoric of heroism: One of the articles on Smith was titled, tellingly, "On African Shores; The Man with an Iron Will" (1894: n.p.).

Smith's story showcases how (African) American self-confidence and -importance was boosted through the missionary movement. This mentality was reinforced by Smith's reports to The Christian Recorder: Smith wrote on his departure, "I was to attempt to travel eighteen thousand miles by sea, single-handed and alone" (Smith 1895b: n.p.). He continued, "I was to endeavor to traverse the West and Southwest Coasts of Africa for more than six thousand miles – to pass through the meridian line and under the equatorial line to a point about five hundred miles south thereof" (ibid). To stress the enormous scale of the enterprise, Smith mentioned that he was to be "borne upon the mighty Congo from Banana Point to Matadi – the southwest terminus of the Congo railroad" (ibid). Smith left no doubt that the Congo signified an Other very far removed from himself, exclaiming, "Strange land, strange people, strange scenes!" (ibid).

The "stars" of the missionary accounts were the missionaries and their superiors[36] themselves. Those who drew their authority from their presence in the Congo

35 The exception is when Fleming represented herself as a potential martyr in her goodbye poem, bidding farewell to her loved ones for the sake of philanthropy: "Millions dying without Christ! [...] This cry has so aroused my heart / That I find here no place; / I must arise and go to them, / O, may they be released!" (Fleming 1887a: n.p.).

36 In the article "Has Methodism Fulfilled its Duty to the Extreme of Society?" from February 2, 1888, The Christian Recorder answered the question posed in the title by comparing the Methodist Bishop William Taylor to Livingstone and Stanley. The latter two were certainly applauded for their "heroic courage" and life-time service to "remove the veil which has so long shut out the light of civilization" (this was the standard discursive mode of The Christian Recorder when it came to white travelers such as Livingston and Stanley). The service by both men, however, faded "into insignificance" (1888a: n.p.), the article claimed, in comparison with the achievements and discoveries made by Taylor. In hyperbolic language, Taylor is described as "the greatest apostle of the nineteenth century, who with the spirit of a Paul and the physical strength of a Sampson, the courage

constantly wrote about their own experience, not the Congo. Their documents attest to their own accomplishments, through which the missionaries presented themselves as fine examples of Black bourgeois life at the turn of the century. These accounts regularly read like straightforward "New Negro" pamphlets. When Fleming published her poetic adieu in The Christian Recorder, she dedicated paragraphs to her "Alma Mater", which she framed as "A home of training dear" (Fleming 1887a: n.p.). A similar connection between education and the missionary spirit is present in the accounts by Sheppard, who also integrated his own life story, emphasizing the (very questionable) racial peace in his home state of Alabama.[37] In addition to this focus on interracial harmony, Sheppard evoked the spirit of uplift by highlighting his fine schooling in Hampton (1917: 16) and at the Tuscaloosa Theological Institute (ibid: 18), which had taught him two things in particular. First of all, it taught him an "ideal of manhood" (ibid: 17) through his interaction with the teachers at those institutions, who carried themselves "erect" and had "deep, penetrating eyes, pleasant smiles and kindly disposition" (ibid). This attitude would be helpful for his own Congolese "children" as well, it was implied. Second, this education incited in him a longing to "do something for the uplift of the colored ministry" (ibid: 18), a desire that resulted in his missionary work. As such, Sheppard emphasized self-reliance, interracial collaboration, education (in short: "uplift") as key elements leading to his missionary engagement.

Why did well-educated, Black, bourgeois Americans undertake a voyage as hazardous and dangerous as the one to the Congo, according to their own texts? Black missionary narratives demonstrate that personal and institutional desires, fascinations, and politics all played an important role. Charles Smith, for instance, explained that he embarked upon his 147-day "tour of the West and Southwest Coast of Africa" (1895a: 5) in order to gratify a "long-cherished desire to see Africa" (ibid). Second on Smith's list of his reasons was his wish to see what Europeans, Africans, and missionaries were actually doing on the continent. Furthermore, Smith said he wanted to "make some meteorological observations" and to "see if there are any openings for employment of the skill and energy of intelligent and industrious young Americans of African descent" (ibid).

Just as his white predecessors had done (cf. previous chapter), Smith justified his travels with a mixture of the scientific, economic, and personal, making his ac-

of a Daniel, the willingness of a Ruth" had turned his back "upon the civilizing influences of his country" (ibid) to go to Africa.

37 Adhering to the interracial harmony propagated by "New Negro" pamphlets, Sheppard wrote in Presbyterian Pioneers in Congo, "The white people were always very kind to us – as they were to all colored people" (1917: 15).

count recognizable and believable to an audience. Like Reade, Stanley, and Livingstone, Smith insisted that his personal observations were scientific. To convince the reader, he laid bare his "sources of information" through which the "intelligent reader" could judge his story of Africa, its ancient races, and the efforts of the Europeans to colonize the continent (ibid: 6). In the retributive tradition of George Washington Williams and E.L. Lewis (see previous chapter), his observations were meant to correct the many errors concerning Africa that had been "propagated in consequence of writers generally not confining the subject of their looks to their own observations" (ibid).

Besides presenting himself as an agent of science and progress, Smith insisted on being considered a privileged eyewitness who deserved credit for having visited Africa. Smith begins the first chapter of Glimpses of Africa with a poem that emphasized just how much authority the eyewitness was considered to obtain in order to shed light on the Congo: "To see Africa from America is one thing; / To see Africa through books and magazines is one thing; / To see Africa through reports and hearsay is one thing; / To see Africa through dreams and visions in one thing; But to see Africa in Africa is another thing" (ibid: 21).

Smith's offhanded remarks throughout his work made it clear, however, that he was first and foremost a systematic reader of Africa and the Congo. Before Smith started traveling, he already acquired knowledge of the Congo that shaped the selection of topics and topoi he mobilized. Many names we encountered in the last chapter resurface in Smith's account: James Tuckey, Leighton Wilson, George Washington Williams, Henry Morgan Stanley, and documents from the ACS, as well as fellow travelers such as W.H. Sheppard. The historical contextualization of the Congo in Smith's work (but also Boone's and Sheppard's), moreover, suggests the extensive use of secondary literature. For instance, Smith wrote at length about the early missionary efforts in the fifteenth and sixteenth centuries through accounts decidedly outside the realm of his own eyewitness observation.

Smith was not alone in admitting his heavy reliance on other authors. This formal characteristic appears in all of the missionaries' accounts, resulting in similar, but not identical texts; to call them "canonized stories", as Poletta does, seems accurate (cf. Introduction). Variations did occur, but they were fairly minimal. In contrast to other missionaries, for instance, Sheppard read the record of Henry Morgan Stanley's voyages into the Congo quite critically. Remembering Stanley's journey near Matadi, the Black missionary "found a road" which had been passed by "Mr. Stanley" (1917: 28). Sheppard was not pleased by what he observed, as he "saw some of Stanley's heavy iron wagon wheels lying by the roadside; also sun-bleached skeletons of native carriers here and there who by sickness, hunger or fatigue, had laid themselves down to die, without fellow or friend" (ibid: 28). Despite these ideological variations, eyewitness accounts very often reproduced existing representations of the Congo. If you've read one travel account, you've read them all, in other words, and it will be shown in what follows what this means in terms of their depiction of the Congo's geography, history, and people.

Geographically, the missionaries described the Congo the way historians and journalists represented it – water-centered and oscillating between the best (rich valley)[38] and the worst one could imagine (impenetrable, mythical[39] "jungle"). The label of the Congo Free State was gradually accepted.[40] Fleming's letter to The Christian Recorder described the "Congo River and country", on the one hand, as "picturesque" and "more beautiful than anything I have ever seen in nature" (1887b: n.p.). On the other hand, the "delightful climate" of the Congo resulted in an "excessive growth and decay of vegetation". Fleming thought that this caused the land to be suffocating, disease-ridden, and deadly: "This I think poisons the air" (ibid). Variations on this ongoing tension between the best and the worst can be found in Boone's and Sheppard's accounts.[41]

---

38 In the course of discussing the potential of the Congo river, the metaphor of the "valley" – very much in vogue in the imperial build-up between 1880 and 1885 (cf. the last chapter) – was repeatedly invoked by The Christian Recorder. For instance, on June 14, 1888, citing a speech of the A.M.E. board of bishops, an article reported on an "opening of the Valley of the Congo" that would bring "to us increased responsibilities, as well as enlarged opportunities" (1888c: n.p.). As soon as the Congo region actually was "opened" for missionary work, however, the "rich valley" was increasingly replaced by its official colonial names, the Congo Free State and the Belgian Congo.

39 Jan Vansina notes that the "jungle" should be considered a "myth" that expresses "the European or North American hostility toward milieux that were utterly foreign to them" (1990: 39).

40 The Christian Recorder had moved to the label of the "Congo Free State" by 1890, for instance when it discussed the death toll of missionaries within it or when it announced the departure of new missionaries out of Spelman (1889b: n.p.; 1890b: n.p.). In the same vein, The Colored American Magazine consistently referred to the region as the "Congo Free State", just as The Chicago Defender systematically moved from the designation of the "Congo Free States" in 1918 to the "Belgian Congo" in 1925 the latest (e.g. 1918b: 4, 1925b: 4). These shifts mattered, as they stabilized the meaning of the Congo from a promising, barren, rich, watery valley to an accepted European possession.

41 The former saw the Congo both as a "land of perpetual spring" (Boone 1927: 8) and the negative emblem of the disease-permeated "'Dark Continent'" (ibid: 47). Sheppard, in

Missionaries produced few new representations of the Congolese; quite often they opposed the geography of the Congo to its inhabitants. Fleming's "admiring eyes" for Congo's nature, for instance, were openly and sharply contrasted "to the benighted minds of the inhabitants" (ibid). Although Sheppard reported more sympathetically and humbly about the Congolese than any other missionary did, his depiction of the Kuba contained topoi similar to those applied by historians and journalists. Whenever he discussed the common natives, their nudity was almost always described, with expressions ranging from "almost naked" and "half-clad" to "naked" (e.g. Sheppard 1917: 21, 48-49, 70, 81, 96). Fleming was subtler on this score, portraying the "dress" of the Congolese as "very simple, consisting only of a loincloth for the common people" (1887b: n.p.).

Fleming and others, however, stressed the existence of another, royal, "good" Congo – that of the "rich" and "the royal families" who "wear long choice skirts down to the ankle and a shoulder wrap besides" (ibid). Sheppard depicted the royal house of the Kuba in favorable terms, as well. At the same time, this allowed him to take up the topoi of the Congo-as-Slave and the Congo-as-Savage. Of particular significance is Sheppard's story about "a slave woman" (1917: 129) who was going to be buried with her recently deceased master. Sheppard "protested and ventured to rescue the woman" (ibid: 130), but was overpowered. His interfering with the men who were dragging the woman to her death was reported to King Lukenga, who was not amused. "He mentioned it to me," Sheppard wrote, saying that "'the burying of the living with the dead was far beyond the Bakete, who only bury goats with their dead, and that is why we bury slaves; they serve us here and then go with us on the journey to wait on us there'" (ibid: 131).

Sheppard's response was scathing: "I told the king in the strongest language I could command that it was wrong without the least shadow of justification" (ibid). Sheppard's response shows how rapidly his benevolence and cultural relativism crumbled in light of rituals he did not understand. Although he would openly state that the "natives" "know death" (ibid: 135), contradicting Gobineau's infamous assertion to the contrary, Sheppard's indignation worked to show that Congolese customs were amoral and evil and dark, and that he, as a bearer of light, must reject them.

Congolese royals and commoners were separated by how they looked, but were re-aligned in terms of their superstitions and idolatry, as well as their tolerance for cannibalism, alcoholism, and gender-bending. "Their religion consists of all kinds of superstitions. They have a different fetich for nearly every thing [sic]," Fleming

turn, assigned a touch of mystery to the Congo forests and jungles, which he described as so "dense and impenetrable" that "everything must be imaginable" (1917: 59).

reported, which she corroborated by recounting the trust Congolese place in "witches" (1887b: n.p.). Cannibalism – a topos already at play in historical texts – is another classic missionary topic. A third returning topic was alcoholism, which also frequently appeared in the missionary discourse of the historians.[42] Gender bending, too, pervaded the accounts by Sheppard, Boone, and Fleming.[43]

Missionaries considered themselves credible eyewitness throughout their accounts, even when describing phenomena beyond their own observational horizon. Depictions of Congolese history, which remain largely unobservable in the field, were integrated in order to provide a credible justification for the missionary enterprise. Smith did this by openly discussing the unsuccessful history of the missionary efforts made by the Roman Catholic Church in order to underscore "how futile are all efforts to Christianize the African without the aid of civilizing forces and to instruct him in matters of religious faith before teaching him the necessity and value of labor" (Smith 1895a: 96). With much of contemporary discourse accusing the Congolese (via the signifier Africa) of being uncivilized and lazy, the missionaries blamed the "natives" for their heathenism, as it was their own "indignity" towards the missionaries that "obliterated every trace of Christianity from the land" (ibid: 101).

Rare were the Black missionary utterances that focused on the history of the Congolese in and by itself. In an exceptional passage, Sheppard provided information on the origins of the Bakuba, whose "real name" (Buxongo) is mentioned, along with their typical appearance, their essential character ("conservative and proud"), their migratory history, and their mythologies (1917: 114). Sheppard's story ran counter to the usual accounts debasing the Congolese. Sheppard took a step back in his story, leaving more space for the Congolese who, he stressed, "do not speak in 'baby language', but in a "full, highly intellectual and musical" one (ibid). Remarks such as these raise the question as to whether Sheppard developed ele-

42 This became a topic in Smith's journey as soon as Congo travelers boarded the ship, an affliction of both Black "civilized natives", as well as white missionaries and traders (1895: 123). Smith noted, "The missionaries confined themselves to wine and beer; the others covered every form of drink that was obtainable" (ibid).

43 "The women, as in all heathen lands," wrote Fleming, for instance, "have all the heavy work of the family to do. The men do the sewing for the family, but the women do all the farming, bring all the water and wood and do the cooking. They do their farm work with the baby of the family tied on their back, as a rule" (1887b: n.p.). The opposition between do-nothing, slightly effeminate Congolese men (who do the "sewing") and sturdy Congolese women was already present in the material investigated in the last chapter and outlasted colonial times.

ments of a counterdiscourse through his interaction with the Congolese. In the end, his critical attitude towards a number of colonial attitudes was outweighed by his many strategies of imperial dehumanization.

Sheppard painted a picture of himself that resembled Livingstone more than Stanley (whose trigger-happy explorations Sheppard remarked upon critically, cf. above). Although the Black missionary aimed for control and command in most of the intercultural encounters, he refused to do so in Stanley's brash, violent fashion. Sheppard stressed instead the importance of remaining a gentleman, whose main characteristics were benevolence, humility, and empathy. "A kind act brings its reward, even in Central Africa", Sheppard remarked when he bought two ducks from a native who remembered Sheppard fondly because he had "given him hippo meat" (ibid: 54). Instead of shooting his way through to the wilderness, as Stanley had literally done, Sheppard tried to mingle with the "natives" and figure out what the Congolese were "thinking" (ibid: 127), as well as learn their language and "curious customs" (ibid: 67).

According to Sheppard's story, paternalistic and bigoted stances towards the natives only brought trouble. "Many times in Central Africa foreigners get into serious difficulties from which they cannot extricate themselves by disregarding the advice of natives" (ibid: 39). Through passages such as these, Sheppard repudiated derogatory portrayals of indigenous people. He also did this, although not exclusively, in order to portray himself as humane and disinterestedly benevolent. Mary Louise Pratt's seminal Imperial Eyes: Travel Writing and Transculturation labels this as an attitude of "anti-conquest" (1993: 37-83). Sheppard's "anti-conquest" strategy also included belittling the Congolese. They might be worthy of some respect, but they most definitely and desperately needed assistance from Sheppard in order to be elevated to his level of civilization. Sheppard took the Congolese seriously in the relativist fashion of his day, which allowed for a discussion of the Congolese as human equals (theoretically at least), while simultaneously deeming their culture inferior. As a consequence, the Congolese mostly function as add-ons in Sheppard's story. The Congolese are Sheppard's informers, the carriers of his supplies, or the subjects of anthropological investigation, whose words and practices were translated and transmitted through Sheppard. This raises the question: To what extent could Sheppard actually translate what he found? Did he actually understand what was going on around him?

Although Sheppard gave the impression that he grasped the language spoken by the "natives" by quoting snippets of their native tongue in his account – a habit that was (and remains) common in ethnographic practice (Fabian 2000b: 135) – what was it that he understood? [44]If he was able to truly read his surroundings, should it not be considered surprising that Sheppard felt isolated in the Congo, despite being surrounded by so many Congolese he would frequently call his "friends" (e.g. 1917: 47, 76, 84)? "Alone with God, no friend, no companion, no one. Alone! Alone!", Sheppard wrote at one point (ibid: 94). Since Sheppard would never talk to the Congolese as equals (he essentialized them, placed them in hierarchies, and depicted them ironically),[45] his isolation was understandable and persistent.

Sheppard's benevolent (but dismissive) take on the Congolese emerges most strongly in his many speeches on Central West Africa in the United States. The Chicago Defender described the first of his spoken accounts on July 6, 1918 in the article "Grace Presbyterian Church Celebrates Thirtieth Anniversary" (1918a: 10). The article discussed a church anniversary on which Sheppard served as the "principal speaker". The title of his speech, "In the Forbidden Land of King Lukenga and into the Camps of the Cannibals", was revealing in terms of how he communicated his own work in the Congo as heroic missionary work caught between a despotic African king and the cannibal Congo masses. The article stated that the returned missionary held the attention of his audience for an hour by telling "how he started with a few school children under a bamboo tree, and after twenty-give years there are now 900 teachers of those same people" (ibid).

Sheppard thus stressed his own cultural proficiency (which should be questioned in the first place). This was to be understood as an amazing achievement, given the enormous challenges he encountered (such as the many "African languages" he had to master). Six years later, The Chicago Defender reported on another speech by Sheppard, this time at Hampton on January, 19, 1923, on the "baffling problems which face the missionaries in Africa" (1923a: 3). As far as just what these problems were, the reader was not told; missionary uplift was "out" by then, and secular civilization efforts were the talk of the day.[46] Cannibalism nevertheless reappeared as a topic in this article. The newspaper reported how Sheppard

44 An epistemic question also raised by Jan Vansina's Paths in the Rainforests: "Outsiders had to rely on inside informants, often on only a single major informant who remains unnamed, and they were likely to misinterpret what they saw and to misunderstand what they were told for lack of knowledge of the local language" (1990: 24).

45 Irony is also part and parcel of Boone's account. "Would you believe me if I tell you that those people have lawyers that plead for their clients; and question the witnesses just as we do in our courts," Boone asked in the section "Habits and Customs" (1927: 31).

46 In that same article, the newspaper described how much the former Congo Free State had changed after "King Albert has come to the throne […] He is building railroads, bridges, hospitals and schools" (1923a: 3).

"vividly described some of his experiences with African wild animals and strange peoples, including the cannibalistic Zappa Zaps" (ibid), therefore again stressing the topic of cannibalism. Only hinting in passing at the highly-cultured Bakubas, Sheppard seems to have continued his lecture, according to The Chicago Defender, by showing a "valuable collection of African curios" which are described as "trophies" of "African customs and superstitions" (ibid), thereby underlining how "heathen" the Congo remained. Sheppard's release from prison after protesting Leopold's regime was discussed as a heroic deed. Sheppard is reported as having said, "When I came out of prison in Leopoldsville after eight days of trial 3,000,000 of our people and yours came out of slavery into the light of liberty and true freedom" (ibid).

If Sheppard's account and that of other missionaries illustrate anything, it is the textuality of eyewitness Congo experiences. Whether authors actually had been in the Congo or not was not decisive in how they wrote about it, in other words, since they were socialized through texts that would shape their vista in very similar ways, almost independent of their experiences. This vista focused on Congolese "lack" – people that should be helped by "us" to overcome their own inability – in an environment that was abundant. This "lack" varied from alcoholism to cannibalism, from the upper to the lower strata of Congolese societies, from changeable to immanent traits. Due to the many textual similarities, the distinction between "new knowledge" and "old knowledge", or between eyewitness accounts (such as Sheppard's) and accounts written by historians in the 19th century (cf. the last chapter) was not as clear-cut as one might suspect. Often, these pieces of knowledge built upon and reinforced each other, turning knowledge on the Congo into a "bricolage", or a reconfiguration of knowledge both from the past and present (Burke 2012: 86).

Despite the production of similar texts by those able to visit the Congo, eyewitness knowledge nevertheless played an important role in Congo discourse. Its emergence led to personal observation becoming increasingly privileged in the discussion of the Congo: It became imperative, in other words, to go to Central West Africa if one wanted to make claims about it, as becomes increasingly apparent in this work (cf. the next chapter and Conclusion). This eyewitness epistemology reinforced the scientific positivism of earlier decades, as discussed in the previous chapter. The belief in understanding other people and their cultures through "imaginative sympathy" (ibid: 77-79), as well as hermeneutics, objective observation by those with the right academic credentials, the right gender, or the right religious or humanist intentions, reached new heights in the colonial age, however. Imperialism profited and drew massively from the eyewitness epistemology. The imperialist knew the Congo: s/he had anecdotes to tell, truths to claim, networks of "natives" to rely on (cf. Said 2003: 112). Imperialism thus increasingly produced a privileged body of knowledge that drew on the authority of those who went to the Congo because they had stakes in it – missionaries, colonists, adventurers. This privileging of those in the "field" versus desktop intellectuals (i.e. academics, activists, editors with no means of actually going to the Congo) became increasingly important in the colonial age (Burke 2012: 35).

Missionaries were extremely credible knowledge brokers and disseminators of truth, both in their own churches and beyond. Hidden behind this knowledge production were interests that went far beyond a humanitarian interest in the Congo, however. The Congo was a template that enabled the casting of oneself, in contrast to it, as heroic, moral, and civilized. In the course of this staging and self-styling, the observable Congo was left by the wayside, producing the Congo in known and very specific and detrimental ways. This instrumental narrative was strengthened by another discursive trait within the broader Congo discourse: The Congo-as-Example, which gained traction when the atrocities of the Congo Free State began receiving public attention.

Second Topos: The Congo-as-Example

White eyewitnesses, particularly missionaries, played an important role in alerting the world to the Congo's forceful transition to global capitalism. Despite the fact that there existed Black Americans who participated in the critique of Belgian imperialism in very concrete ways, exemplified in this section by the historian George Washington Williams (author of History of the Negro Race; see last chapter) and the missionary William Henry Sheppard (author of Presbyterian Pioneers in Congo; cf. previous section), their activism hardly attracted any attention from fellow American intellectuals.

By 1889, George Washington Williams had become increasingly involved in Leopold II's colonial project, leading to a personal encounter with the king, who he initially discussed as "one of the noblest sovereigns in the world" (qtd. in Franklin 1998: 182). Williams even proposed recruiting Black Americans from Hampton, an enterprise that ended disappointingly, since none of the students showed any interest in traveling to the Congo Free State. What was missing from a convincing case to emigrate, according to Williams's biographer John Hope Franklin, was firsthand knowledge of Africa (ibid), and so the historian went there in order to obtain eyewitness authority.

On his way to Africa, Williams visited the White House (where he promised to prepare a memorandum on whether the U.S. should ratify the Berlin Act or not). He also visited the royal Palace in Brussels, where Leopold attempted to dissuade him (in vain) from traveling to the Congo (ibid: 148-179). Both visits illustrate the cultural capital wielded by Williams. Once in the Congo Free State, his two-month stay in 1890 gave him a firsthand impression of the abusive situation there (ibid:180-221). This resulted in "An Open Letter to His Serene Majesty Leopold II, King of the Belgians and Sovereign of the Independent State of Congo" (Wiliamms 1985), as well as "A Report on the Proposed Congo Railway", which was added to the letter (Williams 2006). These texts appear to have been generally accessible and debated in Europe and the United States by the autumn of 1890 (Franklin 1985: 208), making Williams one of the first intellectuals to publish a widely read, all-out indictment of the Congo Free State.

In his "Open Letter", Williams drew on his status as a Congo traveler (and on the observations of other "competent and veracious witnesses"; Williams 2006:121) to firmly dismiss Leopold's humanitarian claims. The claims of acting in the Congo out of "humane sentiments" in order to build a "Christian civilization of Africa" (ibid) were, according to Williams, a travesty. Williams charged Leopold with twelve offences in his "An Open Letter", faulting him for violating the General Act of the Conference of Berlin, permitting the slave-trade to flourish, allowing for the misrepresentation of the Congo as fertile and productive through the works of Henry Morgan Stanley (quite the contrary was true, according to Williams), and lacking the "moral, military and financial strength, necessary to govern a territory of 1,508,000 square miles" (ibid: 125).

Williams depicted the Congolese through discursive elements already used by contemporary Black missionaries, as well as those Morel would employ a few decades later. A double strategy is at work in the depiction of the Congolese in Williams's letter: The Congolese oscillate between innocence and savagery.[47] Williams thus wrote his letter using discursive strategies and rhetoric quite similar to

47 Congolese are, on the one hand, willful executors of "cruelties of the most astounding character", of which Williams foregrounded the atrocity of "burying slaves alive in the grave of a dead chief" (Williams 2006: 125). Stories of cannibalistic cruelty highlighted Congolese savagery: "[B]etween 800 and 1,000 slaves are sold to be eaten by the natives" (ibid). To Williams, the "greatest curse the country suffers" from at the time of writing was the "black soldiers, many of whom are slaves" (ibid: 126), who the Congo Free State hires from Zanzibar in order to do its dirty work. On the other hand, Williams's letter depicts the Congolese as a faceless, majority of silent victims with "unexplained patience, long suffering and forgiving spirit, which put the boasted civilisation and professed religion of your Majesty's Government to the blush" (ibid: 130). This majority did not take militant action against their oppressors – "during thirteen years only one white man has lost his life by the hands of the natives" (ibid).

Morel's and Conrad's, both of whom were in the Congo around that same time (but would publish their seminal work considerably later than Williams's). The letter of Williams, however, did not have the impact that Morel's and Conrad's work did. One reason for this is that Williams's accounts were published more than a decade earlier, when major newspapers such as The New York Times had not yet paved the way for an accepted critical perspective on the Congo Free State. By the time Morel and Conrad published their texts, the Congo Free State had already been discredited.[48] A second reason for the ignoring and open dismissal of Williams's letter was his biography and, above all, his perceived "race". Led by Henry Morgan Stanley and Leopold II, Williams was accused of being a blackmailer of the Belgian king.

48 By May 31, 1897, The New York Times had firmly taken up the term "atrocities" to discuss the brutalities in the Congo Free State. In an article with the title "The Congo Atrocities", the Swedish missionary "Sjoblon" was featured as he spoke in New York on "West African Christian missions" (1897: n.p.; that same missionary already quoted by Morel, albeit with a different spelling; cf. section above). In that same article, The New York Times concentrated almost exclusively on the missionary's view of the brutalities. "He admits many of the charges are true," The New York Times wrote, "such as the mutilations and the severing of hands by the soldiers" (ibid). As with Morel and Williams, the ultimate responsibility for this extreme violence was placed with the Congolese, since "native custom [are] extremely difficult to eradicate", as The New York Times paraphrased the missionary. The newspaper did not issue any kind of verdict on the murderous role of Europeans, even defending the white officials. It indicated that the offences of the natives were punished and that Sjoblon ultimately provided a "justification of the Congo administration." Over time, this apologeticism disappeared in The New York Times. Indeed, as more and more eyewitness came forward, The New York Times covered the Congo Free State increasingly critically. An article on January 3, 1902 reported on an ex-official of Leopold's state (named Captain Burrows) who claimed that the "conditions prevailing in the Congo Free State were a disgrace to civilization" (1902: n.p.). The core of the article was the story of an unnamed "American missionary" who had told the official that the state "employed 500 cannibals" who were used against the natives (ibid). Burrows knew this because he drew from eyewitness stories: "'I have a sworn testimony,'" Capt. Burrows is quoted as having said, "'of the Belgians handing over natives to cannibal tribes for the express purpose of being eaten" (ibid). Similar articles from The New York Times appeared in the same period with revealing titles such as "Oppression in Congo State: Belgian Government gets Rich at the Expense of the Natives" from January 1, 1899 (1899: n.p.). As more and more articles confirmed Williams's analysis of the situation in the Congo Free State, it became harder to dismiss the substance and persuasiveness of his early reports, as also expressed by Morel and Conrad.

Allegations of Williams's criminality were accompanied by racial slurs, as he was dismissed internationally as "a mulatto", a "colonel noir", or an "unbalanced negro" in many media on both sides of the ocean (qtd. Franklin 1998:209-212). The New York Times of April 14, 1890 rounded off this assault on his character (and on the assertions he made in his reports) by framing him as opportunistic and unreliable. A flat-out denial of Williams's claims was the result. "It is reported that some parties here have substantial pecuniary reasons for regretting that Williams ever came here", The New York Times asserted about his presence in Middletown (1891: n.p.).

Unlike Williams, Sheppard was taken quite seriously by The New York Times and other white newspapers. Although Williams and Sheppard reported on similar events in similar ways, Sheppard's accounts was based on his credibility as a missionary (which, at that time, still made a great difference) and were backed up by powerful whites and Blacks. The Times did not allude to his race or doubt the truthfulness of his assertions in the article "Trouble on the Congo". Sheppard's narration of "the reign of terror", as well as "slave raiding and plundering" in the Congo Free State (ibid), was actually conveyed by the white missionary in charge, Morrison, who had spoken to the press about what Sheppard had seen; at the same time, Booker T. Washington supported Sheppard's authority by quoting from his accounts in his own articles on the Congo Free State cruelties. In one of Washington's exemplary articles, "Cruelty in the Congo Country", appearing in the white magazine Outlook on October 8, 1904, Washington cited Sheppard extensively as a reliable "eye-witness" [sic], whom he identified (as he had in his other work) as "a fellow-student at Hampton Institute" (1904: 88). In Sheppard's quote, the cannibalistic atrocities of the Zappo-Zaps were spotlighted. "'Why are the people carved so, leaving only the bones'", Sheppard was said to have asked the chief, who answered "My people ate them" (ibid: 89).

In contrast to white news media such as The New York Times or Outlook, Black American newspapers like The Christian Recorder, The Colored American Magazine, and The Chicago Defender remained nearly silent about the Congo atrocities as they were happening.[49] In the same vein, few Black historians dis-

49 The first mention of the atrocities in The Colored American Magazine appear in October 1909, in the context of the acquittal of the Black missionary William Henry Sheppard of "libel by a Congo concession company" (1909: 248). This charge was made because the missionary publicly faulted the Congo Free State in one of his articles for "tyrannically impressing whole villages for gathering rubber, for levying oppressive taxes and wholesale inhuman torture of the natives" (ibid). In this short text, the magazine showed an awareness of the longevity of the atrocities, as well as the activism against them. Famed

cussed the atrocities in detail. The few exceptions included Pendleton, Woodson, and Du Bois (the latter will be discussed in more detail in the final sections of the chapter).[50] The reluctance of Black intellectuals to focus on the Congo atrocities be-

---

author Sir Arthur Conan Doyle, a long-time critic of the Congo Free State, was said to have "sent to the London Times a ringing appeal" to help free the missionary (ibid). In that same article, the acquittal of Sheppard was discussed as "the most important and perhaps helpful trial ever conducted in the Congo" (ibid). The reason for this is that the Belgian government in reality "admits the heinous crimes to long charged against it" (ibid). With these statements, the magazine hinted at its awareness of the atrocities and indirectly highlighted its silence about them.

50 Pendleton approached the crimes in the Congo from a decidedly Western perspective. Stanley's explorations, as well as the Berlin conference, were interpreted in much the same way as the official rhetoric of the United States' administration had framed them, as exemplified above by John Tyler Morgan's report "Occupation of the Congo Country in Africa" (cf. above). Pendleton discussed the Berlin conference with this idealistic rhetoric by discussing the initial aims of the Congo Free State as the Euro-American push for economic and human freedom: "Trade should be free to all, the navigation of the Congo river should be free and the natives should not be oppressed, but encouraged to make the most of themselves" (1912: 32). Pendleton then contrasted the idealism of the official rhetoric to her perceived reality. This reality entailed, for instance, evil personified by the character of Leopold II. Things went awry in Central West Africa, Pendleton's story went, because the king of Belgium was an amoral leader. Pendleton discussed Leopold as a failed "kind of guardian" (ibid) who could not live up to his philanthropic duty. Leopold "was a wicked, cruel king, sly and crafty and by degrees obtained absolute power over every soul in the Congo" (ibid). "He [Leopold II] claimed that the Congoland and everything in it was his and that the natives were simply his tenants and, strange to say, the thirteen other countries allowed him to do so" (ibid: 32-33). As a cruel, ruthless, absolutist landlord (a slave topos that already appeared in the abolitionist writing of Morel and other Congo Free State activists), Leopold would not hesitate, according to Pendleton, to employ "wicked white men" as heartless and cruel as himself, who in turn would send "cannibal soldiers" to "burn the huts and kill and eat the natives" (ibid: 33). The end of Pendleton's Congo Free State story was a lament on the state of current Euro-American civilization. According to Pendleton, "The terrible things that were reported from the Congo, horrified the civilized world, and more than once Leopold pretended to stop them, but recently accounts of awful conditions have been published" (ibid). The inability to act according to one's own principles is reflected in the works of other historians, too. Historian Carter Woodson confirmed and reiterated this lament, writing, "the civilized world,

trays their refusal to report on the region as a whole. It was not a matter of numbers of victims that guided intellectuals to the topic. The "twelve million natives" (2001: 45) mentioned in Du Bois's The Negro were, in the end, hardly decisive. What mattered was the Congo's usefulness within one's own social and political sphere. The Congo would only be discussed if a credible Black eyewitness from the right walk of life (e.g. Sheppard) happened to be testifying. Central West Africa thus served as a template or an example of a political point that one truly cared about. Congo atrocities would be mentioned to draw attention to the irresponsibility of white civilization, for instance – a deficiency that Black Americans were all too familiar with and to which they would respond. In their discussions of the Congolese, hardly any identification took place with them. The representations of the Congolese oscillated between impotent innocence and murderous savageness – two traits American intellectuals could not incorporate into their own "New Negro" philosophy. This highly selective and instrumental talk about the Congo atrocities foreshadowed Central West Africa's full absorption into an all-out African American local episteme.

Parochial Epistemology

The Congo-as-Example became common sense through the widespread dominance of the local: Whatever happened globally, the local mattered more. This is a phenomenon well known to media scientists, of course. International news is often domesticated and particularized for local audiences by anchoring foreign reports within narrative frameworks that are already familiar and recognizable to those audiences (e.g. Claussen 2004: 25-28). Thus, most reports maintain both global and culturally specific orientations by constructing the meanings of these events in ways that are compatible with the culture and the dominant ideology of societies they serve (ibid: 28). The treatment of the Congo within the American archive goes well beyond "domestication", however. Since the Congo was increasingly absorbed by a variety of American situations, it ultimately and literally became "the American Congo", displacing Central West Africa to such an extent that it became at times almost completely unrecognizable.

As a multifunctional signifier, the Congo was used to designate, first of all, the racially justified mass murder of Blacks by individual white Americans. The correspondence between America and the Congo is quite obvious here. Since the atrocities in the African Congo were understood by African American intellectuals as the responsibility of Leopold II, American situations were labeled as Congo as soon as

then, threw up its hands in holy horror; and the very name of Leopold II became anathema" (1936: 135-136).

they involved a powerful, unscrupulous, murderous, white male in an oppressive, anti-Black context. In the article "First Picture of Georgia Murder Farm" of April 2, 1921, The Chicago Defender recounted the story of John Williams, a plantation owner who "Kills 11; Buries 6 Alive". Like the king of Belgium, Williams is framed as an absolute and ruthless ruler of his farm. The equivalent of severing hands (as was the case in Leopold's Congo Free State) was "pour[ing] acid" in the mouths of Blacks and knocking them unconscious with an ax, after which point they were dumped into the local river (1921b: 1). The Chicago Defender labeled the ruler of this "murder farm" the "Leopold of Georgia" and began the article by telling its readers that "The Belgian Congo has been outdone" (ibid).

The newspaper never clarified why the crime in Georgia ought to be considered worse than those committed in the Belgian Congo. But in the final paragraphs of the article, The Chicago Defender pointed to why it found the analogy fitting. Because John Williams's practice was depicted as "prevalent throughout Georgia in the backwoods towns" (ibid), the newspaper framed the case as a model example of a "system" of anti-Black killing: "Bodies of men have been found in deserted spots all during last year [...] farm hands are separated from their wives and children by white plantation owners as in the days of slavery, and children born out of wedlock are common under the peonage rule" (ibid). The same catchwords employed to describe Leopold's mode of ruling thus reappear in the American context. Leopold's American counterparts treated their subordinates cruelly through a system of exploitation very similar to slavery. The "hands" that were cut off in the African Congo by Leopold were in this way aligned with the maiming and killing of "farm hands" in The Chicago Defender.

The Congo was explicitly mobilized, moreover, to provide a label for the overall system of anti-Black violence in the United States, exceptions to violence against Blacks on the international plane notwithstanding (e.g. Haiti).[51] The Congo therefore designated the economic, social, physical, and psychological violence of Jim Crow laws as a whole – not just individual cases of violence perpetrated by murderous white males. In his seminal The Negro Faces America, the white American writer, Civil Rights activist, and long-term publicity director of the NAACP

51 While discussing a potential "naval base in the Haitian Republic", The Chicago Defender was quick to advocate sending Black American troops. The reason was that Blacks would not make the same mistakes as white American soldiers. "Already we have seen the fruits of American missionary work in Haiti", The Chicago Defender wrote December 11, 1920 in an article titled "The Call of the Blood". It continued, "The investigation now going on at Washington has revealed a condition equaled only in brutality by the treatment meted out to the natives of the Congo by the soldiers of king Leopold of Belgium" (1920b: 12).

(1919-1932) Herbert Seligmann actively used the Congo as a metaphor for this purpose. In a chapter titled "The American Congo", Seligmann lists the "innumerable brutalities" against Black people (1920: 219), ranging from "lynchings" (ibid: 220) and "black codes" (ibid: 221) to all-white courts (ibid: 237) and the peonage system, which kept Blacks in a "condition of servitude and oppression" (ibid: 223).

Seligmann's 1920 book was a remarkable case of how the Congo no longer referred to Africa: The author himself did not mention the continent once in his book. The remarkable malleability of the Congo signifier, therefore, was not only consumed by the signifier "Africa", as demonstrated earlier in this book, but also by the signifier "America", or any part of it that was oppressive enough to earn that label. The Congo stood in practice for many horrific geographies. It could signify the South as a whole, or just a part of it – ranging from whole states, such as Alabama or Georgia, to individual regions, such as St. Louis or the Mississippi area. Central West Africa was thus incorporated into an American geography of horror, including famous judiciary scandals such as the trial of the Scottsboro boys in 1933, which elicited scathing comments in The Chicago Defender, including "Watch Alabama go Congo" (1933b: 1) or "The American ruling class stops at nothing to perpetuate [racial oppression] [...] It has turned the South into an American Congo, inflicting upon the Negro people torture equaled to the most unbridled savagery of the colonies" (1933c: 10).

In contrast to the African American discourse on the atrocities in the African Congo, the American Congo signified brutalities committed by white people only. Whereas "native cannibals" constituted a major factor in the ideological defeat of the Central West African Congo, this was not the case in the discourse of the Congo as a metaphor for national horror. An article from February 12, 1921, titled "Civilized Savages", illustrates this aptly. Using language highly skeptical of missionary work in general, the article asks: "where is missionary work more needed than at home?" (1921a: 12). According to The Chicago Defender, "The sending of missionaries to so-called heathen peoples by the church in America is one colossal joke" (ibid). The reason why this was the case was that some white Americans were more in need of civilization than their Black counterparts abroad: "Are the heathen peoples of Africa and China any worse than the half savage human monsters of the South? Are the bushmen of the Congo or the head-hunting Igorottes of the Philippines any worse than the night-riding Ku-Klux?" (ibid). Just like Morel, who was lauded as an influential activist in The Chicago Defender because he is said to have "expose[d] the horrors perpetuated upon the natives in the Congo under Belgium administration", the newspaper would evoke the topos of "civilized savages" to criticize those involved in the American atrocities. Whereas Morel used this phrase derogatorily in relation to Belgians in the Congo (ibid), the newspaper applied it to oppressive white Americans. In contrast to the discourse on the African Congo, the American Congo offered no active role for Blacks; they were merely the silent victims of white racism.

With this one-sided indictment of white perpetrators, the Congo signifier also enabled a rhetoric of global Black solidarity. As such, the "millions of people of India, the inhabitants of French and British possessions in Africa, and the millions of persecuted of the Belgian Congo" were mentioned in one and the same breath to highlight the need for a "common bond", as The Chicago Defender stated on September 11, 1943 in an article titled "A Common Bond" (1943b: 14). This kind of identification took place when the Congo appeared as an item on a list of other places of horror. Through statements such as these, the Congo again became an example for a crime against Black people in general, rather than a concrete, specific event in Central West Africa. As a consequence, while discussing the military presence of the United States in Haiti in 1922, The Chicago Defender aligned Egypt, India, Morocco, and Korea with the Congo in order to highlight the "same sort of pretensions set up by imperialists in every age" (King 1922: A3). In this passage, the U.S. is said to offer the same excuses "by which King Leopold of Belgium sought to cloak his atrocities and plunder the Congo" (ibid). In what follows, this idea of identification will be taken up in more detail, particularly in terms of how artists linked themselves positively to the Congo, while at the same time distancing themselves from it.

Third Topos: The Congo-as-the-Vital

Handicraft was one of the few elements portrayed positively in Congo discourse between 1885 and 1945, highlighting the importance of folklorist culture as a whole in casting the Congo in a more flattering light. Folklore had strong local elements, too, as will be shown, turning the Congo into a signifier of original "African" energy capable of revitalizing one's own African American culture. Historians such as Washington and Ferris alluded to the Congo in this sense by drawing on the works of Franz Boas, who had related a number of anecdotes on this subject. For instance, Washington's first volume of The Story of the Negro shared the anthropologist's experience with "the artistic industries of the native African" (1909a: 47). "A walk through the African museums of Paris and London and Berlin is a revelation", Washington quotes Boas as saying, "I wish you could see the scepters of African kings, carved of hardwood and representing artistic form; or the dainty basketry made by the people of the Kongo River and of the region of the Great Lakes of the

Nile, or the grass mats of their beautiful patterns" (ibid). Ferris quoted the same passage in the second volume of his 1913 The African Abroad. Additionally, he highlighted "the beautiful iron weapons of Central Africa, which excel in symmetry of form, and many of which bear elaborate designs inlaid in copper, and are of admirable workmanship" (1913b: 550). Congolese handicraft was depicted by Washington and Ferris as "dainty" and "beautiful" – both adjectives possessing positive aesthetic connotations of "taste", "refined" forms, or "delicacy", as Laird & Lee's Webster's New Standard American Dictionary of the English Language (1911) tells us in its entry on "Dainty" (Roe 1911: 324).

From the 1920s onward, craftsmanship was increasingly re-framed and re-interpreted as "art". Against the background of a broader Euro-American "vogue nègre",[52] African tools from the past and of the present were no longer considered curiosities, but works of art. For instance, Alain Locke's seminal "Art Lessons from the Congo", published in the magazine The Survey on February 1, 1927, depicted and discussed Congolese cups, lutes, horns, and other objects of everyday life. In his essay, Locke raised these tools to the level of an "art creed" (as the explanation of one picture of an armlet goes; 1927: 588). This re-evaluation of Congolese craftwork was driven by powerful African American interests rather than a thorough rethinking of Central West Africa. "Art lessons from such a primitive source as this seem ludicrous" (ibid: 587), Locke stated in his article, thus emphasizing that the quintessential drive behind revaluing Congo art is not the art itself. What made Congo art so interesting was its "already mature influence upon the practical technique of modern art", of which Locke mentioned "Cezanne, Picasso, sculptors like Lipcitz [sic] and Brancusi" (ibid). As such, Congo tools became a subject of interest because they had already entered the Western art scene.

The "message" (ibid) of Congolese tools to the American art scene was of great interest to Locke. The "importance of beauty in the ordinary", he suggested, rendered the Congo valuable for "American art" (ibid). This was particularly the case when one considered "the current revival of interest in the decorative and craft arts" (ibid). A second lesson that was to be taken from Congo craftsmanship was that it demonstrated "the superiority and desirability of an art that is native, healthy, useful as well as ornamental, and integral with life, as contrasted with an art that is artificial, borrowed, non-utilitarian, and the exclusive product and possession of cliques and coteries" (ibid). Locke pointed out that Euro-American civilization had a deeply devitalizing trait, which could be countered with African art: "We have discov-

52 As the fashion for Black, primitive, wild, elemental, and erotic art in that same period was termed in urban France, for instance (Boittin 2010: 12-13).

ered that to capitalize Art, we have robbed it of some of its basic values and devitalized its tap-roots in the crafts" (ibid).

This new focus on "Africa" explained why the "Negro" came into style, according to literary scholar Amritjit Singh. What interested Black and white Americans was their nostalgia for a simple, forceful, and unmechanized existence (Singh 2004: 24). Fears of modernity and technology gave the "cult of the primitive [...] an extraordinary foothold on this continent" (ibid). The Congo was part of this cult. The "unexpected source of the folk crafts of Congo tribesmen", as Locke suggested, was considered "an astonishing demonstration of vital art values" (1927: 587).

Elevating Congolese craftsmanship to art produced "counter-stereotypes" (Feith 2004: 278), heightening the sense of history and value of African Americans, not the Congolese. Evoking the well-known topos of the Congo-as-Slave (cf. previous chapter), Locke stressed in his essay that exhibiting Congo art meant that "we are bringing over the cultural baggage of the American Negro that was crowded out of the slave-ship" (1927: 587). Regaining this tradition was akin to rehabilitating "Africa in general esteem and opinion", Locke wrote, once again reducing the Congo to an example of the continent and African American roots, rather than an art scene in and of itself. "More important still," Locke continued, "it has a very vital mission as a recovered and reinterpreted racial heritage, of stimulating and inspiring the expression of the artistic genius of the American Negro, particularly in the arts of his ancestors" (ibid). With these statements, Locke also highlighted the fact that Congo art was artistry from a bygone age, of interest because it stood for a desirable Black American heritage. The Black American might draw great "benefit from this powerful lesson from his own past" (ibid), the author concluded.

When Locke and other proponents of the Harlem Renaissance transformed Congo art into a useful emblem of desirable and essential African roots (building on the idea of the Congo as the original home; cf. previous chapter), a frenzy surrounding Congo naming developed in American (popular) culture. If we take The Chicago Defender as a measure, the mid-20s already bore witness to a massive amount of Congo references in American culture (the break with the pre-20s is considerable).[53] The color of blouses and accessories was described as "Congo brown" and

53 There are only a handful references to Congo naming practices in The Chicago Defender prior to the 20s. The "famed boxer 'Congo Kid'" was the most notable example (e.g. 1914a: 6), who was remembered up until the 40s (1940b: 4). Another exceptional reference to the Congo before the Harlem Renaissance was a dance called the "Congo schottische" (Jefferson 1914: 7).

advertisements tried to market incenses with the name Congo (1936: 6; 1933d: 5).[54] Popular music and night life were particularly prone to the fad. References to events, musicians, and the rise and fall of night clubs bearing the name Congo exploded in the 30s and 40s – from "Club Congo" in Chicago and Milwaukee in the 30s to similarly named clubs in Long Beach, Detroit, and other big cities in the 40s (e.g. Fulton 1937: 2; Hayes 1939: 9).

In the African American dance scene of these days, female dancers were called "Congoettes" and Congo bands and orchestras performed in Congo rooms, Congo lounges, or Congo halls, where they played songs like "Congo Lament" or "I go Congo" (e.g. Levette 1934: 9; Oglesby 1938:19). In the film arena, Oscar Michaux was mentioned and discussed in The Chicago Defender as the director of the film Daughter of the Congo in the late 20s; Paul Robeson was alluded to as a major character in Congo Raid in the 30s; and movies such as Drums of the Congo were announced in the early 40s (1942: 3).

Tracing what exactly the Congo signifies in all these instances is challenging, since these names were hardly accompanied by further explanation. That these names were employed so casually indicates, however, how normalized and naturalized the use of the Congo label in American culture had become. In one case, The Chicago Defender commented on the song "I go Congo" by the composer Clarence Muse as "a tom-tom, measured rhythm melody of powerful, insistent beat" (1933a: 5), connecting the song to emblematic primitiveness ("tom-tom") and to musical sensuousness ("insistent beat"). This reading is supported by texts written by the same Clarence Muse, who would become a Hollywood watcher for The Chicago Defender in the 40s. Throughout his articles, Muse commented on the works of jazz musician Duke Ellington, whose inspiration, according to the author, "will never run dry like the imitators, because he is true to his heritage" (1940: 21). The Hollywood watcher told his readers in subsequent lines what this heritage meant: "He lives and thinks in the culture of brave Blacks, deep in the Congo, close to the beat of the drum" (ibid). The equation of the Congo with the tom-tom, and therefore with a desirable African American heritage, seems to have been the formula behind the naming hype in the cultural industry of the 20s, 30s, and 40s.

The Congo as a designation for one's own commendable primitive origins and cultural legacy was evoked in poetic texts as well, most noticeably in novels, satires, and poems. One of the most famous poetic manifestations of the idea of the Congo as a homeland was Langston Hughes's 1921 "The Negro Speaks of Rivers".

54 Although these instances occurred in the mid-30s, the Congo as a lifestyle label had already popped up in the nineteenth century, when it was marketed as a black tea, as described in the previous chapter.

Through this poem, a timeless and essential Black "soul" is proclaimed that "has grown deep like the rivers" through the ages (1973: 72). Hughes referenced these rivers explicitly and, in doing so, pitted the Congo against the Nile: "I built my hut near the Congo and it lulled me to sleep. / I looked upon the Nile and raised the pyramids above it" (ibid). In this direct comparison, Egypt is associated with cultured and monumental activity ("raising pyramids"), while the Congo is linked to simple, hypnotic sleepiness ("hut", "lulled me to sleep"). Although this sleepiness could be read as a disabling force, it should be interpreted as a reference to the energy of Central West Africa that provides "depth" to African American history and identity. This sense of deep, historic belonging and heritage returned in the poetry published in The Chicago Defender, as well.[55]

Along the same lines as Hughes, Frank Marshall Davis's 1935 poem "Chicago's Congo" evokes the sense of an imaginary Central West African homestead called Congo, which connects to the poet's American home town of Chicago. "From the Congo / to Chicago / is a long trek" goes the refrain, locating the real-and-imagined roots of the Chicagoan Black community in Central West Africa. In the next lines, Davis presents Chicago and the Congo as parallel geographies: "Sing to me of a red warrior moon victorious in a Congo sky... / show me a round dollar moon in the ragged blue purse of Chicago's heavens... / pick me the winners… / in Chicago?…/ in the Congo?" (2002: 5). Whereas the Congo is linked here to a "warrior moon" (ibid), Chicago is discussed as "a round dollar moon" (ibid), thus implying that it is a city that is spoiled, "money mad" (ibid), especially vis-à-vis the simplicity and nobility of the Congo. "Ask me if civilization produces new forms of biting and tearing and killing… / see three million whites and two hundred thousand blacks civilized in Chicago" (ibid), Davis lamented in the next lines his critique of Euro-American civilization. Davis's goal in linking Chicago to the Congo was to celebrate African Americans' assimilation of the capitalist and social mores of the United States, while at the same time retaining the essentially desirable African traits they had brought with them: "You should be proud of me Chicago / I've got a lion's heart and a six-shooter / I've got a fighter's fist and five newspapers / I've got an eye for beauty and another for cash / Nothing you've got I can't have" (ibid: 6). Davis's African American Chicago was thus a desirable cross between the United

55 A reader named "HAMOWI" sent the poem "Lights and Shadows: Mirth" to the newspaper, in which he described "Mother Congo" as a "river of gold". In the same vein as Hughes, the poet expressed a feeling of belonging and inter-racial solidarity based on blood: "deep in my body flows thy blood / for centuries untold have I loved you" (HAMOWI 1928: A2).

Sates and Africa – merging "a lion's heart and a six-shooter", and implying that the rich heritage of Black American rendered them superior to whites.

Claude McKay's 1928 bestselling novel Home to Harlem also evoked a sense of transnational belonging through his celebration of the Congo Club in Harlem, which it describes as "a real throbbing little Africa in New York" (1965: 29). Through this description, McKay allowed the Congo to stand for the overarching sign of Africa and turned it into its synonym. Through the Congo Club the novelist expressed a "blackness" that was as racially exclusive as Hughes's Congo hut. "The Congo was African in spirit and color: no white persons were admitted there" (ibid: 30), McKay writes, and he adds adjectives to his description that were very commonly applied at the time: "[T]he Congo was thick, dark, colorful, and fascinating. Drum and saxophone were fighting out the wonderful drag 'blues' that was the favorite of all the low-down dance halls. In all the better places it was banned. Rumor said it was a police ban" (ibid).

By hinting at the police interference in the Congo Club and by presenting it in contrast to the "better places" (ibid: 36), McKay allowed the place to acquire an air of danger. Although McKay describes the music played at the club as old (which again hinted at its "African" roots), it nevertheless revitalized the African American club scene: "But at the Congo it lived fresh and green as grass. Everybody there was giggly and wriggling to it" (ibid). The cabaret singer Congo Rose is described in Home to Harlem as a "rearing wild animal" (ibid: 71), who "flirted with many fellows" at the night club (ibid: 113). Apart from her promiscuous behavior, the descriptions of Congo Rose suggest a sensuous animality: "[S]he moved down on him like a panther, swinging her hips in a wonderful, rhythmical motion" (ibid: 118).

The texts that produced the Congo-as-the Vital incited a considerable amount of critique. Home to Harlem was faulted in a 1928 review in The Chicago Defender for its tendency to represent Black people the way white people stereotypically saw them: "Again, white people think we are buffoons, thugs and rotters anyway. Why should we waste so much energy to prove it?" (Harper 1938: 6). In the era of "uplift", McKay's representations of the real-and-imagined hedonistic and sexualized side of African American club life were offensive to the idealized bourgeois values promoted by the newspaper. Female authors and poets, such as Anna Julia Cooper and Frances Harper, also questioned this essential, Black, primitive, promiscuous, violent male identity attached to the signifier Congo. They did so very early on, suggesting that this topos had been accumulating for quite some time.[56] The re-

56 One example is Cooper's discussion of "Voodoo Prophecy", an 1892 text by the white poet Maurice Thompson, in Cooper's seminal A Voice From the South. In it, the voice of the "prophet of the dusky race / the poet of wild Africa" (1892: 214) speaks of the sava-

sistance to the Congo signifier as constructed by the Harlem Renaissance reflects the larger opposition to Congo romanticism within the Black community. Jesse Fauset's 1928 novel Plum Bun questioned the tendency to celebrate pure-blooded Congo blackness. "And I can tell you this; I wouldn't care to marry a woman from the Congo," Fauset wrote, "but if I met a coloured woman of my own nationality, well-bred, beautiful, sympathetic, I wouldn't let the fact of her mixed blood stand in my way, I can tell you" (1928: 327). The writer George Schuyler, in turn, expressed discomfort about the mania surrounding the Congo by ridiculing the alleged danger, sensuous spontaneity, and militancy bound up with it. Not coincidentally, Schyler's 1938 Black Empire described the music in the temple of the Black Internationale – a militant Black organization with the goal of taking over Africa and world leadership – as "evil, blood-stirring rhythms born in the steamy swamps of the Congo" that "grew wilder and wilder" (2007: 62). The hyperbole involved in Schyler's

---

gery, heathenism, and feelings of hate and revenge by Black people towards their former slave masters: "As you have done by me, so will I do / By all the generations of your race; / Your snowy limbs, your blood's patrician blue / Shall be Tainted by me, / And I will set my seal upon your face!" (ibid). In times in which Social Darwinian concepts of race purity and degeneration ran rampant, the threat of a militant voice announcing Black mastery and miscegenation was more than disconcerting for whites. It went on: "Yea, I will dash my blackness down your veins, / And through your nerves my sensuousness I'll fling; / Your lips, your eyes, shall bear the musty stains / Of Congo kisses, / While shrieks and hisses / Shall blend into the savage songs I sing!" (ibid). In this poem, "Congo kisses" constituted the zenith of Black boldness, a threat to white supremacy and racial purity. In her discussion in A Voice from the South, Cooper called this poetry "simple and sensuous" and illustrative of a "fine poetic madness" (ibid: 215). At the same time, however, she considered it untruthful. What it did, Cooper asserted, was merely underline the poet's "secret dread and horrible fear" of Black men. "The Negro is utterly incapable of such vindictiveness", Cooper wrote, "such concentrated venom might be distilled in the cold Saxon, writhing and chafing under oppression and repression such as the Negro in America has suffered and is suffering. But the Black man is in real life only too glad to accept the olive branch of reconciliation" (ibid). The trope of "Congo kisses" returned in Frances Harper's "A Fairer Hope, A brighter Morn" from her collection Light beyond the darkness – a poem she wrote as a response to "Voodoo Prophecy". In it, Harper used "Congo kisses" to represent "phantoms of dread and pain" for white people: "fancies wild of your daughter's shriek / With Congo kisses upon her cheek?" (1890: 3). In the end, Harper and Cooper treated the Congo-as-the-Vital as a white fantasy of Black male militancy and sexuality, with little footing in reality.

work, and his description of Congo music in particular, are a sharp critique of the use of the signifier Congo.

When Langston Hughes grew older, he, too, started questioning his Congo essentialism and idealism. He would also turn to satirical irony. As Hughes wanted a glimpse of the continent of origins "to be touched and seen, not merely read about in a book" (1988: 10), he went to Africa as a mess-boy on a freighter in 1923, which he described almost two decades later in his autobiography The Big Sea. Confronted with Africans who considered him a white man, Hughes grew increasingly disheartened about his earlier Pan-African identity claims – a disappointment expressed through the signifier Congo. The pesky and expensive monkey he brought from Africa was dubbed "Congo devil" by his mother in the United States (ibid: 137), for instance. Once Hughes actually had the chance to see the Congo River, moreover, he hardly discussed it, turning the river into a slapstick setting: "A couple of weeks later, I got soaking-wet again, when I fell into the Congo, trying to climb down a rope at Boma. Since I couldn't swim, I got out, without being drowned, by paddling dog-fashion" (ibid: 117). On the one hand, this irony possessed substantial critical potential with regard to the appropriation of the Congo in African American discourse. On the other hand, it was another expression of the stigmatization of Central West Africa. This double action was typical of African American discourse of the time and is elaborated upon in what follows.

Culturalist Epistemology and the Limitations of Reversal

Within the increasingly industrialized mass commodity market of the United States at the turn of the century, the Congo appeared an appealing and useful term. "Congo": Containing two syllables and an internal rhythm, the noun was quickly recognizable, easy to remember, and even faster to sell, qualities that made it particularly tempting for artists and entrepreneurs in search of a broader market. The name Congo was a ready-made and flexible concept. The alliterations constantly formed with it were no coincidence; Congo club, Congo kid, Chicago's Congo, Congo kisses, and so forth were designed for their rhetorical flair. This did not mean that the patchy and stereotypical knowledge of Africa was cast aside altogether. "Congo kid" did not just label himself as such for aesthetic reasons, but also because a believable threat was evoked through the term Congo. "Congo club" applied a similar trick; the hypnotic, spontaneous, wild dancing associated with the name was an asset for nightlife culture.

This versatile Congo signifier was not a fully free-floating one, however. It did have its moral and social limits; not every primitive trait could be assigned to it.

Savageness was acceptable only because of changing social, racial, and cultural politics in the U.S. The morals of Victorian "uplift" were decidedly undermined by the Freudian and anthropological relativist turns. But primitivism was desirable only as long as it could be applied to one's own advantage. Thus Frank Marshall Davis's "Chicago's Congo" was an acceptable metaphor, whereas McKay's Congo Rose was not. "Chicago's Congo" could be easily connected to the Black middle class mainstream of the 30s, which was growing increasingly critical of the idea of Euro-American civilization, interracial cooperation, and unchecked capitalism. By 1938, The Chicago Defender was celebrating Davis by comparing him to the poets of the Harlem Renaissance such as McKay, who, according to The Chicago Defender, wrote in a time "when it was the custom for the smart white literary set and pseudo-intelligentsia who wielded plenty of influence to fawn upon a black person as a genius who was able to scribble his name" (Harper 1938: 6).

Another example of unacceptable primitiveness was the movie Ingagi, a would-be documentary about the "Heart of Africa" produced by Congo Pictures, Ltd.. According to the many articles and letters in The Chicago Defender, the movie was particularly "race-slandering" because it featured Black women mating with a gorilla. As one reader (the director Hilton A. Philips) noted in a letter to the newspaper: "I am an American Negro and have never been to Africa, yet I do not know of any part of Africa where people of our race have offsprings through consorting with gorillas, I do not know anything of Black women 'lower than gorillas themselves' and who fondly caress the wild 'Ingagi' from a husbandly point of view" (Philips 1930: A2). Although the movie depicted the usual primitive Black women in the wilds of Central West Africa, it did not find an appreciative audience because of its animalistic overtones and insinuations of gender-bending running counter to the accepted Black gender roles and respectable Black bourgeois identity (much as McKay's Congo Rose had done).

The Congo-as-the-Vital took up the stereotypes against Black people and turned them upside down. Primitiveness was re-cast as a positive feature that upgraded one's real-and-imagined roots. The reversal of anti-Black stereotypes had serious implications, however. Turning the Congo into a commodity traded in order to construct a certain vision of African American heritage did not rid the signifier of the essentialist, Social Darwinian stereotypes it conjured up. These stereotypes stayed firmly in place and were reaffirmed rather than rejected. Claiming primitiveness as a positive quality was as good as claiming the opposite; the assumption that Central West Africans were "not quite like us" remained.

Desirable savageness should not be read as a decisive turn away from the Social Darwinian idea of modern civilization, as it was by no means irreconcilable with the imperial, colonial times in which Black artists lived. On the contrary – the savage was one of the great ethnographic paradigms developed by European writers during the colonial age of exploration, as Ter Ellingson shows (2001: xiii). The symbolic opposition between wild and domesticated peoples, between savages and civilization was constructed as a part of the discourse of Social Darwinian hegemony. All discourse of savagery, as Ellingson noted, is essentially political, as the term demands a counterbalancing (ibid: 219); savagery, either as an affirmative or a derogatory characteristic, created a polarity that was useful for domination as it required a "civilized" counterpart (ibid). Dealing with civilized or semi-civilized societies required diplomacy and negotiation; dealing with savages, by contrast, required simpler and more direct steps toward conquest, control, territorial extirpation, and, in some cases, extermination (ibid: 220). As such, artistic production also played a useful role in enabling the expansion of colonial control, as it contributed to the growing generalization and dismissal of the savage (ibid). To what extent Black intellectuals were able to counter colonial, Social Darwinian Congo imagery is the topic of the next section, which deals with African American discourse on the Belgian Congo.

Fourth Topos: The Congo-as-Resource

Neither the CFS nor the Belgian Congo managed to become economically successful colonies. This circumstance does not, however, override the long-term idea behind these projects: To mine the Congo for the sake of Western capitalism. The founding fathers of the exploitation of the Congo made it perfectly clear that to think like an empire is to focus on Central West Africa through an economic prism. Livingstone and his militant counterpart Stanley wrote in commercial terms about the Congo, just as the 1884 Senate report "Occupation of the Congo Country of Africa" did (cf. discussion above). Their intentions might also have been humanitarian, but their talk was, first and foremost, oriented towards exploitation. The Senate report, for instance, talked about "all the great commercial nations" (Congress of the United States of America 1884: 7) which were looking for a "new and most inviting field of commerce [...] with the high and noble purpose of opening it freely to the equal enjoyment of all nations alike" (ibid). Only in an apologetic afterthought did the unspecified "blessings to the people of Africa" also receive mention (ibid).

Black historians, missionaries, and journalists made strong humanitarian and moral arguments whenever they talked about Central West Africa. However, their sustained focus on the Congo-as-Resource exemplified how deeply imbedded they were in the imperialistic mainstream of their days. Exemplary historians such as

Washington (1909a und 1909b), Pendleton (1912), Ferris (1913a und 1913b), and Woodson (1936) recounted the story of the Congo in much the same way as official colonial sources. Pendleton's A Narrative of the Negro, for instance, discussed the Berlin conference as an appointment amongst commercial friends for the benefit of the Africans. "Representatives from fourteen countries, the United States included, met and agreed that in that part of Africa, at least, trade should be free to all" (1912: 32). These noble ideals of imperialism and honorable colonial entrepreneurship were also stressed by Woodson, Washington, and Ferris. The latter saw how a "brighter day is rising upon Africa" (Ferris 1913b: 438), and the reason for his optimism was commerce brought by Europeans. Africa's "Congo and her Gambia" were "whitened with commerce, her crowded cities sending forth the hum of business, and all her sons employed in advancing the victories of peace – greater and more abiding than the spoils of war" (ibid: 438-439). Pacification through commerce was Ferris's reading of colonialism, a stance shared by Washington, who added another positive moral-economic aspect to the imperial equation: Congolese Blacks would learn to work and could thus become the backbone of African modernization. Washington proudly asserted, "It is he who builds the railways and the bridges, digs the gold in the South African mines, and collects the rubber in the Congo forests" (1909a: 29). All in all, peace, commerce, and Black workmanship were the keywords with which historians related to their readers the story of colonialism as positive exploitation.

The Chicago Defender openly celebrated the mineral and human wealth of the Congo as a blessing for Euro-American civilization. While King Leopold's regime of forced labor was considered a profit-driven slaughterhouse, the Belgian Congo was increasingly framed as a developing state with high potential. This country was being developed, it was consistently implied, with the aim of managing its wealth efficiently for the benefit of the United States. Initially, skepticism reigned in The Chicago Defender's articles. The newspaper feared the devastating effect of a lack of infrastructure (1922: 13), harsh working conditions (1925b: A1), or a downright return to the protective and abusive days of the Congo Free State. "The present rate of exploitation", The Chicago Defender stated on July 21, 1928 with respect to the "exploitation of the Congolese agricultural and mineral resources", will fully revive "the dreadful days of King Leopold II" (1928c: A1). Those dreadful days of the Congo Free State were mainly an economic issue, an issue boiling down to channeling the wealth of the Congo to a handful of private European shareholders. The anxiety about the Belgian Congo was caused by the fear of not getting a sufficiently large piece of it. The newspaper observed with concern how a "company has been organized with the approval and co-operation of the government" to exploit "territories" of the Congo, for instance (ibid).

Gradually, The Chicago Defender invested more confidence in the "open door" strategies concerning the Belgian Congo, which, by World War II, essentially sought to guarantee the accessibility of Congo resources to the United States. The colony was discussed as one of many nations in Africa which was drilling "sinking holes" to find much-needed oil in the 30s (1930b: 4). By the start of World War II, the Belgian Congo was considered a solid partner of America's, as shown in articles with subtitles such as "Rich Congo Colony Supplies America with Vital Mineral Ore" (1943a: 4). The production of tin, copper, and, above all, radium and uranium was of great interest to The Chicago Defender because of their strategic importance to the United States. In an issue from January 30, 1943, one may read, "In spite of the decline of her glorious civilizations, Africa still has much to give the world" (Willis 1943: 11). The newspaper obviously saw no real civilization in Africa, but did underscore the "practically inexhaustible" copper mines of the Belgian Congo, the production of which was to be "given" to the United States (ibid). In the same vein, the newspaper focused on radium from the Congo because it was instrumental in the "treatment of disease" in the hospitals "of the world and principally in the United States and Great Britain" (Padmore 1943: 4).

All of these news reports based themselves strongly on colonial propaganda. Again and again, one finds in them private or public sources that were close to the colonial project. Lines such as these are not exceptional: "[A]ccording to the 1944 report of the Union Miniere [sic] du Haut Katanga" or "according to the Belgian Information Center in New York" (e.g. Padmore 1945: 5; 1845: 1). Many Defender articles thus easily reveal their reliance on imperial sources. Through the use of these texts from companies and information providers sponsored by the government or privately (such as the Union Minière or the Belgian Information Center), the threat of The Chicago Defender directly adopting the imperial agenda was real.

The incorporation of the colonial prism can also be seen in the gradual decrease in critique of the Belgian Congo vis-à-vis the treatment of the "natives". Lack of decent payment is criticized, but discussed in such a euphemistic fashion that these utterances could have been taken directly from the colonial authorities (which they likely were). The Chicago Defender noted, for instance, in a semi-critical fashion in article titled "Belgium to Enforce Congo 'Status Quo'" from September 23, 1944: "The exploitation of Belgian human and natural resources caused much unrest among the natives before the war" (1944. 18). It then proceeded to water down this already weak opinion by balancing reports of discontented natives with more obedient ones: "With the outbreak of the war, a native army was raised to defend the country and has been praised for its part in the East African campaign" (ibid). Oppression in the Belgian Congo was thus downplayed, and the existence of obedient, successful Black professionals, such as the soldiers mentioned here, emphasized instead.

This focus on the soldiery was no surprise. Whole history books and chapters had been dedicated to the topic, as we have seen already in the previous chapter.[57] This focus on the military continued through the mid-20th century. An article by George Padmore in the 1944 Chicago Defender, "American, African Negroes Get Along Fine In Front Line Foxholes In Italy", discussed how Black troops were bringing down the Nazi regime, also known as the "citadel of racism" (1944: 3). Padmore reported: "From the West will march American Negro troops and famous Senegalese warriors serving with the French Army of Liberation, as well as Congolese forces from the Belgian Congo" (ibid). He continued: "These so-called inferior races are today helping the tear the guts out of the Herrenvolk 'super-men' of Nazi Germany. Such is the irony of history" (ibid). Via this alignment of African and Black American soldiers, a direct attack was launched against the hegemony of Social Darwinian thought, this time dressed up as Nazism. At the same time, an inter-African connection was fabricated through which the Congo could be aligned with a Pan-African professionalism. Above all, the fight by Black soldiers against "the citadel of racism" could and should also be read as a fight against racist America as well, given the ongoing tendency of Black American intellectuals to collapse the Central West African Congo into the American Congo.

In article after article, The Chicago Defender argued along colonial lines and drew upon imperial imagery in order to highlight the need for civilization through economic development. In the process, it downplayed the concrete oppression of Black colonized people and silently condoned the one-sided exploitation of mineral resources. As soon as the oppression of African Americans was addressed,[58] how-

57 Of significance here is George Washington Williams's 1887 A History of the Negro Troops in the War of the Rebellion, 1861-1865 and Norwood Hallowell's 1899 The Negro as a Soldier in the War of the Rebellion. Booker T. Washington's 1900 collection A New Negro for a New century contained chapters on "Afro-American Volunteers and Regiments", both in the past and the present, ranging from soldiers in the Rebellion against Britain and those to the Philippines and Cuba. The same went for Carter Woodson's 1922 The Negro in Our History, which discussed "The Negro in the Civil War" and the "Negro in the World War", inscribing Black soldiers into the major military dramas of American history.

58 In the 1945 Chicago Defender article "Storm Signals at the Golden Gate" from March 10, the end of the world war was considered advantageous for white people only. "Black

ever, the Belgian Congo was turned into a system of intolerable colonial robbery, much in the same way as India and the South Seas were. In other words, as long as the Congo was referred to as a signifier for Central West Africa, oppression was downplayed; whenever the Congo was parochialized and turned into an American signifier, oppression became a real issue.

Were there alternatives to this hierarchy of misery? In the next section, Black anti-imperial thinking will be discussed, mainly as illustrated in the development of W.E.B. Du Bois's thought.

Colonial Epistemology and Anti-Imperialism

Few Black historians formulated a systematic critique of Euro-American imperialism. In fact, they hardly ever used the word imperialism (which implies critique), with the notable exceptions of Carter Woodson's critical chapter on "economic imperialism" in The African Background Outlined and William Ferris's offhanded reference to Kelly Miller's "brilliant pamphlet on Anti-Imperialism" (1913 a:143). Journalists expressed anti-imperial ideas more often, but did not deliver in-depth analysis. The Chicago Defender used the term imperialism primarily to condemn the colonial abuses against the "natives" and to question the appropriation of their territories. When Belgium took over the Congo Free State, the new rulers were described as "10,000 white agents of imperialism" who governed via "savage repression" and "extreme measures of terrorism in the effort to cow the natives and prevent the passing of Nordic power and influence" (1929a: A1). Italy's 1943 invasion of Ethiopia was also systematically referred to as "Italian imperialism" (e.g. Hall 1937: 24).

In all these articles, the term imperialism was used rather offhandedly. The contexts in which the term appears suggest that imperialism signified extremities of colonial rule. Despotic decision-making in the metropolis and foreign ruthlessness were labeled imperialism; economic and human exploitation were not. The United States was therefore generally excluded from the imperial label, since, as The Chicago Defender wrote towards the end of World War II, "we of the democratic na-

America and the colored peoples of the earth" had to prepare for the "outbreak of another war, a bloody racial conflict", the newspaper stated. As the "race problem of America has become part of a world problem [...] the status and standing of Negro America is part and parcel of the color problem of the world, also known as the colonial question" (1945a: 10). This identification based on racial oppression culminated in the assertion that "the Negro is the colonial of America, exploited and robbed of the fruits of his labor just as men of color in the Congo or India or the South Seas" (ibid).

tions are fighting an anti-imperialistic war" (Willkie 1942: A5). As a democracy, the United States supposedly had no imperial ambitions. The Chicago Defender framed the American attitude towards imperialism in the following manner: "We covet no territory. We want no more power than is necessary to prevent a repetition of this slaughter and to maintain a world in which men can be free. We seek to liberate, not to enslave" (ibid).

If the U.S. was considered an imperial power at all, it was linked to an internal or benevolent version of imperialism. In 1923, The Chicago Defender emphasized the existence of an external American imperialism as a necessary evil: "As long as there is an increasing output of American products which are far beyond home consumption foreign markets must be sought; hence a country that enjoys the right of protectorate over another country naturally has a preference of exploiting the markets of that country" (1923b: 12). It went without saying that the "recent acquisitions" of the American empire (Haiti and the Virgin Islands, amongst others) were to be "helped" by America to "advance to a state where they can handle their own affairs with the thorough enlightenment of a modern, free and independent people" (ibid). By 1945, American imperialism was denied altogether (or framed as something that had been overcome).[59]

There were several discursive alternatives available for this particular reading of American foreign policy. The broader discursive field in the United States did contain anti-imperialist writing and activism throughout the period. The Anti-Imperialist League battled against the annexation of the Philippines at the turn of the century by widely circulating anti-imperial propaganda. In doing so, the League reached sizable Black and white audiences (Zinn 2003: 317). Parallel to the agitating activities of the League, numerous white English and American academics, activists, and writers published their critical analyses of imperialism. These books varied greatly in tone and political impetus, offering a wide range of perspectives

---

59 "It has been a long while since the United States had any imperialistic designs toward the outside world", The Chicago Defender noted in 1942 (Willkie 1942: A5). Instead of being faulted for practicing external imperialism, The Chicago Defender accused the U.S. of creating a situation "within our own boundaries" which "amounts to race imperialism" (ibid). Thus, whereas the authors of The Chicago Defender relentlessly attacked the government of the United States for the internal oppression it perpetuated, it would remain largely mute on the topic of American and European expansion abroad, issuing only occasional condemnations of extreme abuse.

and resulting in a considerable output of analytic anti-imperial voices – ranging from conservative to leftist.[60]

Blacks intellectuals were reluctant critics of imperialism. Pauline Hopkins's The Colored American barely mentioned the existence of anti-imperialist thinking, although it reprinted articles by white authors who did. In the midst of the heated debate about the Philippines, for instance, Hopkins published excerpts of the Lewiston Journal article entitled "Negro and Filipino". In it, the authors critiqued anti-imperialist activism more than imperialism itself: "Anti-imperialists who sweat blood because [President] McKinley in obedience to the Senate assumes to place the flag in Manila and to defend it there, are silent over the fact that Louisiana and Mississippi pass laws that admit the vote to white men who cannot read or write and deny it to black men because they cannot read or write" (1900: 5). What one can derive from these comments is that Black intellectuals reluctantly went along with anti-imperial thinking because it was of no real consequence to them or their lives: It addressed oppressive situations abroad that were silently taken for granted at home.

A small number of Black intellectuals did take a more determined stance against imperialism, illustrated here by Kelly Miller's 1900 pamphlet "The Effect of Imperialism Upon the Negro Race" and W.E.B. Du Bois's works "The African Roots of War" (1915), Darkwater (1920), and "Prospect of a World Without Race Conflict" (1944). "The Effect of Imperialism upon the Negro Race", the author of which (Kelly Miller) was a mathematics professor at Howard University and a future editor of the NAACP's The Crisis, was republished in the Anti-Imperialist League's house organ, Anti-Imperialist Broadside, when the Philippine-American War started. Miller attempted to answer the question of why Blacks should care about imperialism. He began by opening his essay with a key idea: The connection between international and domestic issues. "The welfare of the negro race," Miller asserted about Black Americans, "is vitally involved in the impending policy of imperial-

60 The 1912 lectures on imperialism and expansion at Johns Hopkins University by John Basset Moore (Four Phases of American Development) were published alongside John George Godard's collection of articles from the Westminster Review in his 1905 Racial Supremacy: Being Studies in Imperialism. From the American Left, in turn, came an outpouring of socialist and communist pamphlets that in 1923 termed American imperialism a "menace of the Greatest Capitalist World Power" (the title of a pamphlet published by the American Workers Party; Lovestone 1905) and discussed it as a major triggering factor for World War I (e.g. Labor and the Next War: A Study of American Imperialism and its Effects on the Workers, published by the Socialist Party of the United States, O' Neal 1922).

ism" (1900: n.p.). For Miller, oppression abroad would eventually lead to undermining what little liberty Black Americans had at home: "The United States is attempting to force, vi et armis, an alien government upon a unanimously hostile and violently unwilling people. Acquiescence on the part of the negro in the political rape upon the Filipino would give ground of justification to the assaults upon his rights at home" (ibid). According to the author, the African American "would not only forfeit his own weapon of defense, but his friends would lose theirs also. For how, with consistency, could the despoilers of the brown man's rights in Manila, upbraid the nullifiers of the black man's rights in Mississippi?" (ibid).

Miller boiled imperialism down to a domestic racial issue, which he discussed using Social Darwinian rhetoric. If "the Filipino" appeared as a subject at all, it was to assert his or her ability to self-govern, which was at least equal to the "capacity for self-government" possessed by Black Americans (ibid); thus the competence of both groups to determine their own political conditions was highlighted. Linking the Philippines to the United States, Miller considered "the whole trend of imperial aggression" as "a revival of racial arrogance" towards the "feebler races" (ibid). Although he condemned whites as "haughty" in their pretended superiority, Miller's outlook was equally supremacist. The author believed that "natural law" ruled history, through which "the strong will rule the weak, the rich will control the poor, and the wise man will dominate the fool" (ibid). As far as Miller was concerned, inferior people had the ability to govern themselves – whenever they were ready, they should do so, but only in accordance with the central ideas that made the U.S. a democracy. "Any policy which strikes at the vital doctrine of the Declaration of Independence would be [...] like blotting out the sun from the sky," he wrote. Living up to the principles of the Republic meant, in turn, that the United States would not tax the "untaxable[s]" within or without its borders (ibid).

Many anti-imperial texts of this period take up a similar line of argument. For instance, the Anti-Imperialist League discussed American imperialism in its "Declaration" as a test for the values of the republic, and included the statement that "all its citizens are equal under the law; that a government derives its just powers from the consent of the governed, and that there be no taxation without representation" (Atkinson 1976: 23). The ideas of the League were as permeated by Social Darwinian vocabulary and ideas as Miller's text, however, as the League spoke of the dangers American soldiers faced from "physical degeneration, the corruption of the blood" during an occupation of the Philippines (ibid: 24).

The differences between the League's "Declaration" and Miller's pamphlet, however, are instructive as to why Black intellectuals could not have fostered a vigorous anti-imperialism. For one, the League did not understand American imperialism in terms of race.[61] Secondly, the League saw nothing but deception in the "new imperialism" of the United States. It saw the ascendance of "a false philanthropy to set up the law of the might" (ibid). Miller, on the other hand, considered this "law of the might" (and all the suffering it caused to Blacks in the United States, which he described in detail) both a burden and a prerequisite for reaching the "high calling of American citizenship" (Miller 1900: n.p.). Suffering and inequality were just a "temporary obscuration of the light", Miller wrote, deploying the imperialist trope of pitting "light" against "darkness" (ibid). Whereas the League saw nothing but a scam in American imperialism, Miller saw some good in the force it applied. Through the lens of African American history – which he discussed as a progression from savagery to civilized citizenship through the tunnel of forced labor and grief – imperial suffering could, according to Miller, serve the broader good of the Philippine community.

A third reason why African American intellectuals did not wholeheartedly embrace anti-imperialism was that the League considered imperialism to be a primarily economic project of "commercial gain" that would "imperil and delay the settlement of pressing financial, labor, and administrative questions at home" (Atkinson 1976: 23). Miller, in contrast, refused to take up this argument for the Black community. Black people had an interest in politics that "has been moral and not economic [...] the great question of tax and tariff, expansion of trade and commerce, the relative coinage of the precious metals affect him very feebly" (1900: n.p.). The Black community, to Miller, had little stake in the economic ambitions of the "white man" (ibid). Miller contended that "[w]ith manhood rights eliminated" Blacks had no choice but to focus on local economic issues instead of national and international ones: "Local regulations exhaust the whole circle of economic interests in which they live and move and have their being" (ibid). Whereas the nation as a whole might profit from new markets, the Black community did not, and, as such, according to Miller, would not engage in a debate on imperialism.

Even among central Black activists such as labor activist Philip A. Randolph, whose white socialist compatriots were systematically agitating against imperialism, critique of the American empire was scattered and pertained mainly to domes-

61 Du Bois's recounted experience affirms the reluctance on the part of white anti-imperialists to debate the issue racially. "'Should you not discuss racial prejudice as a prime cause of war?'", Du Bois asked at a meeting of the "peace societies in St. Louis", according to this own account in "The African Roots of War" (1915: 712). The secretary was sorry, Du Bois mentioned, "but was unwilling to introduce controversial matters!" (ibid). Again, one re-encounters a potentially important reason why Black intellectuals would not attach themselves to the activism of white anti-imperialists.

tic issues. Randolph published only a handful of anti-imperialist texts. One appeared in July 1921 in his own magazine The Messenger: Here Randolph attacked the racist foreign policy of the United States in an article titled "A Merited Rebuke of American Imperialism". In this text, Randolph demanded the U.S. president "clean house, change habits, make apologies and extend a fitting reparation for our misdeeds and our debauchery of Haiti" (1969: 209). Randolph called these misdeeds "more shameless and inexcusable than the German rape of the Belgian Congo" (ibid) – another instance of how the Congo served as an example of one misery among many.

W.E.B. Du Bois stood as an exception to the general Black intellectual reluctance to address imperialism. Going against the mainstream, Du Bois did take up anti-imperialist thinking, and re-construed it along racial lines. He truly struggled with imperialism – finding it both fruitful to the "natives" as well as detrimental for them – thus producing a range of contradictions in his own writing.

His seminal 1915 essay "The African Roots of War" centered the Congo as the key "to the riches of Central Africa" (1915: 708) and, as a consequence, where the direct cause of imperialism and World War I could be found – all of which Du Bois considered as connected (ibid).

> It all began, singularly enough, like the present war, with Belgium. Many of us remember Stanley's great solution of the puzzle of Central Africa, when he traced the mighty Congo sixteen hundred miles from Nyangwe to the sea. Suddenly the world knew that here lay the key riches of Central Africa. It stirred uneasily, but Leopold of Belgium was first on his feet, and the result was the Congo Free State – God save the mark! But the Congo Free State, with all its magniloquent heralding of Peace, Christianity, and Commerce, degenerating into murder, mutilation, and downright robbery, differed only in degree and concentration from the tale of all Africa in this rape of the continent already furiously mangled by the slave trade. That sinister traffic, on which the British Empire and the American Republic were largely built, cost black Africa no less than 100,000,000 souls, the wreckage of its political and social life, and left the continent in precisely that state of helplessness which invites aggression and exploitation. 'Color' became in the world's thought synonymous with inferiority, 'Negro' lost its capitalization, and Africa was another name for bestiality and barbarism. Thus, the world began to invest in color prejudice. The 'Color Line' began to pay dividends. For indeed, while the exploration of the valley of the Congo was the occasion of the scramble for Africa, the cause lay deeper.

In this remarkable passage, Du Bois tapped into, as well as opposed, the mainstream rhetoric on colonialism in the Congo. He did this in a number of ways. To begin, in his oppositional stance, Du Bois called the officially proclaimed aims of Belgian imperialism (i.e. "Peace, Christianity, and Commerce") what they were: "Magniloquent heralding", which collapsed soon enough into "murder, mutilation, and downright robbery". In contrast to other Black intellectuals (and white ones; see Morel and Conrad, for instance), Du Bois considered this robbery, at least in this text, as the imperialist standard rather than an aberration. This example also reveals, however, the more conformist Du Bois. Here, as elsewhere, the Congo is used as an illustration of how white people within the "British Empire and the American Republic" built their nations on the gains they had gotten from the slave trade, as well as on anti-Black racism. The latter manifested itself, according to Du Bois, in discourse on Africa and Blacks that cast them as inferior, bestial, and barbaric. Du Bois thus mobilized the Congoist strategy of the Congo-as-Example to meta-reflect on issues external to Central West Africa.

In the same vein, Congolese were used by Du Bois to illustrate this economically-driven colonial oppression of Africa, in which they played no significant role. In "Prospect of a World Without Race Conflict" Du Bois asserted, for instance, that "Belgium has held its Congo empire with rare profit during the war, and the home land will recoup its losses in Europe by more systematic rape of Africa" (1944: 455). Congolese opposition to this "rape" – a topic that will return in postcolonial Congo discourses (cf. next chapter) – was hardly acknowledged, apart from a vague warning to whites around the world that "colored people" are "going to endure this treatment just as long as they must and not a moment longer" (1915: 714). The fact that "Africa is being enslaved by the theft of her land and natural resources" (ibid: 713) was expressed without concrete acknowledgment of the substantial resistance in Du Bois's work. Congolese were reduced to "the 'dumb-driven-cattle' stage of labor activity" (ibid) – an ironic designation that is critiqued by Du Bois, but also reproduced in his own texts. Colonial perversion, Du Bois noted in Darkwater, "will have a voiceless continent to conceal it" (1920: 64).

The harsh condemnation of Congolese Blacks by Du Bois does not sit well with his more general unifying stance, and this becomes painfully apparent if one compares Du Bois's take on the Congolese with the following passage. A demand Du Bois repeated often was to "treat black men as human, sentient, responsible beings [...] and treat them as free and equal citizens in a world-democracy of all races and nations" (1915: 712). This quote is exemplary for Du Bois, particularly prior to his move to the Left from the 1930s onward, because of its focus on "a world-democracy". Democratic ideals are mobilized to dismiss imperialism in way that parallels the strategy of the Anti-imperial League and Miller's work: "We must extend the democratic ideal to the yellow, brown, and black peoples [...] we shall not drive war from this world until we treat them as free and equal citizens in a world-democracy [sic] of all races and nations" (1915: 712). Du Bois suggested in Darkwater that this equal treatment entails respect towards the local customs, a continuous striving for a self-governing state, as well as a steady incorporation of the oppressed people into the efforts of "world philanthropy" (excluding, however, "religious conversion"; 1920: 62).

By 1944, when Du Bois published his essay "Prospect of a World without Race Conflict" in the American Journal of Sociology, his thoughts on democratic equality ended in an all-out condemnation of Social Darwinian thought. In the essay, Du Bois interrogated de Gobineau's devastating record of ill-founded "racial assumptions" (1944: 453). The "race philosophy" of the United States and Great Britain was identified, too, as a "philosophy [that] postulates a fundamental difference among the greater groups of people, which makes it necessary that the superior peoples hold the inferior in check and rule them in accordance with the best interests of these superiors" (ibid: 450). Western powers, according to Du Bois, mobilized an amalgam of knowledge in order to keep the "inferior people in check" (ibid: 455). Du Bois mentioned the "social sciences" that were deliberately used as instruments to "prove the inferiority of the majority of the people of the world" (ibid), which was an unusually critical indictment of science in a positivist age. Other academic fields enlisted to construct the inferiority of other races were identified by Du Bois as "history" (which "declared that the Negro had no history"), biology (which "exaggerated the physical differences among men"), and economics, which "even today cannot talk straight on colonial imperialism" as it is unwilling to take up the criticism of socialist thought (ibid).

Through a democratic lens, Du Bois thus advocated equal treatment of Blacks, including the Congolese. This mainly meant asserting their labor rights, installing trade unions in the Congo, and imposing factory legislation, which he called "all of the great body of legislation built up in modern days to protect mankind from sinking to the level of beasts of burden" (1920: 64). From this and other excerpts, however, it becomes clear that Du Bois focused on the colonial African as a "laborer" alone. This economic approach can be partly explained by Du Bois's increasing involvement in Marxist theory and the latter's emphasis on the agency of workers in the course of history. However, in light of Du Bois's rejection of Africa as a "voiceless country", one is prompted to ask how these laborers would achieve agency within the imperialist system?

Du Bois would have pointed to education and labor regulation. However, his deep-seated belief in the anti-Black, anti-worker "scheme of Europe" contradicted the possibility of progress by those means. Du Bois claimed in Darkwater, "The scheme of Europe was no sudden invention, but a way out of long-pressing difficulties" (1920: 43). Colonialism was an economic necessity, since it was key to a "modern white civilization" in which the "white working classes cannot much longer be maintained" (ibid). As such, the history of oppression of the white working class inevitably moved into the direction of empowering workers. Blacks constituted "a loophole" for the ongoing "exploitation on an immense scale for inordinate profit" (ibid). This Black loophole was not just there for the advancement of the super-rich, but also for the middle class and the (white) laborers themselves. "The exploitation of darker peoples" was thus a foundational aspect of colonialism and, according to Du Bois, the real reason behind the World War: "It was this competition for the labor of yellow, brown, and black folks that was the cause of the World War" (ibid: 45). Although he did keep the dissent of Blacks in mind, powerful opposition could hardly develop in a context in which colonized people were assigned so little value.

Despite his open opposition to Social Darwinian thought, Du Bois's language and arguments do betray the deep inroads that it had made in his own writing. A systematic hierarchical division appeared throughout his work between the West and the rest. Just as his contemporaries did, Du Bois framed Africa as a "mysterious" region and a "Dark Continent" whose "dark forests of inmost Africa" were located in the Congo, thereby evoking Conrad's imagery of Central West Africa (e.g. 1915: 707; 1920: 38). There were challenges to this rhetoric, as Mark Twain's "To the Person Sitting in Darkness" (1901) showed.[62]

Du Bois referred to the Congolese as "natives", refusing the distinction that would paint them as citizens (although in theory he advocated for this), who were dominated by the Belgians under a "system of caste and color serfdom" (1920: 65). The Congolese were not agents in their own story, but a Conradian illustration of the "real soul of white culture" (ibid: 39) – a culture described as greedy, murder-

62 Mark Twain's "To the Person Sitting in Darkness" (1901) asked ironically, for instance: "Shall we go on conferring our Civilization upon the peoples that sit in darkness, or shall we give those poor things a rest? Shall we bang right ahead in our old-time, loud, pious way, and commit the new century to the game; or shall we sober up and sit down and think it over first? Would it not be prudent to get over Civilization-tools together, and see how much stock is left on hands in the way of Glass Beads and Theology, and Maxim Guns and Hymn Books and Trade-Gin and Torches Progress and Enlightenment (patent adjustable ones, good to fire villages with, upon occasion), and balance the books, and arrive at the profit and loss, so that we may intelligently decide whether to continue the business or see out the property and start a new Civilization Scheme on the proceeds?" (1901: 164).

ous, and imperial (as opposed to Black culture, it is implied). Thus, Du Bois again reduced the Congo to an example.

Du Bois faulted imperialists for the "invasion" of pre-colonial Congolese "family life the ruthless destruction of every social barrier, as well as the shattering of every tribal law, the introduction of criminal practices" (ibid: 38).[63] Nevertheless, his perspective on Congolese was as inconsistent as that of many contemporary Black and white intellectuals. In much the same way as these contemporaries, Du Bois absorbs the Congolese into more abstract labels such as "Africa", "colonial peoples", "darker nations", "yellow, brown, and black men", or "colored races". Very often, therefore, a merging is enacted of the concrete situation of Congolese with the "coolies in China [...] starving peasants in India [...] black savages in Africa [...] dying South Sea Islanders [...] [and] Indians of the Amazon" (ibid: 47).

This push for the rhetorical unification of people of color had a progressive aim, no doubt. Du Bois's solutions to the colonial oppression of "primitive peoples of Africa and the world" nevertheless contained a vision that resuscitated old Social Darwinian distinctions. He emphasized, for instance, the need for education, thus adhering to the familiar Black bourgeois belief in progress through "uplift and prevention" and "assimilation and uplift" (ibid: 62). "We must train native races in modern civilization", Du Bois asserted in "The African Roots of War" (1915: 713), indicating with these words precisely where he saw their flaws. Within the context of education, Du Bois falls into a number of Congoist traps, condoning imperialism despite its proclaimed evils. Colonialism had its positive sides, according to Du Bois: "Missionaries and commerce have left some good with all their evil. In black Africa today there are more than a thousand government schools [...] all the children of Africa are beginning to learn", Du Bois noted in Darkwater (1920: 65). However, he urged colonial governments to avoid tampering too much in "the curiously efficient African institutions of local self-government through the family and the tribe" (ibid: 71). At the same time, he urged colonial administrations to abolish "deleterious customs and unsanitary usages" (ibid). Confronted with the "unsanitary customs" of the "natives", Du Bois suddenly did believe in the possibility of colonial best practice after all: "The best colonial administrators [...] build on recognized, established foundations" rather than designing colonies "from entirely new and theoretical plans" (ibid).

By 1944, however, Du Bois was voicing serious doubts as to whether this "policy of so educating the colored races" would lead them to "being able to take part in modern civilization", as their training hindered "real acquaintanceship with what

63 He did this by quoting John Hobbis Harris, a Congo traveler and activist for the Congo Reform association.

the more advanced part of the world has done and is doing" (1944: 454). Du Bois thus harbored a deep skepticism about the learning capacities of "the lowest and the most exploited races in the world" (ibid), which had as much to do with their starting point at the bottom of the ladder of civilization as with the education provided by the authorities (the "Negro colleges of the southern United States" exempted, of course; ibid: 455). In the end, Du Bois openly labeled the Congo a "land of silence and ignorance", in which the "modern lifting of the veil of centuries" was hindered both by internal stasis and external incompetence and greed (1992: 392; 1915: 10).

Du Bois's anti-imperial thinking was deeply Congoist. Like Kelly Miller, Du Bois drew from the civilization dichotomy (inferior vs. superior civilizations) to construct a Congo that was an abstract human and mineral resource. Although he searched for a way to stop the anti-Black, anti-African racial prejudice, Du Bois implicitly contributed to it. He claimed that Africa would be self-governing one day and that Africans would become just as good as any white European worker. But until Africa became "the Land of the Twentieth century" (1915: 710), the natives had to be educated, civilized, organized, and politicized. In short, that day was far ahead, and it was unclear in his texts what would make them fight the "War of the Color Line" against whites when the former were considered superior and the latter discussed as backwards. This paradox is quintessentially Congoist, although it takes a subtler form than many of the Congoisms before it. The next chapter investigates to what extent the independence of the Congo contributed to a rhetorical shift surrounding it.

Picturing Congoism: A Conclusion

To summarize and discuss the heterogeneous results of this chapter, a number of photos of the Congo used by Black intellectuals between 1885 and 1945 will be analyzed. There is good reason to take up images in this chapter: By the 1890s, photography had become affordable and portable enough that Black intellectuals often took cameras on their voyages to the Congo. Furthermore, halftone printing had come to be used widely in magazines and newspapers, allowing for the mass circulation of these inexpensive images (Rice 2011: 1). The rise of a "global image economy" (Tucker 2009: 2) also informed the imagery of the Euro-American civilizing mission and the introduction of capitalism through exploitation, modernization, and conversion. From 1904 onward, images of mutilated Congolese were used extensively, and re-energized the nearly obsolete Congo Reform Association and its activism against the "Congo atrocities" (Grant 2005: 66). These images allowed viewers to question the (allegedly) anomalous imperial activity in the Congo Free State. At the same time, they actively promoted the Euro-American presence in the Congo by highlighting the humanitarian aid provided there by medical crews. Captions of pictures in newspapers such as The Chicago Defender highlighted how Westerners, for instance, "Fight Epidemic in Africa" (1928d: A12) or "Fight Plagues in Africa" (1928e: 22). These pictures and captions mostly showed the battle against diseases long conquered in Europe and the United States, such as leprosy, tuberculosis, and sleeping sickness, reinforcing the notion of the Congo as a backward region.

Missionaries such as Sheppard and mass newspapers like The Chicago Defender – the main source of the photos in what follows – actively used pictures to back up their written accounts of life in the Congo. If read critically, these photographs constitute powerful tools for debating the constructedness of the real-and-imagined Central West Africa to be found in texts. These pictures also legitimized the imperial drive for resources through anti-Black imagery, no matter how well-intended they might have been. Pictures will be used in what follows as illustrations of my findings from the written texts. Peter Burke finds this practice problematic, faulting historians for utilizing images to back up "conclusions that the author has already reached by other means" (Burke 2001: 10). Here, however, photographs can be used productively, as they form as much a part of Congoist discourse as the various written accounts of the Congo. Although they use different language codes, which must be acknowledged, visual and written accounts do produce similar tropes and topoi, as they resonate with, and draw from, the same socio-historical context (Bal 2006a: 290, 298; Bal 2006b: 159). From a semantic point of view, there is no essential difference between literary texts and pictures, as Mitchell accentuates (1994: 160-161), which makes both of them readable as "texts" and thus comparable as textual embodiments of Congoism.

While serving as illustrations of Congo discourse, visual material simultaneously provokes new answers to old questions. In contrast to other texts, they allow for a more overt and critical decoding of the "realistic" mode of storytelling than most of the sources applied up until this point. This "realism" provided readers with strong cues to look at the photographs and written texts as truthful eyewitness accounts (Mitchell 1994: 325-326; Bal 2006b: 216). Photographs allow for a more open deconstruction of this mode of storytelling than written accounts due to the unattended details that appear in them, which often escape the attention of their producers and readers. More so than written texts, these details reveal the "tricks, devices, and other lures" (Tagg 1988: 330) that summon up the "power of the real" (ibid: 99). Thus, through a detail-focused reading of these images, the naturalness and unity of the realistic mode can be shown and subverted, as Mieke Bal has noted (2006b: 235; 309).

Congoism as traced in this chapter has been presented as a discourse that created both an unbridgeable distance and an objectifying closeness between Black Euro-Americans and Congolese. The closeness was produced by African American intellectuals' travels to the Congo – as missionaries, journalists, and travel writers in particular. The distance, in turn, was created by capturing the Congolese through the various metaphors of darkness, a darkness in which they wandered blindly and ignorantly, unable to find a way out on their own. Euro-American subjects, in contrast, were poised as the bearers of light whose benevolence allowed "natives" to reach a higher level of civilization, as long as they interacted, engaged, and, in the end, listened to the advice of these Euro-American subjects. The relativism and liberalism of many Black American intellectuals was not a sufficient tool for overcoming the Social Darwinian mainstream of their days, although it did cover up its harshest rhetoric.

Picture one illustrates how hierarchies were both produced and tempered. The image was published in Sheppard's missionary account Presbyterian Pioneers in Congo (1917: 146). It depicts a male dressed from head to toe in white, seated on the grass in what seems to be a rural environment (evoked by the hut-like construction on the left and the hint of a hedge in the background). From other photographs, we recognize this seated figure as Sheppard. He is being worked on with a pencil-like tool by a bare-chested Black male with braided hair, who is seated on his knees and faces Sheppard. In the background, a bare-chested, child-like figure wearing shorts gazes at the two main figures from a distance, covering his/her mouth with both hands. The caption of the picture reads "shaving with a chisel", a phrase with a certain anthropological and objective matter-of-factness, identifying the tool and the activity depicted.

Picture 1: "Shaving with a Chisel"

SHAVING WITH A CHISEL.

Presbyterian Pioneers in Congo, p. 146

The whole pictorial setup creates a contrast between Sheppard and the two other figures. Through visual focalization, Sheppard forms the center of this picture and stands out in many ways. He is fully dressed in white, for instance, and sits leisurely on the ground, his head confidently turned towards the camera. The other figures, in contrast, Black and "half-clad" people (as the parlance of those days went), are rather peripheral entities. Instead of facing the camera, they face Sheppard and are either working for him or observing the overall situation. Through this setup, the picture evokes a master-servant dynamic, deploying many binaries that are by now familiar – dark vs. light, dressed vs. naked, resting vs. working, gazing vs. gazed at, central vs. peripheral, and, ultimately, civilized vs. savage. There is also a tongue-in-cheekiness to the picture that is very much part and parcel of Congoism (see Conclusion, too). The humorous strain of Congoist discourse used irony to override, to some extent, its more overtly paternalistic base. For civilized subjects to allow themselves to be shaved with a chisel by a half-naked native is preposterous, the picture implies, which the "natives" themselves – embodied by the child in the back that covers its mouth out of laughter or embarrassment – confirm. That the Black missionary Sheppard went along with this slightly humorous or embarrassing spectacle shows the benevolence and good humor with which he bore the light of Christ into the "Dark Heart" of the African continent. What is obvious from this picture is that Sheppard mattered to the photographer, and Sheppard alone. This is the egocentric fabric of Congoism – "our" needs, interests, images, desires, and battles are projected on, and debated through, the example of the Congo.

Mastering the uncivilized was a win-win situation, or at least this is what the text corpus from the colonial era appears to espouse. The Congolese had a chance to make something of their "defunct" selves in their rich country; untutored, however, they would have remained ignorant slaves, savages, drunks, gender-benders, and cannibals. There were hardly any attempts to provide real, convincing evidence for these labels. Vague descriptions and suggestive visual material were enough to make audiences believe in the savagery and primitiveness of the Congolese. Most representations of the Congo emerged played straight into a catalog of publicly communicated fears and interests of the ambitious African American middle-class communities. The Central West African Congo turned into a discursive entity that was flexibly used to depict ethical, sexual, political, and behavioral abnormalities in a nexus of class, race, and gender.

The issue of Congolese drunkenness, for instance, was tied up with the large discussion surrounding alcoholism. Du Bois is a good example of how this topic sneaked into the texts of intellectuals. He wrote in The Philadelphia Negro, "One of the chief and most pernicious forms of bribery among the lowest classes is through the establishment of political clubs" (1899: 378). Situating these clubs firmly in the lower strata of African American society, he then described them as "the centre of gambling, drunkenness, prostitution and crime[...] liquor is furnished to 'members' at all times and the restrictions on membership are slight" (ibid: 397). This focus on lower-class alcohol consumption and drunkenness was often combined with references to criminality or gender transgressions (tied to "prostitution" in this quote). Thus, drunkenness was very much at top of the list of undesirable traits among Black Americans who were striving to be accepted as honorable, upright moral citizens. Congolese drunkenness, in other words, was more reflective of the infatuation with alcohol by Black American intellectuals than of any rampaging addiction in Central West Africa.

Picture 2: "Cannibal Dance in the Congo"

CANNIBAL DANCE IN THE CONGO.

Presbyterian Pioneers in Congo, p. 146

Apart from hearsay and the occasional (unchecked and uncheckable) Congo anecdotes, there was little that actually depicted Congolese slavery, savagery, drunkenness, or gender transgressions. For instance, the topos of cannibalism was one of the most dehumanizing assertions made within the Congo discourse. But where was the proof? Picture two, from Sheppard's Presbyterian Pioneers in Congo (1917: 88) provides a visual example of the tension between what was shown and what was signified. The caption here reads "Cannibal Dance in the Congo". To some extent, the "dance" is imaginable: There are drums on the left and an "audience" that is watching the dancing men and women in the foreground of the picture. Some of the "dancers" are bare-chested; some seem to be carrying a baby on their back; most of them show signs of good humor (as do some of the onlookers, who also laugh). Where is the cannibalistic trait in this picture, however? Where are the bodies, the bones, the blood, the eating, or anything that might "prove" it? Or was the reader to believe that the Congolese were perverse enough to sacrifice humans with a smile, dancing happily and publicly before secretly devouring them (and if so, how would this all be known)?

Keeping in mind this lack of proof, some of Jean Jacques Rousseau's comments in his 1754 Discourse on the Origins of Inequality might be applied to African Americans in the colonial era (and to contemporary white writers and writers of color,[64] cf. Conclusion). "In the two or three centuries since the inhabitants of Europe have been flooding into other parts of the world, endlessly publishing new collections of voyages and travel," Rousseau asserted about contemporary travel accounts, "I am persuaded that we have come to know no other men except Europeans" (qtd. in Ellingson 2001: 85). Rousseau found "the ridiculous prejudices, which have not died out even among men of letters" quite significant, since they show "that every author produces under the pompous name of the study of man nothing much more than a study of the men of his own country" (ibid). The description of "characters and customs" by these travelers, according to Rousseau, were merely reflective of "what all of them knew already, and have only learned how to see at the other end of the world what they would have been able to see without leaving their own street" (ibid).

Congoism is a discourse of extremes, balancing the worst and the best of a distanced and not-so-distant Other. In contrast to the Congoism in earlier chapters, the "best" had by this time come to be located not just in the United States, but also in the Congo itself. Congolese no longer merely signified no-good savages and abject slaves, although they also still continued to signify this. They now also embodied unspoiled primitiveness, Black roots, spontaneous wildness, artistic sensuousness, and aesthetic ability. There was, in other words, something to learn from the Congo. This did not shift the frame of reference, which firmly remained the United States and, more specifically, with African American interests, but it did add affirmative qualities to the long lists of defamatory Congolese labels.

This embrace of Congolese ability led to images such as picture three, from The Chicago Defender of September 26, 1914 ("Africa, England, France", 1914b: 1), which showed three men who, as the explanation of the picture describes, "had distinguished themselves in battle". The text on the white person in the middle confirmed him as an English sailor, while the profession of the other two figures remains unspecified. Both the Black and white male have physical contact with the sailor, and are seemingly patting his shoulder. "Note the love the Frenchmen and the African have for their English pal [...] their arms are entwined around him", the accompanying text reads, exaggerating the contact between these men.

With pictures like these, The Chicago Defender could reference a number of abstract desirables, both explicitly and implicitly. The article turned these three men

64 People of color designates non-white racial or ethnic minorities that are tied together through the experience or threat of racism (Ha, Lauré al-Samarei, Mysorekar 2007: 12).

into representatives of "Africa, England, France", as the caption has it. As the Black person on the left was discussed as the "son of a noted merchant of the Congo Free State", Africa was thus embodied by its "heart", the Congo, a strategy of absorption appearing and reappearing conspicuously often throughout this chapter. As such, the Congo continuously stood for something else, both at home and abroad. In the picture of the three men, it stood for the whole of Africa; elsewhere it stood for anti-Black atrocities in the United States, as was shown. At the same time, the image of the three men symbolically celebrated interracial cooperation and the advancement of the race through soldiery – two elements which were integral to the "New Negro" and uplift philosophy of the time.

Picture 3: "Africa, England, France"

The Chicago Defender September 26, 1914

Imperialism turned Congolese into changeable, improvable entities that could be used as examples for the whole "race". As such, they could be lauded as "Fine Specimens of Manhood", too, as the caption of picture four of The Chicago Defender from 1943 states. In this photo, lines of Black men wearing short sleeves and shorts are shown standing erect with their arms spread. The text beneath identifies these men as "soldiers from the Congo and they are really doing a fine job in going through their physical training". The Chicago Defender linked the Congo in "New Negro" fashion to soldiery and education, both of which could be obtained "in army schools in the Congo" where "most of them [the soldiers, that is] can read and write".

Picture 3: "Fine Specimens of Manhood"

The Chicago Defender September 11, 1943

Although recognized as intellectual beings of some sort ("most of them can read and write"), the Congolese were hardly more than a mass of able bodies. This was enough, however, for pro-imperial African Americans intellectuals to use them as emblems for the success of the civilizing missions; these intellectuals insisted on framing locals as human resources that had to be administrated, rather than discussing them as political subjects or colonial citizens bereaved of their rights. Even African American intellectuals who were critical of imperialism, such as Du Bois, thought along similar lines. His relative indifference to local knowledge and his outright contempt for the intellectual or political maturity of the intended beneficiaries of civilizing projects were standard in the colonial period. Through these colonial discursive attitudes, the emiseration of Congolese could be morally rejected, but not politically critiqued. In the end, Black Americans did not have any interest in the Congolese that went beyond using them for their own purposes. To what extent this changed after 1945 will be discussed in the next chapter.

Third Chapter

Revolution, Reform, Reproduction: Strategies and Limitations for Change (1945-Present)

> "Of all words, phrases, and statements connected with Africa, even more than the word 'Africa' itself, the word 'Congo' sets off some very deep vibrations in black hearts, in black souls, in black minds."
>
> E. CLEAVER/REVOLUTION IN THE CONGO 1971

FREEDOM MATTERS: AN INTRODUCTION

In the 60s, the Congo emerged as a geographical hotspot much discussed in the Black American intellectual community. As had been the case in the past, illustrated in the previous chapters through the "atrocities" in the Congo Free State (Second Chapter) and the slave trade (First Chapter), the heightened circulation of the concept and attention paid to the phenomenon of the Congo was driven by certain events (mostly bleak ones in the previous chapters). This time, however, a more joyful occasion, at least at first sight, directed African American intellectuals to the Congo: Central West Africa's transformation from colony to postcolony. This led to the foundation of the Republic of the Congo, founded in 1960, and which was subsequently re-labeled Zaire in 1971, as well as The Democratic Republic of the Congo in 1997 (Nzongola-Ntalaja 2007: 171-213).

The end of colonialism in the Congo was, according to an editorial titled "Some Congo History" from October 1960 in the NAACP's house organ The Crisis, very much "of interest to American Negroes" (1960b: 536). The influential magazine of the groundbreaking Civil Rights organization reminded its readers that African Americans "are not a self-contained group" (ibid), thus framing Black Americans as a more cosmopolitan minority. From this perspective, the plights of "African Negroes" and "West Indian migrants in England" were considered highly relevant to African Americans (ibid).

This sense of socio-cultural connection to Blacks on a global scale was no novelty, of course. Throughout the period covered by this book, real-and-imagined geographies such as Egypt, Haiti, Liberia, and most of all the Congo, were referenced by African American intellectuals. What marked a shift during this time, however, was the systematic engagement with the Congo in more affirmative ways. The Congo was suddenly perceived, albeit mainly in the short period between 1960 and 1975, as a desirable geography due to present aspects of it, and not merely by virtue of vague imaginations of the past or one's deep personal roots in Central West Africa. Although the dystopian version of the Congo re-emerged soon after, the push for change in Congo discourse, beginning in the 60s, cannot be overlooked. It is this change that is of interest in this chapter, which seeks "counterhegemonic" aspects in African American intellectual discourse by tracking the emergence of an "alternative ethical view of society that poses a challenge to the dominant bourgeois-led view" (Cohn 2004: 131).

This new focus on Congo was made possible by an intellectual African American arena that had achieved a heterogeneity and a degree of polarization hardly thinkable in the past. New voices, from within and without, began to intervene in the debates. The Black American intellectual circle had grown and had become increasingly tense due to controversial issues such as integration, affirmative action, and the threat of (anti-Black/anti-white) violence. This chapter demonstrates how the issue of the Congo – its independence, breakdown, and dictatorial regimes – served to further draw out these tensions. Looking at the Congo discourse reveals the emergence of revolutionary and reformist voices in the African American intellectual community that refuted the bourgeois, liberal, and conservative certainties from the present and the past.

The many new voices multiplied how Central West Africa was dealt with discursively and materially. Internationalist cultures, in addition to providing more global perspectives on politics and the African American community, addressed, questioned, and reshaped dominant Congo discourses. Apart from new voices from the African American "lower" social classes – represented by Malcolm X here – the African American intellectual community increasingly included female voices and American Congolese. External voices were integrated, too. Starting from the 60s at the latest, the (formerly) colonized intellectual did indeed speak. Confident, militant activists from Africa and the Caribbean cannot be overlooked in the African American archive. Re-appearing names in leading Black media outlets such as The Chicago Defender were Frantz Fanon,[1] Patrice Lumumba, and Walter Rodney; their talks at and visits to Black universities were announced in these outlets and their books favorably reviewed. Their appearance in The Chicago Defender suggests an interest in these intellectuals that went beyond politicized circles.

The 60s and 70s are presented in this chapter as nothing less than a game changer in terms of the opposition to Congoism. The editorial comments in The Crisis, mentioned above, are a first sign of this. "Some Congo History" shows an understanding of Central West African society and history far superior to that of earlier pieces. Prior to 1945, it would have been unimaginable for editorials to have known leading Congolese officials as a matter of "basic fact" (1960b: 536), such as "Messrs. Lumumba and Tshombe" (ibid).

It would have been similarly inconceivable for African American editors to have taken Congolese politicians seriously enough to call for "sympathetic cooperation of the Free World" (ibid). It would, moreover, have been unfathomable to adopt such a skeptical and disapproving tone with regard to the Belgian colonizers. Although the colonial crimes of the Congo Free State were remembered as horrific, they were hardly conceived of as a problem of colonialism itself. As shown in the previous chapter, the Congo Free State was very often considered the personal wrongdoing of King Leopold II. By the 60s, however, the successor of the Congo Free State, the Belgian Congo, was harshly criticized by the editors of The Crisis because of its colonial politics as such, not because of atrocities it perpetuated. Thus, the Belgian Congo is labeled as economically exploitative, racially biased, politically undemocratic, and educationally unsound. As a final consequence, the blame for the failings of the Congo, in contrast to the past, was placed on the Belgians alone. The final sentence of the editorial "Some Congo History" in The Crisis reads, "Congolese are men who have been pauperized, disfranchised and insulted by the people who annexed them" (ibid: 537).

As the demography of public intellectualism changed (integrating both internal and external newcomers), the representation of the Congo changed, too. To discuss the forms and limitations of discursive change in the post-World War II period, the Black American archive must be traversed differently than in the previous chapters. This chapter is organized around issues such as genre, ethnicity, and gender, which,

1 The magazine Freedomways, which explicitly discussed Fanon's influence, provides a good demonstration of how Fanon was received in more radical African American circles. It remarked upon, for instance, a "growing popularity of Fanon's writing among Afro-American youth and intellectuals" (Jones 1968: 213). The magazine suggested this in an article titled "On the Influence of Fanon", which discussed the "basic theory and strategic theory" of African American activists in 1968 (ibid).

so far, have hardly been addressed on the book's structural level. Who speaks, in what texts is this done, and what does this mean in terms of knowledge production? While discussing fictional texts, non-fiction, and everything in between, the historical context of the African American Congo will be discussed through the Black American primary texts at hand. This can be accomplished with a degree of completeness for the first time in this book, as sufficient texts from a variety of sources and milieus have been produced on the Congo to re-construct a recognizable context for this period. This speaks to, on the one hand, the richness of information provided within Congo discourses from the 60s onward. On the other hand, the textual proliferation surrounding the Congo also underscores (ex negativo) the huge limitations of the African American Congo texts of previous generations, from which nothing close to a general overview of what was happening in Central West Africa could be deduced.

This chapter shows that freedom and empowerment matter: They open up spaces to contest, battle, and reject Black and white intellectual gatekeepers. In a spirit of a sustained revolt against racial, classed, and gendered authority, new understandings and uses of the Congo emerged. The thread that binds this chapter together is the question of how African Americans re-framed a region with such a long discursive history. Were they able to at all? What stones did they have to overturn to do so? And what limits did they encounter? Most of these questions are a matter of focusing on "choice and determination", as Jan Blommaert phrases it (2005: 98). "When people in general are communicating they 'choose' from a range of options," Blommaert states, "they 'select' discourse forms deemed appropriate in the particular context, and they consciously 'plan' the sequential moves, either by 'choosing' to 'follow rules' or by 'flouting' these rules" (ibid). This chapter is about African American intellectuals who try, succeed, and sometimes fail to "flout the rules" in order to create a Congo less dismissive than that of previous generations.

Choice and agency are understood here as complex discursive situations. Freedom of choice is, as Blommaert reminds us, "constrained by normativities, determined by the general patterns of inequality" (ibid: 99). This does not, however, eliminate "creativity, choice, or freedom" (ibid). It merely situates "individual agency in a wider frame of constraints" (ibid). African American intellectuals still had to write and orate within a tangible "frame of constraints", and this will be addressed in what follows. Much truth therefore still lies in Blommaert's assertion that "there is a limit to choice and freedom. It is the interplay between creativity and determination that accounts for the social, the cultural, the political, the historical in communicative events" (ibid). Against the background of decades of discursive determination and newly won freedom and agency, Black intellectuals illustrate that it is possible for individual persons and groups to tackle Congoism, despite such pervasive commonsensical understandings of it.

This chapter therefore shows that Congoism can be identified and countered by those who are surrounded by it. It suggests that it is possible to speak against a discourse from a position within it. Counteragency, however, is hardly ever complete. Most intellectuals in this chapter question certain aspects of Congoism, but reproduce them somewhere else, very often as a parallel move in the same text. Malcolm X, who figures prominently in this chapter, tackled American Congo discourses like no other intellectual before him, for instance, but struggled to disentangle himself from some of Congoism's more winding tentacles. As this chapter shows, many intellectuals since Malcolm X have oscillated between the rejection and reproduction of Congoist tropes, whether they were activists or historians, Civil Rights or Black Power proponents, or modernist or postmodernist writers.

BROTHERS IN ARMS: ACTIVIST NEGATION AND METAREFLECTION

In 1961, the plight of Black America was perceived by African American intellectuals as deeply connected to that of Central West Africa. Exemplary is the novelist-activist James Baldwin's 1961 essay "A Negro Assays the Negro Mood", appearing in The New York Times Magazine. Assessing the importance of "Africa" for the Black community in the U.S., Baldwin underscored the significance of Congo's first prime minister, Patrice Lumumba, who had just been assassinated. Setting his piece against the demonstration of African American activists in the gallery of the United Nations, in "protest against the foul and cowardly murder of Patrice Lumumba" (as John Henrik Clarke phrased it in his essay "The Passing of Patrice Lumumba"; 1962b: 285), Baldwin highlighted Lumumba's great symbolic significance for African Americans. The deceased prime minister, according to Baldwin, had "captured the popular imagination [in Harlem]" (1961: 25).

Many Black intellectuals have used both events in their writings – i.e. Lumumba's death and the "riot" at the United Nations in his honor. Twenty-four years after Lumumba's untimely death, the scholarly journal Callaloo published Amira Baraka's dedication to Larry Neale. In an autobiographical 1985 essay titled "The Wailer", Baraka explains how he himself took part in the demonstration at the UN: "We came together, with a number of others, seeking to raise the level of Black struggle to a more intense expression" (1985: 248). Those who were trying to escalate the Black struggle were, in Baraka's words, "young people who responded to the assassination of Patrice Lumumba by taking to the street, even invading the U.N. (way back when the U.S. controlled it) to show our opposition to U.S. imperialism" (ibid). This anti-imperialist attitude of upping the stakes of the domestic and international Black struggle, according to Baraka and Baldwin, presented quite a departure from earlier days.

An internationally-oriented mindset, combined with self-confident political activism, echoes the assertiveness claimed by the "New Negro" intellectuals at the turn of the century, who, as they told themselves, transcended the politically impotent days of the "Old Negro" (cf. previous chapter). Baldwin claimed, in a similar vein as Baraka, that he no longer wished to adhere to the old activist ways or listen to present leaders. He was tired of seeing Martin Luther King "beaten and assaulted" (1961: 25). Baldwin also contrasted the contemporary post-Lumumba mood in Harlem to bleaker days when he was growing up. Those were the days in which "[n]egroes in this country were taught to be ashamed of Africa [...] they were taught it bluntly by being told, for example, that Africa had never contributed 'anything' to civilization" (ibid: 103). Others, such as activist James Farmer, confirmed that this mood belonged to the past, at least in the African American community.[2] Baldwin asserted that times had changed for good. "Africa" was being self-consciously re-imagined by a broader Black American activist community: Images of "nearly naked, dancing, comic-opera cannibalistic savages in the movies", as Baldwin described them (ibid), made way for an "Africa" that had become a marker of enviable success. This caused serious dissatisfaction with the domestic situation: "'At the rate things are going over here, all of Africa will be free before we can get a lousy cup of coffee" (ibid: 104).

"A lousy cup of coffee" in Baldwin's essay stood for the activist efforts in the early 60s to attempt to "integrate" public institutions, thus opening up the possibility of Blacks using them on equal footing. Activists went about this by reminding Americans of their self-proclaimed core values, such as "liberty and justice for all" (ibid: 25). This "Negro student movement" constituted one end of the African American activist spectrum, according to Baldwin. The opposite end was occupied

2 Farmer confirmed that until the mid-50s, the "mass of American Negroes had little knowledge of Africa" (1965: 132). "Hollywood stereotypes of the dark continent" were all black Americans had: "half-naked black savages dancing around a boiling pot of missionary soup" (ibid: 133). Farmer explains that attitudes first began to change when Haile Selassie visited the U.S. in 1954 and when Ghana and other countries became independent: "Men who would make history must have a history. As the Civil Rights revolution got rolling, it became essential that we locate ourselves within the total saga of mankind, telling of our role in the great story" (ibid).

by the "Nation of Islam", an organization that did "not expect anything at all from the white people [...] they insist on the total separation of the races" (ibid). By discussing activism along these lines (integrationist students vs. the separatist Nation of Islam), Baldwin self-consciously commented on the generally observed split in the "Black Freedom Movement" (as Carson 1991 termed it). To explain this split and reflect upon its consequences (for the Congo discourse) will be this chapter's task.

As a broader phenomenon, the Black Freedom Movement sought de facto and de jure freedom and equality. At the dawn of the 60s, African American citizens were far from possessing equal rights, whether one considers them from a de jure or a de facto perspective. "Jim Crow" apartheid and legalized racial discrimination, as discussed in the last chapter, were firmly in place when the Black Freedom Movement began gaining momentum in the mid-50s. Despite its unifying label, the Black Freedom Movement was anything but a uniform movement with clear cut, common goals (Van Hove 2014: 97-103). Right from the start of the movement, and until its demise in the mid-70s, African American activists debated passionately and perpetually with one another about the tactics, methods, aims, and gender politics of their efforts to improve their legal rights and everyday lives (as expressed through Congo discourse, too). Consequently, political agendas varied. They ranged from outlawing racial discrimination and segregation before the law, most frequently linked to the Civil Rights strand in the Movement, to economic and political self-sufficiency and racial pride, most prominently embodied by proponents of Black Power and Black nationalism.

Within these "camps" there was an enormous amount of heterogeneity, and contemporary African American observers and activist participants constantly commented on this. Black Power proponents, for instance, belonged to secular or religious groups and were internationalist, nationalist, or Marxist in their outlook (as identified in essays such as John Henrik Clarke's 1961 "The New Afro-American Nationalism"). In his essay, Clarke underlines the importance of Lumumba's assassination in nationalist environments: Lumumba helped to "rekindle the flame of Afro-American nationalism" (1961: 286). John A. Morsell's "The Meaning of Black Nationalism" (1962) also highlighted this, albeit ironically: Many Black Power proponents, writes Morsell, had "enshrined" Patrice Lumumba "as patron saint" (1962: 73).

The embrace of Lumumba by Black Power communities draws attention to the differences between the Civil Rights and Black Power movements. Black Power and Civil Rights activists were clearly active in different geographies (urban and rural), attracted a middle- or working-class Black membership, and dealt with racism in their own ways, both within and outside of the political power structures of the U.S. In the more rural American South, for instance, the Civil Rights Movement was characterized by major, well-orchestrated campaigns of civil disobedience, exemplified by the bus boycotts in Montgomery (1955-1956) and sit-ins in Greensboro (1960), as well as numerous mass demonstrations, such as the 1963 "March on Washington for Jobs and Freedom", where Martin Luther King, Jr. gave his emblematic "I have a dream" speech (1991b). In the more urban and industrialized North, by contrast, African Americans pushed for their own political, religious, economic, and cultural institutions to promote African American collective interests, as well as to defend them from racial oppression and violence. This led, for instance, to the success of the Muslim organization Nation of Islam.

In contrast to Southern-based Civil Rights activists such as Martin Luther King, Northern agitators often advocated more militant forms of opposition. The influence of the Nation of Islam's national speaker, Malcolm X, on Black Power proponents and their heirs in Northern metropolitan areas, such as New York and Chicago, was considerable. This caught the grumbling attention of many Black newspapers oriented toward the middle class. Telling, in this respect, was The Chicago Defender's paternalistic introduction to an opinion piece by Eddie Ellis following Malcolm X's assassination, titled "The Legacy of Malcolm X". The paper introduced the article by stating that "the late Malcolm X held a strong appeal for restless, frustrated and disadvantaged youth in the Harlems of New York, Los Angeles and other American cities, as well as for young people of foreign lands" (Ellis 1965: 4). Malcolm X, according to The Chicago Defender, expressed "in impassioned words the feelings of hurt and hope of Harlem youth in the wake of the assassination of Malcolm" (ibid), of which Ellis's text was an obvious example.

Despite the many differences in style, politics, and appeal, the Civil Rights and Black Power movements were never fully separate from each other: The opposition and distinctions between the two, embodied by Martin Luther King and Malcolm X, were never absolute. In fact, as time went by, they inched closer to one another. Although King never endorsed the slogan Black Power, his rhetoric increasingly showed similarities to those who advocated it: "[P]ower is not the white man's birthright," he wrote in 1968, the year of his assassination: "[I]t will not be legislated for us and delivered in neat government packages" (King 1991a: 312). Malcolm X, in turn, never championed King's methods, calling the March on Washington the "Farce on Washington" (X 1999: 284). As time went by, however, Malcolm X did show an increasing amount of interest in King's push for voters' rights, a stance that culminated in Malcolm X's famous 1964 speech "The Ballot or the Bullet", in which he advised his supporters to exercise their right to vote wisely, perhaps even as an alternative to a violent revolution (X 1990c: 23-44).

A key characteristic of the Black Freedom Movement as a whole was that its two strands were deeply self-reflective, and constantly named, categorized, and positioned themselves with regard to political others. In his 1968 Where do We Go from Here: Chaos or Community, Martin Luther King rejects those advocating "Black Power" because of their impatience and "unconscious and often conscious call for retaliatory violence" (1968: 54). King compared and opposed this stance to the peaceful and patient "civil rights movement" (ibid: 169). Black Power proponents, in turn, objected to the "'civil rights' movement" on the grounds that it spoke "to an audience of middle-class whites" and not to the "masses of black people", as Carmichael and Hamilton asserted in their classic 1967 Black Power: The Politics of Liberation in America (1967: 50-51). For the latter two authors, "the goals of integrationists are middle-class goals, articulated primarily by a small group of Negroes with middle-class inspirations or status" (ibid: 53). This issue will return throughout the course of this chapter.

Self-reflection was a serious matter, as Huey Newton (the co-founder of the Black Panther Party) shows in his bestselling To Die for the People (1972). Huey claimed, "We called ourselves Black Nationalists because we thought that nationhood was the answer", only to find out that this label would not do; "Shortly after that we decided that what was really needed was revolutionary nationalism, that is nationalism plus socialism" (1972: 31). After testing the waters, however, Huey "found that it was impractical and even contradictory. Therefore we went to a higher level of consciousness. We saw that in order to be free we had to crush the ruling circle and therefore we had to unite with the peoples of the world. So we called ourselves Internationalists" (ibid). Labeling oneself was taken very seriously, and had equally serious consequences in framing the Congo.

African American activists developed a number of strategies for countering Congoist tendencies. A catalyst in this regard was Malcolm X, who turned epistemology as a whole into a recurring topic. Repeatedly, Malcolm X showed his sensitivity to the issue of knowledge production, especially as fabricated by authoritative institutions such as schools, scientific bodies, and the news media. "They told you and me we came from the Congo", Malcolm X stated powerfully in 1964, "I mean, isn't that what they taught us in school? [...] So we came from the Congo. We're savages and cannibals and all that kind of stuff from the Congo; they've been teaching me all my life I'm from the Congo" (X 1990a. 94). Malcolm X's epistemic activism knew no borders when it came to critiquing "newspapers, commentators, and some of these so-called scientists who are supposed to be authorities" (1970a: 128).

For Malcolm X, "most of the things that we've seen in print usually" were self-serving (ibid: 128). Authorities that produce text thus had a vested interested in depicting the Congolese as savage in order "to justify what the Western powers are doing in the Congo [...] and primarily the presence of the United States" (ibid).

Tackling the imagery of "savages and cannibals", Malcolm X identified central tropes that have also permeated the analyses in this work. Moreover, linking knowledge production to power and discourse, X aligned issues that have returned in contemporary (academic) research. The results of these investigations are not substantially different from Malcolm X's polemic indictment of the American press, for instance. A study by Alison Holder, to take up one example, found that American news channels such as ABC, CBS, NBC, and CNN were very much capable of covering the country when, in the late 1990s and early 2000s, the second Congo war unfolded. However, when the second Congo war began, the State Department ceased to hold daily press briefings on the subject, with the result that the second conflict was underrepresented in the media:[3] While the press corps had reacted instantly to these briefings in 1996, this was not the case during the second war (Holder 2004: 3-4). Holder suggests that Rwanda's role in perpetuating the second war in the Congo created a serious barrier to coverage, as Rwanda had been a staunch U.S. ally (ibid: 4-6).

Malcolm X's analysis in the 60s is strikingly similar to Holder's, although his tone is decidedly more militant. He named, shamed, and categorized the interest groups who pushed and profited from full-blown Congoism in the U.S. The white majority received the brunt of his attacks. After his break with the Nation of Islam, however, the all-out condemnation of white Americans as "devils" gradually softened. "All of them don't oppress," Malcolm X said, "All of them aren't in a position to" (X 1990a: 93; cf. Manning 2012: 389).[4] While differentiating between white communities, Malcolm X also highlighted internal, African American differentiation based on class. Though he never offered a full-fledged analysis of social class in the U.S.,[5] nor used the concept openly as an analytic tool – as might be seen

3 That year, Rwanda, Uganda, Angola, and Kabila's local rebels joined forces to bring down Mobutu, with the blessing of the U.S. (Turner 2013: 46-74).

4 He was quick to add that the "oppressive black people" were "only doing what the white man has taught him" (X 1990a: 92). As a consequence, Malcolm X framed Congoist discourse as an overwhelmingly white problem. If anything, this book has questioned this assertion throughout, demonstrating that Congoism among Black Americans was a mix of Black and white thought.

5 Malcolm X increasingly became sympathetic to socialist class analysis (Manning 2012: 336), but it remains quite difficult to pin one specific class analytic thread on him.

in Franklin Frazier's 1957 Black Bourgeoisie, for instance – Malcolm X did increasingly hint at differences based on wealth, occupation, and privilege. He did so most famously by invoking the terms "house negro" and "field negro". "Just as the slavemaster [...] used Tom, the house Negro, to keep the field Negroes in check," X explained in 1963, "the same old slavemaster today has Negroes who are nothing but [...] twentieth-century uncle Toms to keep you and me in check, to keep us under control, keep us passive and peaceful and nonviolent" (X 1990b: 10).

X framed himself and his followers as "field" Blacks, whereas the "house Negroes" of his own days were the Black bourgeoisie. Within the latter strata, Civil Rights leaders were singled out and derided as the "middle-class so-called Negroes" (qtd. in Manning 2013: 203). It is through his rejection of Black and white bourgeois subjectivity that Malcolm X arrived at a new Congo narrative. Malcolm X lifted the class veil of bourgeois intellectuals by calling them what they were, in the process undermining the "incognito" of the bourgeois (Moretti 2013: 371-372). Revealing bourgeois mentalities and discourse also meant rejecting the Black bourgeois discourse on the Congo.

Malcolm X considered the American press, particularly the white one, as a racist, bourgeois vehicle for the defamation of the Congo that was dangerous and irresponsible. He stated, "The press is so powerful in its image-making role, it can make a criminal look like he's the victim and make the victim look like he's the criminal" (X 1990a: 93). "A good example of what the press can do with its images," according to X, "is the Congo" (ibid). Statements such as these place Malcolm X at the African American vanguard of news media critique on Congo reporting from the early 60s on.[6] Much speaks in favor of X's condemnation of the press.

6 This news critique recurs again and again in the African American archive. In one of its first issues in 1962, the Black arts journal Freedomways published an extensive media critique of the "treatment of Africa and its National Leaders". This treatment had been, as the journal asserted, "little short of scandalous" (Howard 1962: 361). Titled "How the Press Defames Africa", the journal faulted the American and European press for stereotyping the African as a primitive with "rings around his ankles, a spear in his hand, dancing around a boiling pot with a white man in it" (ibid: 362). The journal assured its readers that these stereotypes were produced by biased "American reporters" for the sake of American foreign policy, since they "use their personal influence with leaders there to foster policies they and their governments wish followed" (ibid: 363). The Congo, and Lumumba in particular, stood as proof of the claim that "'good or bad press' can make or break an African leader" (ibid), as Lumumba was obviously boycotted by American journalists. "Lumumba is the best illustration possible", Freedomways wrote, of how the press is used as "a weapon for creating the kind of countries and governments that we

Even liberal and left-leaning white American newspapers were making thinly supported statements about the Congo and its leaders in the early 60s. The widely read "socialist democratic" magazine Dissent (Mills 1994: 15), for instance, framed its only article on Africa's freedom in 1960 (the year of successful mass independence movements on the continent) in an ongoing litany of evolutionary language. The magazine claimed, "Most of these backward territories had not even arrived at a historical level where national feeling was a deep impulse" (Friedenberg 1960: 188). The article in question "An Economic View of Negro African Independence", provided clues as to how the magazine might have framed prime minister Lumumba if it had actually decided to discuss him: "The most dangerous aspect of the new Congo is that the Belgians [...] refused all political and humanistic training to the natives [...] We have the frightening image of a state evolving with embryo political leaders not trained beyond tribal values" (ibid: 199). With this evolutionary view of tribal leaders in an embryonic state, Dissent inscribed itself in the long history of Social Darwinian Congoism, as discussed in the last chapter.

The same can be said about the liberal The New York Times, as well as more conservative magazines such as Life and Time Magazine, which had their tribal characterizations of Lumumba firmly in place even before the conflicts surrounding independence began.[7] Furthermore, they discussed the Congo and Lumumba in articles overwhelmingly filled with violence but devoid of analysis.[8] Malcolm X re-

---

want" (ibid: 364). The net result of all of this, the journal concluded, "is to deprive the average American community of a difference of views on vital questions, leaving an ill-informed public" (ibid: 369). This kind of media critique is still being conducted today, as I show in the remainder of the chapter.

7 For instance, "Messiah in the Congo: Patrice Emery Lumumba", an article published 18 May, 1960 (two weeks before the Congo's independence amidst the formation of the government), describes the Prime Minister as "looking like a dark, bespectacled Davy Crockett under his chieftain's dress – a feathered sheepskin cap [...] He is married to a girl of his neighbourhood in the jungle" (1960: 10). The quotation illustrates how The New York Times painted a portrait of a near-incurable primitive. Conveying an air of objectivity, the vocabulary of the quote can hardly hide that it is a hodgepodge of rumors and hearsay, a mélange of nonsense typical of Congoist discourse. The parade of white people accusing Lumumba in this passage, calling him names, or describing him negatively, culminates in the description of him as a "dark, bespectacled Davy Crockett", a reference to a nineteenth-century larger-than-life American frontiersman with more passion than political intellect.

8 For instance, Life's article "In Chaos, a Deep Fear" from 18 July, 1960, discussed post-independence demonstrations and mutinies in terms of "chaos", "terror", and "mob". The

lentlessly attacked the corporate press for its "Lumumbophobia" (De Witte, The Assassination 49), which led to the ongoing demonization and infantilization of the prime minister in the white U.S. and European media, as Ludo De Witte and others have suggested.[9] Malcolm X exposed this journalistic bias, for instance, in the midst of the Belgian-American intervention in the independent Republic of the Congo. He warned his listeners to "never believe what you read in the newspapers [...] the truth isn't in them. Not when it comes to the Congo" (X 1979d: 135). For Malcolm X, the representation of the American bombings as a "humanitarian project" (1990a: 94) was a deception through which the legitimate struggle of the "brothers in Stanleyville" was reduced to irrational violence or savagery (ibid: 95).

Malcolm X's accusation of misrepresentation draws attention to his insistence on the presence of historical Congo facts against which false claims could be measured. At this point, Malcolm X's discourse shows strong affinities with the "modernist"[10] knowledge tradition within Congoism. Malcolm X emerged as most modern when he attempted to offer a rhetoric and line of reasoning surrounding the Congo that went beyond outright rejection or negation. He thus began mobilizing strategies that had failed African American intellectuals in the past, as demonstrated at length in the previous chapters. Like his predecessors, too, he confused at times, as Richard J. Evans has it, "facts" with "evidence". Whereas the former is a verifiable event that is independent of how it is interpreted, the latter is concerned with using factual accounts to produce a coherent story of some sort by using theory and interpretation (Evans 2000: 76).

Revealing in this respect is Malcolm X's discussion of the historical casualties in the Congo Free State. X maintained, after reading Twain's famous King Leopold's Soliloquy, that the Belgians "butchered" 15 million Congolese (1970a: 128).

---

latter is said to have dangerous mood swings, on the verge of "slaughtering any whites they found … determined to kill" (Snell 160a: 32). The rationale behind violent behavior against whites is linked to the Congo's tribal irrationality, which found an outlet, according to the magazine, in the "anti-white riots" of 1959 which – more accidentally than willfully – led to independence, as the article "IndepenDANCE Dance in Congo" from 11 July, 1960 went (1960: 21).

9 Jean-Claude Williame and Christine Masuy (1997) confirm De Witte's results in their investigation of the Belgian newspaper La Libre Belgique and the American congressional records.

10 I use "modernity" and "modernist" in a philosophical (rather than historical) sense here, i.e. as an amalgam of knowledge practices and institutional knowledge forms, ranging from science to instrumental rationality (e.g. classification, binary oppositions) and positivist objectivity (cf. Cooper 2005: 123).

This number can never be truly verified, of course, which means it cannot be strictly regarded as "fact". X's claim of factuality points, however, to his interests in invoking this number. X was trying to provide evidence for something entirely different. When he cited the number, Malcom X reminded his colonial-friendly white interlocutors of the "remarkable restraint" (ibid) that the Congolese had shown after independence in light of the severity of their oppression. He thereby framed history (the millions that died) through a contemporary lens, turning it into argumentative "evidence". To understand and frame the present, X went back to the Leopoldian regime that had validated the "cutting of the breasts of Black women when they didn't produce their rubber quota; cutting off their hands, cutting of their feet" (ibid: 131). Despite delivering "evidence" for his main point (Congolese restraint), X insisted that his authority was based on "historic fact" (ibid).

Malcolm X the modernist believed in facts delivered by knowledgeable eyewitnesses. To clarify "the deep-rooted hostility that seems to lie in the hearts of our Congolese brothers" toward the "white man" and to debate whether "our brothers are savage" or not, X invited some of "our African brothers and some of our Afro-American brothers [...] who are well-versed in the facts concerning the history of the Congo" (1970d: 135). X relied on eyewitness epistemology (in terms of inviting insiders, i.e. "Africans") to back up his belief in the factuality of the non-savageness of the Congolese. In contrast to earlier generations, however, this eyewitness was not naively mobilized. X clearly differentiated between "well-versed" and naive eyewitnesses.

The result of X's belief in facts delivered by eyewitnesses was that he silently African-Americanized the Congo once again, mobilizing it against bourgeois Blacks. Malcolm X was very consistent in how he approached opponents from other ideological camps. First, he offered claims of his own, against which everyone else could be measured. He repeatedly asserted, for instance, that the Congolese were "just as humane, just as human, and just as intelligent as anybody else on this planet" (1970a: 131). X followed through with this assertion, dividing the Congolese leaders into good and bad ones, thus differentiating and humanizing the Congolese. The bad leaders were embodied by Tshombe and Kasavubu; the good by Prime Minister Lumumba. Whereas Lumumba is labeled "the rightful ruler" and "one of the greatest black leaders" of the Congo, Tshombe is described as "uncle Tom" (X 1970b: 18, X 1970c: 36).[11]

11 By drawing upon the major character of Harriet Beecher Stowe's 1852 novel Uncle Tom's Cabin as a political designation for Tshombe, X invoked a well-known American epithet for slavishness and subservience to white people.

Finally, however, Malcolm X fully Americanized the Congo by turning Tshombe and Kasavubu into puppets of the white political elites of the U.S. X turned Kasavubu and Tshombe into negative symbols of Black liberation, in much the same way as the Civil Rights Movement was framed. Claiming that the U.S. used Tshombe to kill Lumumba, "just like they do with us in this country" (X 1990a: 95), X proceeded to explain how only certain Black leaders are used by whites as a voice for the larger community: "They get a Negro and hire him and make him a big shot – so he's the voice of the community – and then he tells all of them to come on in and join the organization with us, and they take it over" ("ibid). In the next lines, it becomes clear that X is talking about the Nobel Prize-winning Martin Luther King, who is subsequently compared to Tshombe: "Then they give him peace prizes and medals and things. They will probably give Tshombe the peace prize next year for the work he's doing [...] Because he's doing a good job. But for who? For the man" (ibid).

Disappointed in many African American leaders, X turned to the Congo and found Patrice Lumumba, whom he admired, idealized, and identified with for very specific reasons. "He didn't fear anybody," Malcolm X says of the prime minister, "He had those people so scared they had to kill him. They couldn't buy him, they couldn't frighten him, they couldn't reach him" (X 1970c: 64). Thus, X considered Lumumba, in a way that was idolizing and, once again, dehumanizing, "the greatest black man who ever walked the African continent" (ibid), a judgment strongly informed by the individual weaknesses of his Black compatriots and by the systematic defaming of Lumumba as a "tool" of the "Communist World" by the white press, for instance in Life (1961:16). By Americanizing the Congo, X constructed a framework that was dangerously Congoist once again.

Emblematic in this regard is how X discussed the rape of white women following independence. Rape was an ongoing infatuation in the white and Black press alike. The rape of white women was, to Malcolm X, an instance of the "chickens com[ing] home to roost" (1970b: 18), a comment he famously used before in the context of the assassination of U.S. president John F. Kennedy, and which had cost him his prominent place in the Nation of Islam's hierarchy (Manning 2012: 69). Both in the U.S. and the Congo, the chickens came home to roost because of anti-Black violence, X suggested. The parallel between America and the Congo was an obvious one for X: "Lumumba was murdered, Medgar Evers was murdered, Mack Parker was murdered, Emmett Till was murdered, my own father was murdered" (1970b: 25). In passages such as these, X aligns Lumumba with famous African American activists (Evers) and victims of lynching (Till, Parker, and his own father). The African Congo, at this point, has become very much an "American Congo" again. As with the American Congo discourse at the start of the century, Malcolm X explicitly drew a parallel between the Congo and the American South in terms of savagery: "If there are savages in the Congo then there are worse savages in Mississippi, Alabama, and New York City, and probably some in Washington, D.C., too" (1970a: 128).

X's representation of the Congo is thus pervaded with the "tension between what people do with language and what language does to them" (Blommaert 2005: 106). The discursive building blocks and generative discursive tools of X's Congo discourse could not be invented completely from scratch, whether or not X desired to do as much. He had to work with what was historically available to him in order to re-shuffle, re-phrase, and reject these blocks and tools in a way that would lead to a Congo that was acceptable to him. While he remained embedded in the hegemonic discourses on the Congo (in order to be understood), he openly pushed its limits through negation and denial (in order to redraw them). Thus, he African-Americanized the Congo, as previous generations had done, but at the same time humanized its inhabitants and highlighted the geopolitical interests behind Congo's Othering. X applied modernist positivism and eyewitness epistemology to back up his claims; at the same time, however, he deconstructed the manner in which Congo knowledge was produced, thereby underlining the relative value of truth. An awareness of social class enabled X's epistemic critique. In his alienation from non-violent, Christian bourgeois activists, whom he framed as "sellouts", lies an important key for his rethinking of the Congo: Class consciousness allowed Malcolm X to question the bourgeois abjection of the Congo.

Activists and artists who embraced Black Power co-produced and, after his assassination, reproduced X's epistemic novelties. The issue of "brotherhood", observable in X's idolization of Lumumba, is a case in point. X's cultural heirs produced a veritable "'Lumumba Poem' genre" (Dworkin 2003: 206); the prime minister was at once both a concrete historical figure and a topos in these texts. Langston Hughes's 1961 poem "Lumumba's Grave" sets the tone for many other poetic expressions surrounding the prime minister in the following decades: "Lumumba was black / And he didn't trust / The whores all powdered / With uranium dust." (2000: 533). In this poem, Lumumba is racialized right from the first line ("Lumumba was black"). Immediately after that, economic motives ("uranium dust") are suggested for his murder. In the next lines, the topic of remembrance is broached: "They buried Lumumba / In an unmarked grave. / But he needs no marker–," Hughes wrote, "For air is his grave. / Sun is his grave, / Moon is, stars are, / Space is his grave. / My heart's his grave, / And it's marked there. / Tomorrow will mark / It everywhere" (ibid). In these lines, the poem moves from the political to the natural and the personal, as the prime minister is imagined as buried both in the "air" that the writer breathes and in the "heart" of the writer's body. In describing this intricate and intimate connection between writer and prime minister, X's "brotherhood" is re-generated. Similar devices are at work in other contemporary poems.[12]

What is striking about the Lumumba poem genre is that it was dominated by male artists. The few female activists, poets, and playwrights who wrote about the prime minister made something quite different of Lumumba. Disillusion, in these accounts, takes the place of brotherhood. Adrienne Kennedy's 1969 play Funnyhouse of a Negro provides an ideal illustration of this. In the work, Kennedy merges Lumumba with the father of the main character, Sarah, resulting in a flat-out rejection of both: "Her father never hung himself in a Harlem hotel when Patrice Lumumba was murdered. I know the man. He is a doctor, married to a white whore [...] her father is a nigger who eats on a white glass table" (1969: 24). There is no hint at "brotherhood" here. Lumumba exists here as an embodiment of disappointment and deceit (although there are exceptions to this).[13]

Julia Hervé's Orwellian 1973 "A Short Story", appearing in the magazine Black World, provides another female perspective on Lumumba. The story posits the existence of a forgetting pill, or a "technical fix" to make "everybody nonviolent, the pill that would make everybody forget why he wanted to fight, or love or hate, the pill to make everybody forget they have forgotten" (1973: 58). The "political meet-

12 Walter Lowenfels's 1962 poem "Patrice Lumumba Speaks", appearing in Freedomways, aligns Lumumba with the poet with its first line: "I am dead, dead, dead!" (1962: 32). Of course, neither the "I" nor "Lumumba" is truly dead, as Lumumba's "fragments" come together "in you, my brothers, / in the four corners of the world" (ibid). Through Lumumba "the holy Ghost of the Congo" haunted many artists, as Larry Neal put it in his 1974 "Funky Butt, Funky Butt, Take It Away" (1974: 17). Many Lumumba topoi have a longevity among male Black poets that reaches into contemporary times, as Raymond Patterson's 1989 poem "Lumumba Blues" indicates. Evoking the African American blues tradition of lamenting personal misery and social oppression through repetition and call and response, Lumumba is, on the one hand, personalized: "Well, he didn't want much, / just like you and me. / No, he didn't want much, the same as you and me", a typical (blues) line went. In the course of the poem, the African-Americanization of Lumumba, on the other hand, is not just accomplished through style, but also through well-known African American phrases and topoi such as "set my people free" (2001: 239) and "lynched him in the end" (ibid: 240). The theme of remembrance is reinforced with the lines "I won't forget, / Don't think I ever will" (ibid).

13 Shawna Maglangbayan's 1972 monograph Garvey, Lumumba and Malcolm: Black National-Separatists is an example.

ing at the Lumumba Club" (ibid: 60) – which had its real-life counterpart in Angela Davis's Che-Lumumba Club[14] – figures prominently in the narrative as the illustration of the damaging force of forgetting. Drugged amnesiac activists re-frame Mobutu here as a patriot and a follower of Lumumba, instead of remembering him as the prime minister's killer (ibid: 61). Hervé, who, as the biographical note at the end of the story reveals, was an African American in Ghana with a famous émigré father (the novelist and activist Richard Wright), mobilized the story to critique the superficiality and historical shallowness of the Pan-Africanism espoused by African Americans. The story seems to ask: What good is a Pan-Africanist perspective if it is so easily misled by symbolic action (e.g. re-naming streets) that tries to legitimize dictatorship?

Much can be said in favor of Hervé's critique of Black American Pan-Africanist shallowness and commodification if one takes a look at how Black news magazines, such as Jet, discussed the Foreman-Ali Fight in 1974 in Mobutu's Kinshasa. Jet filled its pages with the offhand Pan-Africanist remarks of those involved in the fight. For instance, the official promoter of the event, Don King, went on record stating that he was "offered as much as $1 million to bring the fight to the United States. 'But I was determined to make this fight happen in Africa [...] from the slaveship to the championship'" (Kisner 1974: 52). Although Jet confirmed in that article that both boxers – the aged Ali and the financially destitute Foreman – were offered five million dollars each, this was not just a "clash for cash", as the magazine asserted (ibid). What it was, in the end, was a fight between the materialist Black American Foreman and the proud Black African Ali. Ali's recorded statements did a lot to contribute to this framing. "'When I see George Foreman in front of me,'" Ali was quoted as saying, "'I think about Blacks being enslaved for 300 years. I think if he wins, we (Blacks) stay in chains'" (ibid: 53). The hidden financier and enabler of the event, the dictator Mobutu, was implicitly legitimatized in the course of these events. Hervé's story openly critiqued this kind of commercialized Pan-African shallowness, and offered a type of criticism rarely heard among African American male intellectuals.[15]

---

14 The Che-Lumumba Club became a household name through the ongoing attention lavished on Angela Davis by the Black press of the early 70s, exemplified here by the 1971 article "The radicalization of Angela Davis" in the lifestyle magazine Ebony. This "all-black collective of the Communist party of Sourthern California" (Sanders 1971: 114), as the magazine explained it to its horrified readers, constituted a continuation of the Congo naming practices pervading African American history (cf. previous chapter).

15 An exception is Amira Baraka's tract "The National Black Assembly", which aligned Newark with Zaire in order to juxtapose the African American "bureaucratic élite" to

This is not to say that there was no in-depth, reflective, Pan-Africanist engagement with the Congo to be found. "Brotherhood" was not merely male rhetoric. The most obvious example in this respect was the Black Panther Party, whose chairman, Bobby Seale, wrote in his 1970 memoir, entitled Seize the Time, that the Panthers lived "in the spirit of Nat Turner, Patrice Lumumba, and Malcolm X" (1970: 217). The Panthers walked the walk, sending their minister of information, Elridge Cleaver, to Congo (Congo-Brazaville, that is, not Congo-Kinshasa), dubbed the People's Republic of the Congo in 1971. Cleaver's report, Revolution in the Congo, took up Malcolm X's meta-perspective. In the same vein as X, Cleaver paid special attention to the symbolic significance of the Congo for African Americans: "Of all words, phrases, and statements connected with Africa, even more than the word 'Africa' itself, the word 'Congo' sets off some very deep vibrations in black hearts, in black souls, in black minds" (1971: 9).

The importance of the Congo, which Cleaver called the "heart of Africa" (ibid), a metaphor inherited from the past (cf. previous chapter), was to be found in its relation to African American politics. Cleaver openly reflected on this issue: "Ideologically, Africa was up for grabs" (ibid: 8), he asserted, "one could refer to Africa and make Africa say anything that one was seeking to prove", since as Africa was "not speaking for itself, or because it spoke with so many voices that much confusion resulted in selecting which voice to listen to" (ibid). Cleaver thus critiqued the use of "Africa" and the Congo for one's own purposes, going against the grain of idealized "brotherhood".

However, in true Congoist fashion, which is a deeply contradictory discourse after all, Cleaver's assertions were then followed by statements adhering to the very logic he was critiquing. Building on the typical self-reflective observation of an increasing schism between "cultural nationalists" and "revolutionary nationalists" (ibid: 7) in African American circles, the Black Panther Party decided to go to "Africa, to the Congo [...] to unite the Afro-American liberation struggle more strongly than it has ever been united before [...] to regain that synthesis between the cultural aspects of our Africanness and the revolutionary aspects" (7). To re-unite Black nationalists was thus the function of the Congo voyage, reducing the region to a template for domestic use. Besides unification, the Congo also facilitated the rejection of Black bourgeois leaders, who were called "CIA niggers" and other "uncle Toms in the United States" (ibid: 8, ibd: 27). These Uncle Toms, according to Cleaver, led

"neocolonial Mobutu", who Baraka considered "the murderer of Patrice Lumumba. The Ali-Foreman fight cannot change that! It just announced the open collaboration with U.S. imperialism" (1975: 23). Through this scathing critique, both Mobutu and Black bourgeois leadership in the U.S. were rejected.

by "James Farmer, were sent to Africa in Malcolm's footsteps in order to destroy the effect he was having" (ibid: 8).

To truly appreciate the (both problematic and liberating) novelties introduced by Malcolm X and his heirs (The Black Panther Party, among others), one has to examine some of the rest of the African American activist rhetoric on the Congo. Following Cleaver's lead, let us consider, for instance, James Farmer and his monograph Freedom – When? Despite their differences, it is important to note that Farmer did have more in common with Malcolm X than the latter would have admitted – proof that some of X's strategies did find an audience broader than his own constituency. The first trait they held in common is their interest in the Congo for its own sake. Even in the internationalist times of the 60s, this was not a given, as the example of Martin Luther King shows.[16] The second common trait was their meta-reflection on representations of Central West Africa and their non-acceptance of the authority of news media.[17] Finally, Farmer shared with X a belief in the eyewitness. Especially since his second trip to Africa, Farmer could see "Africa [...]

16 Martin Luther King's public addresses and writings, for instance, hardly contained any reference to the Congo. The exception was his Where do We Go from Here: Chaos or Community? in which King mentioned the Congo while positioning himself against Black Power novelist John O. Killens. The latter considered the violent revolutions in Cuba, North Korea, and China as important political examples for Black America. "Mr. Killens might have some validity in a struggle for independence against a foreign invader. But the Negro's struggle in America is quite different", King asserted (1968: 62). To illustrate the differences between America and colonial countries, King mobilized the Congo ex negativo. "The American Negro is not in a Congo," he claimed, "where the Belgians will go back to Belgium after the battle is over" (ibid). King used this example to emphasize how important his integrationist approach was: "[I]n the struggle for racial justice in a multiracial society where the oppressor and oppressed are both 'at home,' liberation must come through integration" (ibid). The Congo thus served here to counter the threat of violence within the Black Power ideology.

17 In Freedom – When?, Farmer applied the new meta-tactics to his discussion of the Congo. Like X and the Panthers, whose doctrine Farmer called "mistaken and misguided" (albeit with "certain psychological validity"; 1965: 100), Farmer turned the Congo into a cause célèbre of white hypocrisy: "There was a silence in the press during the years in which hundreds of thousands of Congolese were being slaughtered," Farmer asserted, "but then there came huge headlines: FIFTY WHITES KILLED IN CONGO. Why not an airlift to Mississippi, they ask?" (ibid: 100). In essence, both Farmer and X adopted an anti-authority stance typical of much of the anti-Congoism up until today, especially in terms of news media critique.

less emotionally. I could see more dispassionately and rationally – the flaws, the frailties, the power plays, the cruelty, the evil, and the goodness and kindness" (1965: 134-135). By painting a picture of Congolese heterogeneity, Farmer also highlighted their humanity, much as Malcolm X had done.

In contrast to X, however, Farmer casually evoked the Congoist topoi of primitiveness and savagery. When he met the Congolese Prime Minister Moise Tshombe, Farmer found him "more urbane and sophisticated than I had expected him or any Congolese person to be at the present stage of history" (ibid: 148). Farmer's surprise was fed by an evolutionary framework assigning to the Congolese backward, brutish, and rural habits. Farmer's belief in the atrocities of Congolese rebels – chopping off the legs and arms of white and Black alike, as well as eating their hearts and livers (ibid: 149) – reveals the degree to which the idea of the Congo-as-Savage had become entrenched. Through the Congo, and Africa as a whole (which merge frequently, in true Congoist fashion), Farmer propagates his own solution to racial issues in America. In contrast to X, these solutions reflected those of a bourgeois Black culture, hinging on middle class leadership, American nationalism, and education. "As in our own civil rights revolution, the future of the new African nations will depend upon the quality of leaders they produce" (ibid: 143), Farmer proclaimed. Hence his extensive talks with Tshombe and Kasavubu. Farmer had put his trust in the future of Congo into an emerging group of "brilliant university students – the politicians, administrators, and professional classes of tomorrow" (ibid: 162). His hope in this "class" was far more theoretical and ideological than practical, as he seems not to have talked extensively to anyone on his trip other than the Congolese leaders available to him (Tshombe, Kasavubu, and the leaders of their opposition). In a telling exception, Farmer recounted talking to younger East Africans on the issue of the Congo. Many of his younger interlocutors told him that "we [Americans] should get out of the Congo altogether" (ibid: 161). This ran very much counter to Farmer's own opinions. "I thought this nonsense," he wrote, "no major power would withdraw from so important a place as the Congo." The reasons he gives is that "it is both implausible and undesirable, as everyone of the African nations which are nudging Congo affairs along knows" (ibid). This is perfect Congoist non-rationale by Farmer, who seems to be suggesting that "we" are in the Congo because it is inevitable and "normal". Imperialistic attitudes are thus boiled down to the "common sense" rationale that X attempted to counter.

None of the activists mentioned above were entirely successful in countering Congoism in its depth and breadth. The following section examines to what extent historians and journalists picked up on this anti-Congoism in their own work, or developed their own critical ways of dealing with the Congo.

Genre Matters: History, Journalism, and the Limits of Postmodernity

Works of History, Works of Modernity

African American historians have been deeply affected in their depiction of the Congo by the chasm between the Black Power and Civil Rights movements. The most radical strategies for change among works of history appeared in the Black Power camp, which not only challenged contemporary representations of the Congo, but also questioned the validity of historical knowledge more broadly. This challenge came both from within and without a small circle of Black American historians. For instance, in a special issue of the Journal of Black Poetry from 1970, dedicated to the continent of Africa as well as Black nationalism and Pan-Africanism, the sociologist Gerald McWorter (also known as Abd-al Hakimu Ibn Alkalimat) criticized the modernist idea of "history as 'value free' social science" (McWorter 1970-1971: 23). Instead of presuming to be value free, McWorter maintained, history should deal with "the dynamic of a people's reality", rather than coldly assembling a "chronology of personalities and events" (ibid). This critical stance was directed against the pseudo-objective position adopted by bourgeois Black historians and authors of earlier days, and exemplified in this chapter by W.E.B. Du Bois, John Hope Franklin, and Langston Hughes.

McWorter's critical attitude announced the dawn of a new historiographical era. The authority and truth claims of the older generation were radically challenged by young public intellectuals. Most of them were highly strategic and nationalistic in their aims. Frequently, they published shorter and more specialized pieces for a broad audience in independent magazines. As the Congolese gained independence, these authors radically challenged the old ways of writing about Central West Africa by conscientiously filling in the gaps that traditional histories had left open. This becomes clear if one compares and contrasts these new stories to, for instance, a mainstream history such as John Hope Franklin's From Slavery to Freedom: a History of American Negroes. This had been an influential monograph, with the 2010 edition of the work re-published in much the same form as the 1947 edition. In contrast to these new voices, the latter monograph largely ignored the Congo and declared it "impossible to trace with any degree of accuracy the political development of these peoples before Europeanization" (1952: 21). Franklin was by no means an exceptional case in this regard; W.E.B. Du Bois and Langston Hughes made similar claims.[18]

18 The latter, for instance, declared the whole of Africa unknown until some hundred years ago when "darkest Africa" was explored (Hughes 2003: 363). Du Bois, in turn, adopted a

In the 60s, young activist historians did not accept the unknowability of the precolonial Congo and started writing with great force and confidence about it. The historian-columnist Eugene P. Romayn Feldman, for instance, took great issue with "the image of the Congolese as a savage people without culture or history" in a 1965 article in the Negro Digest (1965: 83). According to the author, "historical records reveal that the Congolese had a civilization of their own which was quite well developed and needed least of all the European 'civilizers'" (ibid). In what followed, Feldman listed in detail what remained out of sight (or out of mind) for Du Bois, Franklin, and other historians: The rich corpus of comments and texts on Congo's precolonial past. This corpus included encyclopedias, oral accounts, travelogues by Portuguese explorers from the sixteenth century, and texts by other nationalist Black intellectuals, such as John Henrik Clarke.[19] The "true facts of history", as Feldman termed it positivistically towards the end of his "Truth about the Congo" (ibid: 86), were thus finally revealed.

These were facts that seemed so true, in fact, that even Du Bois began to accept them by the end of his life, thus revising half a century of his own scholarship. Du Bois's revision became obvious, for instance, in a newspaper article titled "A Logical Program for a Free Congo" in 1961, in which he suddenly recognized a substantial pre-colonial history of the Congo. Du Bois's article in The National Guardian illustrates how history is changed and broadened as soon as contemporary concerns create an urgency for it. In "A Logical Program for a Free Congo", Du Bois explained his motivation to write about Congo's past. One element was his desire to counter the widespread depiction of the Congo as a land of savagery during the time of its independence struggle. "The Congo valley is not, as currently painted a nest of howling savages", Du Bois wrote (1961: 6). Ironically, this was the image of the

stance very much like Franklin's in his 1946 The World and Africa by reducing the Congo's colonial prehistory to "Bantu herdsmen" throwing themselves upon Central West Africa in gigantic migratory waves (1972: 78), causing serious mayhem – "they destroyed villages and massacred the inhabitants" (ibid: 48). The home of these scavenging, militant hordes of "Bantus" was the "true 'Heart of Africa'", according to Du Bois, which was located in "the tropical rain forest of the Congo" (ibid: 97). How exactly the kingdom of the Congo fits in this story of brute force and conquest – a historical aside in Du Bois's account that is clearly at odds with the rest of his history (e.g. ibid: 170) – is never really resolved.

19 John Henrik Clarke's essay "The Old Congo" (1962a), which was published in the academic magazine Phylon in 1962, is plagiarized in parts by Feldman. The fourth paragraph is copied without reference, for instance.

Congo he himself had helped shape in much of his oeuvre. Independence, however, had clearly changed this.

Other historians followed suit or themselves reflected self-consciously on this changed attitude towards the Congo, as the example of John Henrik Clarke shows.[20] In the 60s, the Congo also stood for something positive. This required countering the idea, as Du Bois phrased it in the article just mentioned, that "a few half-educated leaders filled with crazy and impossible ambitions" (1961: 6) had taken over the region. A number of Black Power-oriented historians found various means of discrediting this stereotype of primitive savageness. For instance, the historian-novelist-activist John A. Williams' Africa: Her History, Lands and People Told with Pictures (1962) produced one of the first historical accounts that made a point of representing Africa both in its urban modernity and rural tradition. This is exemplified by the cover of the book, which showed three half-naked Black men playing music, all seated in front of an anonymous modern building. In Williams's fact files on the Congo, a picture of a traditional "Muluba dancer" was matched up with photos of Leopoldville's main street, Boulevard Albert, as well as a picture of a copper smelting plant in Elisabethville and a photo of a helicopter that "sprays for mosquitos and flies in Congo city" (1962: 115). The leader of the Republic of the Congo at that point, Adoula, is shown talking to another Black man dressed in a suit (ibid: 113).

The reality and existence of these images served as a powerful impulse to question past representations of the Congo. But the final push to use these depictions was, quite simply, the will to do so. Pictures of Congolese in modern Western clothing had already been published very early on in the century, as was shown in the previous chapter. As Central West Africa was generally considered a useless human landscape that could serve as a marker for original "blackness" or, at best, for primitive, sexually-charged creativity, the Congo could not be incorporated into

20 The discursive influence of concrete events in the Congo was actively contemplated by John Henrik Clarke in "The Afro-American Image of Africa" from the magazine Black World (February 1974). The article discussed the history of the changing Black American image of Africa, attributing the growing interest in Africa to "the rise of independent movements on that continent" and the ongoing reference to this event in "the literature and activities of the civil-rights movement" (1974: 19). This materialized, according to Clarke, into an institutionalization of African history with the development of "Black Studies programs…" (ibid: 20), which in turn strengthened the identification with Africa. Independence, civil rights, and Black Studies, all of which were interconnected, were thus the decisive developments required to broaden the discussion on the Congo, according to Clarke.

any serious history. Once the Congo provided elements that could be helpful for the plight of those writing the histories, however, it became an area of intense focus. This volatility of the Congo signifier also meant that, once the Congo lost its affirmative utility, it was in danger of disappearing from the radar again. This is precisely what happened.

The changing political landscape, both in the U.S. and the Congo, is responsible for the Congo's apparent evaporation in the decades following independence. As the 70s, 80s, and 90s went by, and the Congo slipped into Mobutu's and Kabila's indefensible dictatorships, the Congo disappeared once again from sight. Post-60s historical writing reduced the Congo to the Congo-as-Slave or the Congo-as-the-Vital (cf. previous chapters). Within the latter topos, the pre-modern Congo or the Congo of Lumumba reappear frequently. Molefe Kete Asante's important Afrocentric oeuvre is truly emblematic of this latter treatment of Central West Africa – reducing the Congo in his Encyclopedia of Black Studies to its folklorist leftovers in the U.S and to the symbolic usage of Lumumba. Whenever the contemporary Congo is discussed, it is absorbed into the larger Afrocentric story of "the quest for eternal harmony", as the subtitle of The History of Africa phrases it (Asante: 2007). Thus, the wars in the Congo from the late 90s onward are discussed under the chapter title "Africa consolidates independence". The conflicts made it perfectly clear, however, that the Congo state was politically, militarily, and socially deeply unstable after decades of Western-funded, exploitative Mobutu rule. If anything, the Congo was under pressure by its neighbors, as well as international institutions such as the World Bank, the U.S., and the IMF (cf. Turner 2013).

Apart from the powerful pressures of reality (i.e. independence, the emergence of Lumumba), the changing epistemological orientation within the field of history also contributed to the emergence of fresh representations of the Congo. American history writing was transformed by the introduction of both Black studies and postmodern thought into academia beginning in the mid-1960s. Until then, the study of African Americans hardly ever appeared as a systematic part of university curricula (Banks 1996: 183). When Black Freedom Movement activism hit the campuses, however, the energetic call for the establishment of Black Studies departments became a major rallying point. This resulted, by the early 90s, in the establishment of various programs in over 250 institutions (ibid: 186). In the wake of these came scores of new journals and newsletters. Soon enough, Black studies were "no longer a small affair in the American academy" (Asante/Masama 2005: xx). However, given its central desire to study "the great contributions" of Africans to the "discourse of knowledge", as Asante has it (ibid: xix), Congo knowledge hardly developed within the field.

Parallel to Black Studies, "postmodernist" thought came to the fore in American academia. This body of knowledge challenged and eschewed the self-evidence of reality, as well as the sense of academic objectivity, and called attention to the inadequacy of traditional historiography. One expression of this skepticism was the rise of New Historicism, the proponents of which have acknowledged that their work was driven and inspired by the anti-racist, feminist, and working-class-oriented movements of the 60s and 70s (e.g. Gallagher/Greenblatt 2000: 53). In Practicing New Historicism, Gallagher and Greenblatt underline the importance of the movement's central concerns for their own work – to pluralize, democratize, and revise historical accounts. This involved a new attentiveness to how historiographical sources favor administrative and political accounts from white, European, middle- and upper-class male authors over other kind of sources. Via the social movements of the 50s and 60s, the New Historicists felt the need to broaden the base of historical sources and to try to dislodge the idea that the 'Man' of the administrative and political pamphlets was a universal one (Van Hove 2014).

Although the relationship between postmodern innovations and Black history remained strained (as is shown in what follows), New Historicism's influence in terms of broadening sources considered legitimate is obvious in many African American histories. An excellent example of this is the two-volume To Make Our World Anew: A History of African Americans, which uses traditional archival documentation, as well as journalistic and poetic sources. However, in contrast to African American fiction writers,[21] who systematically set out to correct the limited historical record on slavery through postmodernist fiction writing (Spaulding 2005: 2), Black historians have been reluctant to engage in meta-discussions on fact and fiction. Keith Gilyard suggests in the Encyclopedia of Postmodernism: "Insofar as postmodernism seeks to destabilize notions of fixed or essential truths and identities, it is a body of thought both useful and problematic for the discipline of African American Studies" (2001: 4). The conflict with postmodern thought arises at the point when "foundational truths about all African Americans" are created (ibid).

Molefe Kete Asante's The History of Africa: The Quest for Eternal Harmony is a case in point. The metanarrative of "eternal harmony" is as essentialist as it is anti-postmodernist. Asante knows this, of course, and defends his stance explicitly in the preface. In it, the author frames his history as a "straightforward, illustrated, and factual text [...] a chronological and critical examination of the extensive history of Africa" (2007: xii). In another edited volume by Asante, one of the contributors openly rejects what Asante has called in The African American People: A Global

21 Including Ishmael Reed, Octavia Butler, Toni Morrison, Charles Johnson, Samuel Delany, and Jewelle Gomez, for instance.

History the "current trend in historiography to discover the bizarre, the odd, and the unusual in order to announce something novel" (2012: x). In his Encyclopedia, Asante's anti-postmodernism is performed through Lumumba. "To reread Du Bois, Nkrumah, Lumumba, Cabral, and Fanon in the light of the current state of world affairs," the Encyclopedia states, "implies a reexamination of some of the premises of the current trend of postmodernism" (Mutombo 2005: 52). As such, postmodernist and postcolonial approaches are described as neo-imperial tools, "for it is too obvious that in this imperial era, where 18th- and 19th-century rhetoric has come back to the fore, there is nothing 'post' in the dominant postcolonial discourse of our time, especially when we recall that postcolonies are to a certain extent none other than an Africanization of Western colonies" (ibid).

Apart from the suspicion of neo-imperialist meddling, what other reasons do Black historians have for resisting postmodern tendencies in their writing? One reason for the hesitant response to postmodernist history is no doubt the touch of arrogance with which some postmodernist academics proclaim their importance within African American Studies. For instance, the Encyclopedia of Postmodernism asserts earnestly in its article "African American Studies" that Black Studies can "be regarded as a triumph of postmodernism" (Gilyard 2001: 4). This is a statement that obviously glosses over the ongoing struggle of generations of African Americans. In the end, Gilyard's stance is an anti-postmodernist posture itself. It was precisely the siding of the postmodernists with those who did not fit into the larger, modernist stories – the subordinated and the marginalized – that made its practice and practitioners, as Butler noted, "dissent" (ibid: 15). To give postmodernism credit for the emergence of Black Studies contradicts its own aim to give those subordinated a voice.

Another reason why Asante and others might have refused a postmodernist stance in their histories is the approach's playfulness and relativism. Asante's refusal to go looking for "the bizarre, the odd, and the unusual" (as New Historicists, for instance, tend to do) and to focus instead on the broad brush of African and African American history, is based on the fact that African American historiography has been written with "vindicationist" and "contributionist" aims, or with the aim of inscribing Black Americans constructively into the overall American or African story. Postmodern playfulness, which is often mobilized for epistemic reasons, seems out of place in this deadly serious epistemic-political field. It also seems superfluous, as African American historians have been undermining the alleged objective certainties of historiography all along. They have done so by incorporating their personal stories into their historical work and by openly discussing their political aims (cf. previous chapters).

Moreover, there is not much for Black American historians to gain from the postmodernist tendency to blur fact and fiction. Natalie Zemon Davis's The Return of Martin Guerre is an excellent example of this postmodern merging of personal speculation and archival material in order to fill historical gaps. In her introductory announcement, she reminds her readers that the story of the sixteenth-century French peasant Martin Guerre "is in part my invention, but held tightly in check by the voices of the past" (Davis 1983: 5). This kind of statement cannot be made so easily if one's historiography had been criticized, defamed, and denied for its real-and-imagined subjectivity. The subjective aspect of the writing of Black history has to be defended and addressed even in the present day. Even in the Encyclopedia of Black Studies, Asante is compelled to state that the contributors have "created an encyclopedia that is conceptually driven rather than personality driven" (2005: xxi).

In the same vein, African American history cannot easily absorb Davis's tendency to evoke the "perhapses" and the "may-have-beens" of history (Davis 1983: viii). The reason is that Black history actually matters. It matters politically, personally, and financially to African American communities even now. Whether the real Martin Guerre had come back or not matters very little in Artigat today, whose inhabitants (as Davis reports), "smiled, shrugged their shoulders, and said, 'That's all very well – but that pretty rascal, he lied'" (ibid: 59). African American history, in contrast, is not about smirking about petty stories for the epistemic reason that, as Davis concludes, "it reminds us that astonishing things are possible. Even for the historian who has deciphered it, it retains a stubborn vitality" (ibid: 125). Black history has socio-political consequences that are still felt; the deeply controversial issue of affirmative action, for instance, hinges on the degree to which the rectification of the well-documented, factual wrongs of anti-Black American history, most notoriously slavery, Jim Crow and lynching, is perceived as justified. To question the truth claim of the past, particularly with respect to lynching as Bryant Simon has done,[22] is to potentially undermine political tools for justice in the present.

One wonders if postmodern thought nevertheless provides avenues for anti-Congoist approaches. "The critique of essentialism encouraged by postmodernist

22 Bryant Simon's postmodernist attempt to address a lynching in Blacksburg in 1912 was an attempt to tell "a truer story than the archive reveals" (2004: 152). To do so, Simon turned to fiction full of "perhapses and maybes", just as Davis had done (Davis 1983: 180). The reason for this was that Simon discovered the rather banal truth that newspaper accounts are limited in their potential to tell a full story. I agree with Lubomír Doležel that the "cognitive gain" of filling in the historical gaps of the archive through fiction is quite limited and that it leads to events like lynchings being declared unknowable (2010: 51).

thought is useful for African-Americans" (1990: 28), bell hooks asserted in her 1990 essay "Postmodern Blackness". African Americans, according to hooks, "have too long had imposed [...] from both the outside and the inside a narrow, constricting notion of blackness" (ibid). Postmodern critiques, hooks hoped, would "challenge notions of universality and static overdetermined identity" (ibid). In her very valid remarks, hooks highlights important advantages of postmodern thought hardly applied by Black historians. It is because of this very avoidance of the postmodern that Congoism may have stayed off the radar. As long as African American historians could not write about themselves as subjects at odds with other Blacks (Congolese, lower class Americans, etc.), the move from self-determination to "other-determination" (Butler 2002: 59) could not be made.

Journalism and Postmodern Self-Reflectivity

Contemporary Black journalism provides a partial answer to the question of whether postmodern thought might be a helpful anti-Congoist tool. This genre has embraced postmodern stances and attitudes more overtly than works of Black American history. Journalism, considered more broadly, became amenable to postmodernist tactics in the 60s, when the ideal of objectivity was questioned by the proponents of the New Journalism, such as Tom Wolfe, Truman Capote, Norman Mailer, and Hunter S. Thompson, whose journalistic accounts merged with biographical ones. This challenge by the white New Journalists and the academic postmodernists resulted in a humbler understanding of journalism, as media scholar Stephen Ward explains: "The pillars of truth and objectivity show serious wear and tear due to a post-modern skepticism about objective truth" (2009: 302).

Journalistic partisanship did not need the sanctioning of New Journalists to be carried out on a broad scale, however. African American journalism had done so long before (and defended it as such). Magazines like Ebony, for instance, explicitly and systematically contradicted anti-Black imagery in white-oriented mainstream media. According to the founder and publisher of the magazine, John H. Johnson,[23] his focus on Black life was a new development in post-war America because "there was an almost total White-out" (Johnson/Bennett 1989: 114) on Black news in white media. Johnson explained this in his autobiography as the "unwritten rule [...]

23 Ebony's founder, publisher, and long-standing editorial influence was the African American "entrepreneur of passion" John H. Johnson from Chicago (Summer 2010: 99), who originally knew little about publishing, but was passionate about his main concern: showing the "total Black experience", as Johnson wrote in his autobiography Succeeding Against the Odds (Johnson/Bennett 1989: 157).

that a Black's picture could not appear in the press unless in connection with a crime. There was no consistent coverage of the human dimensions of Black Americans in northern newspapers and magazines" (ibid).

Partisanship reached new heights in the early 60s through the issue of the Congo and especially Lumumba. The white, middle-class magazine Life represented the prime minister more as an abstract idea than a human being. Lumumba was a symbol for violence, irrationality, and communism. All of these topics were narrated against the background of the Congo's monstrousness and tribal chaos. As a response to that particular imagery, Life's Black counterpart Ebony took a more human-interest approach in Lumumba's representation, including lengthy descriptions of his house by the African American correspondent Era Bell Thompson in the article "African Independence 1960" from December, 1960: "The Prime Minister lived in a large frame house on the main boulevard, not far from Parliament" (1960: 148). Thompson continued, "I talked my way past the guards at his gate and met Mrs. Lumumba and their five children. A secretary made an appointment for an interview the next day. When I returned, the tall, scholarly-looking Lumumba shook hands with a room full of foreign delegations and journalists, begged to be excused and dashed off to attend to matters of state" (ibid).

Written in the personable narrative quite typical of the New Journalism, Thompson framed Lumumba in ways recognizable to African Americans. Based on the clues about the "main boulevard" and particularly the "frame house" – a popular kind of suburban home or holiday residence in the American 60s – Lumumba would probably be read favorably as a well-to-do professional who managed to live in a nice area. The passage would also frame Lumumba as an industrious official, one who needs a secretary to manage the many "foreign delegations and journalists" and to organize his urgent "matters of state". His "scholarly-looking" stature would hint at some kind of academic background; his polite excuses would serve as a marker of well-mannered humility; and the presence of his wife and five children in his bustling home office portray him as a family man.

Given the magazine's ongoing celebration of Black success through hard work, education, and effort, chances are high that Lumumba's personality would be recognized and even approved of by Ebony's readers. Ebony's values, as Gußmann suggests, reflected those of its readers, who strongly believed in success, progress, material values (such as owing a house and a car), and responsibility (Gußmann 1998: 97-98). Confidence in American democracy (ibid: 107, 114) and family life were central issues for Ebony's readers, too. According to sociologist Franklin Frazier in his classic 1957 study Black Bourgeoisie, the Black middle class sought compensation for its ongoing rejection and denial by whites by escaping into a world of "make-believe" (1962: 150-151, 189). This fairytale world was driven and perpetuated by the Black press – most prominently, as he claimed, Ebony – which constantly focused on and exaggerated the economic and cultural achievements of Black Americans (ibid). The desire of the Black middle class for recognition may also be seen, for instance, in the continuous interest in African Americans who succeeded in the white world and the strong focus on Africa's increasingly successful anti-colonial struggles and elites.

By opposing Life's Lumumba to that of Ebony's, it becomes obvious that Black journalistic partisanship had both an external and internal aspect. The external aspect turned Lumumba into a symbol of resistance against the white media's anti-Black defamation. The internal aspect, as echoed in Era Bell Thompson's passage, turned Lumumba into a template for Black bourgeois subjectivity. This double move can also be observed in the works of Black journalists who traveled to the Congo in the decades succeeding Congolese independence. During this time, Black American journalists traveled to Central West Africa in bigger numbers than ever before. In contrast to Era Bell Thompson's 1954 monograph Africa, Land of My Fathers: The Story of the Return of a Native Three Hundred Years Later, disappointment and alienation permeated many travel accounts. In Who Killed the Congo (1962), Philippa Schuyler could not establish a sympathetic connection with the Congo as a nation, nor with its inhabitants. Schuyler's apologetic attitude towards Belgian colonialism eventually led to her blame the Congolese for their own misery. "It is a rarely mentioned fact," Schuyler asserted, "that Congolese were very difficult to deal with, and Belgian impatience with them was only too often justified [...] Congolese were maddeningly slow, maladroit and dilatory" (1962: 93).

Under pressure by postmodernist, postcolonial, and African American critical theories, paternalistic passages such as Schuyler's gradually disappeared in Black journalism. Newer journalistic reports on the Congo – exemplified here by Howard French, Keith Richburg, Eddy Harris, and Lynne Duke – tell stories that are skeptical of universality, objectivity, and of the power elites from the U.S. and the Congo. A major feature of contemporary Black journalistic writing on the Congo is self-reflectivity. In the writing of Harris, Richburg, French, and Duke, the personal plays a key role in the larger narrative. The personal here cannot be equated with the private, however, as was the case in some of the postmodern historiography discussed above.[24] Through their life accounts, Richburg, French, Duke, and Harris re-

24 In Simon's attempt to postmodernize lynching historiography, self-reflectivity slips into a private story of how the author enrolled in a fiction class. This account is filled with moderately interesting and hardly relevant details about, for instance, the "prim-looking Southern" teacher who turned out to be "wonderfully generous and open" (2004: 181).

cast contemporary African American activism. Keith Richburg's 1997 Out of America narrates his interest in Africa against the background of his student years at the University of Michigan, where the freshly introduced curricula in African American studies in the late 70s provided him with his first substantial information on Africa (1997: 9). This happened amidst the ongoing activism of the "Black Action Movement", which demanded greater recruiting of minorities for the university's staff (ibid: 17).

The point of this personal reflection is very political. Afrocentric identity politics in his student years made Richburg aware of, and interested in, his own "blackness". Unlike in the 60s, however, this awareness led to a refusal to think racially altogether (which is the whole point of the book, really). Richburg thus trims his identity down to simply American. Richburg flatly denies in his travelogue any type of racial link between the "Africans" he met during his time abroad and himself, in spite of his skin color. Confronted with the ethnic cleansing of Rwanda, with which he prefaces his book, Richburg admits that he was seeing all of "this horror" a bit differently "because of the color of my skin. I am American, but a black man, a descendant of slaves brought from Africa". But there the racial connection stops, Richburg implies. To distance himself from the African identity that was so energetically claimed in the 60s (and continuously re-stated by academics from the Asante circle, for instance) he openly thanks "God" that his ancestors were enslaved so they got away from the genocidal continent (ibid: xvi-xviii). Other journalists begin their accounts with similar assertions of racial non-connection.[25]

The racial disengagement in the journalistic accounts echoes the skepticism of postmodernist thinking about essential connections, identifications, and identities. It is no coincidence that Black journalists integrate the activism of the 60s into their accounts, which gives them the chance to refute the "modernist universalizing agenda" of the Black Freedom Movement, as hooks terms it (1990: 29). In contrast to the activism of the 60s, the authors demand that racial thinking take a backseat as an explanation of social realities. Refusing to accept an essential, Pan-African racial identity does not automatically mean that debates about identity become postmodern, however. The identity of these journalists is not discussed as a result of plural and intersecting discourses, as they would be by postmodernists (Butler 2002: 50-51), nor as the effect of contradictory ideologies. Richburg does not reflect on why

---

There is nothing of that kind of private, narratively irrelevant detail in the Black travelogues mentioned above.

25 Harris, for instance, asserts that "because my skin is black you will say I traveled Africa to find the roots of my race. I did not – unless that race is the human race, for except in the color of my skin, I am not African" (1994: 13).

he dismisses the link between himself and other Blacks (Africans and Americans alike). Reading his text against the grain, one might suggest that if he were actually to do that, he would find that both Africans and Black Americans are a disappointment to him as a bourgeois subject. Africans kill each other without justified cause and refuse to take responsibility for it, Richburg asserts throughout the book. Black Americans, in turn, are also full of excuses concerning the "problems of the black underclass" (1997: 178), which is "still struggling on the streets, hustling just trying to make ends meet" (ibid: 179). To make things even more worse, according to Richburg, "the black underclass" explains its misery by pointing to slavery and the Jim Crow laws.

The disappointment in fellow Blacks found in Richburg's work (and French's, although it is less pronounced)[26] results in the conclusion that "in Africa, there's a lot of that same backward-looking attitude" (ibid: 180). The implication is the same for the U.S.-American Black communities. Richburg's lack of connection "to this strange and violent place" (ibid: 227) ultimately leads to reducing his identity only to his Americanness. This occurs in other accounts, as well. Postmodernist skepticism towards innate Black identity thus leads to reduction, substitution, and apolitical rejection, not to the pluralization or politicizing of identifications and identities.

African American identity politics, as seen through the lens of reductive postmodernism, produces Congo discourses that are divested of the worst derogatory argumentation and rhetoric. In this sense, postmodernist approaches do work. At the same time, the travel accounts by Richburg, French, Harris, and Duke also show that their postmodernist stance, arguments, and language are of no real consequence. These authors remain very much ingrained in the modernist project of constructing conceptual oppositions to make sense of the Congo. The Congo becomes once again rigidly and hierarchically fixed, despite the emphatic and oftentimes critical language with which this is done. Lynne Duke's Mandela, Mobutu and Me contains a textbook example of how this works. While standing on the banks of the Congo, Duke feels "trapped by Africa's wonder and its woe as I watched the river's swells" (2003: 11). This kind of binary rhetoric (wonder vs. woe) is almost always

26 French, too, makes this disappointment in both Africans and his fellow Black Americans obvious in a key scene in his book, where he portrays the Congolese president Laurent Kabila in such a fashion as to resemble a "streetcorner hustler … a genuine thug" (2005: 214), whose "strut" was shown on CNN in an endless loop. To French, who had grown up in a strong middle-class African American family, where pride and self-respect were passed on daily, the street hustler signifies a culturally determined worst-case scenario. The comparison of Kabila with Conrad's Kurtz (ibid: 215) demonstrates just how thoroughly French disapproved of this kind of hustler.

flanked by essentialist stances, as we have seen throughout this book. And it is true here, too. For instance, Duke explicitly frames her time in Africa as the opportunity to receive "a taste of Africa's essence – the surging aspirations and the crushing struggles I was fortunate enough to know" (ibid: 287). These struggles and aspirations are not in Duke's book to humanize Africa, but to naturalize extremes in Africa's "essence". It is not unusual that this leads to a return to traditional "uplift" rhetoric. Richburg, in a manner reminiscent of Booker T. Washington (cf. previous chapter), states: "It seems to me that if the race is ever going to progress, we might start by admitting that the enemy is within" (ibid: 179).

These two examples should not imply that all of these authors reach their conclusions in similar ways. Harris, for instance, truly attempts to overcome the oppositions at work in Duke's and Richburg's texts (American/African, wonder/woe, aspiration/struggle) by positioning himself as more than a "hybrid" – "another race, perhaps, "newborn and distinct, forged in the blast furnace of slavery" (1994: 28-29). Harris's pondering, despite this "right" postmodern, postcolonial language and self-reflectivity, nevertheless quickly slips into binaries: He literally feels like "Jekyll and Hyde" due to his perceived in-betweenness. Harris's postmodernist pondering thus ultimately leads to modernist certainties. One of these certainties is that Harris has more in common "with a handful of whites" than with the "Africans" with whom he is surrounded (which he reads as a denial of his blackness rather than, for instance, a confirmation of class affiliation). Harris discovered this on the banks of the Congo, as many intellectuals did, which was to be "the end of Africa for me" (ibid: 299).[27]

Postmodernist approaches and self-reflectivity have led to cosmetic changes in the language of journalists, but have not led to a radical breach in the Congoist foundations of internal and external Othering. What is missing is an awareness of class and the limitations of genre. As prominent members of the American bourgeoisie, journalists fail to spot their own class biases, especially when newsrooms are packed with people with similar (middle- and upper-) class backgrounds and aspirations, as Cunningham has noted. Moreover, journalistic self-reflectivity never

27 With this gesture, Harris juxtaposed himself with many generations of Americans who went to the Congo and had an epiphany. This included the founding father of American Studies, Perry Miller, as well as a key figure in today's African American Studies, Molefe Kete Asante. "At Matadi, on the banks of the Congo," Perry Miller wrote in his authoritative Errand into the Wilderness, "it was given to me … the mission" of "expounding my America to the twentieth century" (1956: 2). Asante, in turn, decided "to write a narrative history of Africa" while "standing on the banks of the mighty Congo river" as he writes in the preface of The History of Africa (2007: xi).

goes so far as to question whether journalism as a genre should itself be left by the wayside. The economic pressures and commercial interests of newspapers lead to well-known dismissive reporting on the Congo because this reporting has a long and (commercially) successful tradition. "Reporters are biased toward conflict because it is more interesting [...] biased toward sticking with the pack because it is safe," Cunningham asserts, "biased toward event-driven coverage because it is easier [...] biased toward existing narratives because they are safe and easy" (2003: n.p.). These biases are well-known to the most critical of these journalists. French's A Continent for the Taking is permeated with critique towards the news media he had been working for for so long. Despite his attempt "to be different", there he was, French wrote, "just like everyone else, rushing toward another lurid African mess that, thanks to the magic of television, had become the global story of the week" (2005: 59). Like French, many of the Black American journalists are astounded by their own inadequacies, including their own anti-African racism (e.g. Harris 1994 33; Richburg 1997: 248). Welcome as these self-reflections may be, they do not lead to anything substantially different: Congoism is still reproduced in these accounts. Which begs the question: Is "racism" itself, of which Congoism is part and parcel, "becoming reflexive" (Žižek 2000: 6)? This certainly appears to be the case in Black journalism. But does this observation hold for other genres, such as postmodern Black American theater? This will be debated in what follows.

GLOBAL SISTERHOOD: "EVERYDAYING" THE CONGO AND THE FAILED STRATEGY OF SELECTIVE SILENCE

In the period following World War II, a number of Black female writers received unprecedented critical acclaim, as evidenced by the Nobel Prize for Literature won by Toni Morrison in 1993 and the Pulitzer Prizes for Fiction and Drama won by Alice Walker and Lynn Nottage (in 1983 and 2009, respectively). The link to the Congo in Walker's and Nottage's oeuvre is obvious: The latter won her Pulitzer for a 2009 play titled Ruined, which tells the story of a brothel in a war-torn Congolese village; Walker, in turn, wrote a collection of essays (published in 2010) on a number of gender-issues hotspots that she had recently visited, titled Overcoming Speechlessness: A Poet Encounters the Horror in Rwanda, Eastern Congo, and Palestine/Israel. Here, too, the connection to Central West Africa cannot be overlooked.

The link between Morrison and the Congo is an epistemic one. Through her strategy of selective silence – an epistemic issue famously tackled via her 1987 slave novel Beloved – Morrison addresses "unspeakable thoughts, unspoken" (62) revolving around the historical topics of the Middle Passage and slavery (DiPace 1994: 40). In true postmodernist fashion, Morrison told the press that her novel was fiction based on the historical record. She underlined this by dedicating her novel to "the Sixty Million and more" (1987: n.p.) who died in the broader context of the Middle Passage. Asked by Time Magazine whether this number is accurate, Morrison backed up her claim by referring to the vast numbers of Congo slaves: "There were travel accounts of people who were in the Congo – that's a wide river – saying, 'We could not get the boat through the river, it was choked with bodies'" (1994: 257). Morrison thus answered Time's provocative question by referring to eyewitness accounts on the Congo. Notably, she speaks only vaguely of accounts of "people" here, foregoing any specifics. This contrasts to her particularly mentioning the diary of the U.S.-American, slave-owning Burr family, for instance, to which she alludes a few lines later in the interview in order to back up her historical thoughts on slavery at the American end of the ocean (ibid).

Morrison's vagueness regarding the Congo indicates that the finer details of the historical record (e.g. the origins of the slaves) were not her central interest. If this had been the case, she would have mentioned the Congo in Beloved (which she did not). Morisson's project has always been a broader and deeply epistemic one – i.e. to insert slavery as a whole into the American archive by transcending the willed "national amnesia" (ibid) surrounding this issue. In the Time interview, she stated that "I don't want to remember, black people don't want to remember, white people won't want to remember" (ibid). In order to correct the biased American archive, Morrison decided to write intimately on the subject. "This book was not about the institution – Slavery with a capital S," Morisson asserted, "It was about these anonymous people called slaves. What they do to keep on, how they make a life, what they're willing to risk, however long it lasts in order to relate to one another" (ibid).

The Personal, the Political, the Silent

Nottage and Walker, it seems, picked up Morrison's strategy of telling horrific stories in muted and personal ways, thereby attempting to find new ways with which to narrate Congo's unspeakable horrors of rape and war. Nottage's representation of the Congo is part of a broader political agenda. In her introduction to the published edition of Ruined, director Kate Whoriskey explains the play as a tool to "activate change, heal a bit of horror, restore hope and give voice to the silent and unseen" (2009: xiii). The "horror" in question (a well-known topos in discussions of the Congo, as we have seen in the previous chapters) was what Thomas Turner called

"Congo's war against women" (2013: 120-146), or the massive amount of sexual assault perpetrated against women and girls in the course of the second Congo war from 1998 onward. Lynn Nottage's initial intention, as the director Whoriskey explains, of doing "a version of Mother Courage set in the Congo" (2009: ix) places the play in a critical, Brechtian tradition of theater as "social commentary" (ibid). Nottage attempts to execute this agenda, as the director suggests, through a personal and complex narrative "portraying the lives of Central Africans as accurately as [Lynn Nottage] could" (ibid). The ultimate aim is to "examin[e] the spectrum of human life in all its complexities" (ibid: xii).

The narrative of Ruined is personal throughout, as was Nottage's proclaimed intention. This turns the play into an everyday story of how "normal" people get through war times. The story is set in Mama Nadi's bar and brothel in an unnamed mining town in the eastern Congo, from which rebels and government soldiers roam and return. These men are played by the same male actors, thus implying that they are indistinguishable in the crimes they commit. The setting shows, moreover, that "the social contract is utterly tenuous here", as The Feminist Spectator remarks in its review of the play (2009: n.p.). This tenuous social contract leads more than once to the invocation of the well-known Congoist topic of "chaos". This term is also applied in Whoriskey's introduction; the director explains how she and Nottage went to Central West Africa to interview rape survivors in order to find the right "structure" for the play that was "true to our experience" (2009: xi). Interestingly, what they saw was nothing short of "incredible chaos" (ibid: xii).

"Chaos" surfaces frequently in the play, too. "Chaos" is used carefully, however, as a label for very specific situations and exclusively used by male characters. For instance, chaos designates a traffic jam that is experienced by the traveling sales man Christian (Nottage 2009: 6). It also describes the aftermath of a rebel attack on a hospital, as explained by government Commander Osembenga (ibid: 76). Furthermore, the networking pains of the Lebanese diamond merchant Mr. Harari are framed through "chaos". "The man I shake hands with in the morning is my enemy by sundown," the merchant complains, "And why? His whims. Because?! His witch doctor says I'm the enemy. I don't know whose hand to grease other than the one directly in front of me" (ibid: 89). Mr. Harari ends his lament by comparing the current situation to the past: "[A]t least I understood Mobutu's brand of chaos. Now, I'm a relative beginner [...] I must befriend everybody and nobody. And it's utterly exhausting" (ibid).

The way Harari uses the word "chaos" draws attention to the personal investments he has in it. This is the general rule in the play: All the men who use "chaos" profit from it, in one way or another. Christian explains his lateness by mobilizing the word, Osembenga underlines the rebels' lack of morality through the concept, and Harari applies "chaos" to explain the difficulties encountered by businessmen like himself in adapting to changing power relations in the Congo. None of the situations described, however, are "complete confusion and disorder", as the online Oxford Dictionary explains the term "chaos" (n.d., n.p.). Chaos in Ruined is not "a state in which behavior and events are not controlled by anything", as the Dictionary defines it. Instead, chaos describes claims of disorder used to explain shortcomings. Mentioning chaos is a way for Christian, for instance, to keep his business relations with Nadi's brothel alive. He has to somehow justify his long absences, which threatened Mama Nadi's business, so he evokes "chaos" in order to do so. In the same vein, highlighting "chaos" ensures Osembenga's moral high ground with regard to his military opponents; Mr. Harari uses the rationale of chaos in order to trick Mama Nadi into giving up her precious diamond (which he then steals, thus ruining her). "Chaos" in the play, in other words, is a cop-out that allows users to avoid addressing the complexities of the Congo.

Thus, Congoist topoi and topics, such as the Congo-as-Slave and "chaos", are applied with great critical care here.[28] The same goes for other Congo clichés. The assertion of Congolese irrationality and "madness", as Mr. Harari puts it (ibid: 27), are constantly questioned by the cool, collected, and calculated behavior of Mama Nadi. She undermines the brash bluff and the life-threatening ignorance of young Congolese soldiers by addressing them as "men" and not as "monsters", as one of the raped girls, Salima calls them (ibid: 70). "This is a nice place for a drink. Yeah? I don't abide by bush laws," Nadi reacts calmly to the menacing demands for unequal trade by a soldier. "If you want to drink like a man, you drink like a man. You want to behave like gorilla, then go back into the bush" (ibid: 22).

The rhetoric of this passage is disturbingly Congoist, of course, evoking the old dehumanizing topoi of Congolese men as "gorillas" from the "bush". Nadi's goal, however, is to address the soldiers as "men" in order to keep her business afloat in

28 When Christian discusses two pieces of merchandise for the price of one with Mama Nadi, he is referring to two abused young women (Sophie and Salima). Mama Nadi first refuses to take Sophie, as she has been "ruined": Rebels have raped her with a bayonet and destroyed her genitals. Although Nottage demonstrates multiple times that Nadi has more heart and shrewder politics than she first appears to, her survey of the two women recalls the behavior of a slave auctioneer. This is, however, not simply another unreflective use of the Congo-as-Slave, a well-known topos from the past. Nottage raises the topic of Congolese involvement in slavery in a way that allows her to humanize the Congo. Telling the "full story, the positive alongside the negative" (Whoriskey 2009: xii) is indeed a strategy that works well to achieve this.

an orderly manner. Nadi does not insult them with these stereotypes, nor does she reduce them to subpersons (which, ultimately, would be quite counterproductive; these men do have guns, after all). From Nadi's point of view, these soldiers are not inherently gorilla-like, as Congoism would have it, but have to decide whether they want to be gorillas or not. This is the difference to authors in the past writing about the Congo, who have portrayed Congolese men as inherently beastly (cf. previous chapters). Congoist language is thus used to show the relative power and fleeting meaning of stereotypes – they can do good, too, by inciting order in potentially explosive situations.

Ruined is committed to showing the Congo as a tangible, albeit problematic, "home" of and for the Congolese. It is a home in which "people were determined to survive and build lives", as the director phrased it (Whoriskey 2009: xii). Thus, Nottage builds the characters slowly and carefully, delivering information about the setting and the specific political moment in time. This is done with reference to a number of American topics, and most prominently African American pop culture. There is a casual reference to a "poster of a popular African American pop star" hanging over the bed of one of the brothel's girls, for instance (Nottage 2009: 30). Another example is Nottage's framing of menacing soldiers as young gangster rappers who chase off Congolese coltan diggers in the area they control: "Dirty poacher been diggin' up our forest, we run 'em off. Run them good, gangsta style: 'Muthafucka run!'" (ibid: 21). This use of the African American vernacular and of typical pop cultural topoi such as the "gangsta" is reinforced by the behavior the stage comments suggest for the soldiers: "The Rebel Soldier strikes a hip-hop 'gansta-style' pose" (ibid).

Telling the full and personal story was part of Nottage's critique of the corporate news media, which, as the director puts it, too often focuses solely on "the violence, the poverty and the AIDS crisis" (Whoriskey 2009: xii). Again, then, we encounter the media critique which has been gathering steam since the 60s and has continuously entered critical Congo texts. This, in fact, has truly become the new standard in Congo discourse. There is absolutely no lack of commentary on the Congo's extraordinarily paltry coverage. This critique is so widespread that it has even become the standard in the news media itself. Exemplary here is how CBS's 60 Minutes introduced a 2008 documentary titled "War Against Women: The Use Of Rape As A Weapon In Congo's Civil War". "You probably haven't heard much about it" (CBS News 2008), the voiceover mentioned at the start of the film, followed by the assertion that this is now going to change by directing serious attention to "the deadliest conflict since World War II" (ibid).

Quite typical of contemporary media coverage of the Congo rapes is allowing victims to narrate their own misery in the most painstaking detail. In the CBS documentary, for instance, Lucienne M'Maroyhi talks about her own harassment. "I was lying on the ground, and they gave a flashlight to my younger brother so that he could see them raping me," she recalled (ibid). "They were telling your brother to hold the flashlight?" CBS journalist Anderson Cooper asked. M'Maroyhi confirmed and told Cooper that "they raped me like they were animals, one after another. When the first one finished, they washed me out with water, told me to stand up, so the next man could rape me" (ibid). The story in the reportage finished, painstakingly, with Cooper's voice telling his audience how Lucienne was "then dragged through the forest to the soldier's camp. She was forced to become their slave and was raped every day for eight months. All the while, she had no idea where her children were" (ibid).

Baaz and Stern justifiably call this kind of journalism a "pornography of violence" (2013: 92). This concept will be used here to frame how American attention towards the Congo increasingly revolves around cruelty, leading to mass media coverage that highlights violence, linking condemnation to a constant, obsessive replaying of horrible sequences. The problem with these unceasing replays of violence is that certain limits "of respect, piety, pathos" (Behar 1996: 2) are crossed, leading to a representation of the Congolese that is deeply disrespectful (ibid).

Nottage attempts to avoid reproducing the media's sensationalist Congo reporting on mass rape. She refuses to go into detail regarding the specifics of rape, for instance. When Christian sells Sophie to the brothel, the crimes against her are silenced. "Militia did ungodly things to the child, took her with [...] a bayonet and then left her for dead," Christian tells Mama Nadi (2009: 13). As soon as he wants to continue the story, Nadi interrupts him forcefully: "I don't need to hear it. Are you done?" (ibid). Silence and ellipsis return frequently in these moments,[29] echoing Toni Morrison's strategy of bespeaking the unspeakable through hints rather than description.

Alice Walker echoes Morrison, too, albeit with less success than Nottage. In discussing her work Overcoming Speechlessness in an interview with Democracy Now!, Walker explains the origins of her own speechlessness: "Things can be so horrible that people lose the ability to talk about them" (Walker 2010b) To exempli-

29 For instance, in one of their first interactions, Nadi offers a glass of liquor to Sophie to help against "the pain down below. I know it hurts, because it smells like the rot of meat. So wash good" (Nottage 2009: 17). Sophie herself interrupts another traumatized girl, Salima, from talking about her destroyed family: "Stop it! We said we wouldn't talk about it" (ibid: 38).

fy this, Walker dug into the Congo past, on which she had "written a thesis of sorts" when she went to college (2010a: 8). Speechlessness set on in her own experience when "she learned that the King of Belgium had decided that if the Africans in the Belgian Congo could not fulfill their rubber quota that he had imposed on them, he could order their hands to be chopped off" (Walker 2010b). The effect of this story on Walker as "a student, as an eighteen- and nineteen-year-old" was that she "couldn't speak about it. I just – I put it somewhere that I left for many years" (ibid). This strategy, Walker asserted, was applied by many of her contemporaries, too, in light of the recent atrocities in the Congo and Rwanda: "[T]hey encounter these brutalities and they literally can't talk about them, and so we don't speak. But if we don't speak, then there's more of it, and more people suffer. So it's a call to overcoming speechlessness" (ibid).

Walker alludes to the same paradox described by Teresa Behar, who discusses "the central dilemma of all efforts at witnessing" (1996: 2): What should one do, she asks, "in the midst of a massacre, in the face of torture, in the eye of a hurricane, in the aftermath of an earthquake" (ibid). Should one "stay behind the lens of the camera, switch on the tape recorder, keep pen in hand?" Or should one do the opposite: Mute oneself, as documentation, too, easily slips into voyeurism, egocentrism, and dehumanization (ibid)? Walker is paradigmatic of how this paradox is too often reconciled in the context of the Congo. Her story, as it turns out, seems to be an easily resolvable personal matter, not a difficult epistemic struggle. Her speechlessness, in other words, does not seem that big of a deal, as it is mainly a matter of personal "healing" through a "sangha, a Buddhist circle of support" (Walker 2010a: 17). Shallow reflection of this kind leads, once again, down the Congoist path. If one does not relentlessly reflect on the ethico-political implications of one's own representations, debasement is reproduced, as Walker's example demonstrates. To avoid Congoist discourse, one must continuously ask, as Illan Kapoor does (building on Spivak's "Can the Subaltern Speak?"), "to what extent do our depictions and actions marginalize or silence [...] what social and institutional power relationships do these representations, even those aimed at 'empowerment', set up or neglect? And to what extent can we attenuate these pitfalls?" (2008: 42).

Walker does not place her own representational involvement with the Congo front and center. What becomes central are her identity and "tears of hopelessness" (Walker 2010a: 17). Thus, the author frames victims of rape in her terms, not in those of the Congolese. Indeed, Walker re-asserts that she would rather not talk about the atrocities that women in general, and a Congolese woman named Generose in particular – experienced. "It has been almost impossible to speak of it" (ibid: 16), she writes, and causes her to despair of "humanity" (ibid). But the author had to speak up in order to help this Congolese "sister" who "understood the importance of speech, speech about the unspeakable, and is a source of my ability to share the following story, a story that has propelled me into a period of speechlessness" (ibid: 12-13). Thus, Generose's story is told as the Congolese woman herself wanted it, Walker suggests. The simplicity and clarity of this argument allows Walker here to resume Congoist business as usual.

What Generose describes to Walker is this: This "proud woman [...] who reminded me of a young Toni Morrison" related how her husband was hacked into pieces by "gunmen who also carried machetes" and who chopped off her own leg (ibid: 14). Walker goes on, "They cut off her leg, cut it into six pieces, and began to fry it in a pan [...] they tried to force her son to take a bite" (ibid). As the son refused to do so, he was shot dead. The daughter, however, did bite into a piece of her mother's body and had since disappeared" (ibid: 15). This was the child that Generose hoped Walker could help her find through the latter's connection to the NGO Women for Women International (ibid).

The pornographic elements of Walker's story render "speechlessness" and "selective silence" suspect as an effective anti-Congoist strategy. To her credit, Walker's story deviates from CBS's, as she focuses on the atrocities surrounding the rape of Generose, not on the act itself. On the other hand, Walker's account is not all that different from CBS's in terms of its detailed narration of almost unthinkable acts of violence that cannot be understood properly by reading her story alone. Walker presents a worst-case sexual violence scenario to a Western audience that is motivated to respond with benevolence towards those "poor" Congolese "sisters".

Nottage's silence departs radically from Walker's. The playwright refuses to narrate horror openly, for instance. In contrast to Walker, silence does have some bearing with regard to the larger story, thus protecting the fictional Congolese women from exhibitionist external gazing and giving them some agency in a war-torn, male dominated environment (an agency most notably embodied by Mama Nadi). Despite this difference, however, it is striking how similar Nottage's buzz words are to those taken up by Walker and CBS. As in the efforts of the latter, Ruined offhandedly mentions "coltan" numerous times (e.g. Nottage 2009: 13, 21, 25, 31, 89), as well as "blue helmets" (ibid: 95) and "aid workers" (ibid: 80, 88, 90, 91). The Congolese gynecologist Dr. Mukwege makes an appearance both in the preface to Ruined (Whoriskey 2009: xii) and in the CBS documentary.[30] In the same vein as the CBS reportage, the published edition of Ruined contains frontal pictures of the (crying) Congolese rape survivors with whom Lynn Nottage spoke, whose "painful

30 Mukwege founded and works in Panzi Hospital in Bukavu, where he specializes in the treatment of women who have been gang-raped.

narratives [...] in the gentle cadence and the monumental space between their gasps and sighs" (2009: n.p.) can, according to the conclusion, be found in the play. As in the news media narratives, it seems that stories of Congolese rape survivors require photographs of victims in order to attract readers – pictures which would be unthinkable if these were European or American rape survivors, as Baaz and Stern righly remark (2013: 92).

These similarities between CBS and Ruined highlight a real problem in the overall strategy of selective silence: It does not work if an audience has no notion at all about what might be happening in the moments of quiet. Ultimately, the theatergoer must have some background knowledge of Central West Africa in order to fill in the gaps. As a strategy, "unspeakable thoughts, unspoken" (Morrison 1983: 62) does not quite work as a way of describing the Congo's complexity, or at least not without alluding to other narratives, such as those offered by the media. Ruined is an excellent example of how a certain set of discursive events and explanations used by the media return in a work of fiction. And they must return in order to even understand the fiction, in this case.

The idea of rape as a "weapon of war", which has achieved a near-hegemonic status in terms of explaining sexual violence in Central West Africa, as Baaz and Stern explain, translates problematically into theater. In Ruined, it culminates in Salima exclaiming to her male harassers that "you will not fight your battles on my body anymore" (Nottage 2009: 94). Although "rape as a weapon of war" discourses grant a certain rationality to Congolese men (they rape as a strategy to enrich themselves), it does, in the end, reproduce a known trope surrounding Congolese men: Congolese as subhuman abusers of women. In Ruined, women like Mama Nadi may possess some authority as she brings soldiers and miners to order in her regulated establishment. In the end, however, these men miserably fail the women, and are goodhearted losers at best. Salima's husband, for instance, was buying a new pot when the rebel soldiers overran their village and attacked her. Finding herself pregnant after the attack, she cries that she's carrying the "child of a monster" (ibid: 70). As her husband pleads with Mama to allow him to see Salima, he holds a pot in his hand, a pitiful symbol of the reparations he's unable to make.

All in all, in contrast to what it suggests through its use of the rape-as-a-weapon-of-war discourse, Ruined is not a "gendered" reading of war-torn Congo, but a "sexed one". It is, in other words, about one sex (men) abusing and failing the other (women). "God, I don't know what those men did to you," the traveling salesman Christian says to Mama Nadi, who is financially ruined, "but I'm sorry for it. I may be an idiot for saying so, but I think we, and I speak as a man, can do better" (ibid: 101). A consequence of Christian's stance, which is the also the one assumed by the play, is that the rapes in the Congo can be solved when men better themselves individually and morally (by becoming less greedy, less violent, and more thoughtful, for instance). Apart from this obvious bourgeois individualist take on social matters (which echoes Walker's), the sexed story in Ruined thrives on the dichotomy between, on the one hand, men as abstract perpetrators and, on the other, women as concrete, everyday victims and survivors of sexual assertions of male power. Dauphinée is right in stating that this stance dehumanizes rapists in the face of their actions: "[W]e abandon the perpetrator. The perpetrator becomes Other" (2007: 119). Congolese women, in turn, are also Othered by the shameless taking and publicizing of their photographs, the pressure exerted on them to tell their stories for Western interests, and the denial of a humanity more readily granted to Euro-American women.

Gendering the story of the Congo is one way of humanizing the Congolese involved – both men and women. In their interviews with male Congolese soldiers and officers, Baaz and Stern heard truly repellent stories of desperation, disappointment, humiliation, and violence which they endured and committed. Against this background, the authors ask how one should "write of the subject who commits rape" (2013: 37) when this subject himself is marked by human suffering. How does one understand, in other words, the suffering of those who rape and are raped without condoning the former's violent act (ibid: 39)? These are compelling questions, which, however, neither the media nor Ruined can or will ask. What one is confronted with instead is an oversimplification of the rape story, blaming men in ways that do not cast them as parts of a larger social picture. With these reductive explanations, the anti-male "gendercide"[31] in the Congo wars has remained off the radar, as has the systematic recruitment of male child soldiers whose families were murdered by the same people who turn them into warriors (Turner 2013: 144). There is very good reason to believe that other topics remain unaddressed because of explanations that simply blame men. Rape in these accounts is seldom discussed as a part of a broader "culture of violence" (ibid: 132) that accepts rape and male violence as "normal" or even fetishizes it.

Radical Historicism

Tackling Congoism necessitates thinking historically and radically historicizing eyewitness reports. Ruined, however, explains the sexual violence in the Congo solely through a contemporary lens. Nottage (like Walker and Cooper) is misguided

31 Or the targeted killing of young males, especially non-combatant men who have been and continue to be the most frequent targets of mass killing and genocidal slaughter.

in believing that visiting the Congo and personally talking to victims will allow direct access to the complex truth behind the brutalities. This becomes very clear in a number of concrete narrative situations. The returning story of Generose is one such case. Walker's version of Generose's story (cf. above) revolves around the topos of cannibalism, for instance – a well-known and empirically extremely poorly documented infatuation, which featured in many media reports on Congolese rape (Stern/Baaz 2013: 91). One must express skepticism as to whether this topos was invoked by Generose to represent her reality or to grab Walker's and her readers' attention. This skepticism may not be easy to maintain, but is, nevertheless, legitimate – especially since Generose's story appears in another book on Congolese rape survivors, namely Lisa J. Shannon's A Thousand Sisters, whose author is active with the same NGO as Walker (Women for Women International).

In Shannon's book, Generose narrates her story in a strikingly different manner: In Walker's version, Generose is at home with her two children and her husband. In Shannon's account, on the other hand, Generose said to be there with "six children, one was my sister's child" (2010: 150). Walker tells her readers that the husband was chopped into pieces; Shannon states that he was shot. Walker mentions that Generose's leg was fried in a pan, while in Shannon's it was "burnt in the fire" (ibid). Most importantly, in Shannon's story there is no hint of a lost child who must subsequently be found. Shannon tells us that the next time Generose saw her children was "two months and a week" later (ibid). Why does Shannon's story deviate so dramatically from Walker's? Did Shannon and Walker not listen carefully, or did Generose give Shannon and Walker different accounts?

These irreconcilable stories are indicative of a systemic problem: Shannon's and Walker's rape stories (and other texts building on them, such as Nottage's Ruined) have become commodities. As a global issue, conflict-related rape has over the last decade become a multimillion-dollar industry in which Congolese women have been "encouraged to represent themselves as survivors of rape in order to establish themselves as legitimate recipients of humanitarian aid" (Baaz/Stern 2013: 99). In Generose's specific situation, it is quite possible that she framed the deeply traumatic story of the loss of her husband and her leg (the overlapping topics in Walker's and Shannon's stories) as an experience of rape in order to get hold of much-needed support for the survival of her family. The willingness of Nottage, Walker, and others to "save brown women from brown men", as Spivak famously phrased it (1988: 101), leads to deeply unbalanced communicative situations that rule out the possibility of Congolese women speaking for themselves on their own terms (cf. Kapoor 2008: 41). This epistemic challenge remains mostly unacknowledged in Walker's and Nottage's texts. They disavow their own determinations, such as their "favourable historical and geographic position" (ibid: 46). When Walker and Nottage, naively or knowingly, pretend to have no determination apart from being a woman, they are silently justifying self-interest through the voice of the sister-other.

Self-interest renders accurate, truthful human communication extremely difficult, if not impossible. Shannon's engagement and writing are motivated by the personal desire to overcome her banal former life, which she describes in her book, and to finance her new one in the service of the NGO Women for Women International. The benefits for Generose framing herself as a rape victim in her interactions with Shannon surface regularly in her story, too. Generose tells Shannon: "Already the benefit has been more than a hundred dollars, which I used to buy a cow" (Shannon 2010: 151). On top of that, Shannon offers to pay for an operation on Generose's leg, which, as the author explains, is rotting from a "life-threatening bone infection" (ibid: 149). Naive eyewitness epistemology combined with a luminous rhetoric of "global sisterhood" hides, but does not erase, the power difference between the Euro-American activists and the "object" of their writing, which, in its most extreme cases, results in outright abduction by humanitarian organizations.[32]

Ruined falls into the trap of ahistoricism. Thomas Turner's observations regarding a historically determined Congolese "culture of violence, rape and impunity" (2013: 131) must lead to an investigation of the broader Congo archive to understand the present disaster. Rape in the Congo has a history that goes beyond the brutal "now" of "Africa's world war" (ibid: 17). A deep understanding of the historicity of sexual violence is a prerequisite for grasping it as a real-and-imagined Central West African phenomenon. Nancy Rose Hunt, for instance, links the 2003 "angry mass rape [...] on some 200 girls and women in a village named Nsongo Mboyo" (2008: 220) to the brutalities of the Congo Free State in that same village. Hunt explicitly makes the case that the rape of the present had its roots in the much-neglected wife abductions,[33] "hostage houses", mutilations, and sexual abuses that

32 Euro-American humanitarian organizations resort to sheer force, as Baaz and Stern remind us, in order to showcase their victims to donors (2013: 97), thereby abusing them to secure funding for their own organizations in the lucrative business that Congolese rape has become in the wake of its increasing commercialization (ibid: 88-106). Unintentionally, the isolation of Congolese rape victims and, in some cases, their outright abduction reminds us of the hostage houses for women of the Congo Free State.

33 Hunt notes that pictures of non-sexual mutilation have been favored over those of sexual abuse, especially sexual abuse of women (2008: 222-223). Mutilation was more sayable, according to Hunt – and more photographable – than either rape or forced incest. Morel's Red Rubber, as discussed in the previous chapter, indeed confirms this bias. Sexual muti-

occurred from 1892 onward, when the violent rush for raw rubber began (cf. previous chapter).

The most compelling element in Hunt's research is that she shows how Congolese rape cases raise serious questions regarding the "duration, reproduction, and repetition in history and historical writing" (ibid: 221). Memories of the crimes of the Congo Free State could have easily persisted for decades, as Hunt concludes, leading to stories and attitudes that still have an effect today. The words of women such as Boali and Mingo, whose voices were registered in depositions before King Leopold's Commission of Inquiry in 1905 and 1906, are very similar to contemporary rape stories.[34] Many topoi in Boali and Mingo's narratives overlap with that of Generose's (e.g. the absent husband, the violent house visitation by a soldier, the chopping off of legs, and other stories of absurdly painful sadism and cannibalism).

The similarities of past and present rape accounts draw attention to sexual violence as a discursive ritual in the overall Congo discourse, ready to be told in similar wording for reasons that have little foundation in the present Congo itself. To be sure, rape is very likely to be endemic in the Congo, and thus is very "real". But looking at the African American Congo archive, which is permeated by all sorts of gendered violence committed by Congolese men against "their" women, it must at least be acknowledged that rape hardly ever signifies Congolese sexual violence alone, but also points to domestic issues of those who write about the Congo. To understand the Congo, one must, in other words, historicize both the Congo and one's own involvement in the broader realm of sexual violence.

The historicization of the Congo through Black American perspectives must include, for instance, a reflection on the embattled significance of rape within the African American community as a whole. In the 60s, for instance, the "myth that all black men were rapists" was very much alive (hooks 1981: 63). Thus, as soon as independence troubles started in the Congo, white middle-class magazines such as

lation by "the agents of the Anversoise" (ibid), for instance, receive scant attention, whereas other forms of violence permeate his account.

34 "One day when my husband went into the forest to gather rubber, the sentry Ikelonda came," Boali stated, "finding me in my hut where I stayed, and asked me to give myself to him". Boali "rejected his proposition" and the sentry became enraged and "fired a gun shot at me, which gave me the wound whose trace you can still see". The story ended with Ikelonda thinking "I was dead", only to realize that the torture had just started when the sentry "cut off my right foot" in order to rob her of her bracelet (Boali of Ekolongo 1905, qtd. in Hunt 2008: 225). Mingo's story, in turn, mentioned how sentries made "me take off my cloth and put clay in my sexual parts which made me suffer a lot" (Mingo of Ilua 1906, qtd. in ibid: 236).

Life were ready to start spreading suggestive images and stories about the systematic rape of white women by Congolese soldiers. This eagerness was reminiscent of the will to believe that lynched Blacks in the South at the turn of the century were truly rapists (cf. previous chapter). These media stories, of both African American and Congolese rapists, have since been discredited and disregarded as nonsense.[35]

However, if one wants to discredit those rape stories, more has to be done than insist on their falseness (which, theoretically, can easily be refuted in turn). To understand Congolese rape stories through an American lens, one must examine one's own historical attitudes towards rape. African American sexual violence has always been a deeply contentious discursive battleground. This becomes obvious if one takes a look at African American news media such as The Chicago Defender. The paper discussed Congolese rape in the 60s the way Black intellectuals had done throughout their history: by questioning the legitimacy of the rape charge, as shown by Ida B. Wells-Barnett in the previous chapter. In the early 60s, rape was explained as a political act of resistance, as echoed in the title of The Chicago Defender's article from August 13, 1960, "Congolese Claim: 'Belgians Mistreat Our Women; We Mistreat Theirs; Now We Equal' (Siggins 1960: 160).[36] Attempts to rationalize Black rape were in great demand in the 60s and 70s, as bell hooks explains (1981: 70). Elridge Cleaver's confessions in his bestselling Soul on Ice (1991) are a case in point. In the book, Cleaver claimed to have become a rapist for political reasons. "Rape was an insurrectionary act," the author stated (ibid: 33), "It delighted me that I was defying and trampling upon the white man's law, upon his system of values, and that I was defiling his women – and this point, I believe, was the most satisfying to me because I was very resentful over the historical fact of how the white man has used the black woman. I felt I was getting revenge" (ibid). Behind this smoke screen of "avenging themselves against racism" Black men were

35 Stories about the "hundreds of white women, even children of 12" who had been raped, "many repeatedly", as one correspondent of Life wrote in an attention-grabbing 1960 article titled "Faces of Terror in Congo" (Snell 1960b: 32), had hardly any correspondence to the situation in the Congo, as even the colonialism-friendly 2002 Belgian monograph Weg uit Congo (Verlinden 2002) confirms. The trouble with these narratives is, however, that they stay in the archive, awaiting recollection and re-inscription.

36 In this story, The Chicago Defender blamed the Belgian women for wearing shorts that were too short and offering their "apples too freely to lusty 'Adams'" (Siggins 1960: 2). Rape thus ceased to be a flat-out questionable event (as it had been when African Americans were involved in early twentieth century), but became an occurrence that was to be explained racially and sexually, by, among other tactics, blaming or ignoring the real-and-imagined victims.

expressing "exploitative feelings about white women and finally all women", as hooks argues (1981: 70).

Here, too, we might examine Nottage's framing of Congolese rapists as hip hop youngsters, amongst other framings. Obviously, this framing is an instantiation of the ongoing African-Americanization of Central West Africa. Discussions of sexual violence (including rape) within contemporary hip hop culture have been indicative of a larger gender crisis within the Black community. This crisis was already foreseen by the Black Power movement in the 60s, as hooks has it, when Black Power proponents "disassociated themselves from chivalrous codes of manhood" and started embracing "those men who exploited and brutalized women" (1981: 106). As Tricia Rose also maintains, contemporary hip hop culture produces tropes of aggressive Black promiscuity for mainly white audiences that have helped to "justify the violence and domination of black people", "including the rape of black women" (2008: 179). With rape as such an embattled African American signifier, Nottage's particular framing of Congolese rapists is striking: She addresses both the Congo rape crisis as well as the African American one. It is at this point that Nottage's strategy of "everydaying" the Congo, or of giving the everyday in the Congo a voice through personal narratives and respectful silences, crumbles under the weight of self-indulgent, parochial interests.

All in all, the most progressive aspect of Nottage's theater lies in the way she evokes her stories through a disciplined, non-damaging use of language. This becomes evident if one compares Nottage's work to the CBS documentary, which is filled with Congoist language and attitudes: "Right now there's a war taking place in the heart of Africa, in The Democratic Republic of Congo," CBS journalist Anderson Cooper introduced his topic in "heart of darkness" fashion, "and more people have died there than in Iraq, Afghanistan, and Darfur combined [...] more than five million people have died and the numbers keep rising" (CBS News 2008). Nottage refused Cooper's (and Walker's) numbers game for good reason, since this strategy easily "depersonalize[s]" via the "mark of the plural", as Memmi phrases it, allowing people to "drown in an anonymous collectivity" (Memmi 1991: 687). Nottage circumvented the "crushing objecthood" (Fanon 2005: 101) of the plural by confining herself to the personal mode of narrating.

Mama Nadi's brothel is thus unapologetically center stage. This allows, to a great extent, for stereotypical Western interests in the story to be side-stepped. Lynn Nottage's infatuations (nor those of the African American community) do not play a main role in Ruined. This contrasts with Alice Walker's essay, which hinges on "overcoming speechlessness", that is, her own speechlessness, rather than that of Congolese rape survivors. Nottage's strategy of decentralizing herself and remaining "close" to the perceived everyday Congo is a key prerequisite for producing knowledge on the Congo, rather than on oneself. Congolese women are the ones that are "ruined", not Nottage. Quite the contrary, in fact, as the work won Nottage a Pulitzer.

Nottage's play thus shows that being somewhere that is not the Self (Kapoor 2008: 57) is possible, no matter how incomplete this somewhere may be. Ruined, despite all its inadequacies in terms of the Congoist fallacies it takes up, indicates that it is possible to resist the temptation to produce an Other to suit one's own interests alone. Although Nottage's work goes far to counter Congoism by purging her language of the usual Congoist tropes and topoi (and if they are used, they are applied critically), and through her devotion to telling stories for their own sake, there remains the problem of the transferability and coherence of what lies beyond the author. In the end, Nottage speaks for the Congolese women. The question becomes: Can Congolese Americans break through this barrier?

SUBALTERN CONGOISM

According to the 2000 U.S. census, about 3800 individuals in America originated from the Congo (Bureau of the Census 2000). This number describes those who emigrated from the Congo in the last few decades – not the hundreds of thousands who became enslaved in the 18th and 19th centuries. This number might have tripled since then, as a 2013 report by the European Resettlement Network mentions 10.000 new Congolese refugees in the United States (European Resettlement Network 2013: n.p.). Among the Congolese diaspora in the U.S. are highly prolific intellectuals, such as the historian Georges Nzongola-Ntalaja and the novelist Emmanuel Dongala. Both work at American universities and have gained considerable critical acclaim for their work, Nzongola for his 2002 history, The Congo from Leopold to Kabila: A People's History, and Dongola for his tales of Liberian child soldiers in the 2006 novel Johnny Mad Dog.

In what follows, the lesser known Congolese American writers Albert Makelele and the Ngwala brothers will be examined – particularly Makelele's 2008 autobiography This is a Good Country: Welcome to the Congo and the latter's 2012 novel Congo: Spirit of Darkness. These authors will be discussed because (and not despite) the fact that their works are located at the fringes of the American Congo corpus. Neither of them can be called professional writers with a substantial oeuvre, nor do they have systematic backing from a powerful community (academic or otherwise): There are no quotes from fellow writers, for instance, praising their work on the covers of their books. In fact, both of them funded the publication of their books themselves. This makes their texts rougher, but also less constrained by the usual pressures of the publishing process. These books are nevertheless sold on Amazon.com, and are therefore widely available. Because of their "freer" status, the books theoretically have more ideological and methodological leverage to re-shape, re-think, and reject existing Congo discourses. A final criterion for the selection of these two works is that they are epistemic opposites: The modernist work of Makelele contrasts sharply with the postmodernist approach assumed by the Ngwalas.

Makelele and the Ngwalas are mediocre writers: Neither of their books are easy reads. Makelele starts off his memoirs with an imaginative road trip through his home town of Stanleyville in 1944. This trip is, as Makelele confesses on the cover of his book, an "arduous" start for the "uninitiated" (2008: n.p.). "There are numerous reference to some rather esoteric and indigenous names and terminologies," the author explains, "purposely laid down for recording" (ibid). Indeed this is the case; Makelele's quirky compilation of historical, academic, and personal narrative is difficult to get through at times. The Ngwala brothers, in turn, wrote a historic novel whose main narrator is, at least in theory, Susan Baily Dawson, a 100-year-old English abolitionist, whose youth in the Congo is related. In practice, however, Dawson's life story only loosely frames the mélange of "native" Congolese and Euro-American stories. Working on the novel on "many late nights and weekends" (2012: n.p.), as the Ngwalas' acknowledgments state, does have an effect on the overall presentation, and turns the novel into a text that struggles to maintain a consistent narrative focus.

Difficult or unpleasant to read as it may be, Makelele's memoir does intriguing things with the Congo. To be sure, this is the life story of a perfectly assimilated Black middle-class Congolese American. As in many previous generations of the Black bourgeoisie, the issues of a stable family life, a fruitful career, and an excellent American education (courtesy of a scholarship) are discussed and celebrated, crowned by a large selection of family pictures in which the Makeleles present themselves as middle-class subjects in much the same vein as past generations of African American intellectuals. The pictures show Albert as a well-dressed, well-to-do, proud pater familias who presides over a large family of well-groomed children and grandchildren, while not forgetting to have fun as well (there are holiday pictures of Albert, for instance).

Despite this bourgeois self-fashioning, oppositional stances come to the fore in Makelele's work. He is well aware, for instance, of the "negative notions" (Makelele 2008: 170) surrounding the Congo, as well as the "prejudices" and the aspects of "doom and gloom" (ibid) which cast "an abject and base affront to the very humanity of the African considered" (ibid). Makelele applies a number of strategies to avoid reproducing Congoist clichés. He renders his own knowledge of the Congo relative, for instance, by reducing his eyewitness authority to local phenomena and local insights (which does not mean that he cuts out the global altogether, as we will see). Being Congo-born does not give him the license to talk about the whole, vast country (this is in contrast to many Black and white Euro-American journalists; cf. the Conclusion of this book). Makelele focuses on his hometown of Stanleyville (Kisangani in postcolonial times) and refrains from making sweeping statements, at least at the start of the book. But even on Kisangani, a place which "could not be traded in with any other places anywhere on this planet" (ibid: 74), Makelele has no universal knowledge claims to make. This goes not only for himself, but for those surrounding him.

Makelele begins his account in 1944, when he actively began "knowing the city of Kisangani" (ibid). Watching his father work as a longshoreman, he witnessed how the "wealth of the Congo float[ed] down the river to destinations unbeknown to me, at the age of five or six" (ibid: 75). The issue of "not knowing" frequently returns in Makelele's account, as, for instance, when he comes to the issue of the colonial economy of the Congo. Information regarding trade relations between the Congo and South Africa was "not readily available to the average Congolese" (ibid: 5), thus turning the rubber economy activity into an activity that was hardly understood. The same goes for the exportation of animals. Makelele admits that "no one had a precise answer" as to where to all the animals were shipped (ibid: 76): Makelele states, "One's guess was as good as another's" (ibid). Makelele thus hints at the limitations of Congolese accounts of historical topics, which are not very well understood by many European or American travelers who interview Congolese on their voyages (cf. the Conclusion).

Makelele's book highlights the textuality of Congolese eyewitness accounts, too. Congolese like himself had to read up on historical topics to make sense of what had happened around them. Although he is aware of evoking the trope of the "happy native" (ibid: 77), Makelele insists on discussing the bulk of Congolese as politically ignorant, as they "cared less concerning what was happening outside the country and around the world, be it for lack of political awareness or simply pure ignorance, whatever the case might be" (ibid). Makelele thus considers Congolese knowledgeable only if they possess the possibilities of knowing accurately by virtue of their geographical proximity or through archival experience. It therefore follows that Congolese can err in their evaluation of the accuracy of what they're saying. Every so often, the subaltern who draws his social and historical capital from his perceived identity as a Congolese is just plain uninformed or wrong, Makelele suggests.

Makelele's position of talking and knowing is a humble one, as he understands the limits of lived historical experience – this only starts to make sense to him in combination with profound archival knowledge. The transnational links between Congolese and African Americans, for instance, are made clear to him through the archive. Makelele can only make sense of his first contact with African Americans in the 40s through his research in libraries. Three Black Americans had visited his school in Kisangani, and the author recalls the Americans having an "intriguing, mystical effect on us [...] we were taken by an inner compulsion to touching them as to find out whether they were for real" (ibid: 69); the Americans, in turn, are said to have been "benignly looking at and scrutinizing one then the other" (ibid: 18). The second encounter took place a few years later, when "a group" of Black Americans (ibid) were sent to his home town by the Rockefeller Research group, "investigating all that was rumored about the Congo and its fabulous wealth" (ibid). After they left, corporate investments – in colonial collaboration with Americans and Belgians – followed, of which Makelele provides a short list. Makelele can provide this information, not because he experienced this first hand, but because he went looking for knowledge in the archive.

Makelele's stories, which are produced through textual and experiential knowledge, underpin the tension between the author and the Black American visitors, who are depicted as cultural or economic proxies of colonialism. Underlying these stories is a divide between Makelele and African Americans as a whole, which surfaces in passages that express the alienation Makelele feels. As soon as Makelele arrived in the U.S., for instance, he found out "how uniformly and consistently across the board American Blacks long ago had fixated ideas regarding Africans in general" (ibid: 108). On a more general level, Makelele's archival research shrewdly points out the "decades of bombardments by newspapers, poetry, novels, radio, movies and television" that have preconditioned Americans in "thinking negative, disassociate them from or just hold lukewarm sentiment, at best, towards matters African" (ibid: 110). Makelele therefore sees a "deep gulf of mass ignorance and misinformation" regarding Africa in general and the Congo in particular (ibid: 111). This, according to the author, has created a chasm between Africans and African Americans. His own attempts to counter the many stereotypes "fell on deaf ears or rather should I say that I was listened to with a strain of a benign disbelief" (ibid: 109). Makelele thus found what this book has also unearthed: a long and rich tradition of the defaming of the Congo in the African American archive.

Does Makelele's recognition of a long history of denigrating the Congo help him to avoid it himself? It does for large stretches of his work. However, in his self-fashioning, Makelele at times slips into a paternalistic, moralistic attitude towards contemporary Congolese. In the harshest Congoist fashion, Makelele condemns his fellow countrymen for supposedly living in a "fanciful, imaginary fairy world" (ibid: 166), especially in terms of "the process of production, acquisition and accumulation of material and consumer goods, the creation of wealth" (ibid: 166). The solution for the all-pervading "passive, receptive attitudes [...] towards life" must be, according to Makelele, "mass education of the people, including adult education" (ibid: 168). On top of that, Congolese must be "taught that production (i.e. hard work and labor) is what brings the wealth of the nation" (ibid: 166). Appealing to young Congolese to start the "great task of the great march forward" (ibid: 169), Makelele slips into the well-known framework of evolutionary progress, turning once again to Congoist stereotypes.

"It will be a great tragedy for Africans not to be thinkers, writers and Universalists," Makelele asserts, "given the resounding magnitude of backwardness at the arduous race toward world modernism [...] they remain without recourse in their ability to help themselves" (ibid: 174). In the same Congoist vein, Makelele concludes that all these bad Congolese qualities are particularly saddening, given the Congo's resources. It is a point of irony that he cannot fail to be amazed by (e.g. ibid: 174-175), as the Congo-as-Resource topos demands. The Congoist orientation is rounded off by a rather uncritical usage of Stanley's and Conrad's texts, of which the latter is quoted to underline the timeless quality of Congolese poverty – today's misery is "nothing much different from the days of Joseph Conrad's voyage on the river boat when he noticed the exact same thing" (ibid: 174).

Makelele's hope for the Westernization of the Congo leads to him advocating that the Congo adopt Euro-American recipes for success: He highlights the need for free enterprise and an expanding market, secularism, and a pluralist electoral democracy. This prescription silently assumes the superiority of the capitalist system, which, however, is never addressed. If there are problems in the Congo, these are, as far as Makelele is concerned, home-grown. The Congolese are thus made responsible for their own condition and are not viewed as part of a larger economic system that depends on external factors to succeed. Samir Amin is right in that it is "futile to speak of the decisive role of internal factors" in light of dominant external ones (ibid: 183), which are decisive in the history of capitalism. This will return in the concluding part of this book, too.

The novel by the Ngwalas, Congo: Spirit of Darkness, might be considered the polar opposite of Makelele's modernist work. In the acknowledgments, the authors claim that "truth and fiction have been merged harmoniously" (2012: n.p.), thus aligning themselves with a long tradition of writers of postmodern fiction[37] (and postmodern historians, as was discussed above). Fictionalizing the Congo and its inhabitants within a "genuine" academic setting (however problematic this claim may be in light of my hypothesis of the existence of academic Congoism) has the advantage of enabling the reader to imagine a certain "progressiveness". The Ngwalas' novel presents the zenith of imaginative possibilities, taking the reader on board a pirate ship whose captain is a Django-like former Congolese slave who attacks one of Leopold II's ships (named Spirit of Darkness La Caprice). The Congolese revenger does this for profit, but also, as he states, to avoid seeing "more of my people killed" (ibid: 232). He himself has created a human laboratory for racial equality on his ship: "My crew is made up of free men. I welcome Europeans and Africans as equals on my craft [...] I teach my crew to become sailors without turning them into slaves. This is the way of my world [...] we are pirates, blind to colour" (ibid: 234). This self-determined Congolese pirate is the militant counterweight to the frightened and victimized Congolese women and children who are whipped into slavery throughout the rest of the novel. In contrast to the pirate, they "could do nothing but watch, helplessly wailing in terror" (ibid: 117).

In addition to the Congolese captain, there is plenty more progressive characterization to be found in the novel, some of which borders on pure fantasy. For instance, on board Leopold's ship is a German academic who transcends the racism of his days by questioning the "ill-speak of the Dark Continent" (ibid: 211). That same academic explains African witchcraft to the journalist Dawson, the main character of the book (ibid: 207), as an understandable social act. Dawson, in turn, takes up the defense of the "natives" by revealing that colonialism leads to nothing but "excellent servants and slaves" (197). Given the list of secondary literature at the end of the book, the novel suggests that a Congolese pirate, an anti-racist German scientist, and an abolitionist female journalist could have existed, could have met,

37 Exemplary here are the first lines of Barbara Kingsolver's bestselling novel The Poisonwood Bible: "This is a work of fiction. Its principal characters are pure inventions with no relations on this earth, as far as I know. But the Congo in which I placed them is genuine" (1999: ix). Oddly enough, the "genuineness" of the Congo that Kingsolver proclaimed is based on academic works of history, a list of which is published in a long bibliography at the end of the book. This is done in Michael Crichton's Congo, too, and is alluded to in Ronan Bennett's The Catastrophist. A Novel (the latter, however, does not explicitly catalogue the literature he used, but merely acknowledges the "debt I owe it", 1997: n.p.). It is in this tradition that the Ngwalas published their book, including a long list of secondary literature at the end to attest to the genuineness of their account.

or could have least developed stances as progressive as those portrayed in the novel. This must, however, be questioned. If one takes seriously what is known about the period in question (the late 19th century, that is), it is unlikely that things could have unfolded in this way or been discussed in the terms presented by the book. As was shown in the previous chapter, there were hardly any deviant opinions among Black and white European or American intellectuals in the late 19th century on the issue of Africa and the Congo. Thus, the passages in question emerge as anachronistic, echoing today's hopes instead of the past's possibilities.

The impression of fantasy gone wild becomes more acute if one takes a closer look at the bibliography. One finds strange bedfellows there, which make the historical characterization of the pirate and the scientist even more unlikely and ill-founded. The list of literature places academic texts (e.g. from the well-known Africanist Basil Davidson) alongside scholarship written for a broader audience (e.g. Adam Hochschild's work on the Congo Free State). In the same vein, the novel links children's literature (e.g. Taplin's Pirate's Handbook) to the travelogues of Stanley and Schweinfurth. The overall effect of this hodgepodge makes it appear as if these texts should all be taken equally seriously. Although the Ngwalas are certainly not the only ones in the history of Congo writing to use faulty information, this seldom occurs so blatantly.

The Ngwalas have attempted to write a historical novel in the postmodern tradition. The list of heterogeneous texts in their bibliography avoids any privileging, allowing all of the texts to be read as if they were merely literature, each producing their own truths in their respective intellectual circles (Butler 2002: 24). None of these texts, it is suggested, have a unique or reliable relation to the world, nor any certain correspondence with reality: "They are just another form of fiction" (ibid: 15).

This opens up enormous space for the free play of the imagination. The knowledge value of this strategy, however, is probably negligible to none. What do the lengthy conversations in Congo: Spirit of Darkness between "natives" of "the untarnished heart of Central Africa" (2012: 2) bespeak in the end? The question becomes especially relevant if these conversations sound as if they are produced by contemporary American suburbanites (with a primitive edge), who discuss their lives as American middle-class subjects might, "absorbed by their work and the stories of the day" (ibid: 4). The most noticeable difference between the Congolese and the middle-class Americans, however, is the former's attention to and belief in the world of spirits, witchcraft, sorcerers, and voodoo (a belief Euro-American characters in the book share, emphasizing how true this belief must be). This again can be understood as a postmodern wink, upgrading the "irrational" in the struggle with one's own despair regarding the "Enlightenment-derived public functions of reason" (Butler 2002: 9). In the Ngwalas' novel, if villagers had listened to the sorcerer Ndoki's warning to run as "the devil lures [...] take your children" (Ngwali 2012: 3), they would have been spared enslavement and death. Thus the assumption that a sorcerer's powers are nothing more than meaningless superstition (as we have encountered many times in the African American archive) is actively countered.

Despite its progressive quality, the postmodernist method comes with its drawbacks. The infatuation with the "surreal" deprives the Congo of its history of all-too-rational colonial exploitation: Again, Central West Africa becomes an unknowable place of mysterious forces and similarly strange peoples. Everything is possible in such a place, including Black pirate avengers or, as is the case in Crichton's Congo, killer apes who violently protect the lost city of Zinj in the jungles of Central West Africa against Euro-American capitalists and explorers. In a Euro-American archive filled with so much nonsense, one should ask whether the Congo is an appropriate template for giving reign to one's own epistemic infatuations.

CONGOISM, CLASS, CREATIVITY: A CONCLUSION

This chapter has addressed the novel ways in which 20th-century African American intellectuals began to approach the Congo. None of these attempts has been entirely free of Congoist tendencies, however. Confident female Congolese voices were shown to have been promising opponents of Congoism, but also at times its reproducers. Works of history, journalistic texts, and theater plays proved equally unsuccessful in countering Congoism. Class was revealed as far more than background in this chapter because of the urgency with which this issue was attended to by proponents of Black Power. Wallerstein reminds us, "I know of no serious historical interpretation of this modern world of ours in which the concept of the bourgeoisie, or alternatively of the middle classes, is absent" (1988: 98). It would have, indeed, been difficult to tell the story of intellectual Congo discourses in African America without outing its main protagonist, the Black bourgeoisie.

However, class remains, as bell hooks asserts in her reflections in Where We Stand: Class Matters, a much-neglected perspective in explaining African American communities (cf. the Introduction): "Collectively, black folks in the United States have never wanted to highlight the issue of class and class exploitation, even though there have always been diverse caste and class groups among African-Americans" (2000: 89). For bell hooks, the reason why "it has been difficult for black folks to talk about class" is this (ibid: 8): "Acknowledging class difference destabilizes the notion that racism affects us all in equal ways. It disturbs the illusion of racial solidarity among Blacks, used by those individuals with class power to ensure that their class interests will be protected even as they transcend race behind the scenes" (ibid).

Texts that pushed back against the intellectual authority of Black bourgeois subjects tended to go far in their critique of Congoism, too. Anti-Congoist creative practice has always existed on the periphery of existing class hegemonies. While this creativity developed within existing hegemonic discourses (and had to in order to be understood), it also attempts to alter the hegemonic discourse "by shifting the borders and by creating new (contrasting) forms of consciousness; it produces 'supplements' to what is already in the 'archive', so to speak" (Blommaert 2005: 106). The center of this process can be located in "the individual agent, a subject often living with idiosyncratic ideas and concepts, fantasies and nightmares, who out of his/her own personal experience in society starts to feel that dominant understandings do no longer work" (ibid). One of the central anti-hegemonic agents in this chapter was Malcolm X. In the discussion of the man and select heirs to Black Power, the extremely classed nature of Congoism emerges more clearly. X's focus on and advocacy on behalf of the lower strata of the African American community highlighted the impetus behind the Black bourgeoisie's creation of a "homogeneous Other" (Spivak 1988: 84). Furthermore, X allowed the Congo to shift from an entity that was utterly dismissed (the bourgeois version of the Congo) to one of admiration and humanity (the anti-bourgeois version). In the end, X, too, struggled to overcome the long history of Congoism, as he took up strategies of the past to idealize the region.

What can we learn from Black intellectuals in terms of undermining Congoism? As shown, an important aspect has been the need for historical, archival, and personal meta-reflection. The example of Malcolm X illustrated that rejection and negation of the Congoist standard began with an epistemic awareness of historical truth production and of the historical Congo archive. X openly discussed, condemned, refuted, and re-framed this tradition of denigrating the Congo; he therefore overturned the image of the Congo as a place of cannibalism and savagery and made it a place as humane as any other, populated by good and bad Congolese (exemplified by Lumumba and Tshombe). This kind of socio-political "creativity" – a concept I use in Csikszentmihalyi's sense of introducing a socially relevant new idea that "changes some aspects of the culture" (1997: 25) – requires that individuals master the historical field and see patterns within it. This is precisely what Malcolm X, as a passionate autodidact, did; he studied African and American history continuously and critically (cf. Manning 2012) and was thus able to introduce variations on it.

The tactic of meta-reflection also proves helpful in positioning authors ideologically and intellectually with regard to others who discuss the Congo. X harshly criticized Martin Luther King and others for their take on the Congo. Through his classed perspective, X recognized Civil Rights advocates as the executors of, in the words of bell hooks, "a class-based [...] struggle whose ultimate goal was to acquire more freedom for those black folks who already had a degree of class privilege, however relative" (2000: 92). This recognition of significant political others, including their reasons for writing on the Congo (or not writing at all), is a prerequisite to countering Congoism. It calls attention to the "geo-political determinations" of those talking about the Congo, as Spivak terms it (1988: 66), and highlights their "complicity" with, and dependence on, Congoism. This is especially true if those engaged in reflection also include themselves in this practice. X questioned the Congo discourse of others, but hardly cast any doubt on his own engagement with the Congo. His own complicity remained unaddressed, and this became a manner by which to evade it. What is more, by stressing his own factuality, X put himself outside history and inside Congoist discourse.

The truly creative person (X in this case) attempts to convince his "constituency" of the truthfulness and importance of the discovered novelty, that is, to provide a fresh perspective on the Congo, as Csikszentmihalyi describes it (1997: 28). Once this is achieved, this "constituency" will then subsequently incorporate this novelty into its own writing, thinking, and orating: "The next generation will encounter this novelty as part of the domain they are exposed to, and if they are creative, they in turn will change it further" (ibid). This kind of socially transmitted, cumulative, and challenging creativity occurred to some extent in the Black Power scene of the 60s and 70s. This scene took up X's rhetoric of Congolese "brotherhood", which led ultimately to Elridge Cleaver's voyage to Central West Africa. Cleaver might be considered the next stage of development in X's philosophy of American-Congolese brotherhood – moving from X's abstract brotherhood to a more concrete version of it. X's multi-leveled criticism and creativity has been passed down to a generational base much broader base than that of the Black Power scene. While rejecting Black Power politics, liberal Civil Rights-oriented journalists, such as Howard French, took up some of X's critical stances and motivations.

Anti-Congoist activity also depends on the genre in which it appears. "Never believe what you read in the newspapers [...] the truth isn't in them. Not when it comes to the Congo" (1970d: 135), X stated in the early 60s, openly challenging the authority of the media and questioning their ability to change their dispositions.

Drawing on Csikszentmihalyi once again, the level of creativity of individuals depends on "how well suited the respective domains and fields are to the recognition and diffusion of novel ideas" (1997: 31). As shown throughout this chapter, journalists struggle to produce innovative discourse. The self-serving political economy behind the corporate press inevitably leads to, amongst other things, an "if it bleeds, it leads" approach to the Congo (Van Hove 2010). This does not preclude the emergence of critical utterances on the role of the press by those who are part of the guild. Critical voices are numerous. Mostly, however, these utterances are meaningless, as those who communicate them do not follow up on their own critique. Critique in this sense is a way to continue what intellectuals have been doing all along, minus a number of cosmetic changes, predominantly on the level of language.

Finally, this chapter has shown that the "female" and "postmodern" perspectives on the Congo do not inevitably lead to creatively novel results. Nottage's "sexed" reading falls short because it is not postmodern (or "gendered") enough. Writing the Congo in a mode that is too postmodern, however, does not lead to immediately novel results either, as was discussed in relation to the Ngwala brothers. In the end, it becomes clear that the pursuit of knowledge of the Congo still takes place in an epistemic minefield. This raises the question of whether one should (or can) write about the Congo in any meaningful manner at all. How one might speak about a Congo that has "a lot of baggage" (cf. Kapoor 2008: 42) will be dealt with in the Conclusion of this book. In this final section, the potential non-narratability of the Congo will be debated, as will the misguided expectation that it can be fully comprehended.

Conclusion

Doing Damage, or Re-Writing Central West Africa

How to investigate a discursive presence, such as the "Congo", that keeps emerging in a heterogeneous corpus of African American texts, but has been ignored as a major topic within (African) American intellectual circles throughout the last two hundred years? This book chose to take a Foucauldian approach (cf. Introduction) through which a substantial amount of (African) American texts and practices were assembled that possessed at least one commonality: They produced utterances about the Congo. These texts and practices were then read "widely" and "closely" against and alongside one another, showing that the Congo discourse in which many texts operated determined to a great extent what and how they communicated. Through constant critical evaluation and an ongoing combination of many analytic categories – specifically race, class, gender, ethnicity, and capitalism, with class as the most systematic thread – this book's approach enabled an empirically-led theoretization of the Congo, leading to the neologism "Congoism".

Congoism, as a term, has its roots in 19th-century America, as was shown in the First Chapter. If anything, the emergence of a discursive phenomenon like Congoism echoes the longue durée influence that discourses in general can have – my book truly attests to the power of discourse in general and the U.S. American Congo discourse in particular. Congoism's discursive forms may have altered, its epistemic foundation may have changed, but its function has remained similar throughout the decades: Designating what "we", bourgeois subjects, do not want to be and do not want to be framed as: dysfunctional, alienating, savage, ugly, enslaved. As was shown throughout the book, Congoism proved extremely malleable in its form, epitomized by the ever-changing (but also ever-returning) topoi of the Congo as Slave, the Congo-as-Savage, the Congo-as-Darkness, the Congo-as-the-Vital, and the Congo-as-Resource. Congoism thus functioned as, to paraphrase Foucault, a discursive truth regime of rejection – both of internal and external Others.

One central Congoist strategy, starting in antebellum America, has been the Congo's separation from, and unification with, the signifier "Africa". The strategy of evoking an "African" homogeneity, while at the same time dividing it into favorable and less favorable regions, recurs in many works by African American intellectuals. Another strategy has been the constant catering to the epistemic mainstream, whatever it happened to be. Congoism is an extremely conformist discourse, which attaches itself to the intellectual standard and forces the Congo to fit into the frameworks provided by it. This turned the Congo into a recognizable and convincing signifier that reflected the dominant knowledge paradigms – from classicism and romanticism in the First Chapter to science in the Second and postmodernism in the Third.

Congoism also thrived on the strategy of hierarchization. Paradigms of objectivity and firsthand observation (in the First and Second Chapters), as well as self-reflectivity and meta-critical stances towards the Congo text production within one's own intellectual circle (as seen in the Third Chapter), provided clarity as to where Central West Africa should be placed in comparison to "us". This unbridgeable distance between "us" and "them", along with the continuation of an asserted closeness to the Congolese, are revealed by and produced through the aforementioned topoi and through modes of narration, such as tongue-in-cheekiness: Suggestions of closeness through humorous encounters merely override the more overtly paternalistic base of Congoism, as was shown from the Second Chapter onward. The attempts to break through the dismissive American Congo discourse have been noticeable, especially in the Third Chapter, which investigated whether identity-based (and genre-oriented) text selection can open up spaces of dissent, but showed that both men and women, American-born and Congo-born African Americans, activists, and journalists participated in the reproduction of Congoism. Reproduction was thus far more common than effective opposition through strategies of "negation", "reversal", "everydaying", or "meta-reflection"

This book has also demonstrated to what extent (Black) American intellectuals have been grappling with the Congo for centuries in an ongoing and confrontational dialog with white American and European intellectual discourse. This transnational and transcultural aspect has continued to exist up to the present day. What has changed since 1800 are the authors – those, in short, who actually produce Congoism (against the backdrop of a large, dismissive Congo archive), despite their attempts to treat the Congo fairly. Due to past and present activisms, as well as globalization and changing schools of thought, the American cultural mainstream has undeniably become more diverse.

This is reflected in the highly profitable Congo book industry, which is now permeated by POC ("people of color") – a term that designates non-white racial or ethnic minorities that are tied together through the experience or threat of racism (Ha/Lauré al-Samarei/Mysorekar 2007: 12). If one searches "Congo" on Amazon.com, for instance, bestselling white American writers are listed alongside lesser-known Black and foreign-born ones. Michael Crighton's popular novel Congo shows up at the top of the Amazon list, together with the Ngwalas' Congo: Spirit of Darkness (cf. Third Chapter). In the non-fiction department, one finds a travelogue by the Indian-born Anjan Sundaram titled Stringer: A Reporter's Journey in the Congo, general histories like the Belgian journalist-author David Van Reybrouck's Congo: The Epic Story of a People, Michael Deibert's 2003 The Democratic Republic of Congo: Between Hope and Despair, a new edition of Arthur Conan Doyle's 1900 critique of the Congo Free State, titled The Crime of the Congo, and Jason Stearns's 2011 Dancing in the Glory of Monsters (cf. First Chapter).

The current diversity among authors writing on the Congo is a continuation of the transcultural aspect of Congoism. The dichotomous, dismissive character of Congoism continues, as well – tropes of hope and despair, darkness and light persevere, as the titles mentioned above already suggest. Congoism clearly cuts through geography, time, and identity. Congolese, Black Americans, American Congolese, Indian Americans, and Belgian writers do not engage in the Congo discourse in ways that differ all that radically from earlier times, it seems. While these monographs exist predominantly outside the immediate realm of the African American intellectual community, a discussion of these books, and Van Reybrouck's Congo history in particular, will help to reveal the broader contemporary relevance of this study and will, once again, underscore the transcultural and transnational aspects and connections of Congoism. African American intellectuals, as was shown, interacted very actively with each other, but also with major schools of historic thought and with their socio-political environments. Individual white Euro-American intellectuals exercised a massive influence on Black intellectuals, who, in turn, have often acknowledged the effect of white American and European discourses and traditions on their own Congo writing. What holds true for African American intellectuals also proves relevant to a great extent for white Euro-American ones, it seems. This is due to the fact that Congo authors – both in the past and in the present – tend to base their texts on similar epistemological convictions and sources, leading to a very similar discourse.

One book in particular embodies this stasis, namely David Van Reybrouck's Congo: The History of an Epic People, published in English in 2014, which truly mines U.S. American sources. Van Reybrouck's book is a model example of how historical works from outside the U.S. incorporate and reflect the Congo discourses within the U.S. Van Reybrouck actively acknowledges the American influence on the Central West African Congo in numerous instances, ranging from the fact that "[W]ords like steamer and boy, due in part to the influence of British and American missionaries, never disappeared" (2014: 63) to the very explicit mentioning of U.S. political influence and the presence and effect of Black political discourse and individuals in the Congo (e.g. Bishop William Taylor, ibid: 48; Marcus Garvey, ibid: 150; Du Bois, ibid: 180; Obama ibid: 174 and 533-534). The references to the United States continue throughout, culminating in quotes which, for instance, link the "colonial city" in the Congo with urban settings in the United States: "There was more space and freedom, the distances were greater, the lanes broader, the lots roomier. From the very start, these cities were planned with the automobile in mind. It had something American about it, many whites felt" (ibid: 166). The author continues the comparison by stating: "Léopoldville with its various urban nuclei but no clear city center looked more like Los Angeles than like the medieval towns of Belgium or the 19th-century middle-class neighborhoods of Brussels or Antwerp" (ibid).[1] Van Reybrouck even frames W.E.B. Du Bois as a "radical American civil rights activist" (ibid: 180) – thus echoing the ongoing internal categorization that takes place within African American activist circles. This highlights the extent to which the author is part and parcel of an American discourse, consciously or unconsciously.

In what follows, this book will be discussed in relation to this book's findings on the African American Congo discourse. Although it is certainly true that Van Reybrouck writes against a very different background than African American intellectuals have done in the last two hundred years, it is equally true that strong overlaps in rhetoric, epistemic attitudes, and sources do systematically occur. Again, this is mainly determined by the archives that the author mines. According to Foucault, historical sources are primarily indicators for, and reflectors of, the social conditions under which they were produced. By analyzing sources in a Foucauldian manner, fundamental aspects of social relationships may be revealed. "Why have certain discourses been produced and not others?" is a central question here; the same is true for Van Reybrouck.

In the four years since its first Dutch/Flemish edition in 2010 (originally titled Congo: een geschiedenis/Congo: A History), Van Reybrouck's book has become a phenomenal success in terms of sales and critical acclaim. The book has been translated into six languages so far (English, French, Danish, Norwegian, Swedish, and

1 This kind of comparison appears in the book, e.g. "Léopoldville in those years was a kind of New Orleans" (Van Reybrouck 2014: 168).

German) and has been awarded numerous prestigious prizes, such as the 2010 Libris Geschiedenis Prijs (Netherlands and Flanders), the 2012 Prix Médicis essai (France), and the 2012 NDR Kultur Sachbuchpreis (Germany). In the Low Countries, the book was an instant hit, published to coincide with the celebrations of fifty years of Congolese independence. More than 150.000 copies were sold within less than half a year, a substantial amount in the Benelux (Geysels and Van Baelen 2010).

Merging the research qualities of an academic, the writing skills of an acclaimed novelist, and the interviewing skills of a journalist, Van Reybrouck produced a work that continuously walks the line between various text genres, as well as that between fact and imagination. The book's perceived "newness" was constituted by the many aesthetic and empathetic aspects in Van Reybrouck's writing (cf. Van Hove 2011). Supporters of the book frequently emphasized the beauty of its language and composition, as well as its "empathy" (e.g. Hendrickx 2010).

Van Reybrouck's work also impressed reviewers because of his heterogeneous source material, combining scholarly works and "personal stories", as The New York Times wrote (Ledgard 2014: n.p.). In his review for The Washington Post, Martin Meredith emphasized the legitimacy of the author's claims by highlighting Van Reybrouck's "10 visits to the country" in which he "managed to find Congolese veterans with memories of early white missionaries and colonial officials, and tales of religious uprisings and resistance movements" (2014: n.p.). Meredith continues to praise the work by mentioning that "his witnesses from more modern times included musicians, footballers, political activists, warlords and child soldiers. The result of all this is a vivid panorama of one of the most tormented lands in the world" (ibid). Eyewitness epistemology, as discussed in previous chapters, convinced the reviewers that Van Reybrouck's book should be taken seriously, a claim that I have questioned throughout.

The anecdotal quality of Congo: The Epic Story of a People is also responsible for the book's appeal. Van Reybrouck openly went for the small stories within "history", including his own father's, who worked as an engineer in secessionist Katanga (Van Reybrouck 2010b: n.p.). Despite this inclination toward the anecdotal, Van Reybrouck indicated in his interviews that he did not wish to shy away from constructing more traditional "big stories" (ibid: n.p.). The author positioned himself in this context explicitly in opposition to postmodernist writing, which tends to stay "close to one self, to tell one's own little story, hoping that out of all these images and fragments some mosaic like picture will emerge" (ibid). A final element of perceived newness was Van Reybrouck's open break with the "traditional narrative schemes" of Belgian and Dutch Congo historiography (ibid). This post-ideological writing caused the author to distance himself from researchers like De Witte and Hochschild who, according to Van Reybrouck, write in "an old school, left-wing engagement which brought with it a certain black-white thinking" (ibid).

Van Reybrouck's post-ideological approach does not produce a wholly uncritical history, however. Congoism and critique are not mutually exclusive. "To at least challenge the Eurocentrism that I would doubtlessly find on my path" (2014: 2), he writes, Van Reybrouck promises to be critical towards "the shaky compass" of written sources (ibid: 4). These written sources, according to the author, have tended to tell Central West African history only starting from colonialism onward (an observation this work shares). "To place Congo's history in the hands of a European. How Eurocentric can one be?" (ibid: 16), Van Reybrouck asks rhetorically. In contrast to these earlier accounts, the author begins his history in the prehistoric Congo and counters Eurocentric history by tackling Congoist language, amongst other phenomena: "If a heart of darkness existed [in the pre-colonial Congo], it was sooner to be found in the ignorance with which white explorers viewed the area than in the area itself. Darkness, too, is in the eye of the beholder" (ibid). The author also embraces an anti-Eurocentrism by occasionally integrating contemporary urban Congo history, as well as history works by "Congolese voices", into his story (ibid: 2).

Who are these Congolese that Van Reybrouck cites? He mentions Congolese academics (ibid: 561), along with "everyday people whose lives had been marked by the broader scope of history" (ibid: 3). In doing the latter, Van Reybrouck announces that his narrative is a "bottom-up history", based on interviews "with those whose perspectives usually do not make it into the written sources" (ibid: 563). Van Reybrouck hoped that this "archive" (ibid) of "local perspectives" (ibid: 3) would provide new insights and "a fuller, more tangible picture than textual information does" (ibid). To ensure the accuracy of those Congolese voices, Van Reybrouck restricted his interviews to the material aspects of "ordinary lives" (i.e. what Congolese "had eaten [...] the clothes they'd worn, what their house looked like"). This kind of non-textual information often exhibits greater permanence than remembered opinions and attitudes, according to the author: "Nothing is so contemporary as our memories" (ibid).

Thus, throughout his Introduction, Van Reybrouck applies several strategies of critique that had been taken up by African Americans in previous decades. Like Lynn Nottage, he highlights the "everyday"; like John Williams, he rejects the topos of Heart of Darkness and underlines the existence of a modern Congo; like Malcolm X, Van Reybrouck clearly espouses a critical meta-perspective on Congo discourse. However, it is also in the same manner as many African American intellectuals that Van Reybrouck's well-intentioned announcements crumble in the course of his Congo history. Forceful rhetorical rejection and offhanded reproduction of Congoism have been bedfellows all along, as was shown in previous chapters. And so it goes with Congo: The Epic Story of a People.

Overtly rejecting the Conradian Congo analogies is one thing; stepping outside of this rhetoric (and the discourse and archive it belongs to) itself is quite another, as Van Reybrouck's work proves (like that of many Black intellectuals before him). Van Reybrouck's introduction frequently reproduces reductive Congo imagery, for instance. For Van Reybrouck, the Congo river flows into the Atlantic as "someone who slashes his wrists and holds them under water – but then eternally" (ibid: 2); Kinshasa is compared to a "termite queen, swollen to grotesquery and shuddering with commotion" (ibid: 4); the equatorial forest he likens to a "head of a broccoli" (ibid: 12); the map of the Congo resembles "a balloon" (ibid: 8); and manioc roots sold on the markets remind the author of "sawed off tusks [...] as though the subsoil is barring its teeth, angry and fearful as a baboon" (ibid: 5). This ironic, animalistic rhetoric is lent strength by his systematic use of comparisons. The "peaceful maritime delta" of the Nile is contrasted with the violent one of the Congo (ibid: 2); The Democratic Republic of the Congo's capital is compared to its twin sister Brazzaville, which is "smaller, fresher, shinier" than Kinshasa (ibid: 4), and whose soil is black, not red, "as in other parts of Africa" (ibid: 5). To round off these rather random comparisons, Van Reybrouck contrasts the rural Congo of the sixteenth century with Renaissance-era Italy (ibid: 20). The message of Congolese backwardness can hardly be overlooked, a message this book has focused upon in the Congo archive throughout the last 200 years.

Failing infrastructure and the awkward clothing of Congolese are reappearing topoi in Van Reybrouck's work, a fascination he shares with African American works (cf. the Third Chapter) and the other books on the Amazon.com list, as we will see. Dysfunctional roads and inadequate train services justify Van Reybrouck's rule of thumb that "a journey that took one hour during the colonial period now corresponds to a full day's travel" (ibid: 15); (bleak) postcolonial times are thus pitted up against a (better) colonial period. This implicit privileging of colonial aspects returns throughout the story. Van Reybrouck's rule of thumb echoes the Belgian "model colony" discourse mentioned in the Introduction – a discourse which highlights the structural progressiveness of the Belgian Congo without mentioning that this relied upon forced or poorly paid labor by, for instance, Congolese cantonniers who kept the roads free (cf. Butcher 2008: 138). Thus, Van Reybrouck's implicit charge against the Congo – why has everything gone downhill since colonialist times? – is very much part of an internal Belgian discussion (just as African American Congo discourses and topoi had been). At this point, if not earlier, Van Reybrouck proves intimately bound up in Belgian ideological negotiations about the meaning of the Congo.

There is a strong class element in Van Reybrouck's focus on the real-and-imagined struggle with Congolese public infrastructure, too. Failing infrastructure is such a dominant topos because it goes against the grain of major bourgeois values, such as efficiency, regularity, continuity, and precision, as Moretti has it (2013: 18). On an epistemic plain, the ongoing attention directed at damaged roads is the expression of how private and public commodities became the new "principle of bourgeois validity: "consensus has been increasingly built on things, not men – let alone principles", as Moretti framed it (ibid: 21). Commodities (new and "whole" ones, favorably) confer legitimacy on Van Reybrouck. If these things are not there, as is the case with the Congo, the place tends to become illegitimate.

Van Reybrouck's depiction of the Congolese is permeated with strategies of commodification. In his text, we also find the recurring topos of "friendship" encountered in the accounts of 19th-century Black travelers or in texts of female anti-rape activists, for instance. In the same vein as these missionaries and activists, the distance between Van Reybrouck and his interview partners is revealed and reinforced throughout by his rhetoric. This underlines repeatedly the lack of connection between those involved. The author's narrative reveals that the class distance between him and the Congolese in fact precludes any form of truthful communication. A case in point is the friendship of the author with Nkasi, allegedly born in 1882, whom Van Reybrouck visits at home a number of times. Van Reybrouck considers Nkasi and his family as quintessentially "poor people", however – people without whole commodities. Their relationship is thus mediated through things; things that are missing, things that are broken, things that Van Reybrouck brings as gifts, as "poverty cannot be combated with powdered milk alone" (ibid: 26). Tellingly, Nkasi is introduced in Van Reybrouck's narrative with reference to his "scratched lenses", which are "attached to his head with a rubber band" (ibid: 10). Descriptions of Nkasi's family members are limited to their taste for soft drinks and cheap Euro-American clothes. "One of them had a sweater that read Miami Champs", Van Reybrouck observes (ibid: 10). Congolese people are judged, tongue-in-cheek, through their relationship with "things".

Van Reybrouck also reproduces Congoism by losing sight of, or interest in, his own principles of knowledge production. We have seen this among Black intellectuals, too, by, for instance, calling for Black unity while simultaneously abjecting, ignoring, and reducing the Congo Blacks. Van Reybrouck's treatment of Patrice Lumumba illustrates how this operates in his own text. In the introduction, the author proclaims his interest in using the Congolese as an oral archive for obtaining information on material traces of the past. This principle breaks down in the characterization of Lumumba. Van Reybrouck talked to Jamais Kolonga, for instance, who is a Congolese musician and participant-eyewitness of Congo's independence ceremonies, during the course of which Kolonga contrasts the "calm, cultivated, and respectful" president Kasavubu with the "irresponsible" prime minister Lumumba (ibid: 274-275). Van Reybrouck qualifies Kolonga offhandedly as ethnically biased because he was "a native of Bas-Congo" (ibid: 274). But the author nevertheless cites Kolonga's opinion in a lengthy passage. This kind of knowledge production contradicts Van Reybrouck's own historical approach, in which he professes to use Congolese eyewitnesses as a source for material factuality alone, not for their opinions. Kolonga suggests in his conversation with the author that his opinion is more than just the voice of one person: It also stands for the opinion of "old people in Bas-Congo", who regard Lumumba as "empty-headed, affected, and rude" (ibid: 275).

Kolonga's account is a typical instance of a native informant who is allowed to speak about topics he cannot judge properly because they are beyond his knowledge horizon (cf. previous chapter, too). Van Reybrouck does assert that "fourteen million people rarely share the same opinion" (ibid: 274), but these words prove to be rather empty. Through Van Reybrouck's source selection from an already deeply flawed Congo archive, Congolese are ultimately homogenized and portrayed as speaking in a single voice critical of Lumumba. In a list of rather negative quotes, Kolonga's opinion is strengthened by and aligned with Euro-American voices, such as the Belgian chief commander General Émile Janssens and American deputy secretary of state Douglas Dillon. The latter called Lumumba "messianic" and "irrational" – a judgment which was shared by many news media in the 60s (cf. previous chapter) – while the former is said to have evaluatd the prime minister as follows: "moral character: none; intellectual character: entirely superficial; physical character: his nervous system made him seem more feline than human" (ibid: 301). Subpersonhood "made in the U.S." thus finds its way without any critical footnote into Van Reybrouck's account, again highlighting the transtemporal and transcultural quality of Congoism that makes it so difficult for individual writers to escape it.

Against this background of a "normalized" Congo discourse as well as a "standardized" way of dealing with a flawed Congo archive, Van Reybrouck's Lumumba account barely meets the standard of a trustworthy historical depiction. If racist caricatures of Lumumba's opponents turn out to be acceptable historical utterances, it is worth trying to map out some of the potential processes involved in this depiction of a democratically elected, brutally murdered prime minister. One potential reason for Van Reybrouck's framing of Lumumba lies in the author's opposition to critical historians such as De Witte and Hochchild. This reveals itself in interviews (cf. above), as well as in writing. The author tends to implicitly differentiate or contradict the openly partisan narratives of De Witte (who turned the prime minister into a heroic, revolutionary figure). Van Reybrouck's Lumumba story thus becomes a way to position himself against ideological others, in much the same fashion as earlier Black intellectuals.

Congo-born scholar Valentin Mudimbe describes Van Reybrouck's book on its back cover as a "well-documented and passionate narrative which reads like a novel. [...] As an eye, a judge, and a witness, a talented writer testifies" (ibid: n.p.). With this kind of praise, Van Reybrouck's book is fictionalized ("narrative", "novel", "writer") and rendered simultaneously a well-researched effort ("well-documented"; "witness"). Despite the author's explicit critique of postmodernist historians, Van Reybrouck seems to end up as one himself. Due to this variety of attitudes, De Witte's careful analysis of Van Reybrouck's many factual mistakes can thus be met with silence (cf. De Witte 2020).

Unverifiable stories produced by Congolese permeate Van Reybrouck's history – similar to the many Black historians in the past – and are dealt with as if they were authoritative narratives. Thus, Nkasi figures prominently in Van Reybrouck's book, as does the man who stole the Belgian king's sword during the Congo's independence festivities. Van Reybrouck seems to realize that he is on thin ice with respect to the reliability of his informants: "Ngwadi's fantasy knew no bounds", the author states about the man who claims to have stolen the king's sword (2014: 277). To counteract the danger of integrating a voice that is "talking rubbish" (as Butcher put it in his own account, 2008: 109) Van Reybrouck puts the 1882-born Nkasi to the test to figure out whether he is indeed "one of the oldest people ever. In the Congo, no less" (2014: 7), where the average life expectancy barely scratches 50 and whether he is telling the truth by means of "check and double check" (ibid). With this in mind, Van Reybrouck's account becomes a relevant example of how Congo writing has been rendered superficially postmodern, but remains modernist at heart (cf. also the previous chapter). Van Reybrouck indicates that the structural questions raised by postmodernist thinkers remain unaddressed and unresolved, including those relating to binary thinking, rationality, the "grand narratives" of progressive development, and the fraught relation between reality and language. Van Reybrouck's particular use of interviews, eyewitness accounts, and his own observations deeply depends, so it seems, on a "logocentric" belief (as Derrida would have it; cf. Butler 2002: 15-23) in terms of the correspondence of "voice" and reality.

Van Reybrouck's history tends to be as inconsistent and paradoxical as many offered by Black American intellectuals. His deep investment in the "will to truth" and the "will to knowledge", to paraphrase Foucault in his History of Sexuality (1998: 12-13), leads to a writing attitude of hubris, and to the authorial self-confidence in knowing for sure (despite the impossibility of this claim). In the same vein as Herskovits in the Second Chapter, Van Reybrouck recognizes the inherent limitations of knowledge production as a whole as pertains to the Congo, but produces alleged truths nevertheless. Other authors on the Amazon list do so, too. Stearns's Dancing in the Glory of Monsters provides a case study of certainty in the midst of deep-rooted doubts. The number of times that Stearns relativizes his own knowledge is telling.[2] Despite this theoretical recognition of the complexity of producing truthful Congo texts, Stearns insist on knowing in the end. And that is the whole point of Congoism: Claiming to know despite the impossibility of knowing. Stearns "knows", for instance, that the horror stories he recorded in the Congo – including well-known topoi of cannibalism, rape, senseless murder, and other savagery (Stearns 2011: 6, 28, 263) – all happened as they were told to him: "All of these stories are true" (ibid: 328). This paradoxical espousal of massive doubt, on the one hand, and absolute certainty about one's own ability to speak truthfully about the Congo, on the other, is quite typical of contemporary Congoism.

The works on the Amazon.com list attest to Congoism's continued existence and "common sense" status. To step outside it proves more challenging than staying within it. Congoism is not an inevitable fate, however. It is possible both to recognize and to address it through historical awareness, skeptical reading and writing strategies, and the careful scrutiny of subtle and overt Othering processes through racial, classed, and gendered perspectives. The works on the Amazon.com list prove that change is possible. If postmodernism taught most of the authors appearing on it anything, it is to believe in the power of language. Stearns has gone the furthest in addressing the historicity, depth, ideology, and scope of Congo rhetoric. In his role as a critic, Stearns stresses the complexity of the Congo, which "eludes simple definition, with many interlocking narrative strands" (ibid: 5). With this in

2 A selection of examples: "It is difficult to separate Mariam's myth from reality" (Stearns 2011: 99); "It is difficult to tell how well war stories separate fact from fiction" (ibid: 124); "As always in the Congo, the myth reveals a bit of the man, but not much" (ibid: 219); "Of course, this is not what really happened. The truth is buried under hundreds of competing rumors and may never be entirely uncovered" (ibid: 308); "Sometimes it seems that by crossing the border into the Congo one abandons any sort of Archimedean perspective on truth and becomes caught up in a web of rumors and allegations, as if the country itself were the stuff of some postmodern fiction" (ibid: 282).

mind, he criticizes, among other actors, corporate media for ignoring and simplifying the Congo (ibid: 5-6, 327).[3]

Like Lynn Nottage (cf. last chapter), Stearns gives an example of how language works through particular words, for instance through the concept of "chaos" (a concept constantly invoked in other works as well; cf. the last chapter). "The words 'chaos', 'mess', and 'confusion' recurred in my discussions with the general," Stearns writes, "they contrasted with his refrain that all he tried to do during this time was obey orders and uphold discipline. They were two conflicting ways of absolving himself from responsibility, but also means of coping morally and psychologically with the killing around him" (ibid: 19-20). Passages such as these, along with the epitaph by Mbembe in the concluding chapter, suggest that Stearns is more than aware of the importance of how one captures the Congo through language, as well as the role language plays in constituting realities and how pervaded it is by personal and ideological interests.

To have read Mbembe, as Stearns seems to have done, is not enough, however. First of all, because Mbembe himself is speaks about Africa in general, and not the Congo specifically (a problem of homogenization within postcolonial theory, as was suggested in my Introduction). Secondly, because Stearns constantly reproduces the very problem that Mbembe criticizes – the metaphorical use of Africa as "generally of lesser value, little importance and poor quality" (qtd. in Stearns 327). The author's attempt to depict the Congo in terms of a "joint humanity" (to paraphrase Mbembe) and not as "the abject mess" that "western media" has made it to be (ibid: 327) crumbles within the first few pages of Stearns's account. Various strategies of irony and ridicule creep into the author's depiction of the Congo.

Stearns focuses constantly on plastic flip-flops, for instance. Numerous people of rank are described as wearing them – from ministers and community leaders to President Kabila (ibid: 59, 132, 187). Stearns's Boasian proclamation (cf. previous chapter) of understanding the Congo "on its own terms" (ibid: 328) collapses in his own perpetual flip-flopping in his relation to the Congo. Flip-flops matter. To explicitly discuss Congo's leaders as wearing sandals also ridicules their politics. The concentration on flip-flops frames them, moreover, as unsteady, cheap, and untrustworthy. The literal meaning of flip-flops (in the sense of president Kabila wearing an open sandal that is) is overshadowed by its metaphoric meaning (flip-flopping as in suddenly changing to an opposite opinion). Flip-flops reinforce the idea of Kabila's awkwardness and unsuitability as President, as he is depicted as having been "superstitious" and as having had some "funny ideas" anyway. "Don't

3 This media critique is, as was discussed in the previous chapter, increasingly becoming the standard in Congo storytelling.

wear flip-flops at roadblocks", as one of Kabil''s former child soldiers mentions in his interview with Stearns (ibid: 151). Stearns's suggestion that even the Congolese air is filled "with the rumble of thousands of flip-flops and bare feet on the hot tarmac" (ibid: 14) turns Kabila's flip-flopping into a broader Congolese phenomenon. The overall effect is that this so-called literal truth is shown, on closer inspection, to be metaphorical.

How to avoid Congoism? Reflecting earnestly on one's language use is a way of confronting one's own beliefs, motivations, and limitations. An analogy, an explanation, or a metaphor that sounds inappropriate in the depiction of Euro-American regions is likely inadequate for the Congo as well. Reflecting on language ideally leads to transcending the metaphysics of presence, or the unshakable confidence held by many authors in language as a reliable mirror of present Congolese reality. One way in which this belief manifests itself is the infatuation of many Congo writers with capturing truth and reality by visiting the place. This is and remains deeply flawed against the background of the importance of textuality for almost all books about the Congo available on Amazon.com.

Many contemporary eyewitness reports, most prominently Van Reybrouck's work, highlight a serious engagement with Euro-American texts on the Congo before and after their interviews with Congolese. Like 19th-century Black Congo missionaries such as William Sheppard, traveling to the Congo must thus be considered a deeply intertextual occupation. This has resulted in the ongoing reproduction of historically contingent Congo discourse – interests, rhetoric, and infatuations will be shared and updated, and sometimes even rejected. At the same time, intertextuality reduces the Congolese to providers of soundbites and interesting couleur locale in accounts that could have been written without them. It is true that the subaltern speaks in these books. But who is there to listen and understand, really, as was also addressed in the previous chapter?

The production of Congo knowledge has reached a degree of epistemic complexity that resists the typical writing process of reading-critiquing-experiencing-writing. This process places the Congo interpreter front and center – not the vicious, historically entrenched, and politically entangled Congo discourse. This kind of hermeneutic understanding, according to Shklar, "makes sense only if there is a known and closed whole, which can be understood in terms of its own parts" (2004: 657–658). The works on the Amazon.com list suggest that neither the whole nor the parts have been understood by these many bestselling or academic authors, however, thus rendering this hermeneutic process obsolete. Interviewing Congolese will not enable a break-through, either. Due to the widespread acceptance and dissemination of Congoism by many Congolese, talking to them is far from a matter of mining sources that enable a way out of Congoism.

Instances of how Congolese reproduce past discourse on themselves are provided by the work of Thomas Turner. In Turner's experience, many Congolese tend to describe their "diversity in terms of a taxonomy that derives from 19th-century European raciology" (2013: 75). This is also relevant in the postcolonial era, in which the Congolese inherited a state with a colonial economy of forced or poorly paid labor and white supremacist schooling (ibid: 9)." Congolese leaders (of which Mobutu and Joseph Kabila are the most prominent examples) have been willing to pander to the ethnic prejudices and preferences of Euro-American elites in order to secure their power (ibid: 40). Many authors take the ethnic discourse of many Congolese at face value, however, while ignoring other, more valid or fruitful categories of analysis. The fragmentation of the Congolese social landscape into the urban super-rich and rural super-poor can hardly be overlooked, but remains insufficiently discussed (Trefon 2011: 109).

The epistemic complexities of Congolese knowledge production and subjectivity remain deeply unacknowledged by many contemporary authors. "Extreme secrecy, discreet but constant surveillance [...] the manipulation of rumor" (ibid: 18) are contrivances that often seem to escape the attention of Euro-American authors in their communication with, and representation of, Congolese. After decades of propaganda and the ongoing destruction of archives and other forms of information (ibid: 97), Congolese "have low expectations on being informed of trivial matters and even lower expectations regarding important national issues", according to Trefon (ibid: 112). He continues: "Even fairly well-documented events are relegated to the realm of suspicion and disbelief, such as the circumstances surrounding the murder of Patrice Lumumba" (ibid). Congolese communication often boils down to "cultivating confusion and misunderstanding, reformulating official explanations with updated ones and sending conflicting messages are clearly identifiable trends" (ibid).

None of these communicative aspects are addressed by the authors mentioned above. On the contrary – even many of the well-known problems of fieldwork are neglected in the final version of their books. Fieldwork is hardly ever portrayed as "a period of deep frustration, disappointment and confusion, sometimes even of bitter tears," as Blommaert and Dong assert, adding that "people contradict each other, and just when you think you found the key to the whole thing, the whole thing changes again" (2011: 25). This is particularly true of fieldwork in the Congo, which mostly takes place in "doubly" traumatic postwar contexts. Congolese were already traumatized by structural violence before the full-blown wars compounded it and tore communities apart through fear, resentment, jealousy, and rage (Turner 2013: 137-138).

Without a more modest understanding of the possibility of "knowing" the Congo, there can be no way out of Congoism. The will to truth and the push for knowledge has to be suspended, rejected, or replaced by more modest expectations of the ability to understand the Congo. To represent the Congo can also mean not writing at all. There is hardly a way around this suggestion, given the complexities of discussing the Congo. And if one must write, the attempt should indeed not be, as Fabian has it, to avoid doing damage to Central West Africa" (2000a: 260). Instead, one should try to "do damage" to the manner in which the Congo is discussed – "to shake, subvert, and alter at least those ideological certainties" that have contributed to the overt and silent sanctioning of imperialism in its many forms (ibid).

References

Primary Works

Alexander, William T. (1888): History of the Colored Race in America, Kansas City: Palmetto.

Anthropological Review (1864): Review of Savage Africa: Being the Narrative of a Tour in Equatorial, South-Western, and North-Western Africa; With Notes on the Habits of the Gorilla; On the Existence of Unicorns and Tailed Men; On the Slave Trade; On the Origin, Character, and Capabilities of the Negro, and on the Future Civilisation of Western Africa by W. Winwood Reade, Vol. 2.5 (May), pp. 123-126.

Asante, Molefe Kete/Mazama, Ama (2005): "Preface." In: Molefe Kete Asante/Ama Mazama (ed.), Encyclopedia of Black Studies. London: Sage, pp. xix-xxii.

Asante, Molefe Kete (2007): The History of Africa: the Quest for Eternal Harmony, New York: Routledge.

Asante, Molefe Kete (2012). The African American People: a Global History, New York: Routledge, 2012.

Atkinson, Edward (1976). "Anti-Imperialist League: Declaration of Principle and Preliminary Organization." In: Gerald E. Markowitz (ed.) American Anti-Imperialism 1895-1901, New York: Garland, pp. 23-24.

Baldwin, James (1961): "A Negro Assays the Negro Mood." In: The New York Times' Magazine March 12, pp. 25, 103-104.

Baraka, Amiri (1975): "The National Black Assembly and the Black Liberation Movement." In: Black World (March), pp. 22-27.

Baraka, Amiri (1985): "The Wailer." In: Callaloo 23 (Winter), pp. 248-256.

Bennett, Ronan (1997): The Catastrophist: a Novel, New York: Simon & Schuster.

Blyden, E.W./Lewis, D.D. Taylor/Dwight, Theodore (1871): The People of Africa: A Series of Papers on Their Character, Condition, and Future Prospects, New York: Anson D.F. Randolph & Co.

Boas, Franz (1921 [1911]): The Mind of Primitive Man, New York: The MacMillan Company.

Boone, Clinton C. (1927): Congo as I Saw It, New York: J.J. Little & Ives.

Brawley, Benjamin (1918): Africa and the War, New York: Buffield & Company.

Brown, William Wells (1863): The Black Man: His Antecedents, His Genius, and His Achievements, Boston: James Redpath.

Brown, William Wells (1867): The Negro in the American Rebellion, His Heroism and His Fidelity. Boston: Lee & Shepard.

Brown, William Wells (1880): My Southern Home: Or, The South and its People, Boston: A.G. Brown & Co.

Brown, William Wells (1882). The Rising Son; or, the Antecedents and Advancement of the Colored Race, Boston: A.G. Brown & Co.

Bruce, William Cabell (1891): The Negro Problem, Baltimore: J. Murphy & Co.

Butcher, Tim (2008): Blood River: A Journey to Africa's Broken Heart, London: Vintage.

Campbell, Ellen (1841): "A Tale of Domestic Life." In: Godey's Lady's Book. April 1841, n.p.

Carmichael, Stokeley/Hamilton, Charles (1967). Black Power: The Politics of Liberation in America, New York: Random House.

Carroll, Chas (1900): The Negro: A Beast, St. Louis: American Book and Bible House.

CBS News (2008): "War Against Women: The Use Of Rape As A Weapon In Congo's Civil War." January 13 (http://www.cbsnews.com/news/war-against-women/).

Clarke, John Henrik (n.d). "The Life and Death of Patrice Lumumba." In: Schomburg Center for Black Research, New York.

Clarke, John Henrik (1961): "The New Afro-American Nationalism." In: Freedomways 1961 (Fall), pp. 285-295.

Clarke, John Henrik (1962a): "The Old Congo." In: Phylon 23.1. (Spring), pp. 61-65.

Clarke, John Henrik (1962b):"The Passing of Patrice Lumumba." In: Journal of Human Relations 1962 (Summer), pp. 383-393.

Clarke, John Henrik (1974): "The Afro-American Image of Africa." In: Black World (February), pp. 19-21.

Cleaver, Elrdige (1971): Revolution in the Congo, London: Stage 1.

Cleaver, Elridge (1991 [1968]): Soul on Ice, New York: Random House.

Cockey, Thomas (1778): "Two Hundred Dollars Reward." In: The Pennsylvania Packet October 29, n.p.

Congress of the United States of America (1884): "Occupation of the Congo Country of Africa." 48th Congress, Senate Report No. 393, 1st Session. March 26. n.pag.

Conrad, Joseph (2006 [1902]): Heart of Darkness, in: Paul B. Armstrong (ed.), Heart of Darkness: A Norton Critical Edition, New York: Norton.

Cooper, Anna Julia (1892): A Voice From the South by a Black Woman of the South, Xenia: Aldine.

Crighton, Michael (1993 [1980]): Congo, London: Arrow.

Crogman, W.H/Kletzing, A.M (1920 [1898]): Progress of a Race, or the Remarkable Advancement of the Afro-American Negro, Atlanta: J.L. Nichols.

Crummell, Alexander (1969 [1862]): The Future of Africa: Addresses, Sermons, etc., etc, New York: Negro Universities Press.

Davis, Frank Marshall (2002 [1935]): "Chicago's Congo: Sonata for an Orchestra." In: John Edgar Tidwell (ed.), Black Moods: Collected Poems, Chicago: University of Illinois, pp. 5-7.

Davis, Natalie Zemon (1983): The Return of Martin Guerre, Cambridge: Harvard University.

De Buffon, Georges-Louis Leclerc/ Goldsmith, M. et al. (1810): A History of the Earth and Animated Nature: From M. De Buffon, Goldsmith and Others. Ed. W. Davison. Vol. 1. Appollo Press.

De Gobineau, Arthur (1915 [1853]): The Inequality of Human Races, transl. Adrian Collins, London: William Heineman.

Deibert, Michael (2013). The Democratic Republic of Congo: Between Hope and Despair, New York: Zed.

Delany, Martin R. (2004 [1852]). The Condition, Elevation, Emigration, and Destiny of the Colored People of the United States and Official Report of the Niger Valley Exploring Party, New York: Humanity Books.

Dongola, Emmanuel (2006): Johnny Mad Dog, New York: Picador.

Douglass' Monthly (1859a): "American Civilization Illustrated: A Great Slave Auction. "April, n.p.

Douglass' Monthly (1859b). "Miscellaneous News Items." August, n.p.

Douglass' Monthly (1859c): "Slave Breeding vs. the Slave Trade." August, n.p.

Douglass' Monthly (1861a): "Secret History of the African Slave Trade." March, n.p.

Douglass' Monthly (1861b): "Conviction of a Slave Trader." December, n.p.

Douglass' Monthly (1861c). "Dealings with Slavery and the Contrabands: Facts, Scenes and Incidents." December, n.p.

Douglass' Monthly (1863): "Native Africans Enlisting." April, n.p.

Doyle, Arthur Conan (2015 [1900]): The Crime of the Congo, London: Leopold Classic Library.

Du Bois, W.E.B. (1899): The Philadelphia Negro, Boston: Ginn & Co.

Du Bois, W.E.B. (1915): "The African Roots of War." In: The Atlantic Monthly 115.5 (May), pp. 707-714.

Du Bois, W.E.B. (1920): Darkwater: Voices from Within the Veil, New York: Harcourt, Brace, and Howe.

Du Bois, W.E.B (1944): "Prospect of a World Without Race Conflict." In: American Journal of Sociology 49.5 (March), pp. 450-456.

Du Bois, W.E.B (1961): "A Logical Program for a Free Congo." In: National Guardian May 15, p. 6.

Du Bois, W.E.B. (1972 [1946]): The World and Africa: An Inquiry into the Part Which Africa Has Played in the World. An Enlarged Edition, with new Writings on Africa by W.E. Du Bois, 1955-1961, New York: International Publishers.

Du Bois, W.E.B. (1992 [1925]): "The Negro Mind Reaches Out." In: Alain Locke (ed.), The New Negro: Voices of the Harlem Renaissance., New York: Touchstone, pp. 385-414.

Du Bois, W.E.B. (2001 [1915]): The Negro, Philadelphia: University of Pennsylvania Press.

Du Chaillu, Paul B (1861): Explorations & Adventures in Equatorial Africa; With Accounts of the Manners and Customs of the People, and of the Chase of the Gorilla, Crocodile, Leopard, Elephant, Hippotamus, and Other Animals, London: John Murray.

Duke, Lynne (2003): Mandela, Mobutu, and Me: A Newswoman's African Journey, New York: Doubleday.

Easton, Hosea (1837): A Treatise on the Intellectual Character, and Civil and Political Condition of the Colored People of the U. States: And the Prejudice Exercised Towards Them: With a Sermon on the Duty of the Church to Them, Boston: Isaac Knapp.

Ellis, Eddie (1965): "The Legacy of Malxolm X." In: The Chicago Defender March 11, p. 4.

Farmer, James (1965): Freedom – When? New York: Random House.

Fauset, Jessie Redmon (1928). Plum Bun, New York: Frederick A. Stokes.

Feldman, Eugene P. Romayn (1965). "The Truth About the Congo." In: Negro Digest (May), pp.83-86.

Ferris, William (1913a): The African Abroad or His Evolution in Western Civilization. Vol. I, New Haven: Tuttle, Morehouse & Taylor.

Ferris, William (1913b): The African Abroad or His Evolution in Western Civilization. Vol. II, New Haven: Tuttle, Morehouse & Taylor.

Fleming, L.C. (1886): "Letter from the Congo." In: The Christian Recorder July 8, n.p.

Fleming, L.C. (1887a): "The Missionary's Adieu." In: The Christian Recorder March 17, n.p.

Fleming, L.C. (1887b): "A Letter from the Congo Valley." In: The Christian Recorder December 8, n.p.

Franklin, John Hope (1952 [1947]): From Slavery to Freedom: a History of American Negroes, New York: Alfred Knopf.

Frazier, Franklin E. (1962 [1957]): Black Bourgeoisie: The Rise of a New Middle Class in the United States, New York: Macmillan.

Frazier, Franklin E. (2007 [1929]): "La Bourgeoisie Noire." In: Henry Louis Gates Jr./Gene Andrew Jarrett (eds.), The New Negro: Readings on Race, Representation, and African American Culture, 1892-1938. Princeton: Princeton University, pp. 137-141.

Frederick Douglass' Paper (1851a). "The Slave Trade." September 4, n.p.

Frederick Douglass' Paper (1851b): "Soft Iron." November 27, n.p.

Frederick Douglass' Paper (1852a): "Meeting of the Colored People of New York." February 5, n.p.

Frederick Douglass' Paper (1852b): "Mrs. Stanton's Address." May 13, n.p.

Frederick Douglass' Paper (1852c): "Negro Shot." September 3, n.p.

Frederick Douglass' Paper (1853a): "The Editor." February 18, n.p.

Frederick Douglass' Paper (1853b): "Slavery: Colored National Convention." November 25, n.p.

Frederick Douglass' Paper (1855a): "Our Correspondents." January 12, n.p.

Frederick Douglass' Paper (1855b): "Profits from Bees." July 6, n.p.

Freedom's Journal (1827a): "Marriage Customs, & C. of Various Nations." October 5, n.p.

Freedom's Journal (1827b): "Letter from Bishop Allen." November 2, n.p.

French, Howard (2005): A Continent for the Taking: The Tragedy and Hope of Africa, New York: Vintage.

Friedenberg, Daniel M. (1960): "An Economic View of Negro African Independence." In: Dissent VII.2 (Spring), pp. 188-200.

Fulton, Alexander (1937): "Fulton's Facts." In: The Chicago Defender February 6, p. 21.

Garnet, Henry Highland (1848): The past and the Present Condition, and the Destiny, of the Colored Race, Troy: Steam Press.

Garnet, Henry Highland (2003 [1843]). "An Address to the Slaves of the United States of America." In: Bill Lyne/Vernon D. Johnson (eds.), Walking the Talk: an Anthology of African-American Studies, Up per Saddle River: Pearson, pp. 115-120.

Garvey, Marcus (2006 [1914]): "Booker T. Washington's Program." In: The Philosophy and Opinions of Marcus Garvey, New York: Routledge, p. 41.

Godard, John George (1905): Racial Supremacy: Being Studies in Imperialism, Edinburgh: Geo A. Morton.

Goodrich, Chauncey A./Porter, Noah (1886a): "Country." In: Webster's Complete Dictionary of the English Language. With Various Literary Appendices and Numerous AdditionalIllustrations, London: George Bell & Sons, p. 303.

Goodrich, Chauncey A./Porter, Noah (1886b): "Land." In: Webster's Complete Dictionary of the English Language. With Various Literary Appendices and Numerous Additional Illustrations, London: George Bell & Sons, p. 749.

Goodrich, Chauncey A./Porter, Noah (1886c): "Nation." In: Webster's Complete Dictionary of the English Language. With Various Literary Appendices and Numerous Additional Illustrations, London: George Bell & Sons, p. 875.

Goodrich, Chauncey A./Porter, Noah (1886d): "Tribe." In: Webster's Complete Dictionary of the English Language. With Various Literary Appendices and Numerous Additional Illustrations. London: George Bell & Sons, p. 1411.

Graham, Lorenz B. (1925): "Natives of Africa not Uncivilized." In: The Chicago Defender March 7, p. A1.

Hama, Ben E./Kattiaa/mojo12 et. Al (n.d.): "Congo." In: urbandictionary.com, n.d, (http://www.urbandictionary.com/define.php?term=Congo).

Hall, Chatwood (1937): "Watchdog of Italian Imperialism." In: The Chicago Defender May 29, p. 24.

Hallowell, Norwood P (1897): The Negro as a Soldier in the War of the Rebellion. Bonston: Little, Brown, and Company.

Hamilton, Joseph (1810). "Chronological Table of Remarkable Events, Discoveries, and Inventions." In: Johnson's Dictionary of the English Language, in Miniature. To Which are Added, and Alphabetical Account of the Heathen Deities, and a Copious Chronological Table of Remarkable Events, Discoveries, and Inventions; Boston: West & Blake; pp. 263-276.

Hamilton, William (1998 [1815]): "O' Africa." In: Philip S. Foner/Robert James Branham (eds.), Lift Every Voice: African American Oratory: 1787-1900, Tuscaloosa: Alabama University, pp. 91-97.

HAMOWI (1928): "Lights and Shadows: Mirth." In: The Chicago Defender April 21, p. A2.

Harper, Frances E.W. (1890): "A Fairer Hope, A brighter Morn." In: Light beyond the darkness, Chicago: Donohue and Henneberry, p. 3.

Harper, Lucius C. (1938): "Dustin' off the News." In: The Chicago Defender September 10, p. 6.

Harris, Eddy L. (1994): Native Stranger: A Black American's Journey into the Heart of Africa, New York: Penguin.

Hayes, Bob (1939): "Here and There." In: The Chicago Defender July 8, p. 9.

Herskovits, Melville J. (1941): The Myth of the Negro Past, New York: Harper and Brothers.

Hervé, Julia (1973): "A Short Story." In: Black World (May), pp. 56-64.

Hilton-Simpson, Melville William (1911): Land and Peoples of the Kasai; Being a Narrative of a Two Years' Journey among the Cannibals of the Equatorial Forest and Other Savage Tribes of the South-Western Congo, London: Constable.

Hopkins, Pauline E. (1988): Of One Blood: Or, the Hidden Self. 1902-03. In: Hazel V. Carby (ed.), The Magazine Novels of Pauline Hopkins, New York: Oxford University, pp. 439-621.

Houston, Drusilla Dunjee (2007 [1926]). Wonderful Ethiopians of the Ancient Cushite Empire, New York: Forgotten Books.

Howard, Charles P. Sr. (1962): "How the Press Defames Africa." In: Freedomways (Fall), pp. 361-370.

Hughes, Langston (1973 [1921]): "The Negro Speaks of Rivers." In: Arnold Adoff (ed.), The Poetry of Black America: Anthology of the twentieth Century, New York: Harpers, p. 72.

Hughes, Langston (1988 [1940]): The Big Sea, New York: Thunder's Mouth.

Hughes, Langston (2000 [1961]): "Lumumba's Grave." In: Arnold Rampersad (ed.), The Collected Poems of Langston Hughes, New York: Alfred A. Knopf, 2000, p. 533.

Hughes, Langston (2003 [1960]). The First Book of Africa. In: Arnold Rampersad et al. (eds.), The Collected Works of Langston Hughes. Works for Children and Young Adults: Poetry, Fiction, and other Writing, Vol. 11, Columbia: University of Misouri, pp. 360-393.

Hutchinson, Margarite (1881). "Introduction." In: Margarite Hutchinson (ed./transl.), A Report of the Kingdom of Congo and of the Surrounding Countries; Drawn out of the Writings and Discourses of the Portugese Duarte Lopez by Filippo Pigafetta, in Rome 1591, London: John Murray, pp. xi-xxi.

Jefferson, N.H. (1914): "Latest New York News." In: The Chicago Defender December 5, p. 7.

Johnson, Harvey (1891): "The Question of Race: A Reply to W. Cabell Bruce", Baltimore : Printing Office of J.F. Weishampel.

Johnson, James Weldon (1927): Native African Races and Culture, s.l/s.n.

Johnson, James Weldon (1969 [1933]): Along this Way: the Autobiography, New York: Viking.

Johnson, John H./ Bennett, Lerone Jr. (1989): Succeeding Against the Odds, New York: Warner.

Jones, John Henry (1968): "On the Influence of Fanon." In: Freedomways (Third Quarter), pp. 209-213.

Kant, Emmanuel (2000 [1804]): "Physical Geography." In: Emmanuel Chukwudi Eze (ed.), Race and the Enlightenment: a Reader, Malden: Blackwell, pp. 58-64.

Kelley, D.G./ Lewis, Earl (2005a): To Make Our World Anew: A History of African Americans to 1880, Vol 1., New York: Oxford University.

Kelley, D.G./ Lewis, Earl (2005b): To Make Our World Anew: A History of African Americans to 1880, Vol 2., New York: Oxford University.

Kennedy, Adrienne (1969): Funnyhouse of a Negro. A Play in One Act, New York: Samuel French.

King, Judson (1922): "U.S. Marines Revive Slavery in Haiti." In: The Chicago Defender June 10, pp. A3-A4.

King, Martin Luther Jr. (1968): Where do We Go from Here: Chaos or Community? Boston: Beacon.

King, Martin Luther Jr. (1991a): "Black Power Defined." In: James M. Washington (ed.), A Testament of Hope: The Essential Writings and Speeches of Martin Luther King Jr., New York: Harper One, pp. 303-312.

King, Martin Luther King Jr. (1991b): "I Have a Dream." In: James M. Washington (ed.), A Testament of Hope: The Essential Writings and Speeches of Martin Luther King Jr., New York: Harper One, pp. 217-220.

Kingsolver, Barbara (1999). The Poisonwood Bible. London: Faber and Faber.

Kisner, Ronald E. (1974): "Foreman and Ali Stage Africa's Biggest Fight." In: Jet 26 September, pp. 50-53.

Levette, Harry (1934): "Clarence Muse Leads Cast of 2,000 in Song Festival." In: The Chicago Defender August 18, p. 9.

Lewis, R.B. (1844): Light and Truth; Collected from the Bible and Ancient and Modern History, Containing the Universal History of the Colored and the Indian Race, from the Creation of the World to the Present Time, Boston: A Committee of Colored Gentlemen.

Lieber, Francis (1830): "Congo." In: Francis Lieber (ed.), Encyclopaedia Americana. A Popular Dictionary of Arts, Sciences, Literature, History, Politics and Biography, Brought Down to the Present Time; Including a Copious Collection of Original Articles in American Biography; on the Basis of the Seventh Edition of the German Conversations-Lexicon, Vol. III, Philadelphia: Carey and Lea, pp. 425-426.

Lieber, Francis (1835): "Tea." In: Francis Lieber (ed.), Encyclopaedia Americana. A Popular Dictionary of Arts, Sciences, Literature, History, Politics and Biography, Brought Down to the Present Time; Including a Copious Collection of Original Articles in American Biography; on the Basis of the Seventh Edition of the German Conversations-Lexicon, Vol. VII., Philadelphia: Desilver, Thomas, & Co., pp.160-162.

Life Magazine (1960): "IndepenDANCE Dance in Congo." 11 July, p. 21.

Livingstone, David (1875): A Popular Account of Dr. Livingstone's Expedition to the Zambesi and Its Tributaries; and of the Discovery of Lakes Shirwa and Nyassa, 1858-1864: Abridged from the Larger Work, London: John Murray.

Locke, Alain (1927). "Art Lessons from the Congo." In: The Survey February 1, pp. 587-589.

Locke, Alain (1992 [1925]): "The New Negro." In: Alain Locke (ed.), The New Negro: Voices of the Harlem Renaissance, New York: Touchstone, pp. 3-18.

Lord, Eliot/Trenor, John J.D./Barrows, Samuel J. (1905): The Italian in America, New York: B.F. Buck & Company.

Los Hombres Calientes (2001): New Congo Square, Basin Street, compact disc.

Lovestone, Jay (1905): American Imperialism: The Menace of the Greatest Capitalist World Power, Chicago: American Workers Party.

Lowenfels, Walter (1962): "Patrice Lumumba Speaks." In: Freedomways (Winter), p. 32.

Lowie, Robert H. (1938): "Subsistence." In: Franz Boas (ed.), General Anthropology, Boston: D.C. Heath and Company, pp. 282-326.

Lyons, Daniel (1899a). "Barbarian." In: Daniel Lyons (ed.), The American Dictionary of the English Language: Based on the Latest Conclusions of the Most Eminent Philologists, New York: Peter Penelon Collier, p. 29.

Lyons, Daniel (1899b): "Coenogamy." In: Daniel Lyons (ed.), The American Dictionary of the English Language: Based on the Latest Conclusions of the Most Eminent Philologists, New York: Peter Penelon Collier, p. 67.

Lyons, Daniel (1899c): "Cruel." In: Daniel Lyons (ed.), The American Dictionary of the English Language: Based on the Latest Conclusions of the Most Eminent Philologists, New York: Peter Penelon Collier, p. 87.

Lyons, Daniel (1899d): "Extermination." In: Daniel Lyons (ed.), The American Dictionary of the English Language: Based on the Latest Conclusions of the Most Eminent Philologists, New York: Peter Penelon Collier, p. 135.

Lyons, Daniel (1899e): "Frank." In: Daniel Lyons (ed.), The American Dictionary of the English Language: Based on the Latest Conclusions of the Most Eminent Philologists, New York: Peter Penelon Collier, p. 181.

Lyons, Daniel (1899f): "Gorilla." In: Daniel Lyons (ed.), The American Dictionary of the English Language: Based on the Latest Conclusions of the Most Eminent Philologists, New York: Peter Penelon Collier, p. 201.

Lyons, Daniel (1899g): "Horde." In: Daniel Lyons (ed.), The American Dictionary of the English Language: Based on the Latest Conclusions of the Most Eminent Philologists, New York: Peter Penelon Collier, p. 224.

Lyons, Daniel (1899h): "Introduction." In: Daniel Lyons (ed.), The American Dictionary of the English Language: Based on the Latest Conclusions of the Most Eminent Philologists, New York: Peter Penelon Collier, pp. v-vii.

Lyons, Daniel (1899i): "King." In: Daniel Lyons (ed.), The American Dictionary of the English Language: Based on the Latest Conclusions of the Most Eminent Philologists, New York: Peter Penelon Collier, p. 257.

Lyons, Daniel (1899j): "Native." In: Daniel Lyons (ed.), The American Dictionary of the English Language: Based on the Latest Conclusions of the Most Eminent Philologists, New York: Peter Penelon Collier, p. 280.

Lyons, Daniel (1899k): "Savage." In: Daniel Lyons (ed.), The American Dictionary of the English Language: Based on the Latest Conclusions of the Most Eminent Philologists, New York: Peter Penelon Collier, p. 377.

Lyons, Daniel (1899l): "Tribe." In: Daniel Lyons (ed.), The American Dictionary of the English Language: Based on the Latest Conclusions of the Most Eminent Philologists New York: Peter Penelon Collier, p. 455.

Makelele, Albert (2008): This is a Good Country: Welcome to the Congo, Bloomington: Authorhouse.

Marrant, John (1998 [1789]): "You Stand on the Level of the Greatest Kings on Earth." In: Philip S. Foner/Robert James Branham (eds.), Lift Every Voice: African American Oratory: 1787-1900, Tuscaloosa: Alabama University, pp. 27-37.

Marsalis, Winston/Jacub, Addy (2007): Congo Square, Jazz at Lincoln Center, compact disc.

Mather, Frank Lincoln (1915): "Pendleton, Leila Amos." In: Frank Lincoln Mather (ed.), Who's Who of the Colored Race: A General Biographical Dictionary of Men and Women of African Descent, Vol. One, Chicago s.n., p. 214.

McKay, Claude (1965 [1928]): Home to Harlem, New York: Pocket Books.

McWorter, Gerald (1970-1971): "Common Problems, Common Solutions: Toward a Pan African Ideology." In: Journal of Black Poetry, pp. 23-37.

Mead, Margaret (1928): Coming of Age in Samoa: A Psychological Study of Primitive Youth for Western Civilization, New York: William Morrow & Company.

Miller, John (1887): Theology, Princeton: Evangelical Reform.

Miller, Kelly (1900): "The Effect of Imperialism Upon the Negro Race. Ably Set Out by a Colored Man." In: Anti-imperialist Broadside 11, Boston, 1900. n.p.

Moore, John Basset (1912): Four Phases of American Development: Federalism – Democracy – Imperialism – Expansion, Baltimore: John Hopkins.

Morel, Edmund Dene (1904): King Leopold's rule in Africa. London: W. Heinemann.

Morel, Edmund Dene (1919): Red Rubber: The Story of the Rubber Slave Trade Which Flourished on the Congo for Twenty Years, 1890-1910, Manchester: National Labour.

Morrison, Toni (1987). Beloved, London: Chatto.

Morrison, Toni (1994): "Interview with Angelo Benno in Time Magazine." In: Danille Taylor-Guthrie (ed.), Conversations with Toni Morrison, Jackson: University of Mississippi, pp. 255-261.

Morsell, John A. "The Meaning of Black Nationalism." The Crisis February, 1962.

Muse, Clarence (1940): "What's Going On in Hollywood." In: The Chicago Defender May 4, p. 21.

Mutombo, Nkulu N'Sengha (2005): "African Philosophy." In: Molefe Kete Asante/Ama Mazama (eds.), Encyclopedia of Black Studies, London: Sage, pp. 45-53.

Neal, Larry (1974): "Funky Butt, Funky Butt, Take it Away." In: Hoodoo Hollerin' Bebop Ghosts, Washington: Howard University, pp. 2-18.

Newton, Huey P (1972): To Die for the People, New York: Random House.

Ngwala, Alain/ Ngwala, Mayi: Congo: Spirit of Darkness, Langham: Genet.

Nietzsche, Friedrich (1968 [1901-1910]): The Will to Power: A New Translation, Walter Kaufmann/R.J. Hollingdale (transl.), New York: Random House.

Nottage, Lynn (2009): Ruined, New York: Theatre Communications Group.

Oglesby, Jack (1938): "Just Don't Develop Without Able Arrangers." In: The Chicago Defender March 5, p.19.

O'Neal, James (1922): Labor and the Next War: A Study of American Imperialism and its Effects on the Workers, Chicago: Socialist Party of the United States.

Padmore, George (1943): "Africa Gives World 90% of All its Radium." In: The Chicago Defender August 28, p. 4.

Padmore, George (1944): "American, African Negroes Get Along Fine in Front Line Foxholes In Italy." In: The Chicago Defender August 19, p. 3.

Padmore George (1945). "Africa Holds Key to Atomic Future; World's Uranium Supply." In: The Chicago Defender September 8, p. 5.

Patterson, Raymond R (2001 [1989]): "Lumumba Blues." In: Tony Medina/Louis Reyes Rivera (eds.), bum rush the page: a def poetry jam, New York: Three Rivers Press, pp. 239-240.

Paul, Nathaniel (1827): "Address, Delivered on the Celebration of the Abolition or Slavery, in the State of New York, July 5, 1827", Albany: Johny B. Van Steenbergh, n.p.

Pendleton, Leila Amos (1912): A Narrative of the Negro, Washington: Press of R.L. Pendleton.

Pennington, James W.C (1841): A Text Book of the Origin and History, &c. &c. of the Colored People, Hartford: L. Skinner.

Perry, Rufus L (1887): The Cushite; or, the Children of Ham (the Negro Race), as Seen by the Ancient Historians and Poets, New York: Literary Union.

Philips, Hilton A. (1930): "From 'Ingagi': What the People Say." In: The Chicago Defender July 19, p. A2.

Pickens, William (1916): The New Negro: His Political, Civil and Mental Status and Related Essays, New York: Neale.

Pickens, William (1969 [1906]): "Talladega College." In: Negro Periodicals in the United States, 1840-1960, New York: Negro University, pp. 244-247.

Pigafetta, Filippo (1881 [1591]): A Report of the Kingdom of Congo and of the Surrounding Countries; Drawn out of the Writings and Discourses of the Portugese Duarte Lopez by Filippo Pigafetta, in Rome 1591, in: Margarite Hutchinson (ed./transl.), London: John Murray.

Plato, Ann (1988 [1841]): "Education." In: Essays; Biographies and Miscellaneous Pieces, in Prose and Poetry, New York: Oxford University, pp. 26-33.

Porter, Noah (1884): "Valley." In: Noah Porter (ed.), A Practical Dictionary of the English Language, Giving the Correct Spelling, Pronunciation, and Definitions of Words with an Appendix Containing Various Useful Tables, Chiefly Derived from Webster's Unabridged Dictionary, New York/Chicago: Ivison, Blakeman, Taylor, and Company, p. 482.

Randolph, Philip (1969 [1921]): "A Merited Rebuke of American Imperialism." In: The Messenger (July), New York: Negro University, p. 209.

Reade, Winwood (1864): Savage Africa: Being the Narrative of a Tour in Equatorial, Southwestern, and Northwestern Africa; with Notes of the Habits of the Gorilla; on the Existence of Unicorns and Tailed Men; on the Slave-Trade; on the Origin, Character and Capabilities of the Negro, and on the Future Civilization of Western Africa, New York: Harper & Brothers.

Reade, Winwood (1872): The Martyrdom of Man, New York: Truth Seeker Company.

Richburg, Keith B. (1997): Out of America: A Black Man Confronts Africa, San Diego: Harvest.

Roe, E.T (1911): "Dainty." In: E.T. Roe (ed.), Laird & Lee's Webster's New Standard American Dictionary of the English Language, Chicago: Laird & Lee, p. 324.

Rollin, Frank A. (1883): Life and Public Services of Martin R. Delany, Boston: Lee and Shepard.

Sanders, Charles L (1971): "The Radicalization of Angela Davis." In: Ebony (July), pp. 114, 120.

Schuyler, George (1991 [1938]): Black Empire, Boston: Northeastern University.

Schuyler, George (2007): "The Rise of the Black Internationale." In: Louis Henry Gates/Gene Andrew Jarrett, The New Negro: Readings on Race, Representation, and African American Culture, 1892-1938. Princeton: Princeton University, pp. 149-156.

Schuyler, Philippa (1962): Who Killed the Congo? New York: Devin-Adair.

Seale, Bobby (1970): Seize the Time: The Story of the Black Panther Party and Huey P. Newton, London: Hutchinson.

Seligmann, Herbert J. (1920): The Negro Faces America, New York: Harper & Brothers.

Shannon, Lisa J. (2010): A Thousand Sisters: My Journey into the Worst Place on Earth to be a Woman, Berkeley: Sea.

Sheppard, William Henry (1917): Presbyterian Pioneers in Congo, Richmond: Presbyterian Committee of Publications.

Shufeldt, R.W. (1907): The Negro: A Menace to American Civilization, Boston: Gorham Press.

Siggins, A.J. (1960): "'Congolese Claim: 'Belgians Mistreat Our Women; We Mistreat Theirs; Now We Equal'" In: The Chicago Defender August 13, pp. 1-2.

Smith, Amanda (1893): An Autobiography; the Story of the Lord's Dealings with Mrs. Amanda Smith, the Colored Evangelist; Containing an Account of Her Life Work of Faith, and Her Travels in America, England, Ireland, Scotland, India, and Africa, as an Independent Missionary, Chicago: Meyer & Brother.

Smith, Charles Spenser (1895a): Glimpses of Africa, West and Southwest Coast: Containing the Author's Impressions and Observations During a Voyage of Six Thousand Miles from Sierra Leone to St. Paul de Loanda and Return, Including the Rio Del Ray and Cameroons Rivers, and the Congo River, from Its Mouth to Matadi, Nashville, n.l: Publishing House, A.M.E. Church Sunday School.

Smith, Charles Spenser (1895b): "Letter No. 1." In: The Christian Recorder January 10, n.p.

Snell, David (1960a): "In Chaos, a Deep Fear." In: Life Magazine 18 July, pp. 31-32.

Snell, David (1960b): "Faces of Terror in Congo." In: Life Magazine 25 July, pp. 32-33.

Spencer, Herbert (1867): The Principles of Biology, Vol. II, n.l.: Williams and Norgate.

Spencer, Herbert (1897): The Principles of Sociology, New York: Appleton.

Stanley, Henry Morgan (1878): Through the Dark Continent; or, the Sources of the Nile, Around the Great Lakes of Equatorial Africa, and Down the Livingstone River to the Atlantic Ocean: in Four Volumes. Asher's collection of English authors, British and American, Hamburg: Grädener.

Stanley, Henry Morgan (1891): In Darkest Africa; or, The Quest, Rescue and Retreat of Emin, governor of Equatoria, London: S. Low, Marston, Searle and Rivington.

Stearns, Jason (2011): Dancing in the Glory of Monsters: the Collapse of the Congo and the Great War of Africa, Philadelphia: Perseus Running.

Still, William (1872): The Underground Railroad A Record Of Facts, Authentic Narratives, Letters, &C., Narrating The Hardships, Hair-Breadth Escapes And Death Struggles of the Slaves in Their Efforts For Freedom, As Related by Themselves And Others, Or Witnessed by the Author, Philadelphia: Porter & Coates.

Sundaram, Anjan (2014): Stringer: A Reporter's Journey in the Congo, New York: Random House.

Tayler, Jeffrey (2000): Facing the Congo: A Modern-Day Journey into the Heart of Darkness, New York: Three River.

The Chicago Defender (1914a): "Kid Dixon Fights Tonight at Memphis." May 23, p 6.

The Chicago Defender (1914b): "Africa, England, France." September 29, p. 1.

The Chicago Defender (1915): "Great Thinker Liked Pie." November 27, p. 3.

The Chicago Defender (1918a): "Grace Presbyterian Church Celebrates Thirtieth Anniversary." July 6, p 10.

The Chicago Defender (1918b): "Yonkers Gleanings." September 21, p. 4.

The Chicago Defender (1919a): "Riot Sweeps Chicago." August 2, p. 1.

The Chicago Defender (1919b): "Reaping the Whirlwind." August 2, p. 16.

The Chicago Defender (1920a): "Dies Aged 104 Years." October 9, p. 1.

The Chicago Defender (1920b): "The Call of the Blood." December 11, p. 12.

The Chicago Defender (1921a): "Civilized Savages." February 12, p. 12.

The Chicago Defender (1921b): "First Picture of Georgia Murder Farm: Kills 11; Buries 6 Alive." April 2, p. 1.

The Chicago Defender (1922): "Africans Seek Railroad Aid." October 14, p. 13.

The Chicago Defender (1923a): "Belgian Congo Growing Better Lecturer Says." January 20, p. 3.

The Chicago Defender (1923b): "American Imperialism." October 13, p. 12.

The Chicago Defender (1924): "Darker Races Lose Friend as Congo Hero Passes out." Nov 29, p. 1.

The Chicago Defender (1925a): "How Africa is Rising." May 2, p. 13.

The Chicago Defender (1925b): "Missionary Leaves for Belgian Congo." June 6, p. 4.

The Chicago Defender (1925c): "Mister Congo is en route to U.S." November 7, p. 13.

The Chicago Defender (1926): "Tells of Her Mission Work over Africa." April 3, p. 2.

The Chicago Defender (1928a): "Dark Continent Lures." January 14, p. 2.

The Chicago Defender (1928b): "On with Democracy." June 30, p. A2.

The Chicago Defender (1928c): "Organize Company to Exploit the Congo." July 21, p. A1.

The Chicago Defender (1928d): "Photo Standalone 9." November 10, p. A12.
The Chicago Defender (1928e): "Fight Sleeping Sickness in Africa." December 15, p. 22.
The Chicago Defender (1929a): "Atrocities Still Rule Belgian Congo." January 5, p. A1.
The Chicago Defender (1929b): "Edmond D. Morel Freed Belgian Congo Slaves." March 23, A1.
The Chicago Defender (1930a): "Southern Savages." September 27, p. 14.
The Chicago Defender (1930b): "It's Oil now as 5 Nations Drill Africa." December 27, p. 4.
The Chicago Defender (1931a): "Defender Agent Dies." May 2, p .2.
The Chicago Defender (1931b): "C.H. Congo, Leland Contractor, Buried." May 9, p. 3.
The Chicago Defender (1931c): "California Pastor will Take Cruise to Liberia." June 20, p. 13.
The Chicago Defender (1931d): "D.C. Nite [sic] Club Opening as Notables out." October 21, p. 5.
The Chicago Defender (1931e): "Peyton out as Head of Club Congo." December 5, p. 5.
The Chicago Defender (1933a): Muse Writes another Hit Song Number." February 18, p. 5:
The Chicago Defender (1933b): "The Week." April 1, p. 1.
The Chicago Defender (1933c): "A Lynch Verdict." April 15, p. 10.
The Chicago Defender (1933d) "All Seven for only one dollar." April 15, p. 5.
The Chicago Defender (1935a): "Says Africa Not A Dark Continent." November 2, p. 10.
The Chicago Defender (1935b): "From the Defender Files: 11 Years ago." November 30, p. 16.
The Chicago Defender (1936): "Mitchell-Talbot Nuptials Held Wednesday." August 22, p. 6.
The Chicago Defender (1938): "Spelman Grad, Back From Home In Africa, On Visit." October 29, p. 3.
The Chicago Defender (1940a): "Dean Kelly Miller's Death." January 20, p. 14.
The Chicago Defender (1940b): "Life Term is Given Boxer in Dual Slaying." April 6, p. 4.
The Chicago Defender (1940c): "The Man of the Hour." November 16, p. 14.
The Chicago Defender (1941): Leonard Reed to Produce New Plantation Show in Detroit." June 7, p. 21.
The Chicago Defender (1942): "Bledsoe Recovering from Leg Broken in Film Work." January 24, p. 3.

The Chicago Defender (1943a): "Other 8." January 23, p. 4.
The Chicago Defender (1943b): "A Common Bond." September 11, p. 14.
The Chicago Defender (1943c): "Fine Specimen of Manhood." September 11, p. 20.
The Chicago Defender (1943d): "Methodists Plan to Train Native African Pastors." December 18, p. 22.
The Chicago Defender (1944): "Belgium to Enforce Congo 'Status Quo'." September 23, p. 18.
The Chicago Defender (1945a): "Storm Signals at the Golden Gate." March 10, p. 10.
The Chicago Defender (1945b): "Negro Scientists Help to Split Atoms." August 18, p. 1.
The Chicago Defender (1963): "Malcolm X Suspended." December 5, pp. 1-2.
The Chicago Defender (1975): "Activist Talks Here." April 22, p. 4.
The Christian Recorder (1861a): "Blind Tom." June 22, n.p.
The Christian Recorder (1861b): "A Sermon Delivered in Saint Thomas' Church, Fifth Street, Philadelphia, July 17th, 1794." October 19, n.p.
The Christian Recorder (1863): "A Bird's Eye View of Missions in Africa." May 30, n.p.
The Christian Recorder (1866): "Something About Woman's Work." June 16, n.p.
The Christian Recorder (1872): "Christianity at Large." November 9, n.p.
The Christian Recorder (1874a): "African Exploration." January 22, n.p.
The Christian Recorder (1874b): "Princeton: A Difference." July 23, n.p.
The Christian Recorder (1875a): "Lake Tanganyika Outlet." April 1, n.p.
The Christian Recorder (1875b): "Central Africa." May 20, n.p.
The Christian Recorder (1875c): "Livingstone, the Friend of Africa." May 27, n.p.
The Christian Recorder (1875d): "The Outlook's View of American Slavery." September 16, n.p.
The Christian Recorder (1876a): "Brevities." February 17, n.p.
The Christian Recorder (1876b): "Cameron's Discoveries in Africa." August 31, n.p.
The Christian Recorder (1877): "Further from Stanley." March 22, n.p.
The Christian Recorder (1878a): "Stanley's Defender." February 14, n.p.
The Christian Recorder (1878b): "Brevities." April 18, n.p.
The Christian Recorder (1880): "Anderson, the Great Liberian Adventurer." December 23, n.p.
The Christian Recorder (1881a): "The Twentieth Century." June 16, n.p.
The Christian Recorder (1881b): "Personal." December 8, n.p.
The Christian Recorder (1882a): "The Colored People – Different Races." May 18, n.p.

The Christian Recorder (1882b): "The Brotherhood of Man." June 8, n.p.
The Christian Recorder (1882c): "Dr. Blyden's Letter." September 28, n.p.
The Christian Recorder (1882d): "Personal." November 9, n.p.
The Christian Recorder (1882e): "Foreign." November 23, n.p.
The Christian Recorder (1883a): "A History of the Negro Race in America from 1619 to 1880 Negroes As Slaves, As Soldiers and As Citizens." January 11, n.p.
The Christian Recorder (1883b): "Williams History [sic] of the Negro." January 18, n.p.
The Christian Recorder (1883c): "A Society has been Established at London." June 7, n.p.
The Christian Recorder (1883d): "Whipped by Germany, and Outwitted by England." June 7, n.p.
The Christian Recorder (1883e): "Personal." July 5, n.p.
The Christian Recorder (1883f): "Portugal is Inclined to have her Say." November 15, n.p.
The Christian Recorder (1884a): "Bethel A.M.E. Church" January 21, n.p.
The Christian Recorder (1884b): "It Looks as if Ethiopia Would Stretch Forth her Hands." May 8, n.p.
The Christian Recorder (1885a): "The Destiny of the English-Speaking Race." March 19, n.p.
The Christian Recorder (1885b): "Missionary Day." March 5, n.p.
The Christian Recorder (1885c): "Missionary Day." March 26, n.p.
The Christian Recorder (1885d): "The Continent of Africa." April 9, n.p.
The Christian Recorder (1885e): "The Duty of the Hour." April 23, n.p.
The Christian Recorder (1885f): "Progress of Protestant Missions in the Dark Continent." April 16, n.p.
The Christian Recorder (1885g): "Bethel A.M.E. Church Saved From a Grasping Heir in Suit at Law." April 30, n.p.
The Christian Recorder (1885h): "We are now Offering a 'The History of the Negro Race in America.'" September 10, n.p.
The Christian Recorder (1886a): "The Present Domain of Slavery." February 18, n.p.
The Christian Recorder (1886b): "Rev. Peter Bowman." February 25, n.p.
The Christian Recorder (1886c): "Thomasville (Ga.): Notes." May 13, n.p.
The Christian Recorder (1886d): "Has Methodism Fulfilled its Duty to the Extreme of Society?" February 2, n.p.
The Christian Recorder (1888a): "The Dark Continent Made Darker." May 24, 1888. n.p.
The Christian Recorder (1888b):"Quadrennial Address." June 14, n.p.

The Christian Recorder (1889a):"The Dark Races and the Dark Methodists." June 20, n.p.

The Christian Recorder (1889b):"Of 800 White Persons who Settled in the Congo Free States, Africa." September 5, n.p.

The Christian Recorder (1890a):"The W.C.T.U. – its Relation to the Verities and the Negro Problem." February 27, n.p.

The Christian Recorder (1890b):"Notes of Interest." May 8, n.p.

The Christian Recorder (1891):"Africa-its Resources and Possibilities." September 10, n.p.

The Christian Recorder (1894):"On African Shores; The Man with an Iron Will." November 29, n.p.

The Colonizationist and Journal of Freedom (1834): "Abduhl Rahamann." Boston: Geo W. Light, pp. 29-31.

The Colored American Magazine (1837): "Schooner Amistad." September 7, n.p.

The Colored American Magazine (1839a): "Power of the Free States." May 18, n.p.

The Colored American Magazine (1839a) "From the Herald of Freedom." September 28, n.p.

The Colored American Magazine (1840a) "National Reform Convention of the Colored Inhabitants of the United States of America." July 25, n.p.

The Colored American Magazine (1840b) "The New York State Convention." August 29, n.p.

The Colored American Magazine (1900) "Editorial and Publisher's Announcements." October 27, p. 5.

The Colored American Magazine (1909) "The Month." October, p. 248.

The Crest Musical Bulletin (2002). "Negro Minstrelsy from its Origin to the Present Day." In: Karl Koenig (ed.), Jazz in Print (1859-1929): An Anthology of Early Source Readings in Jazz History, Hillsdale: Pendragon, pp. 81-83.

The Crisis (1960a): "Editorials: African College Students." October, p. 536.

The Crisis (1960b): "Editorials: Some Congo History." October, pp. 536-537.

The Liberator (1831): "Objections to Colonization." November 19, n.p.

The Liberator (1836): "Light and Truth." November 26, n.p.

The Liberator (1843): "Moral Suasion and Law Won't Mix, Any Way You Fix it." June 9, n.p.

The National Era (1850): "Women's Rights Convention." September 19, n.p.

The National Era (1851): "Slave Cases." January 2, n.p.

The New York Times (1891): "Williams in Middletown: He Prospered for a Time, But his true Character was Learned." April 15, n.p.

The New York Times (1897): The Congo Atrocities: Lame Reply to the Charges of Missionary Sjoblon." May 31, n.p.

The New York Times (1899): "Oppression in Congo State: Belgian Government gets Rich at the Expense of Natives." January 1, n.p.
The New York Times (1900): "Trouble on the Congo." February 22, n.p.
The New York Times (1902): "Congo State Atrocities: An Ex-Official Says Conditions are Worse than ever Before." January 3, n.p.
The New York Times (1960): "Messiah in the Congo: Patrice Emery Lumumba." 18 May, p. 10.
The North Star (1847): "To our Oppressed Countrymen." December 3, n.p.
The North Star (1849a): "Capture of a Slaver." January 5, n.p.
The North Star (1849b): South Carolina." January 12, n.p.
The North Star (1849c): "Extracts." April 13, n.p.
The North Star (1849d): "The Captive Dreams." May 4, n.p.
The North Star (1849e): "The Law of Human Progress." September 14, n.p.
The North Star (1851): "The African Slave Trade." January 16, n.p.
Thompson, Era Bell (1954a): Africa, land of my fathers: The Story of the Return of a Native Three Hundred Years Later, New York: Doubleday.
Thompson, Era Bell (1954b): "African Independence 1960." In: Ebony, December, pp. 144-152.
Tillinghast, Joseph Alexander (1902): The Negro in Africa and America, New York: Negro University.
Truth, Sojourner (2011 [1867]). "Address to the First Annual Meeting of the American Equal Rights Association." In: Henry Louis Gates, Jr/Jennifer Burton (eds.), Call and Response: Key Debates in African American Studies, New York: Norton, pp. 242-243.
Truth, Sojourner (1878): Narrative of Sojourner Truth; a Bondswoman of Olden Time, Emancipated by the New York Legislature in the Early Part of the Present Century; With a History of Her Labors and Correspondence Drawn From Her "Book of life", Battle Creek: n.p.
Turner, Henry McNeal (1893): African Letters, Nashville: Publishing House A.M.E. Church Sunday School.
Twain, Marc (1901): "To the Person Sitting in Darkness." In: The North American Review 172.531 (February), pp. 161-176.
Twain, Marc (1905): King Leopold's Soliloquy, Boston: P.R. Warren.
Van Reybrouck, David (2010a): Congo: een geschiedenis, Amsterdam: Bezige Bij.
Van Reybrouck, David (2010b): "Tussen zwijgen en brullen zit altijd de dialoog. Interview with Bas Heijne." In: NRC Handelsblad 3 August (https://www.nrc.nl/nieuws/2010/07/30/tussen-zwijgen-en-brullen-zit-altijd-de-dialoog-11925880-a337363).
Van Reybrouck, David (2014): Congo: the Epic Story of a People, transl. Sam Garrett, London: Fourth Estate.

Verlinden, Peter (2002): Weg uit Congo: het drama van de kolonialen, Leuven: Davidsfonds.

Vidal, Koen (2010): "Congo, hart van licht en duisternis." In: De Morgen 11 October, p.34.

Walker, Alice (2010a): Overcoming Speechlessness: a Poet Encounters the Horror in Rwanda, Eastern Congo, and Palestine/Israel, New York: Seven Stories.

Walker, Alice (2010b). "Alice Walker on 'Overcoming Speechlessness: A Poet Encounters the Horror in Rwanda, Eastern Congo and Palestine/Israel.'" In: Democracy Now! April 13 (https://www.democracynow.org/2010/4/13/alice_walker_on_overcoming_speechlessness_a).

Walker, David (1830): Walker's Appeal, in Four Articles; Together with a Preamble, to the Coloured Citizens of the World, but in Particular, and Very Expressly, to Those of the United States of America, Written in Boston, State of Massachusetts, September 28, 1829, Boston: David Walker.

Walters, Joseph Jeffrey (2004 [1894]): Guanya Pau, in: Gareth Griffiths/John Victor Singler (eds.), n.l.: Broad View Press.

Warne, Frank Julian (1904): The Slav Invasion and the Mine Workers: A Study in Immigration, Philadelphia: J.B. Lippincott Company.

Ward, Herbert (1891): Five Years with the Congo Cannibals, London: Chatto & Windus.

Washington, Booker T. (1900): A New Negro for a New Century. An Accurate and Up-To-Date Record of the Upward Struggles of the Negro Race. Chicago: American Publishing House.

Washington, Booker T. (1909a): The Story of the Negro: The Rise of the Race from Slavery, Vol I, New York: Association.

Washington, Booker T. (1909b): The Story of the Negro: The Rise of the Race from Slavery, Vol II, New York: Association.

Washington, Booker T. (1979 [1904]): "Cruelty in the Congo Country." In: Booker T. Washington /G. & Harlan McTigue, Booker T. Washington Papers, Volume 8, Champaign: University of Illinois, pp 85-90.

Washington, Booker T. (2011 [1895]): "The Atlanta Exposition Address." In: Henry Louis Gates, Jr/Jennifer Burton, Call and Response: Key Debates in African American Studies, New York: Norton, pp. 206-208.

Webster, Noah (1834a): "Morocco." In: Noah Webster (ed.), Elements of Useful Knowledge. Vol. III. Containing a Historical and Geographical Account of the Empires and States in Europe, Asia and Africa with Their Colonies. To Which is Added, a Brief Description of New Holland, and the Principal Islands in the Pacific and Indian Oceans, New Haven: Bronson, Walter & Co., pp. 255-256.

Webster, Noah (1834b): "Coast." In: Noah Webster (ed.), An American Dictionary of the English Language; Exhibiting the Origin, Orthography, Pronunciation, and Definitions of Words: By Noah Webster, LL. D. Abridged from the Quatro Edition of the Author: To Which are Added, A Synopsis of Words Differently Pronounced by Different Orthoëpists; and Walker's Key to the Classical Pronunciation of Greek, Latin, and Scripture Proper Names, New York: N. and J. White, p.156.

Webster, Noah (1834c): "Congo." In: Noah Webster (ed.), An American Dictionary of the English Language; Exhibiting the Origin, Orthography, Pronunciation, and Definitions of Words: By Noah Webster, LL. D. Abridged from the Quatro Edition of the Author: To Which are Added, A Synopsis of Words Differently Pronounced by Different Orthoëpists; and Walker's Key to the Classical Pronunciation of Greek, Latin, and Scripture Proper Names, New York: N. and J. White, p. 178.

Webster, Noah (1834d): "Country." In: Noah Webster (ed.), An American Dictionary of the English Language; Exhibiting the Origin, Orthography, Pronunciation, and Definitions of Words: By Noah Webster, LL. D. Abridged from the Quatro Edition of the Author: To Which are Added, A Synopsis of Words Differently Pronounced by Different Orthoëpists; and Walker's Key to the Classical Pronunciation of Greek, Latin, and Scripture Proper Names, New York: N. and J. White, p. 200.

Webster, Noah (1834e): "Golden." An American Dictionary of the English Language; Exhibiting the Origin, Orthography, Pronunciation, and Definitions of Words: By Noah Webster, LL. D. Abridged from the Quatro Edition of the Author: To Which are Added, A Synopsis of Words Differently Pronounced by Different Orthoëpists; and Walker's Key to the Classical Pronunciation of Greek, Latin, and Scripture Proper Names, New York: N. and J. White, p. 381.

Webster, Noah (1834f): "Land." In: Noah Webster (ed.), An American Dictionary of the English Language; Exhibiting the Origin, Orthography, Pronunciation, and Definitions of Words: By Noah Webster, LL. D. Abridged from the Quatro Edition of the Author: To Which are Added, A Synopsis of Words Differently Pronounced by Different Orthoëpists; and Walker's Key to the Classical Pronunciation of Greek, Latin, and Scripture Proper Names, New York: N. and J. White, p. 484.

Webster, Noah (1834g): "Shore." An American Dictionary of the English Language; Exhibiting the Origin, Orthography, Pronunciation, and Definitions of Words: By Noah Webster, LL. D. Abridged from the Quatro Edition of the Author: To Which are Added, A Synopsis of Words Differently Pronounced by Different Orthoëpists; and Walker's Key to the Classical Pronunciation of Greek, Latin, and Scripture Proper Names, New York: N. and J. White, p.752.

Week, John H. (1913): Among Congo Cannibals: Experiences, Impressions, and Adventures During a Thirty Year's Sojourn Among the Boloki and Other Congo Tribes, with a Description of their Curious Habits, Customs, Religion, and Laws. Philadelphia: J.B. Lippincott.

Wells, Collin D. (1907): "Social Darwinism." In: American Journal of Sociology 12.5, pp. 695-716.

Wells-Barnett, Ida B. (1996 [1895]): "A Red Record: Tabulated Statistics and Alleged Causes of Lynching in the United States." In: Jacqueline Jones Royster (ed.), Southern Horrors and Other Writings: The Anti-Lynching Campaign of Ida B. Wells, 1892-1900. Boston: Bedford/St. Martin's, pp. 73-157.

Whoriskey, Kate (2009): "Introduction." Ruined, New York: Theatre Communications Group, pp. ix-xiv.

Williams, Fannie Barrier (1900): "The Club Movement Among Colored Women of America." In: Booker T. Washington (ed.), A New Negro for a New Century. An Accurate and Up-To-Date Record of the Upward Struggles of the Negro Race, Chicago: American Publishing House, pp. 379-405.

Williams, George Washington (1885): History of the Negro Race in America From 1619 to 1880. Negroes as Slaves as Soldiers, and as Citizens. Together With a Preliminary Consideration of the Unity of the Human Family, an Historical Sketch of Africa, and an Account of the Negro Governments of Sierra Leone and Liberia, New York: G.P. Putnam's Sons.

Williams, George Washington (1985 [1885]): "A Report on the Proposed Congo Railway." In: John Hope Franklin, George Washington Williams: A Biography, Durham: Duke University Press, pp. 255-263.

Williams, George Washington (2006 [1890]): "An Open Letter to His Serene Majesty Leopold II, King of the Belgians and Sovereign of the Independent State of Congo." In: Paul B. Armstrong (ed.), Heart of Darkness, New York: Norton, pp. 120-130.

Williams, John A. (1962): Africa: Her History, Lands and People Told with Pictures, New York: Cooper Square Publishers.

Willis, Beatrice (1943): "Africa Subject Of Bud's Book Review." In: The Chicago Defender January 30, p. 11.

Willkie, Wendell (1942): "Race Imperialism must Go!" In: The Chicago Defender September 26, p. A5.

Wilson, J. Leighton (1856): Western Africa: Its History, Condition, and Prospects, New York: Harper & Brothers.

Wood, J.G (1870): The Uncivilized Races of Men of All Countries of the World. Hartford: J.B. Burr and Company.

Woodson, Carter (1922): The Negro in Our History, Washington: Associated Publishers.

Woodson, Carter (1936): The African Background Outlined; Or Handbook for the Study of the Negro, Washington: Association for the Study of Negro Life and History.

X, Malcolm (1970a [1964]): "An Exchange on Casualties in the Congo." In: George Breitmann (ed.), By Any Means Necessary, Speeches, Interviews and a Letter by Malcolm X., New York: Pathfinders Press, pp. 127-131.

X, Malcolm (1970b [1964]): "Answers to Questions at the Militant Labor Forum." In: George Breitmann (ed.), By Any Means Necessary, Speeches, Interviews and a Letter by Malcolm X., New York: Pathfinders Press, pp. 14-32.

X, Malcolm (1970c [1964]): "The Founding Rally of the OAAU." In: George Breitmann (ed.), By Any Means Necessary, Speeches, Interviews and a Letter by Malcolm X., New York: Pathfinders Press, pp. 33-67.

X, Malcolm (1970d [1964]):"The Homecoming Rally of the OAAU." In: George Breitmann (ed.), By Any Means Necessary, Speeches, Interviews and a Letter by Malcolm X., New York: Pathfinders Press, pp. 133-155.

X, Malcolm (1990a [1964]): "At the Audubon." In: George Breitman (ed.), Malcolm X Speaks. Selected Speeches and Statements, London: Secker & Warburg, pp. 89-104.

X, Malcolm (1990b [1963]): "Message to the Grassroots." In: George Breitman (ed.), Malcolm X Speaks. Selected Speeches and Statements, London: Secker & Warburg, pp. 3-17.

X, Malcolm (1990c [1964]): "The Ballot or the Bullet." In: George Breitman (ed.), Malcolm X Speaks. Selected Speeches and Statements, London: Secker & Warburg, pp. 23-44.

X, Malcolm (1999 [1964]): The Autobiography of Malcolm X: As Told to Alex Haley, New York: Ballantine Books.

Secondary Works

Aberjhani/Sandra L. West (2003a): "The Chicago Defender." In: Aberjhani/Sandra L. West (eds.), Encyclopedia of the Harlem Renaissance, New York: Facts on File, pp. 61-62.

Aberjhani/Sandra L. West (2003b): "The Colored American Magazine." In: Aberjhani/Sandra L. West (eds.), Encyclopedia of the Harlem Renaissance, New York: Facts on File, p 65.

Achebe, Chinua (2006 [1977]): "An Image of Africa: Racism in Conrad's Heart of Darkness." In: Paul B. Armstrong (ed.), Heart of Darkness: A Norton Critical Edition, New York: Norton, pp. 336-349.

Alcoff, Linda Martin (2007): "Epistemologies of Ignorance: Three Types." In: Shannon Sullivan (ed.), Race and Epistemologies of Ignorance, Albany: State University of New York, pp. 39-58.

Amin, Samir (2009 [1988]). Eurocentrism: Modernity, Religion, and Democracy. A Critique of Eurocenrism and Culturalism, transl. Russell Moore/James Membrez, New York: Monthly Review.

Anderson, Benedict (2006 [1983]): Imagined Communities: Reflections on the Origin and Spread of Nationalism, London: Verso, 2006.

Anderson, Talmadge/Stewart, James (2007): Introduction to African American Studies: Transdisciplinary Approaches and Implications, Baltimore: Imprint Editions, pp 1-29.

Appiah, Kwame Anthony (1992): In my Father's House: Africa in the Philosophy of Culture, London: Methuen.

Baaz, Eriksson Maria/Stern, Maria (2013): Sexual Violence as a Weapon of War? Perceptions, Prescriptions, Problems in the Congo and Beyond, New York: Zed Books.

Bair, Barbara (2005): "Though Justice Sleeps: 1880-1900." In: D.G. Kelley/Earl Lewis, To Make Our World Anew: A History of African Americans Since 1880, Vol 2, New York: Oxford University, pp. 3-66.

Bal, Mieke (2006a): "Reading Art?" In: A Mieke Bal Reader, Chicago: University of Chicago Press: pp. 289-312.

Bal, Mieke (2006b): Reading Rembrandt: Beyond the Word-Image Opposition, Amsterdam: Amsterdam Academic Archive.

Bal, Mieke (2009): Narratology: Introduction to Theory of Narrative, Toronto: University of Toronto.

Banks, William M. (1996): Black. Intellectuals: Race and Responsibility in American Life, New York: Norton.

Barkan, Elazar (1992): The Retreat of Scientific Racism: Changing Concepts of Race in Britain and the United States Between the World Wars, New York: Cambridge University.

Baßler, Moritz (2005): Die kulturpoetische Funktion und das Archiv: Eine literaturwissenschaftliche Text-Kontext-Theorie, Tübingen: Francke.

Bay, Mia (2000): The White Image in the Black Mind: African-American Ideas about White People, 1830-1925, New York: Oxford University.

Bean, Annemarie/Hatch, James V./McNamara, Brooks (1996): "Editor's Preface." In: Annemarie Bean/James V. Hatch/Brooks McNamara (eds.): Inside the Minstrel Mask: Readings in Nineteenth-Century Blackface Minstrelsy, Hanover: Wesleyan University, pp. xi-xiv.

Bederman, Gail (1995): Manliness & Civilization: a Cultural History of Gender and Race in the United States, 1880 – 1917, Chicago: The University of Chicago.

Behar, Ruth (1996): The Vulnerable Observer: Anthropology That Breaks Your Heart, Boston: Beacon.

Berressem, Hanjo (2007): "On the Matter of Abjection." In: Konstanze Kutzbach (ed.), The Abject of Desire, Amsterdam: Rodopi, pp 19-48.

Beyan, Amos J. (2005). African American Settlements in West Africa: John Brown Russwurm and the American Civilizing Efforts, New York: Palgrave Macmillan.

Birmingham, David (1981): Central Africa to 1870: Zambezia, Zaïre and the South Atlantic, London: Cambridge University.

Blommaert, Jan. Discourse: a Critical Introduction (2005), Cambridge: Cambridge University Press, 2005.

Blommaert, Jan/Dong, Jie (2011): Ethnographic Fieldwork: a Beginner's Guide, Bristol: Multilingual Matters.

Boittin, Jennifer Anne (2010): Colonial Metropolis: the Urban Ground of Anti-Imperialism and Feminism in Interwar Paris, Lincoln: University of Nebraska.

Borstelmann, Thomas (2001): The Cold War and the Color Line. Cambridge: Harvard University.

Bourne, Randolph (1916): "Trans-National America." In: Atlantic Monthly 118 (July), pp. 86-97.

Brantlinger, Patrick (1985): "Victorians and Africans: The Genealogy of the Myth of the Dark Continent." In: Critical Inquiry 12.1, pp. 166-203.

Braudel, Fernand (1995 [1966]): The Mediterranean and the Mediterranean World in the Age of Philip II, Vol I, transl. Sian Reynolds, Berkeley: University of California Press.

Breisach, Ernst. Historiography (2007 [1983]): Ancient, Medieval, and Modern, Chicago: University of Chicago.

Broeck, Sabine. "(Post)Slavery, Abjection and the Genealogy of Gender as White Epistemology." Bremen: forthcoming.

Bührmann, Andrea/Schneider, Werner (2008): Vom Diskurs zum Dispositiv: Eine Einführung in die Dispositivanalyse, Bielefeld: Transcript.

Bureau of the Census (2000): "Democratic Republic of the Congo (Zaire)." (http://www.census.gov/population/socdemo/ancestry/ancestry_q_by_DAC_2000.xls).

Burke, Peter (2001): Eyewitnessing: The Uses of Images as Historical Evidence, Ithaca: Cornell University Press.

Burke, Peter (2012): A Social History of Knowledge From the Encyclopédie to Wikipedia, Vol. II, Cambridge: Polity.

Burton, Vernon (2001): "Civil War and Reconstruction, 1861-1877." In: William L. Barney (ed.), A Companion to nineteenth-Century America, Malden: Blackwell, 2001, pp. 47-60.

Butler, Christopher (2002): Postmodernism: A Very Short Introduction, New York: Oxford University.

Carson, Clayborne (1991): The Eyes on the Prize – Civil Rights Reader: Documents, Speeches, and Firsthand Accounts from the Black Freedom Struggle, 1954 – 1990, New York: Penguin.

Chasmar, Jessica (2014): "Joe Biden Wants the 'Nation of Africa' to Prosper."In: The Washington Times August 6 (http://www.washingtontimes.com/news/2014/aug/6/biden-wants-nation-africa-prosper/).

Chibber, Vivek (2013): Postcolonial Theory and the Specter of Capital, London: Verso.

Claussen, Lisbeth (2004): "Localizing the Global; 'Domestication' Processes in International News Production." In: Media Culture Society 26.25, pp. 25-44.

Cline, Catherine Ann (1981): E.D. Morel 1873-1924: The Strategies of Protest, Belfast: Blackstaff.

Cohn, Theodore H. (2004): Global Political Economy: Theory and Practice. London: Longman.

Cooksey, Susan/Poynor, Robin/Vanhee, Hein: Kongo Across the Waters, Gainsville: University Press of Florida.

Cooper, Frederick (2005): Colonialism in Question: Theory, Knowledge, History, Berkeley: University of California.

Csikszentmihalyi, Mihaly (1997): Creativity: Flow and the Psychology of Discovery and Invention, New York, Harper.

Cunningham, Brent (2003): "Re-Thinking Objectivity." In: Columbia Journalism Review July 11 (http://archives.cjr.org/feature/rethinking_objectivity.php).

Dagbovie, Pero Gaglo (2010): African American History Reconsidered, Urbana: University of Illionois.

Dauphinée, E. (2007): The Ethics of Researching War. Looking for Bosnia, New York: Manchester University, 2007.

Davis, Johnny (2011): "In Praise of Urban Dictionaries." In: The Guardian 21 April (https://www.theguardian.com/books/2011/apr/21/in-praise-urban-dictionaries).

Derricourt, Robin M. (2011): Inventing Africa: History, Archaeology and Ideas, London : Pluto.

De Witte, Ludo (2001 [1999]): The Assassination of Lumumba, transl. Ann Wright, London: Verso.

De Witte, Ludo (2010): "David Van Reybrouck masseert westerse bemoeienissen in Congo weg." In: Apache Newslab 18 Mai (https://www.apache.be/2010/05/18/david-van-reybrouck-masseert-westerse-bemoeienissen-in-congo-weg/).

DiPace, Angela (1994): "Toni Morrison's Beloved: "Unspeakable Things Unspoken." In: Sacred Heart University Review 14.1, pp. 40-52.

Dirks, Nicholas B. (2001): "Postcolonialism and Its Discontents: History, Anthropology, and Postcolonial Critique." In: Joan W. Scott/Debra Keates (eds.), Schools of Thought: Twenty-Five Years of Interpretive Social Science. Princeton: Princeton University, pp. 227-251.

Dirlik, Arlif (1994): "The Postcolonial Aura: Third World Criticism in the Age of Global Capitalism." In: Critical Inquiry 20.2, pp. 328-356.

Doležel, Lubomír (2010): Possible Worlds of Fiction and History: The Postmodern Stage, Baltimore: John Hopkins University.

Donnelly, Mabel Collins (1986): The American Victorian Woman: the Myth and the Reality. New York: Greenwood.

Driver, Felix (2001): Geography Militant: Cultures of Exploration and Empire, Malden: Blackwell.

Du Bois, W.E.B. (1999 [1903]): The Souls of Black Folk, New York: Norton.

Dunn, Kevin C. (2003): Imagining the Congo: The International Relations of Identity, New York: Palgrave Macmillan.

Ugrešić, Dubravka (1996): "The Realisation of a Metaphor." In: The Culture of Lies: Antipolitical Essays, London: Phoenix, pp. 55-65.

During, Simon (2005): Cultural Studies: A Critical Introduction, New York: Routledge.

Dworkin, Ira (2003). "American Hearts: African American Writing on the Congo, 1890-1915." Diss. City University of New York.

Dworkin, Ira (2012): "On the Borders of Race, Mission, and State: African Americans and the American Presbyterian Congo Mission." In: Steven van Wolputte (ed.), Borderlands and Frontiers in Africa, Berlin: LIT, pp. 151-182.

Dworkin, Ira (2017): Congo Love Song: African American Culture and the Crisis of the Colonial State, Chapel Hill: The University of North Carolina.

Edgerton, Robert B (2002): The Troubled Heart of Africa: A History of the Congo, New York: St. Martin's.

Ellingson, Ter (2001): The Myth of the Noble Savage, Berkeley: University of California.

Ellison, Ralph (1966 [1953]): Shadow and Act, New York: Signet Book.

Emery, Lynne Fauley (1988): Black Dance from 1619 to Today, London: Dance Books.

Ernest, John. Liberation Historiography (2004): African American Writers and the Challenge of History, 1794-1861, Chapel Hill: the University of North Carolina.

Ernst, Wolfgang (2002): Das Rumoren der Archive: Ordnung aus Unordnung, Berlin: Merve.

Evans, Freddi Williams (2011): Congo Square: African Roots in New Orleans, Baton Rouge: University of Louisiana.

Evans, Richard J. (2000 [1997]): In Defence of History, London: Granta Books.

Everill, Bronwen (2013): Abolition and Empire in Sierra Leone and Liberia, Basingstoke: Palgrave Macmillan.

Eze, Chukwudi (2000): "Introduction." In: Eze Chukwudi (ed.), Race and the Enlightenment: a Reader, Malden: Blackwell, pp 1-9.

Fabian, Johannes (1990): "Presence and Representation: The Other and Anthropological Writing." In: Critical Inquiry 16.4. (Summer), pp. 753-772.

Fabian, Johannes (2000a): "Dilemmas of Critical Anthropology." In: Time and the Work of Anthropology: Critical Essays, 1971-1991, Amsterdam: Barwood, pp. 245-264.

Fabian, Johannes (2000b): Out of Our Minds: Reason and Madness in the Exploration of Central Africa, Berkeley: University of California.

Fairhead, James (2003): African-American Explorations in West Africa: Four Nineteenth-Century Diaries, Bloomington: Indiana University.

Fanon, Frantz (2005 [1961]): The Wretched of the Earth, New York, Grove.

Feith, Michel (2004): "The Syncopated African: Constructions of Origins in the Harlem Renaissance (Literature, Music, Visual Arts)". In: Harold Bloom (ed.), Harlem Renaissance, Broomall: Chelsea, pp. 275-294.

Feminist Spectator (2009): "Ruined, by Lynn Nottage." March 16 (https://feministspectator.princeton.edu/2009/03/16/ruined-by-lynn-nottage/).

Finkelman, Paul (2006a): "Colonization." Encyclopedia of African American History 1619-1895: From the Colonial Period to the Age of Frederick Douglass, Volume 2, New York: Oxford University, pp. 315-317.

Finkelman, Paul (2006b): "Franklin, John Hope." Encyclopedia of African American History 1619-1895: From the Colonial Period to the Age of Frederick Douglass, Volume 1, New York: Oxford University, pp. 263-269.

Firchow, Peter Edgerly (2000): Envisioning Africa: Racism and Imperialism in Conrad's Heart of Darkness, Lexington: University Press of Kentucky.

Foner, Eric (2010): The Fiery Trial: Abraham Lincoln and American Slavery, New York: Norton.

Foucault, Michel (1998 [1976]): History of Sexuality, Volume 1: An Introduction, transl. Robert Hurley, New York: Pantheon.

Foucault, Michel (2010 [1972]): The Archaeology of Knowledge, transl A.M. Sheridan Smith, New York: Vintage.

Frankel, Noralee (2005): "Breaking the Chains: 1860-1880." In: D.G. Kelley/Earl Lewis (eds.), To Make Our World Anew: A History of African Americans To 1880, Vol 1, New York: Oxford University, 227-280.

Franklin, John Hope (1998 [1985]): George Washington Williams: A Biography, Durham: Duke University.

Füllberg-Stolberg, Katja (2003): Amerika in Afrika: Die Rolle der Afroamerikaner in den Beziehungen zwischen den USA und Afrika 1880-1910, Berlin: Klaus Schwarz.

Gaines, Kevin K. (1996): Uplifting the Race: Black Leadership, Politics, and Culture in the Twentieth Century, Chapel Hill: The University of North Carolina.

Galbraith, John Kenneth (2009 [1954]): The Great Crash 1929, Boston: Mariner.

Gallagher, Catherine/Greenblatt, Stephen (2000): Practicing New Historicism, Chicago: Chicago University.

Gates, Henry Louis Jr./Gene Andrew Jarrett: "Introduction." In: Henry Louis Gates Jr./Gene Andrew Jarrett (eds.): The New Negro: Readings on Race, Representation, and African American Culture, 1892-1938, Princeton: Princeton University, pp. 1-22.

Gehrmann, Susanne (2003): Kongo-Greuel: Zur literarischen Konfiguration eines Kolonialkritischen Diskurses (1890-1910), Hildesheim: Georg Olms.

Geysels, Jos/Van Baelen, Carlo (2010): "Vertalen, ok, maar met welk geld? Groot success Congo-boek nekt subsidiekansen." In: De Standaard 22 December (http://www.standaard.be/cnt/t63417nr?word=geysels%20congo).

Gilyard, Keith (2001). "African American Studies." In: Victor E. Taylor/Charles E. Winquist (eds.), Encyclopedia of Postmodernism, New York: Routledge. pp. 4-5.

Gilroy, Paul (1993): The Black Atlantic: Modernity and Double Consciousness, Cambridge: Harvard University.

Gomez, Michael A (1998): Exchanging our Country Marks: The Transformation of African Identities in the Colonial and Antebellum South, Chapel Hill: University of North Carolina.

Gondola, Didier Ch. (2002): The History of Congo, Westport: Greenwood.

Gooding-Williams, Robert (2006): "Foreword: Supposing Nietsche to be Black – What then?" Jacqueline Scott/Todd A. Franklin (eds), Critical Affinities: Nietzsche and African American Thought, New York: New York State University: pp. vii-xviii.

Gossett, Thomas F. Race (1997 [1963]): The History of an Idea in America, New York: New York University.

Gould, Stephen Jay (1996 [1981]): The Mismeasure of Man, New York: Norton.

Graeber, David (2014): "Anthropology and the Rise of the Professional-Managerial class." In: Hau: Journal of Ethnographic Theory 4.3, pp. 73–88.

Grafton, Anthony (1997): The Footnote: a Curious History, Cambridge: Harvard University.

Gramsci, Antonio (1999 [1971]): Selection from the Prison Notebooks, London: Elecbook.

Grant, Kevin (2005): A Civilized Savagery: Britain and the New Slaveries in Africa, 1884-1926, New York: Routledge.

Grossman, James R. (2005): "A Chance to Make Good: 1900-1929." In: D.G. Kelley/Earl Lewis (eds.), To Make Our World Anew: A History of African Americans Since 1880, Vol 2, New York: Oxford University, pp. 67-130.

Gruesser, John C. (2000): Black on Black: Twentieth-Century African-American Writing about Africa, Lexington: University of Kentucky.

Guldi, Jo/Armitage, David (2014): The History Manifesto, Cambridge: Cambridge University.

Gußmann, Katharina (1998): "The Silent Power of the Possible – Ebony magazine: Ein halbes Jahrhundert schwarzes Selbstverständnis." Diss. Humboldt-Universität zu Berlin.

Ha, Kien Nghi/Lauré al-Samarei, Nicola/Mysorekar, Sheila (2007): Re/visionen: Postkoloniale Perspektiven von People of Color auf Rassismus, Kulturpolitik und Widerstand in Deutschland, Münster: Unrast.

Hafter, Daryl M. (1979). "An Overview of Women's History." In: Marie Richmond Abbott (ed.), The American Woman: Her Past, Her Present, Her Future, New York: Holt, Rinehart and Winston, pp. 1-27.

Hall, Gwendolyn Midlo (2005): Slavery and African Ethnicities in the Americas: Restoring the Links, Chapel Hill: University of North Carolina.

Hall, Stephen G. (2009): A Faithful Account of the Race: African American Historical Writing in Nineteenth-Century America, Chapel Hill: University of North Carolina.

Hall, Stuart (2003a [1997])."Introduction." In: Stuart Hall (ed.), Representation: Cultural Representations and Signifying Practices, London: Sage, pp. 1-12.

Hall, Stuart (2003b [1997]). "The Spectacle of the 'Other'." In: Stuart Hall (ed.), Representation: Cultural Representations and Signifying Practices, London: Sage, 223-290.

Hall, Stuart (2003c [1997])."The Work of Representation." In: Stuart Hall (ed.), Representation: Cultural Representations and Signifying Practices, 1997. London: Sage, pp. 13-74.

Hallet, Wolfang (2010): "Methoden kulturwissenschaftlicher Ansätze: Close Reading and Wide Reading." In: Ansgar Nünning and Vera Nünning (eds.), Methoden der literatur- und kulturwissenschaftlichen Textanalyse, Stuttgart: Metzler, pp. 293-316.

Hargreaves, J.D. (1957): "Winwood Reade and the Discovery of Africa." In: African Affairs 56.225 (October), pp. 306-316.

Harms, Robert W. (1981): River of Wealth, River of Sorrow: The Central Zaire Basin in the Era of the Slave and Ivory Trade, 1500-1891, New Haven: Yale University.

Harris, Susan K. (1988): "Review of The Ideal of Real Womanhood in Mid-Nineteenth-Century America, by Frances B. Cogan, and After the Fall: The Demeter-Persephone Myth in Wharton, Cather, and Glasgow, by Josephine Donovan." In: American Literature 62.2, pp. 330-333.

Harrison, Donald (2001): Spirits of Congo Square, Candid, Compact disc.

Hartman, Saidiya (2007): Lose Your Mother: A Journey along the Atlantic Slave Route, New York: Farrar, Straus and Giroux.

Harvey, Bruce A. (2001): American Geographics: U.S. National Narratives and the Representation of the Non-European World, 1830-1865, Redwood: Stanford University.

Hawkins, Hunt (2006): "Heart of Darkness and Racism." In: Paul B. Armstrong (ed.), Heart of Darkness: A Norton Critical Edition, New York: Norton, pp. 365-375.

Hendrickx, Sébastien (2010): "La Belgique congolaise: de Congohype herbekeken." In: rekto:verso (http://www.rektoverso.be/artikel/la-belgique-congolaise-de-congohype-herbekeken).

Henriques, Julian et al. (1984): Changing the Subject: Psychology, Social Regulation, and Subjectivity, New York: Methuen.

Herren, Madeleine (2012): "Introduction: What is Transcultural History?" In: Madeleine Herren (ed.), Transcultural History: Theories, Methods, Sources, Berlin: Springer, pp. 1-10.

Hewlett, Richard G./Anderson, Oscar E. (1962): The New World, 1939–1946, University Park: Pennsylvania State University.

Hobsbawm, E.J. (1991 [1987]): The Age of Empire:1875-1914, London: Macdonald.

Hochschild, Adam (1998): King Leopold's Ghost: A Story of Greed, Terror, and Heroism in Colonial Africa, New York: Mariner.

Hodges, Graham Russell (1999): Root and Branch: African Americans in New York and East Jersey, 1613-1863, Chapel Hill: University of North Carolina.

Hofstadter, Richard (1993 [1944]): Social Darwinism in American Thought, Boston: Beacon.

Holder, Alison (2004): "Forgotten or Ignored? News Media Silence and the Conflict in the Democratic Republic of Congo (DRC)", Diss. London School of Economics.

hooks, bell (1981): Ain't I a Woman: Black Women and Feminism, Boston: South End Press.

hooks, bell (1990): "Postmodern Blackness." In: Yearning: Race, Gender, and Cultural Politics, Boston: South End Press, pp. 23-31.

hooks, bell (2000): Where We Stand: Class Matters, New York: Routledge.

Horne, Gerald (2009): Mau Mau in Harlem. The U.S. and the Liberation of Kenya, New York: MacMillan.

Hunt, Nancy Rose (2008): "An Acoustic Register, Tenacious Images, and Congolese Scenes of Rape and Repetition." In: Cultural Anthropology 23.2, pp. 220-253.

Hutton, Frankie (1993): The Early Black Press in America, 1827 to 1860, Westport: Greenwood.

Iggers, Georg G. (2007 [1993]): Geschichtswissenschaft im 20. Jahrhundert: Ein kritischer Überblick im internationalen Zusammenhang, Göttingen: Vandenhoeck & Ruprecht.

Inikori, Joseph (2000): "Capitalism and Slavery, Fifty Years After: Eric Williams and the Changing Explanations of the Industrial Revolution." In: Heather Cateau/S.H.H. Carrington (eds.), Capitalism & Slavery Fifty Years Later: Eric Eustace Williams – A Reassessment of the Man and His Work, New York: Peter Lang, pp. 51-80.

Iriye, Akira (2004): "Transnational History." In: Contemporary European History 13, pp. 211-222.

Jäger, Siegfried (2004): Kritische Diskursanalyse: Eine Einführung, Münster: Unrast.

Jardins, Julie Des (2003): Women and the Historical Enterprise in America: Gender, Race, and the Politics of Memory, 1800-1945, Chapel Hill: The University of North Carolina.

Joseph, Peniel E. (2006): Waiting 'Til the Midnight Hour: A Narrative of Black Power in America, New York: Henry Holt.

Kapoor, Illan (2008): The Postcolonial Politics of Development, New York: Routledge.

Karl, Rebecca (2007): Staging the World: Chinese Nationalism at the Turn of the Twentieth Century, Durham: Duke University.

Kellner, Bruce (2004): "'Refined Racism': White Patronage in the Harlem Renaissance." In: Harold Bloom (ed.), Harlem Renaissance, Broomall: Chelsea, pp. 53-66.

Kisangani, Emizet Francois/Bobb, Scott F. (2010): Historical Dictionary of the Democratic Republic of the Congo, Lanham: Scarcecrow.

Klein, Herbert S. (1999): The Atlantic Slave Trade, Cambridge: Cambridge University.

Kocka, Jürgen (2013): Geschichte des Kapitalismus, München: Beck.

Kolchin, Peter (2003): American Slavery, 1619-1877, New York: Hill and Wang.

Koselleck, Reinhart (1972):“Einleitung.” In: Otto Brunner, Werner Conze, Reinhart Koselleck (eds.), Geschichtliche Grundbegriffe: Historisches Lexikon zur politisch-sozialen Sprache in Deutschland, Vol.1, Stuttgart: Klett-Cotta. pp. XIII-XXVIII.

Koselleck, Reinhart (2006): “Sozialgeschichte und Begriffsgeschichte.” In: Begriffsgeschichten, Frankfurt a.M.: Suhrkamp, pp. 9-31.

Kühl, Stefan (1994): The Nazi Connection: Eugenics, American Racism, and German National Socialism, New York: Oxford University.

Lake, Obiagele (2003): Blue Veins and Kinky Hair: Naming and Color Consciousness in African America, Westport: Praeger.

Lapsansky-Werner, Emma J. (2006): “The Christian Recorder.” In: Paul Finkelman (ed.), Encyclopedia of African American History: 1619-1895. From the Colonial Period to the Age of Frederick Douglass, Vol. 2, New York: Oxford University Press, pp. 268-269.

Ledgard, J.M. (2014): “History's Stranglehold: David Van Reybrouck's ‘Congo’.” In: The New York Times May 1 (https://www.nytimes.com/2014/05/04/books/review/david-van-reybroucks-congo.html?_r=0).

Levine, Joseph M. (1991): The Battle of Books: History and Literature in the Augustan Age, New York: Cornell University.

Littlefield, Daniel C. (1991): Rice and Slaves: Ethnicity and the Slave Trade in Colonial South Carolina, Urbana: University of Illinois.

Littlefield, Daniel C. (2005): “Revolutionary Citizens.” D.G. Kelley/Earl Lewis (eds.), To Make Our World Anew: A History of African Americans to 1880, Vol 1, New York: Oxford University, pp. 103-168.

Loomba, Ania (2005 [1998]): Colonialism/Postcolonialism, New York: Routledge.

Manning, Marable (2012): Malcolm X: A Life of Reinvention, London: Penguin.

Maset, Michael (2002): Diskurs, Macht und Geschichte: Foucualts Analysetechniken und die historische Forschung, Frankfurt: Campus.

Masuy, Christine (1997): “De l'indifférence à l'effroi: le Congrès américain et Patrice Lumumba (1959-1961).” In: Pierre Halen/János Riesz Patrice (eds.), Lumumba entre dieu et diable: Un héros africain dans ses images, Paris: L'Harmattan, pp. 199-213.

Mbembe, Achille (2004): On the Postcolony, Berkeley: University of California.

McDonald, Robert M.S. “Early National Politics and Power, 1800-1824.” In: William L. Barney (ed.), A Companion to nineteenth-Century America, Malden. Blackwell, pp. 5-18.

Memmi, Albert (1991 [1957]): The Colonizer and the Colonized, Boston: Beacon.

Meredith, Martin (2014): "'Congo: The Epic History of a People' by David Van Reybrouck." In: The Washington Post April 4 (https://www.washingtonpost.com/opinions/congo-the-epic-history-of-a-people-by-david-van-reybrouck/2014/04/04/4090eb20-aa1b-11e3-b61e-8051b8b52d06_story.html?utm_term=.69f4a7aabf10).

Meriwether, James H. (2002): Proudly We Can Be Africans: Black Americans and Africa, 1935-1961, Chapel Hill: University of North Carolina.

Miller, Christopher L (1985): Blank Darkness: Africanist Discourse in French, Chicago: University of Chicago.

Miller, Joseph C. (1976): "The Slave Trade in Congo and Angola." In: Martin L. Kilson/Robert I. Rotberg (eds.), The African Diaspora, Cambridge: Harvard University, pp. 75-113.

Miller, Joseph C. (1988): Way of Death: Merchant Capitalism and the Angolan Slave Trade: 1730 – 183, London: Currey.

Miller, Joseph C. (2012): The Problem of Slavery as History: A Global Approach, New Haven: Yale University.

Miller, Perry (1956): Errand into the Wilderness, Cambridge: University of Harvard.

Mills, Charles (1999 [1997]): The Racial Contract, Ithaca: Cornell University.

Mills, Charles (1998): Blackness Visible: Essays on Philosophy and Race, Ithaca: Cornell University.

Mills, Nicholaus (1994). "Preface." Legacy of Dissent: 40 Years of Writing from Dissent Magazine, New York: Simon and Schuster, pp.1-15.

Mills, Sara (1997): Discourse, London: Routledge.

Mitchell, W.J.T. (1994): Picture Theory, Chicago: University of Chicago.

Morgan, Kenneth (2007): Slavery and the British Empire: From Africa to America, New York: Oxford University.

Moretti, Franco (2013): The Bourgeois: Between History and Literature, London: Verso.

Morrison, Toni (1992): Playing in the Dark. Whiteness and the Literary Imagination, Cambridge: Harvard University.

Mudimbe, V. Y. (1988): The Invention of Africa: Gnosis, Philosophy, and the Order of Knowledge, Bloomington: Indiana University.

Mudimbe, V.Y. (1994): The Idea of Africa, Bloomington: Indiana University.

Myrdal, Gunnar (1944): An American Dilemma: The Negro Problem and Modern Democracy, New York: Harper and Brothers.

Nathan, Hans (1996): "The Performance of the Virgina Minstrels." In: Annemarie Bean/James V. Hatch/Brooks McNamara (eds.), Inside the Minstrel Mask: Readings in Nineteenth-Century Blackface Minstrelsy, Hanover: Wesleyan University, pp. 35-42.

Nelson, Samuel H. (1994): Colonialism in the Congo Basin:1880-1940, Athens: Ohio: University Center for Internationa Studies.

Newman, Louise Michele (2005): "Religion, Reform, and Radicalism in the Antebellum Era." In: Nancy A. Hewitt (ed.), A Companion to American Women's History, Malden: Blackwell, pp. 117-131.

Nzongola-Ntalaja, Georges (2007 [2002]): The Congo from Leopold to Kabila: A People's History, London: Zed Books.

Nzongola-Ntalaja, Georges (2010):"Vijftig jaar Congo in dertien vragen." In: Rekto:Verso 42, August (http://www.rektoverso.be/artikel/vijftig-jaar-congo-dertien-vragen).

Obeyesekere, Gannath (2005): Cannibal Talk: The Man-Eating Myth and Human Sciences in the South Seas, Berkeley: University of California.

Oxford Dictionaries: "Chaos." n.d. (https://en.oxforddictionaries.com/definition/chaos).

Patterson, Orlando (1982): Slavery and Social Death, Cambridge: Harvard University.

Pauw, Jacques De (1997): Into the Heart of Darkness: Confessions of Apartheid's Assassins, Johannesburg: Jonathan Ball.

Pease, Donald E. (1993): "New Perspectives on U.S. Culture and Imperialism." In: Amy Kaplan and Donald E. Pease (eds.), Cultures of United States Imperialism, Durham: Duke University Press: pp. 22-40.

Petermann, Werner (2004): Die Geschichte der Ethnologie, Wuppertal: Peter Hammer.

Poletta, Francesca (2006): It was Like a Fever: Storytelling in Protest and Politics, Chicago: University of Chicago.

Pratt, Mary Louise (1993): Imperial Eyes: Travel Writing and Transculturation, London: Routledge.

Proctor, Robert N. (2008): "Agnotology: A Missing Term to Describe the Cultural Production of Ignorance (and Its Study)." In: Roberrt N. Proctor and Londa Schiebinger (eds.), Agnotology: The Making and Unmaking of Ignorance, Stanford: Stanford University, pp. 1-36.

European Resettlement Network (2013): "Refugees from the Democratic Republic of the Congo." 1 August (http://www.resettlement.eu/resource/refugees-democratic-republic-congo).

Rice, Mark (2011). "Colonial Photography Across Empires and Islands." Journal of Transnational American Studies 3.2., pp. 1-22.

Richards, Jennifer (2007): Rhetoric, New York: Routledge.

Roger, Jacques (1997): Buffon: A Life in Natural History, Ithaca: Cornell University.

Rose, Tricia (2008): The Hip Hop Wars: What We Talk about When We Talk about Hip Hop – and Why It Matters, New York: Basic Books.

Ryden, David Beck (2009): West Indian Slavery and British Abolition, 1783-1807, Cambridge: Cambridge University.

Said, Edward W. (1994 [1993]): Culture and Imperialism, New York: Vintage.

Said, Edward W. (2003 [1978]): Orientalism, New York: Vintage.

Sawyer, Keith R. (2002). "A Discourse on Discourse: An Archaeological History of an Intellectual Concept." In: Cultural Studies 16.3, pp. 433-456.

Sekula, Allan (1989): "The Body and the Archive." In: Richard Bolton (ed.), The Contest of Meaning: Critical Histories of Photography, Cambridge: MIT, pp. 342-388.

Sexton, Jay (2011): The Monroe Doctrine: Empire and Nation in Nineteenth-Century America, New York: Hill and Wang.

Seymour, Richard (2012): American Insurgents: A Brief History of American Anti-Imperialism, Chicago: Haymarket Books.

Shklar, Judith N. (2004): "Squaring the Hermeneutic Circle." In: Social Research 71.3, pp. 655-678.

Shohat, Ella/Stam, Robert (2008 [1994]): Unthinking Eurocentrism: Multiculturalism and the Media, London: Routledge.

Simon, Bryant (2004): "Narrating a Southern Tragedy: Historical Facts and Historical Fictions." In: Alun Munslow/Robert A. Rosenstone (eds.), Experiments in Rethinking History, New York: Routledge, pp. 156-182.

Sinclair, Andrew (1977): The Savage: A History of Misunderstanding, London: Weidenfeld & Nicolson.

Singh, Amritjit (2004): "Black-White Symbiosis: Another Look at the Literary History of the 1920s." In: Harold Bloom (ed.), Harlem Renaissance, Broomall: Chelsea, pp. 23-34.

Smithson, Michael J. (2008): "Social Theories of Ignorance." In: Robert N. Proctor and Londa Schiebinger (eds.), Agnotology: the Making and Unmaking of Ignorance, Stanford: Stanford University Press, pp. 209-220.

Soja, Edward W (2000 [1996]): Thirdspace: Journeys to Los Angeles and Other Real-and-Imagined Places, Malden: Blackwell.

Spaulding, Timothy A. (2005): Re-Forming the Past. History, the Fantastic, and the Postmodern Slave Narrative, Columbus: Ohio State University.

Spivak, Gayatri Chakravorty (1988): "Can the Subaltern Speak?" In: Marxism and the Interpretation of Culture, Bassingstoke: Macmillan, pp. 271-313.

Spurr, David (1993): The Rhetoric of Empire. Colonial Discourse in Journalism, Travel Writing, and Imperial Administration, Durham: Duke University.

Stansell, Christine (1986): City of Women: Sex and Class in New York City, 1789-1860, New York: Knopf.

Summer, David E (2010): The Magazine Century: American Magazines since 1900, New York: Peter Lang.

Tagg, John (1988): The Burden of Representation: Essays on Photographies and Histories, New York: MacMillan.

Thompson, E.P (1995a). "Class and Class Struggle." In: Patrick Joyce (ed.), Class, New York: Oxford University, 133-142.

Thompson, E.P. (1995b): "The Making of Class." In: Patrick Joyce (ed.), Class, New York: Oxford University, 131-132.

Thompson, Farris (2005): "Kongo Influences on African American Artistic Culture." In: Joseph E. Holloway (ed.). Africanisms in American Culture, Bloomington: Indiana University, pp. 283-325.

Thornton, John (1991): "The African Dimensions of the Stono Rebellion." In: The American Historical Review 96.4, pp. 1101-1113.

Tillery, Alvin B. (2011): Between Homeland and Motherland: Africa, U.S. Foreign Policy, and Black Leadership in America, Ithaca: Cornell University.

Trafton, Scott (2004): Egypt land: Race and Nineteenth-Century American Egyptomania, Durham: Duke University.

Trefon, Theodore (2011): Congo Masquerade: the Political Culture of Aid Inefficiency and Reform Failure, London: Zed.

Trotter, Joe William Jr. (2005): "From a Raw Deal to a New Deal?: 1929-1945." In: D.G. Kelley/Earl Lewis: To Make Our World Anew: A History of African Americans Since 1880, Vol.2, New York: Oxford University, pp.131-166.

Tucker, Jennifer (2009): "Entwined Practices: Engagements with Photography in Historical Inquiry." In: History and Theory 48, pp. 1-8.

Turitz, Shari (1993): Confronting the Heart of Darkness: An International Symposium on Torture in Guatemala, Washington.

Tyner, James A. (2006). The Geography of Malcolm X: Black Radicalism and the Remaking of American Space, New York: Routledge.

Turner, Thomas (2013): Congo, Cambridge: Polity.

Tuttle, William M. Jr. (1970): Race Riot: Chicago in the Red Summer of 1919, New York: Atheneum.

Tyrrell, Ian (2009): "Reflections on the Transnational Turn in United States History: Theory and Practice." In: Journal of Global History 4.3, pp. 453-474.

United States Board on Geografic Names (https://geonames.usgs.gov/).

Van Hove, Johnny (2009): "Kuifje in Afrika 2.1? De Productie van Congo-verhalen in Amerikaanse en Vlaamse mainstream media." In: Media & Racisme, Brussels: Epo, pp. 13-29.

Van Hove, Johnny (2010): "Belgisch-Congo een modelkolonie hoezo?" In: De Wereld Morgen 29 June (http://www.dewereldmorgen.be/artikels/2010/06/29/belgisch-congo-een-modelkolonie-hoezo).

Van Hove, Johnny (2011). "Narrating Violence Empathetically: a Narratological Investigation of the Slave Trade in David Van Reybrouck's Congo: a History." In: Institut für postkoloniale und transkulturelle Studien (INPUTS) January (http://www.fb10.uni-bremen.de/inputs/pdf/narrating_violence_empathetically.pdf).

Van Hove, Johnny (2014): "The New Historicism in Action: Tracing the Black Freedom Movement via African American Novels." In: Elizabeth Kovach/ Ansgar Nünning (eds.), Key Concepts and New Topics in English and American Studies - Schlüsselkonzepte und neue Themen in der Anglistik und Amerikanistik, Trier: WTV, pp. 97-113.

Vansina, Jan (1990): Paths in the Rainforests: Toward a History of Political Tradition in Equatorial Africa, Madison: University of Wisconsin.

Vansina, Jan (2010): Being Colonized: The Kuba Experience in Rural Congo. 1880–1960, Madison: University of Wisconsin.

Vanthemsche, Guy (2006): "The Historiography of Belgian Colonialism in the Congo." In: Csaba Lévai (ed.), Europe and the World in European Historiography, Pisa: Pisa University, pp. 89-119.

Veysey, Laurence (1979): "The Autonomy of American History Reconsidered." In: American Quarterly 31.4, pp. 455-477.

Von Eschen, Penny M. (2006): Satchmo Blows Up the World: Jazz Ambassadors Play the Cold War, Cambridge: Harvard University.

Wallerstein, Immanuel (1988): "The Bourgeois(ie) as Concept and Reality." In: New Left Review 1.167 (January-February), pp. 91-106.

Ward, Martha C. (1986): Poor Women, Powerful Men: America's Great Experiment in Family Planning, Boulder: Westview Press.

Ward, Stephen J.A. (2009): "Journalism Ethics." In: Karin Wahl-Jorgensen/ Thomas Hanitzsch (eds.), The Handbook of Journalism Studies, New York: Routledge, pp. 295-309.

Weinberg, Meyer (2003): A Short History of American Capitalism, Chicago: New History Press.

Welter, Barbara (1966): "The Cult of True Womanhood: 1820-1860." In: American Quarterly 18.2 , pp. 151-174.

West, Russell (2007): "Abject Cannibalism: Anthropophagic Poetics in Conrad, White, and Tennant – Towards a Critique of Julia Kristeva's Theory of Abjection." In: Ed. Konstanze Kutzbach (ed.), The Abject of Desire, Amsterdam: Rodopi, pp. 235-254 .

White, Deborah Gray (2005): "Let My People Go: 1804-1860." In: D.G. Kelley/ Earl Lewis (ed.), To Make Our World Anew: A History of African Americans To 1880 Vol 1, New York: Oxford University, pp. 169-226.

White Pages (http://www.whitepages.com/).

Willaert, Thijs (2012): "Postcolonial Studies After Foucault: Discourse, Discipline, Biopower, and Governmentality as Travelling Concepts", Diss. University of Gießen.

Williame, Jean-Claude (1997): "La diabolisation symbolique de Patrice Lumumba dans La Libre Belgique." In: Pierre Halen/János (ed.), Riesz, Paris: L'Harmattan, pp. 189-195.

Williams, Eric (1944): Slavery and Capitalism, Chapel Hill: University of North Carolina.

Williams, Raymond (1983): "Bourgeois." In: Keywords: a Vocabulary of Culture and Society, New York: Oxford University, pp. 45-48.

Williams, Vernon J. (1996): Rethinking Race: Frans Boas and His Contemporarie, Lexington: University Press of Kentucky.

Williams, Walter L. (1982): Black Americans and the Evangelization of Africa: 1877-1900, Madison: University of Wisconsin.

Williams, Linda (2001): Playing the Race Card: Melodramas of Black and White from Uncle Tom to OJ Simpson, Princeton: Princeton University.

Winterer, Caroline (2002): The Culture of Classicism: Ancient Greece and Rome in American Intellectual Life, 1780-1910, Baltimore: John Hopkins University.

Wood, Peter H (2005): "Strange New Land: 1619-1776." In: D.G. Kelley/Earl Lewis, To Make Our World Anew: A History of African Americans To 1880, Vol 1, New York: Oxford University, pp. 53-102.

Woodruff, Nan Elizabeth (2012): American Congo: The African American Freedom Struggle in the Delta, Chapel Hill: University of North Carolina.

Wright, Donald R. (2001): "African Americans." In: William L. Barney (ed.), A Companion to nineteenth-century America, Malden: Blackwell, pp. 195-208.

Zimmerman, Andrew (2010): Alabama in Africa: Booker T. Washington, the German Empire, and the Globalization of the New South, Princeton: Princeton University.

Zinn, Howard (2003 [1980]): A People's History of the United States: 1492-Present, New York: Harper Collins.

Žižek, Slavoj (2000): The Fragile Absolute, or, Why is the Christian Legacy Worth Fighting for? London: Verso.

Geschichtswissenschaft

Manfred E.A. Schmutzer

Die Wiedergeburt der Wissenschaften im Isla

Konsens und Widerspruch (idschma wa khilaf)

2015, 544 S., Hardcover
49,99 € (DE), 978-3-8376-3196-8
E-Book
PDF: 49,99 € (DE), ISBN 978-3-8394-3196-2

Pascal Eitler, Jens Elberfeld (Hg.)

Zeitgeschichte des Selbst

Therapeutisierung – Politisierung – Emotionalisierung

2015, 394 S., kart.
34,99 € (DE), 978-3-8376-3084-8
E-Book
PDF: 34,99 € (DE), ISBN 978-3-8394-3084-2

Thomas Etzemüller

Auf der Suche nach dem Nordischen Menschen

Die deutsche Rassenanthropologie in der modernen Welt

2015, 294 S., kart., zahlr. z.T. farb. Abb.
29,99 € (DE), 978-3-8376-3183-8
E-Book
PDF: 26,99 € (DE), ISBN 978-3-8394-3183-2

Leseproben, weitere Informationen und Bestellmöglichkeiten finden Sie unter www.transcript-verlag.de